W9-DGQ-916

CIA.

From Diocletian to the Arab Conquest

Professor J.H.G.W. Liebeschuetz

J. H. G. W. Liebeschuetz

From Diocletian to the Arab Conquest:
Change in the Late Roman Empire

VARIORUM

British Library CIP data   Liebeschuetz, J. H. G. W.
From Diocletian to the Arab conquest:
change in the late Roman Empire. —
(Collected studies series; CS310)
1. Roman Empire, 395-476
I. Title   II. Series
937'.09

ISBN 0-86078-258-1

Published in Great Britain by   Variorum
Gower Publishing Group
Gower House, Croft Road
Aldershot GU11 3HR

Printed in Great Britain by   Galliard (Printers) Ltd
Great Yarmouth Norfolk

COLLECTED STUDIES CS310

CONTENTS

This volume contains xiv + 336 pages

PUBLISHER'S NOTE

The articles in this volume, as in all others in the Collected Studies Series, have not been given a new, continuous pagination. In order to avoid confusion, and to facilitate their use where these same studies have been referred to elsewhere, the original pagination has been maintained wherever possible.

Each article has been given a Roman number in order of appearance, as listed in the Contents. This number is repeated on each page and quoted in the index entries.

INTRODUCTION

These papers were written over a period of thirty-one years. Most of them were preliminary studies for my books: *Antioch* (Oxford, 1982), *Continuity and Change in Roman Religion* (Oxford 1979) and *Barbarians and Bishops* (Oxford 1990). It is not difficult to see which article is linked with which book. In spite of this I hope that the collection has a certain cohesion of its own. Certainly all but one of the articles share unity of time in that they deal with problems of Late Antiquity. 'The religious position of Livy's History' is the exception. The relevance of this paper is that Livy's reconstruction of the healthy institutions of early Rome was read and admired in Late Antiquity, and that his brand of traditional religion, combining piety, patriotism, nostalgia and literary culture, still made a powerful appeal to educated Romans under Christian emperors. 'Livian' religion was a retarding factor in the progress of Christianisation in the West. Admirers of Livy formed part of the audiences to which panegyrics were addressed. The paper 'Religion in the *panegyrici Latini*' is concerned, among other things, to show that the speakers used religious phraseology which was acceptable to Christians and pagans alike, because it expressed concepts common to both religions, so that the speech would satisfy the Christian emperor as well as those of his important subjects who remained loyal to ancestral cults. 'Ammianus, Julian and divination' illustrates how belief in traditional techniques for receiving communications from the gods continued through the 4th century, contradicting the view that what strength remained in paganism at that time was derived from mystery religions.

The two papers on the fall of John Chrysostom examine a conflict of a kind previously unknown to the Ancient World, made possible by the advance of Christianity. The Christian empire contained two hierarchies – one secular, the other religious. Friction of some kind was inevitable. Things were made worse by the fact that Constantine and his successors encouraged the clergy to look to the emperor to settle their conflicts and divisions, and thus made sure that the state would get involved in whatever dispute divided the Church – and that such disputes were made more intractable. Chrysostom had many opponents among the clergy but what doomed him was that the Eastern government supported his enemies.

When Chrysostom's followers were persecuted, a number fled to Rome where they found aristocratic patrons. The same Roman group also supported Pelagius [see Peter Brown (1970)]. This was not a coincidence. The ascetic and moral teachings of Pelagius, with their persistent call to the rich to use their wealth to alleviate the miseries of the poor, are both in spirit and substance close to the sermons of Chrysostom, some of which were in fact translated into Latin by Pelagian clergy. My two 'Pelagian' papers are immediately concerned to refute interpretations put forward respectively by J.N.L. Myres and John Morris. If they have a more general interest it is that each illustrates the Pelagian drive for deeper Christianisation of the Roman senatorial class. It was not sufficient for Pelagius – as it was not for Chrysostom – that society should have become nominally Christian, but conversion ought to be followed by the adoption of comprehensively Christian views and attitudes. The article 'Epigraphic evidence on the Christianisation of Syria' argues that the acceptance of Christianity by the country population in Syria was much slower than has generally been thought. A feature of Christianised Syria is that the planning of monasteries in the territory of Antioch was outward-looking while those around Apamea tend to form a totally enclosed, inward-looking complex. Paper IX discusses reasons for the difference.

The articles of Part II are concerned mainly with secular themes related to a profound transformation of Late Roman civic and military institutions which took place between the 4th and 6th centuries. 'Government and administration in the Late Empire' is a general account of the administrative structure of the Empire as it was set up by Diocletian and his immediate successors. There follow three papers in which administrative problems of Antioch in the 4th century are discussed on the basis of evidence provided by Libanius. The focus is on the 4th century but there is attention to subsequent developments. The two papers on Synesius illustrate conditions in cities which were no longer run in the standard Diocletianic manner. The council seems to have ceased to function as a collective authority. Society is dominated by competing magnates. The bishop is on the way to becoming the real leader of the city. The army is no longer able to keep raiders out of the province, and has lost part of its monopoly of defence to private levies organised by magnates, like Synesius himself.

It is possibly a consequence of changes in social organisation that our evidence for the 5th century is quite different from that for the 4th. The paper 'Antioch and the villages of Northern Syria in the 5th and 6th centuries' has little information about decurions and the administration of cities. What we are able to describe is the growth of villages, the founding of monasteries and the deepening division between Christians who accepted the Council of Chalcedon and those others, the monophysites, who did not. Papers XVII and XVIII return to aspects of the government of cities. They are based on papyrus evidence which enables us to study phenomena which, whether they were more widespread or not, are visible to us only in Egypt. The office of the pagarch is seen as part of the reforms undertaken by Anastasius in order to make good the damage done to the administration of the Empire by the financial and social decline of the curial class. He attempted to involve non-curial magnates in the holding of civic offices, notably those of *defensor*, corn-buyer and *curator*. It is argued that the Egyptian pagarch was a post created at this time to direct the collection of taxes. The new system seems to have involved a reduction in the power of provincial governors, and eventually in a considerable role in city government falling to the garrison commander, a post which might be combined with that of pagarch.

Paper XIX is an attempt to explain the origins of the *bucellarii* who formed an important part of field armies of the time of Justinian. The argument is that from the late 4th century generals personally recruited federates for impending campaigns, and that as these men were enrolled for the duration of the war rather than a lifetime of military service, they needed some assurance that they would not be totally discarded once the campaign was over. The bucellariate established a formal patron-client relationship between commander and men. It meant that the latter undertook continuing responsibility for their men's welfare without the state having to take on an expensive permanent obligation. Paper XX shows how much the 6th-century military organisation of Syria and Mesopotamia, for both defence and attack, had changed since the age of Diocletian and Constantine. The line of frontier forts seems to have been to a large extent abandoned. An essential part in the guarding of frontiers was now left to Arab allies. When a powerful field army was needed it had to be specially assembled. The eastern army seems to have been scattered in small garrisons of fortified towns. When I wrote this article I was not aware of the profound changes successive outbreaks of the plague seem to have produced in Syria after 542 AD. In this respect paper XX is superseded by the more recent XVI.

The last thirty years have produced much work on Late Antiquity. This is not the place to list everything published on the topics treated in my articles. It must suffice to list some more recent publications which would certainly have modified my views if they had been available at the time. The books of Simon Price (1984) and Robin Lane Fox (1986) must influence anybody writing on paganism. Sabine MacCormack (1975) and (1976) has similar importance for the study of panegyrics and ceremony, and there is now also a valuable introduction and commentary to Pacatus' panegyric of Theodosius (C.E.V. Nixon 1987). It is safe to say that nobody's views on Ammianus will be unaffected by J.F. Matthews' forthcoming *The Roman Empire of Ammianus*. Themes touched on in my Pelagius articles have been fully developed in the well-known papers of Peter Brown (1961), (1968) and (1970), and in a stimulating article by R. Markus (1986). There have been very important books on Synesius by D. Roques (1987) and S. Vollenweider (1986). A great deal of new insight into the whole complex of problems involving Synesius, Chrysostom and Gainas will be provided by the forthcoming book of Alan Cameron, Jaqueline Long and Lee Sherry, *Barbarians and Politics at the Court of Arcadius* (U. of California P.) The last few years have produced a lot of work on Syria in Late Antiquity. Some is mentioned in article XVI, more is cited in Hugh Kennedy (1985). Late Roman administration has not been a particularly popular object of research in recent times, but there has been movement in the area of taxation and the related area of city-finance. A. Cerati (1975) has shown that A.H.M. Jones's *Later Roman Empire* does not contain the last word on *iuga, capita* and the Late Roman system of taxation. J. Gascou's work on the interrelation of city, state and great estates in Byzantine Egypt (1985), and the very intelligent, if controversial writings of W. Goffart on the related topics of late taxation and barbarian settlement (1974 and 1980) raise fundamental issues. The stimulating effect of Goffart's work is illustrated by the recent volume of the Austrian Academy edited by H. Wolfram and A. Schwarcz (1988), and especially the contribution of J. Durliat (1988).

So discussion continues: 'inque brevi spatio mutantur saecla animantum et quasi cursores vitai lampada tradunt.' (Lucretius II.77–8)

*
*　*

It remains for me to thank the editors and publishers of the books and journals in which the articles first appeared for generously giving permission to Variorum Reprints to reproduce them in this volume: The Roman Society, London (I); Akademie-Verlag, Berlin (II); Verlag Peter Lang, Frankfurt a. M. (III); *Nottingham Medieval Studies*, University of Nottingham (IV, XVI); the Australian Association for Byzantine Studies (V); *Latomus*, Brussels (VI); Franz Steiner Verlag Wiesbaden GmbH, Stuttgart (VII, XI); Akadémiai Kiadó, Budapest (VIII); Basil Blackwell, Oxford (IX); Associated Book Publishers (U.K.) Ltd, London (X); C.H. Beck Verlag and the *Byzantinische Zeitschrift* (XII, XVIII); J.D. Sauerländer's Verlag, Frankfurt a. M. (XIII); *Byzantion* (XIV, XV); the *Rocznik Papirologii Prawniczej (Journal of Juristic Papyrology)*, University of Warsaw (XVIII); and the Rheinisches Landesmuseum, Bonn (XX).

J.H.G.W. LIEBESCHUETZ

Nottingham,
August 1989

Works mentioned in Introduction

Brown, Peter (1961) 'Aspects of the Christianisation of the Roman aristocracy', *J.R.S.* LI, 1–11.

———— (1968) 'Pelagius and his supporters', *J. Theol. St.* n.s. XIX, 93–114.

———— (1970) 'The patrons of Pelagius: the Roman aristocracy between East and West', *J. Theol. St.* n.s. XXI, 56–72.

———— (1972) *Religion and Society in the Age of Saint Augustine*, London: Faber, 161–226 = reprints of the 3 above cited articles.

Cameron, Alan; Long, Jacqueline; Sherry, Lee (forthcoming) *Barbarians and Politics at the Court of Arcadius*, U. of California Press.

Cerati, A. (1975) *Caractère annonaire et assiette de l'impôt foncier au Bas-Empire*, Paris.

Durliat, J. (1985) 'Le salaire de la paix sociale dans les royaumes barbares, Ve-VIe siècles', in H. Wolfram and A. Schwarcz (1988), 21–72.

Gascou, J. (1975) 'Les grands domaines, la cité et l'état en Égypt byzantine', *Travaux et Mémoires* IX, 1–90.

Goffart, W. (1974) *Caput and Colonate, towards a History of Late Roman Taxation*, Toronto.

———— (1980) *Barbarians and Romans AD — 584 the Technique of Accommodation*, Princeton.

Kennedy, Hugh (1985) 'The last century of Byzantine Syria: a reinterpretation', *Byzantinische Forschungen* X, 141–83.

Lane-Fox, R. (1986) *Pagans and Christians*, London.

MacCormack, S.G. (1976) 'Latin prose panegyrics: tradition and discontinuity in the Later Roman Empire', *Revue des études augustiniennes* XXII, 29–77.

———— (1981) *Art and Ceremony in Late Antiquity*, Berkeley: U of California Press.

Markus, R.A. (1986) 'Pelagianism: Britain and the Continent', *J. Eccl. Hist.* XXXVII, 191–204.

Matthews, J. (1990) *The Roman Empire of Ammianus*, Berkeley and London.

Nixon, C.E.V. (1987) *Pacatus, Panegyric to the Emperor Theodosius*, translated with an introduction by C.E.V. Nixon, Liverpool University Press.

Price, S.R.F. (1984) *Rituals and Power, the Roman imperial cult in Asia Minor*, Cambridge.

Roques, D. (1987) *Synésios de Cyrène et la Cyrénaique du Bas-Empire*, Paris: CNRS.

Vollenweider, S. (1985) *Neuplatonische und Christliche Theologie bei Synesios von Kyrene*, Göttingen.

Wolfram, H. and Schwarcz, A. (1988) *Anerkennung und Integration*, Österreichische Akademie der Wissenschaften, Phil.-Hist. Kl., Denkschriften no.193.

I

THE RELIGIOUS POSITION OF LIVY'S HISTORY

The History of Livy is extraordinarily full of references to the gods and their worship. In this way it differs strikingly from the writings of Sallust and Tacitus, not to mention the Commentaries of Caesar. This fact has been interpreted in various ways. Kajanto has argued that, the frequent references to religious matters notwithstanding, events in Livy's History are mainly determined by human beings, not by gods and fate.[1] Bayet sees in Livy a pure agnostic who has grasped the importance of the religious factor in history.[2] On the other hand, Stübler maintains that Livy was traditionally orthodox and supplemented tradition with a belief in the mission of the emperor Augustus as a god and son of a god to save Rome.[3] An intermediate position is taken up by Walsh who sees in Livy a Stoic who can continue to respect traditional beliefs and practices because they have been given a symbolic place in a comprehensive philosophical system.[4]

A considerable part of the difficulty in penetrating to Livy's personal attitudes lies in the fact that Livy's History has been profoundly influenced by earlier narratives. The narrative of numerous events of Roman history had long been shaped into a pattern which would teach a civic or religious moral. It was an important function of historiography at Rome to convey such lessons [5] and Livy, when rewriting the earlier narratives, will have been reluctant to omit or change beyond recognition too many of the well known *exempla*.[6] In addition, it has been shown that earlier histories not only furnished Livy with a factual basis for his narrative but also strongly influenced the whole character of sections based on them.[7] On the other hand Livy's most individual contribution to the History is generally agreed to consist of the episodes, single scenes, or sequences of scenes, into which he has organised the traditional material.[8]

In the present paper a number of Livy's episodes are examined in detail. I shall argue that thorough-going rationalism and earnest advocacy of religion are closely associated. Livy would appear to have been unaware that one was inconsistent with the other and to have made no attempt to save Roman religion by associating it with a more rational system such as that of the Stoics. It will be suggested that Livy's attitude, a reflection of the overwhelmingly public character of Roman religion, was shared by many educated Romans of the age and survived into much later periods.

I. LIVY'S THOUGHT REVEALED IN EPISODES

Livy's handling of an episode can be studied in the narrative of the Caudine Forks disaster. Livy based his version on an elaborate older account, with many details derived from the events connected with the Numantine treaty of 137—an exceptionally clear example of the reconstruction of the Roman past on the model of more recent events.[9] This account

---

* I should like to thank Dr. P. G. Walsh and Professor A. D. Momigliano for suggestions and corrections.

[1] I. Kajanto, *God and Fate in Livy* (1957). Use of this work has been made throughout this paper. cf. W. Warde Fowler, *Roman Ideas of Deity* (1914), 134–58.

[2] J. Bayet, Budé edition of *Livy* 1, xxxix; 5, 137–8.

[3] G. Stübler, *Die Religiosität des Livius* (1941).

[4] P. G. Walsh, *Livy, his historical aims and method* (1961), 46–81 ; also ' Livy and Stoicism ', *AJP* LXXIX (1958), 355–75 ; also in T. A. Dorey (editor), *Latin Historians* (1966), 115–42.

[5] cf. Cicero, *de Or.* 2, 36 ; *Or.* 120. His use of *exempla* : M. Rambeau, *Cicéron et l'histoire romaine* (1953), 25–54. Augustus collects *exempla* : Suet., *Aug.* 39, 2. Polybius noted that Roman history contained many stories of exemplary patriotic behaviour like that of Horatius Cocles : Pol. 6, 54, 6—55, 4.

[6] Some older *exempla* : Dream of Latinius, Liv. 2, 36, 1 ff. and Cic., *Div.* 1, 55 ; Macr., *Sat.* 1, 11, 3. Defeat of Flaminius, Liv. 22, 3, 4 ff. and Cic., *Div.*

1, 77. Temple of Locri, Liv. 29, 8, 9 ff. ; 29, 18, 1–16 and Diod. 27, 4.

Camillus' generosity to Falerii already an *exemplum* in 171 : Liv. 42, 47, 6 ; Diod. 30, 7, 1. A. Momigliano, *CQ* XXXVI (1942), 110–20, esp. 113 ; = *Secondo contributo alla storia degli studi classici* (1960), 89–104.

[7] Walsh, *Livy* 124–6, 131–5. See also A. H. McDonald, *PCPhS* 186 (1960), 43–8, especially 45 on ' scissors and paste ' composition ; R. M. Ogilvie, *A Commentary on Livy, Books 1–5* (1965), 7–16.

[8] E. Burck, *Die Erzählungskunst des T. Livius* (reprint of 1964 with up-to-date bibliography), 182 ff. ; Ogilvie, o.c. 17 ff. ; K. Witte, *RhM* LXV (1910), 270 ff. and 359 ff. A single scene, death of Romulus : 1, 15, 6–16, 8. A sequence of scenes forming a unit : 1, 8, 4–13, 8 (Sabine women).

[9] 9, 1–12, 4. See H. Nissen, 'der Caudinische Frieden ', *RhM* LXV (1870), 43 ff. While there can be no doubt that the detail of the renunciation of the Caudine treaty is based on events of 137/6, the surrender of the sponsors of the Caudine treaty was already considered a precedent in 136 : Plut., *Ti. Gracchus* 8 ; App., *Ib.* 83.

had already suggested that the Roman disaster had been incurred as retribution for the arrogant refusal of a Samnite offer of peace.[10]

We can conclude from his many references to *fetiales*, or the justness or otherwise of war,[11] that this was a lesson which Livy considered important. It is not surprising therefore that he developed it to the best of his ability. The arrogance of the Romans, the injustice of their cause and the appropriateness of the punishment are made abundantly clear.[12] But the episode does not end with the lesson. The second and longer part, the description of how the Romans reacted to disaster and humiliation, is developed to provide an impressive example of Roman character, of the pride and sense of honour which made the Samnites' rejection of the advice of Herennius Pontius a disastrous mistake.[13]

In this second half of the episode the topic of the just war is still relevant but Livy has handled it differently so as to allow no clear lesson to emerge. He insists that the agreement which the Romans renounced was a *sponsio* not a *foedus* and thus eliminates the offence against the gods.[14] He reports two speeches in which the ex-consul Postumius proposes and defends the renunciation of the treaty. But he also records the objections of certain tribunes and repeats them in a speech assigned to the Samnite leader, Gaius Pontius himself.[15] The moral issue has thus been turned not into a lesson but into a debate—a debate whose outcome is inconclusive.

After the renunciation of the treaty, the surrendered sponsors are rejected by the Samnites and return home *forsitan et publica, sua certe liberata fide*.[16] This cautious phrase surely implies that Livy felt considerable doubt as to the morality of the Roman action. It is necessary to add that the inconclusiveness of the debate is hardly allowed to reflect on the Roman decision. The reader has already been fully convinced that a people such as the Romans have been shown to be could not possibly live at peace after so great a humiliation. The Romans are felt to be humanly if not morally justified.

Taking the episode as a whole, we see that the moral interest is central throughout—surely there is very little constitutional or historical interest—but the straightforward moral lesson occupies only a portion of the episode. Livy has shown himself eager to build up suitable material to teach an appropriate lesson but also aware that much history is not suitable and that issues like the renunciation of the Caudine treaty are too complex for simple approval or condemnation.

An example of an episode in which religion occupies a central place is provided by the narrative of the deification of Romulus. This brilliantly evokes the psychological atmosphere in which a new cult becomes accepted.[17] The disappearance of Romulus in the midst of a sudden storm, followed shortly after by a return to bright sunshine, leaves the actual fate of Romulus mysterious, while the accompanying natural phenomena suggest supernatural processes.[18] The explanation that Romulus has been taken up to heaven is assigned to senators who were standing nearest and is represented as evoking an outburst of religious emotion in the frightened people.[19] Nowhere does he state that it was an illusion. Nowhere does he state that an alternative version, which had darkly survived to his time, according to which Romulus had been killed and dismembered by the senators, was the true one.[20] But indirectly he unmistakably shows that this was the version he favoured. Early in his account he states that Romulus was dearer to the people than to the

[10] Dion. H. 15, 9 (13). Dio 8, 8–10 ; Zonar. 7, 20. App., *Samn.* 1–2.

[11] 1, 24, 3 ff.; 1, 35, 5 (cf. Ogilvie, o.c. 127) ; 3, 71 ; 4, 30 ; 7, 31 ff. ; 21, 5 ff. ; 21, 10, 9 ; 21, 19, 6 ; 31, 8, 3 ; 35, 16, 1 ; 36, 3, 9 ; 38, 42, 7 ; 39, 2, 1–3. This concern for the justness of wars was already found in Livy's predecessors. See N. Erb, *Kriegsursachen und Kriegsschuld in der ersten Pentade des T. Livius*, (1963) ; M. Gelzer, ' Römische Politik bei Fabius Pictor ', *Hermes* LXVIII (1933), 129–66 = *Kl. Schr.* 3, 51–92. Polybius' interpretation : Pol. 36, 2.

[12] 9, 1, 3–11 ; end of lesson, 9, 7, 12.

[13] 9, 3, 5–13 ; ibid. 12, 2–4.

[14] 9, 5, 2 : ' non ut volgo credunt Claudiusque etiam scripsit foedere pax Caudina sed per spon-

sionem facta est.' cf. Cic., *Inv.* 2, 30, *foedus summae religionis*.

[15] 9, 8, 3—9, 19 ; cf. Cic., *Off.* 3, 10, 109 ; *Rep.* 3, 18, 28. C. Pontius : Liv. 9, 11, 1–13.

[16] 9, 11, 13.

[17] 1, 15, 6—16, 8 ; cf. J.-C. Richard, ' Énée, Romulus, César et les funerailles impériales ', *MEFR* LXXVIII (1966), 67–78.

[18] Not only the thunder but also the rapid restoration of *serena et tranquilla lux*, cf. 2, 62, 2 *tranquilla serenitas* and 26, 11, 3 *mira serenitas cum tranquillitate*. In *religionem ea res ... versa est*. According to Dion. H. 2, 56, 2 such detail is found in accounts that are μυθωδέστερα. Livy uses it to make his rationalist account psychologically plausible.

[19] 1, 16, 2–3.

[20] 1, 16, 4; cf. Dion. H. 2, 56, 3 ; Cic., *Rep.* 2, 10 (20).

senators and that he kept a bodyguard.[21] This information in this position must be intended to prepare the reader for Romulus' murder by the senators. Next the report of his apotheosis is expressly assigned to senators, and the fact that it prevailed is ascribed to the panic of the moment and to the admiration of Romulus' qualities—nothing is said about its truth.[22] Finally Proculus Iulius claims that the deified Romulus has appeared to him. But this action is motivated or at least its circumstances are indicated by *sollicita civitate desiderio regis et infensa patribus*,[23] which strongly suggests that the vision was made up with the political aim of calming the people and reconciling them to the senate, an aim which, we are expressly told, it achieved.[24]

So Livy did not believe that Romulus was actually raised to heaven.[25] But this does not mean that he refused him divine honours. The section dealing with his death begins by asserting that none of the actions of Romulus' life was in contradiction of the belief held after his death of his divine origin or of his divinity.[26] This statement is echoed by the phrase which opens the last scene of Romulus' life, *his inmortalibus editis operibus*,[27] and again by the statement that *admiratio viri* induced people to believe in his apotheosis.[28] Moreover the supposed vision is given a perfectly valid divine message for the Roman people : . . . *caelestes ita velle ut mea Roma caput orbis terrarum sit : proinde rem militarem colant.* . . . It is plain that Livy did not consider that to show the purely human origin of a cult was enough to discredit it. Quite the contrary. Great public benefits deserved religious commemoration. It is quite consistent that the religious rite described after the account of the foundation of Rome is not directed towards one of the great gods but to Hercules, represented as a deified man.[29]

Another episode in which religion plays a great part is the narrative of the great Latin War,[30] culminating in the *devotio* of the consul Decius in the decisive battle. The religious features were already in Livy's source, but we can observe some of his modifications.

After hearing the impudent demands of the Latins the consul Manlius turns to the image of Jupiter with the words : ' Hear these wicked proposals, Jupiter, hear them, Law and Right (*ius fasque*)! Will you, Jupiter, observe foreign consuls and a foreign senate in your consecrated temple, yourself a prisoner and defeated ? '[31] The language is religious but also demagogic and recalls the arguments used to oppose the political advance of the plebeians.[32] Livy is critical of this particular example of demagogy. He describes Manlius as *par ferociae* of the Latin envoys, and thus recalls his condemnation of the Roman envoys who had provoked the great attack of the Gauls.[33] The traditional account, or Livy's particular source, then moved to a climax : the Latin envoy scorns Jupiter and receives instant and dramatic punishment. Livy tones down the supernatural elements with a *proditur memoriae* and states as a fact only that the envoy fell down the steps of the temple. A miracle is reduced to an omen. As for the rest he comments *et vera esse et apte ad repraesentandam iram deum ficta possunt*. But the traditional point remains. The war whose successful outcome proved a turning point in Roman history was a thoroughly just one.[34]

In the account of the *devotio* Livy first reveals his rationalism by dissociating himself from the account of a vision seen by each of the consuls with a *dicitur*.[35] Then the consul's

---

[21] 1, 15, 8.
[22] 1, 16, 4.
[23] 1, 16, 5 continues ' et *consilio* . . . unius hominis addita rei dicitur fides '.
[24] 1, 16, 8 ; cf. Cic., *Rep.* 2, 10 (20).
[25] There is not even an assurance of the survival of the soul of Romulus, which seems to be accepted by Dion. H. 2, 56, 6 ; ibid. 2, 56, 3 ; Cic., *Leg.* 2, 8, 19 ; ibid. 2, 11, 27 ; *ND* 2, 24, 62 ; but mocked by Cotta in *ND* 3, 15, 39. Also Dion. H. 2, 63, 3 seems to be acquitting Julius of inventing the vision.
[26] 1, 15, 6 ; cf. Cic., *Rep.* 2, 10 (17).
[27] 1, 16, 1.
[28] 1, 16, 4.
[29] The message : 1, 16, 7 ; Hercules : 1, 7, 15. Does Livy's attitude imply a readiness to deify the living Augustus ? This is not clear ; cf. 4, 20, 7 (Ogilvie, o.c., n. 7, 563–4), *prope sacrilegium* not to accept Augustus' version of the Cossus inscription— but this is perhaps humorous and Livy did not alter

his version. See also 9, 18, 4 *vanitatem ementiendae stirpis* (of Alexander the Great) and 26, 19, 6–8.
[30] Liv. 8, 3, 8–11, 1 On location of battle see note in *O.C.T.* on 8, 8, 19.
[31] 8, 5, 8.
[32] 6, 41, 4 ff.
[33] 5, 36, 1.
[34] 8, 6, 3. Livy regularly dissociates himself from narratives of miracular occurrences, e.g. 1, 31, 4 *traditur* followed by *certe* when he resumes his account of facts ; cf. 1, 55, 3 *traditur* ; ibid. 5 *dicitur* ; 2, 7, 2 *adiciunt miracula* . . . *creditam* . . . *certe* ; 7, 6 (Marcus Curtius) *dicitur* . . . *ferunt* . . . Omission of Dioscuri from battle of Lake Regillus : cf. Liv. 2, 20, 12 with Ogilvie's commentary and Cic., *ND* 2, 2 (6). News of Pydna : cf. Liv. 45, 1 and Cic., *ND* 2, 2 (6). On whole subject see Kajanto, o.c. n. 1, 25 ff.
[35] 8, 6, 9 ; 8, 9, 1.

self-sacrifice is described in terms of the effect it has on the soldiers of the two armies. Charging into the enemy on horseback, the consul appeared ' a victim sent from heaven to appease all divine anger and to turn destruction away from his side to that of the enemy ', for fear and panic accompanied him into the Latin ranks and there first upset the front line and then the rest of the army. Thus the *devotio* achieved its effect—but this could be explained in purely psychological terms.[36] This is also true of its effect on the Romans, who, we are told, *exsolutis religione animis* renewed their attack. The sight of the ritual victim freed the Romans from worry about the intentions of the gods.[37]

But in Livy's account the *devotio*, though beneficial, is not decisive. Even after the death of Decius, in some parts of the battle the Latins were still superior and the Roman victory was only achieved by a well-timed charge of the *triarii* on the orders of the surviving consul.[38] Either side might have won if it had been under the leadership of T. Manlius.[39] So Livy leaves the possibility open that the battle was decided by purely military factors.

To sum up the outlook revealed in the episodes examined so far, Livy has shown himself very much interested in morality, especially the observation of *fides* in private, public and international affairs,[40] but also aware that moral issues are not always straight-forward. We have also found Livy a strong supporter of religion and prepared to develop certain events as examples of the advantages of religious observance. But he is also willing to explain the effectiveness of religious rites psychologically or sociologically.

The sociological approach to religion is very prominent in Livy's treatment of Numa. When we compare his account with that of Dionysius of Halicarnassus we see that Livy has magnified Numa's share in the establishment of the state religion,[41] perhaps primarily from the literary motive of gaining a sharp character-contrast between Romulus, the great military leader, and Numa, the man who founded the state anew *iure . . . legibusque ac moribus*.[42] But the result of this method of composition, that Roman religion appears as something deliberately established by a king to serve as a foundation for the social order of a state at peace, must be intended. It is likely that this widely held view of the origin and purpose of Roman religion was already found in Livy's source, perhaps Antias.[43] But Livy does nothing to obscure it. On the contrary he states it as clearly and unambiguously as possible ' positis externorum periculorum curis ne luxuriarent otio animi, quos metus hostium disciplinaque militaris continuerat, . . . rem ad multitudinem imperitam et illis saeculis rudem efficacissimam, deorum metum iniciendum ratus est '.[44] And since this fear could not be made to descend into their minds without the aid of ' some invented marvel ' he pretended that he had nocturnal meetings with the goddess Egeria and that it was she who had inspired his religious regulations.

And Numa achieved his aim. The people, the *multitudo*, became so preoccupied with appeasing the gods in the correct way that their thoughts turned away from force and violence. More positively, since it was felt that the gods took an interest in human affairs, such piety filled the hearts of all that *fides ac ius iurandum* could regulate social relationships without the support offered by the penalties of the laws.[45] Livy returns to the topic of *fides* when he describes Numa's institution of the cult of that goddess. By including in the chapter on Numa's religious innovation, alone of numerous perhaps equally picturesque rites, a description of part of the ritual of *Fides*, he once again emphasises that this is the most valuable product of Roman piety—in the private field at any rate.[46]

It has been suggested that Livy's rationalism is restricted to the superstition of the lower orders,[47] but of this there is insufficient evidence. Admittedly, he provides many examples of the social use of religion to keep the people in order,[48] or to oppose political change,[49]

[36] 8, 9, 9–13. Other examples of psychological effectiveness of ritual acts : 1, 12, 5–6 ; 10, 26, 11 ; 10, 19, 17 ; 2, 62, 1–2 ; 26, 11, 2–3.
[37] 8, 9, 13.
[38] 8, 10, 4 ff.
[39] 8, 10, 8.
[40] cf. nn. 11, 45, 46.
[41] Dion. H. 2, 18–23 assigns basic religious regulations to Romulus. Livy 1, 7, 3 ' sacra dis aliis Albano ritu, Graeco Herculi ut ab Euandro instituta erant facit'.
[42] 1, 19, 1 ; Ogilvie, o.c. 30–1.

[43] Cic., *Rep.* 2, 14 ; *Leg.* 2, 7 (16) ; Dion. H. 2, 63 ff. cf. Ogilvie, o.c. n. 7, 90–1 ; F. W. Walbank, *Commentary on Polybius* Vol. 1 (1957), 741–2 ; W. Fowler, *Roman Ideas of Deity* 81 ff.
[44] 1, 19, 4.
[45] 1, 21, 1–2. Similarly Pol. 6, 56, 13–15.
[46] 1, 21, 4 on *fides* ; cf. 3, 20, 5 and two famous *exempla*, *Per.* 18 (Regulus), 24, 18, 5 (prisoners of Cannae).
[47] Walsh, *Livy* 48.
[48] 5, 55, 1 ; 6, 1, 10.
[49] 4, 2, 5 ff. ; 5, 14, 2 ; 6, 41, 4 ff. ; 7, 6, 10.

and gives no indication that he considers this an abuse. But neither does he at all suggest that he distinguished between aspects of the religion of the Roman people which were merely socially useful and those which had a more truly religious or philosophical significance.

In Livy's history there are few examples of that higher religion implied in Varro's saying that the superstitious man fears the gods but the truly religious person reveres them as parents.[50] He will not even allow religious merit to the contemplative vigils of Scipio Africanus in the temple of Jupiter. There is no place in this history for knowledge of the gods derived from contemplation of the regular motions of the heavens, which according to Stoic doctrine can be the source of piety and justice and of a happy life.[51] Livy did not develop the idea of Natural Religion,[52] although the account of religious acts before Numa might have given him an opportunity.

Livy certainly appears to criticise some manifestations of religion; all forms of religious hysteria or excess,[53] religious individualism, even on the part of a national hero,[54] mystery cults,[55] the excesses of foreigners.[56] But in rejecting these things he is merely restating the traditional Roman distinction between religion and superstition,[57] not introducing a philosophic distinction between higher and lower forms of religion. Livy's rationalism must therefore be taken to operate over the whole range of the religion of the Roman people. But it would nevertheless be a mistake to deduce that Livy intends to invalidate Roman religion. Surely the piety of so many heroes of Livy's History is pointed out as not the least of the exemplary features of this most exemplary period of Roman history.

II. BOOK V: ELABORATE ADVOCACY OF RELIGION

Any doubts as to whether Livy is not after all using religion for purely literary purposes that may remain in the mind of the reader of Books I–IV of the History are surely removed by a reading of Book V. This book, which has as its double theme the capture of Veii by the Romans and of Rome by the Gauls, is not only by far the longest sustained religious episode in the History, but also one which through its place at the end of the first pentad, concluding the obscure early history, occupies a particularly emphatic position.[58] But in this episode each of the three main happenings, the capture of Veii, the capture of Rome, and the Roman recovery, follows a narrative in which the impious acts of the defeated and pious acts of the victors have been carefully recorded.[59] The moral, that national piety leads to success, is made to follow quite naturally from the narrative, but Livy also makes the point explicit, as in the sentences that herald the capture of Veii.

'And now the games and the Latin festival had been repeated, now the water had been let out from the Alban lake upon the fields and now her fate was seeking Veii out. Accordingly, the leader fated to bring about the destruction of that city and to save his country, Marcus Furius Camillus, was appointed dictator. The change in command instantaneously changed the entire situation.'[60] In this summing up, which is surely Livy's own, the contribution to victory of various ritual acts and of the generalship of Camillus are put absolutely parallel and on the same level. Each contributes to victory in the same way and to the same degree.

A similar tendency is implicit in the treatment of the second episode of the book, the capture of Rome by the Gauls. Before the disaster the Romans replaced a deceased censor,

[50] Varro in Aug., *CD* 6, 9.
[51] Scipio : 26, 19, 9 ; contemplation of heavens : Cic., *ND* 2, 61 (153) ; *Div.* 2, 72 (148–9).
[52] Cic., *Leg.* 1, 8 (24) ; Dio Chr. 12, 39 ; Varro in Aug., *CD* 4, 31.
[53] e.g. 6, 5, 6 ; 7, 3, 1–4 ; 25, 1, 6 ff. ; 26, 9, 7–8 ; 27, 23, 2 ; 27, 37, 1 ff. ; 28, 11, 1 ; 29, 10, 4 ; 29, 14, 1–2.
[54] 1, 31, 7 ; cf. 1, 20, 6–7 ; also on Scipio Africanus 26, 19, 9.
[55] 39, 8 ff. (Bacchanal scandal). cf. G. R. Reitzenstein, *Die Hellenistischen Mysterienreligionen* (1927), 101 ff. ; K. Latte, *Römische Religionsgeschichte* (1960), 270 ff.
[56] In the episode 10, 38 ff. Livy contrasts the

Samnites' barbarous abuse of religion (38, 5–13) with the good sense of the Roman who acts on the report of favourable auspices even though the report is proved false (40), and vows a thimbleful of mead (42, 7). See also abuse of religion in mass suicides : 28, 22, 5–11 (Astapa) ; 31, 17 (Abydos). On Abydos contrast Polybius 16, 31–3, cf. F. W. Walbank, *JRS* LV (1965), 11.
[57] Cic., *ND* 2, 28 (72) ; *Div.* 2, 72 (149). On the origin, K. Latte, o.c. 268.
[58] A. Klotz, *RE* XIII, 819. Walsh, *Livy* 173. Second Preface : 6, 1, 1–3.
[59] Analysis : Burck, o.c. n. 8, 109–36 ; Ogil o.c. n. 7, 626.
[60] 5, 19, 1–2.

took no notice of a divine warning, and expelled their ablest general Camillus. Finally Roman ambassadors, in flagrant breach of the *ius gentium*, took part in fighting against the Gauls and were subsequently not surrendered to the Gauls but elected to office.[61] The ensuing disastrous war is thus shown to have been a thoroughly unjust one.

The theme that the Romans defeated at the Allia were fighting in an unjust cause Livy found in his sources.[62] But he used all the resources of his art to impress it on his readers. ' Now even though so heavy a weight of calamity was looming over them—to such an extent does fortune blind men when she does not want her gathering might to be resisted and scattered . . . ', the Romans did not appoint a dictator, did not levy adequate forces, did not fortify a camp before battle, consulted neither auspices nor entrails before engaging the enemy and were defeated almost without a fight.[63] Even though Livy never makes the point explicit, a reader familiar with the idea of dramatic justice [64] cannot avoid feeling that the Romans were defeated because they had acted impiously and that the blindness inflicted on them was an act of just retribution.[65]

But with the entry of the Gauls into the city a complete reversal of Roman morale took place. Henceforth, the Romans showed the utmost respect for all matters concerned with religion.[66] Now the Gauls have put themselves in the wrong.[67] They are then defeated as effortlessly as they had previously conquered the Romans.[68] Finally, the moral of all these events—that the Romans fare well when they heed the gods but badly when they spurn them—is drawn in Camillus' great concluding speech.[69]

But the fact that Livy has composed his narrative to teach a religious moral does not mean that the form of this or similar narratives is to be taken at its face value, as a literal account of the way the gods reward piety and punish impiety. Such naivety would be unthinkable on the part of the author of the episodes discussed earlier. Then, many of the religious topics, the prophecies and their appeasement, the acts of piety after the battle of the Allia, perhaps the arguments for not moving the city to Veii,[70] were so tightly bound up with the subject matter of Book V that only an aggressive secularist could have written the book on a purely profane plane—and we know that Livy was not that. Finally, Book V is by far the longest passage in which metaphysical reward and punishment plays such a central role. Such passages become progressively rarer in the later books.[71] This in itself suggests that Livy felt most free to use such motifs when the events he was describing contained a considerable proportion of myth—as he believed to be the case with Roman history up to the capture of Rome by the Gauls [72]—and could thus be shaped more freely into effective examples.

One must also consider literary convention. Since the Hellenistic period, or even earlier, historians had used religious motifs without theological implications for moralising or even purely literary ends.[73] Thus the history of Agathocles found in Diodorus, but probably derived from Duris,[74] employs many of Livy's themes : divine signs,[75] the political use of religion,[76] and the psychology of crisis religion.[77] The account also includes a fulfilled oracle [78] and examples of supernatural retribution.[79] Another section of Diodorus' History, probably based on Philinus, presents the disaster suffered by Regulus at the hands of the Carthaginians as a punishment for his earlier arrogance in refusing terms of peace.[80]

---

[61] 5, 31, 6 ; 32, 6 ; 36, 8.

[62] 5, 36. cf. Diod. 14, 113, 3–7. Dion. H. 13, 12.

[63] 5, 37, 1–3 ; 38, 1 ; 38, 5 ff. This detail is not found in other versions.

[64] For Greek tradition: Ogilvie, o.c., on 5, 37, 1 ; cf. also Livy 44, 6, 14 ; 6, 17 (from Polybius ?) ; 29, 8, 11 ; 18, 12–15 (temple of Locri).

[65] cf. Cic., *Har. Resp.* 39. Blindness as gift of fortune : Cic., *Am.* 15 (54).

[66] 5, 39, 8 ff. ; cf. 5, 47, 4 and Plut., *Camillus* 27, 3 on sacred geese.

[67] 5, 48, 9.

[68] ibid. 49, 5, ' iam verterat fortuna, iam deorum opes humanaque consilia rem Romanam adiuvabant. igitur primo concursu haud maiore momento fusi Galli sunt quam ad Alliam vicerant'.

[69] 5, 51, 5–10. But Kajanto, *God and Fate* 35–7, argues that Livy merely gives Camillus the arguments which a pious Roman of the old times would have used.

[70] cf. Plut., *Cam.* 31, 3 ; 32, 1.

[71] Walsh, *Livy* 55. Kajanto, o.c. 52–3, 62–3, 98–100.

[72] *Praef.* 7 (cf. Cic., *Leg.* 1, 1–5) ; Liv. 6, 1, 2 ff. ; 7, 6, 6, '. . . fama rerum standum est, ubi certam derogat vetustas fidem '. On the First Decade as ' prose epic ' cf. McDonald, o.c. n. 7 above, 166–8.

[73] References to religion hold attention : Cic., *Inv.* 1, 23. cf. F. W. Walbank, *Bull. Inst. Cl. St.* 1955, 4 ff. and *Historia IX* (1960), 216–34 ; B. L. Ullman, *TAPA* (1942), 25–53.

[74] *RE* v, 2, col. 1855 *s.v.* Duris (E. Schwartz) ; P. Oxy. XXIV, n. 2399.

[75] Diod. 19, 2, 2 and 19, 29.

[76] ibid., 20, 7 and 20, 11.

[77] ibid., 20, 14.

[78] ibid., 20, 29, 3.

[79] ibid., 19, 103, 5 ; 20, 70.

[80] Diod. 23, 15, 1–6 ; cf. Pol. 1, 35. F. W. Walbank, *CQ* XXXIX (1945), 1–18.

Even Polybius made use of the full machinery of tragedy, furies, blindly self-destructive actions and agony, to make the unhappy last years of Philip V of Macedon appear to be a retribution for the crimes of the earlier years of his reign.[81] But in Polybius the features are clearly not meant to be statements about the moral government of the universe, but similes, impressing the reader that his particular history was as terrible and sad as any he might see on the stage.

This use of religion also came to Rome. Roman historians took over many of the dramatic devices of the ' tragic ' historians, and among them metaphysical causation. Livy's predecessors had already presented the Caudine disaster and the defeat of Regulus [82] as retribution for arrogance. The defeat of Gaius Flaminius at Lake Trasimene was shown to have been deserved by the consul's impiety.[83] Responsibility for the destruction of Carthage seems to have been assigned by Valerius Antias to Nemesis.[84] The capture of Rome in 390 appears to have been treated in one version as a punishment for an earlier act of hubris, the refusal by the Romans of a Veiian offer to surrender.[85] This theme was not taken up by Livy, but that of the guilty envoys which plays so important a part in his narrative had also been previously used by one or more of his predecessors.[86] It would seem that this particular feature of dramatic writing appealed to Roman historians because it provided a convenient way of putting into history the moral lessons which, as we have seen, it was one of the functions of historiography at Rome to supply.[87]

Thus Livy's scheme of composition in Book V would not be thought to have committed him personally to any particular view about providence and its ways with men. Educated readers certainly would have recognized it as part of his dramatic literary technique.[88] As literary technique it is extremely effective. Livy's demonstration of the benefits that result to the Roman people when Roman virtue and Roman religion together determine the behaviour of Rome's citizens is all the more convincing because it suggests an immediate if naive explanation of why these benefits result. But as this explanation is not explicitly stated, but in accordance with Livy's normal technique [89] merely made to arise out of the events, the reader remains free to supply his own more sophisticated explanation.

III.   LIVY AND STOICISM

It has been suggested [90] that the sophisticated explanation which enabled Livy himself to argue the continued validity of traditional cults was Stoic philosophy, in the form in which it was current at Rome and is expounded in Cicero's *De Natura Deorum* : that Reason, which according to Stoic doctrine pervades all nature,[91] might be personified, as Ceres on the land, for instance, or Neptune in the sea, and could thus be thought to provide a rational justification of the gods of the city state.[92] Stoic doctrine could also provide a new basis for morality in that by virtue of his share of the universal reason was in a position to harmonise his conduct with the end towards which the world was tending.[93] Finally the Stoic doctrine of providence [94] could be adapted to supply a higher justification for the Roman empire. Stoic philosophy was therefore well suited to serve Livy [95] as a metaphysical framework for his narrative as a whole, as well as to explain the effectiveness of religious acts. But it does not seem to me that Livy has used Stoicism, or indeed any other philosophy, in this way.

[81] F. W. Walbank, *JHS* LVII (1938), 55–68.

[82] Livy, *Per.* 19. On development of the *exemplum* : *RE* II, 2086 ff., *s.v.* Atilius 51 (P. v. Rhoden).

[83] Livy 21, 63, 1 ff. ; 22, 3, 7 ff. ; Cic., *Div.* 1, 35. Walsh, *Livy* 68.

[84] App., *Lib.* 85, cf. Walsh, *Livy* 122.

[85] Cic., *Div.* 1, 44 (100) ; Dion. H. 12, 13 (17).

[86] Diod. 14, 113 ; Dion. H. 13, 12 (18–19) ; cf. Ogilvie, o.c. n. 7, 716.

[87] The technique is likely to have fitted well with the theatrical aspect of Roman state religion noted by Polybius 6, 56, 8–11 (cf. Walbank, *CQ* XXXIX (1945), 9–10), and exploited by Cicero before the people but not the senate, *Cat.* 3, 18–23 ; cf. 2, 13. R. Syme, *Sallust* (1964), 247.

[88] On Livy's use of dramatic technique : Burck,

Erzählungskunst 176 ff. On Tarquinius' tragedy : Ogilvie, o.c. n. 7, 186–7, 196–7.

[89] I. Bruns, *Die Persönlichkeit in der Geschichtsschreibung der Alten* (1898), 12–27.

[90] Walsh, o.c. n. 4 above.

[91] Cic., *ND* 2, 19 (end) ; cp. Fowler, *Religious Experience* 365 ff.

[92] Cic., *ND* 2, 28 (70–72).

[93] Cic., *Leg.* 1, 7 (22).

[94] Cic., *ND* 2, 13 (36).

[95] Leaving aside the problem of the depth to which a Roman's outlook might be affected by Greek philosophy. Obviously Lucretius was profoundly affected, but Cicero or Varro very much more superficially. cp. W. Fowler, *Roman Ideas of Deity*, 81–2.

In spite of his method of indirect characterization Livy is always careful to make the point of his lesson perfectly, even pedantically, clear. If therefore he intended his story to be interpreted in terms of a system of philosophy, he would surely have provided some quite unmistakable indication that he had a particular system in mind. But there are no unmistakable references to Stoic philosophy in the History. Such Stoic themes as philosophical religion, natural religion, or the harmony of the natural order,[96] do not occur at all. Some expressions which can be understood in a Stoic sense are found. But they are too scattered, too obscure and too ambiguous to be taken for the philosophical key to the whole. These defects, for instance, limit the significance of certain final or comparative clauses which carry the implication that the endless succession of troubles suffered by the Romans in their early years were purposively sent to school the people for greatness.[97] Certainly a doctrine of providence can be read into them. But in no case is it a primary [98] function of the passage to make a statement about providence.

More prominent, through numbers and context, are the forty references to fate, and it is indeed tempting to see in them a pointer to a Stoic doctrine of providence.[99] But examination of individual passages in their context does not suggest that the idea of a purposeful providential order is the central concept underlying them all. Instead, they naturally seem to fall into two groups : passages where fate represents the divine will as expressed in oracles,[100] and those where it personifies inevitable destruction, or the power responsible for sending it.[101] In the passages of the second group fate is often a near synonym for death.[102] In a number of passages fate represents the destiny of an individual, but mostly in contexts where the possibility at least of death is being contemplated.[103]

Fate is most prominent in Book V and here the passages fall very clearly into these two groups. The *libri fatales* are the books containing the oracular lore of the Etruscans and the *fata* are the prophecies contained in them or in a reply of the Delphic oracle.[104] Secondly, *fatum* or *fata* appear in the role of remorseless and inevitably approaching calamity—or the power responsible for it.[105] The relative prominence of *fatum* in Book V is a consequence of the relevance of each of the meanings to the subject matter of the book. In the narrative of no other event in Roman history do oracles play so essential a part as in the narrative of the conquest of Veii. On no other occasion were the Romans unable to avoid the crowning calamity of the capture and burning of their city. Each of the two

---

[96] See above, nn. 50–2.

[97] As argued by Walsh, *Livy* 52–3. The relevant passages are 3, 10, 8 (cf. 6, 21, 2) ; 6, 34, 5 ; 7, 1, 7 ; 7, 27, 1 ; and 10, 6, 3. cf. also 1, 46, 3, the most significant. The relative insignificance of the final clauses is illustrated by 6, 34, 5 where after relating the failure of plebeians to stand for the consular tribunate Livy comments ' ne id nimis laetum parti alteri esset ' and proceeds to relate the beginning of the Licinian-Sextian agitation. Surely providence was pursuing more profound aims in this matter than to prevent excessive joy over a political triumph.

[98] e.g. 6, 21, 2 ' Volscos . . . velut sorte quadam prope in aeternum exercendo Romano militi datos ' distinguishes *Volsci* from more occasional enemies. In 3, 30, 2, Livy's comment on the cessation of civil strife as a result of a hostile raid expresses his belief in the importance of *metus hostilis* for the preservation of internal peace at Rome. See I. Kajanto, *Arctos* 11 (1958), 56–63, esp. 61–2 with ref. to Liv. 2, 54, 2 ; 3, 9, 1 ; 1, 19, 4 ; cf. the debate over the destruction of Carthage : Plut., *Cat. Ma.* 27, 3 ; App., *Lib.* 69 ; Diod. 34, 33, 4–6 ; Sall., *Cat.* 10. Of all the passages only the statement about the Ligurians (39, 1, 1) is part of a longer development (cf. speech of Manlius, 38, 17). But even this should probably be taken to mean no more than that Livy thought constant effort good for the Romans.

[99] Stoic interpretation : Walsh, *Livy* 53–5 ; Ogilvie, o.c. n. 7, 48, on 1, 4, 1. A contrary view : Kajanto, *God and Fate* 53–63. The following argument owes much to Kajanto.

[100] e.g. 1, 7, 11 ; 8, 6, 11 ; 8, 24, 11 ; 21, 22, 9 ; 29, 10, 8. See also below, n. 104.

[101] e.g. 8, 24, 4 ; 10, 28, 12. See also below, n. 105.

[102] 3, 50, 8 ; 9, 1, 6 ; 10, 29, 3 ; 26, 13, 17 ; 42, 11, 5 ; 42, 52, 7.

[103] 1, 7, 15 ; 5, 40, 3 ; 8, 24, 2 ; 9, 18, 19 ; 8, 7, 12 ; but in 9, 33, 3 only the recurring feuds between the tribunes and the Claudii.

[104] 5, 14, 4 *fatalibus libris* ; 5, 15, 4 *proprior interpres fatis oblatus*, a man to interpret a *prodigium* ; 5, 15, 9 *excidium patriae fatale*, inevitable if the Romans were to drain the Alban lake according to the *libri fatales* and the *disciplina Etrusca* ; 5, 16, 8 *desperata ope humana fata et deos spectabant*, *fata* is the reply from Delphi ; 5, 16, 10 *ex his quae nunc panduntur fatis*—the decree of the gods revealed at Delphi.

[105] cp. (a) the impressive phrase *fato(-is) urgente (-ibus)* : 5, 22, 8 ; 5, 36, 6 ; 22, 43, 9 (for the same phrase rather than an echo : Virgil, *Aen.* 2, 635 ; Lucan, *Phar.* 10, 30 ; Tacitus, *Germ.* 33, 2). (b) closely related : 5, 19, 1 *fata adpetebant* ; 5, 33, 1 *adventante fatali . . . clade* ; 5, 37, 1 *vim suam (fortunae) ingruentem* ; 5, 32, 7 *ingruente fato*. (c) where fate is an agent of unavoidable destruction —or the destruction itself : 8, 7, 8 ; 25, 16, 4 (Gracchus could not avoid fate though forewarned) ; 26, 29, 9 (Marcellus driven by fate to meet Hannibal and his death). In 1, 42, 4 *fati necessitatem* in the immediate context refers to Servius' failure to appease the hostility which was to lead to his death—not to the expulsion of the kings and the introduction of *libertas* (otherwise Walsh, *Livy* 54).

aspects of fate logically presupposes a belief in predestination, but there is nothing specifically Stoic about either of them. Oracles and doom, after all, already occur in Homer.[106]

But in a few passages fate seems to have been assigned a wider and more positive role. So in four well-known passages the three greatest leaders of the Roman people, Aeneas, Camillus and Scipio Africanus are each in turn associated with fate.[107] At first sight it would appear that Livy wishes to demonstrate the special care of providence for the Roman people revealed by the gift of providential leaders at hours of national crisis. But a closer examination shows that fate does not play an identical role in all four passages. The providential association is very strong when, shortly after the battle of Cannae, Scipio is described as *iuvenis fatalis dux huiusce belli*.[108] But when later in the war the Carthaginians are described as dreading Scipio *velut fatalem . . . ducem in exitium suum natum*[109] the proximity of *exitium* detracts from the providential association. Scipio may still be the heaven-sent leader, but he is also the agent of inevitable destruction. The role of fate is shrinking to that which we have found so prominent in Book V. The context in which Camillus is described as *fatalis dux* is very similar.[110] A powerful implication is that he is the leader who will bring inescapable doom to Veii and its as yet quite unsuspecting citizens. Of course a providential interpretation is not excluded, but the author is in no way committed to it.

Aeneas is not given the epithet *fatalis dux*, but the fates are said to have led him ' in his wanderings to Italy and the beginnings of a greater development '.[111] Here the idea of a directing providence is clear. But a Roman reader confronted with the ' fates ' was quite likely to think no further than the divine signs which directed Aeneas' movements and his settlement in Latium.[112] The purpose of this passage, like that of a number of other passages—including one ' fate ' passage—in Book I[113] is to add significance to the events described by forecasting the greatness which will be their eventual outcome.

To sum up the use of fate in the History : for Livy the strongest associations of the concept of fate are not with providential government of the world but with inevitable calamity and with oracles. He does not use *fatum* and *fatalis* as sign-posts to a providential interpretation of his history, but for limited literary aims. Of course a Stoic interpretation is not excluded, but it will be the reader's, not the author's contribution.[114]

It is true that the reader of Livy's history feels himself transported into ' an ordered and intelligible universe '.[115] But this, I would argue, is due to the subject-matter rather than to the cumulative effect of a comparatively small number of passages open to a Stoic interpretation. It would be hard to write an account of the steady growth of Roman power over the centuries without making it appear pre-ordained and inevitable. Moreover, the principal Roman institutions and ideals are presented so vividly and consistently that the reader is indeed transported into an orderly world sign-posted with stable institutions and civic virtues—but the order is that of a somewhat idealized Rome, not of an underlying philosophical system.

IV. THE OUTLOOK OF LIVY

The fact that Livy felt able to commend religion without justifying it in terms of a more philosophical view of the world is in itself significant. Evidently Livy felt that a rationalist outlook on the world could coexist with complete affirmation of the religion of the Roman people. In contrast to his firm adherence to public religion Livy's personal religion remains elusive. We can be sure that he enjoyed traditional ceremonies and that

[106] Homer, *Il.* 22, 303 μοῖρα or 365 κήρ. See also Kajanto, o.c. n. 1, 53 on μοῖρα.
[107] cf. Walsh, *Livy* 54. Ogilvie, o.c. n. 7, 671.
[108] 22, 53, 6.
[109] 30, 28, 11.
[110] 5, 19, 1 ' Veiosque *fata* adpetebant. igitur *fatalis* dux ad excidium illius urbis servandaeque patriae . . . dictator dictus '. The *fata . . . fatalis* effect is, surely, one reason for the choice of the epithet.
[111] 1, 1, 4 ' sed ad maiora rerum initia ducentibus fatis primo in Macedoniam venisse inde . . . '.
[112] cf. Servius on *fato profugus* in *Aen.* 1, 2, ' sane non otiose fato profugum dixit Aeneam verum ex disciplina Etruscorum '. On the signs, Dion. H. 1, 55–57.

[113] 1, 4, 1 ' sed debebatur, ut opinor, fatis tantae origo urbis '. Other forecasting passages : 1, 7, 10 ; 1, 16, 7 ; 1, 55, 5–6.
[114] The only case with a definitely Stoic link is 25, 6, 6 ' fato cuius lege immobilis rerum humanarum ordo seritur '; but this is said by the survivors of Cannae, to evade responsibility—not by Livy. Contrast the much clearer use of *fatum* in a philosophical sense by Lucan, e.g. 1, 33 ; 1, 70 ff. ; 2, 2 ff. ; 2, 226. *Fortuna* is not given a providential role either : see H. Erkell, *Augustus, Felicitas, Fortuna* (1952), 172–3 ; Kajanto, o.c. n. 1, 98–100.
[115] Walsh, *Livy* 81.

54

he was capable of entering imaginatively into the state of awe and reverence induced by sacred objects or rites. I would suggest that it was this capacity, exercised on the ceremonial of contemporary religion, rather than an intellectual grasp of the importance of the religious factor in history, that enabled him to describe Roman religion in action in the early years of the Roman state. But further it is difficult to go. For a reader whose conception of religion is derived from the Bible it is almost impossible to assess the relative strength of strictly religious, as opposed to political, antiquarian, or literary elements in his outlook.

But the elusiveness of his personal religion is not peculiar to Livy. In the *De Natura Deorum*, Cotta, the representative of the New Academy, and Balbus, the Stoic speaker, while philosophically at opposite extremes, are agreed on the necessity of maintaining the Roman state religion. Cotta, who puts forward the agnostic view, is willing to engage in rational discussion of religion, but in practice he feels bound to follow the tradition of his ancestors, and the arguments of the philosophers are irrelevant.[116]

Cicero himself was neither what we would recognize as a religious man, nor was he a firm adherent of any single philosophical sect.[117] Moreover he has written some devastating criticism of important aspects of Roman state religion.[118] Nevertheless in a public role he acted and spoke with strict orthodoxy, and when he came to draw up a constitution and laws for his ideal state, he went back to the combination of religious and secular institutions that he supposed to have existed in Rome in its golden age.[119] So the validity of the Roman state religion was common ground among Romans of otherwise very different religious or philosophical attitudes.[120] Livy's aims as a historian are comparable with those of Cicero as a political theorist, and his appeal is to the same common ground.

But while the precise character of the religion of Livy, and of men like him, may be debated, its existence cannot be ignored. Only a strong and widely shared sense that the traditional religion was an essential part of the Roman state can explain its long survival in the face of rational criticism. Some of the rites revived by Augustus may have declined into mere romantic masquerading by members of the Roman aristocracy,[121] but two hundred years later the paganism attacked by Tertullian was still, in the first place, the state cult of the Roman people, not the teaching of philosophers or the rites of mystery religions.[122] Moreover, even in this late age sceptical rationalism was not felt to be an enemy of traditional religion. Quite the contrary. In the *Octavius* of Minucius Felix the spokesman of paganism bases his unsuccessful case on the argument that, since reason cannot provide certainty about the nature of the government of the world, it is best to maintain the religion handed down by one's forefathers.[123] The combination of scepticism with respect for ancestral *auctoritas* recurs in the plea Symmachus delivered to the Christian emperor Theodosius for the restoration of the Altar of Victory.[124] This attitude has found its classical expression in Livy's History and this fact itself may have contributed to its power of survival.

Livy would certainly have wished his work to have such an effect.[125] Whether he really believed that the institutions he had revived in his narrative could be restored to life is another matter. The preface suggests a fundamentally pessimistic outlook.[126] The

[116] *ND* 3, 2 (5–6). On this cf. G.E.M. de Ste Croix, *Past and Present* 26 (1963), 6–31, esp. 29–31; S. Weinstock, *JRS* LI (1961), 209–10.
[117] J. Ferguson, 'The religion of Cicero', in *Studies in Cicero*, Rome 1962, 83–96; F. Cumont, *After-life in Roman Paganism* (1922), 31–3; K. Latte, *Religionsgeschichte* 285–6.
[118] Notably in *Div.* 2.
[119] Cicero and public religion: *II Verr.* 1, 46; *Font.* 46; *Har. Resp.* 18 ff.; *ad Att.* 1, 18, 3. The ideal state: *Leg.* 2, 10 (23). *Ius divinum*: *Leg.* 2, 18–22.
[120] Sallust was not a religious author, *Cat.* 30, 2; *Iug.* 90, 1. Yet *deos neglegere* is a symptom of decline, *Cat.* 12, 3; 10, 4 (on which passages see R. Syme, *Sallust*, 1964, 247). cf. also Varro's attitude in Aug., *CD* 4, 31.
[121] K. Latte, o.c. 309 ff.
[122] Tert., *Ap.* 10, 3 ff.; 13, 1 ff.; 25, 1 ff.
[123] Min. Fel., *Oct.* 6, 1 'cum igitur aut fortuna certa aut incerta natura sit, quanto venerabilius ac melius antistitem veritatis maiorum excipere dis-

ciplinam, religiones traditas colere . . .' In his case this includes the religious examples of Roman history, ibid. 7. cf. G. Lieberg, *RhM* CVI (1963), 62–79.
[124] Symmachus, *Rel.* 3, 8 'nam cum ratio omnis in operto sit unde rectius quam de memoria atque documentis rerum secundarum cognitio venit numinum? Iam si longa aetas auctoritatem religionibus faciat, servanda est tot saeculis fides et sequendi sunt nobis parentes, qui secuti sunt feliciter suos'.
[125] *Praef.* 10 '. . . inde . . . quod imitere capias. . . .'
[126] ibid. 4 '. . . ut iam magnitudine laboret sua, . . . ad haec nova, quibus iampridem praevalentis populi vires se ipsae conficiunt'. ibid. 5 '. . . ut me a conspectu malorum quae nostra tot per annos vidit aetas . . . avertam'. ibid. 9 '. . . donec ad haec tempora quibus nec vitia nostra nec remedia pati possumus, perventum est'. ibid. 11 '. . . . nec in quam civitatem tam serae avaritia luxuriaque immigraverint'. On this cf. Kajanto, *Arctos* II (1958), 55–63.

past had been better than the present.   Moral decline came to Rome late, but it comes to all states.   This mood recurs in several comments in the body of the History.[127] Descriptions like the *devotio* of Decius read like an attempt to evoke something which belonged to a long-vanished state of mind.[128]   Such descriptions add archaic colour to the narrative.   More significantly, they display valuable patriotic or moral attitudes.[129] But this does not necessarily mean that Livy thought that a revival of the rites would restore the attitudes in the very different Rome of his own time.   The health of so political a religion could not be independent of that of the body politic as a whole.

This brings us to the question of Livy's attitude to Augustus and his revival of the Roman state.[130]   The fact that Augustus remained on good personal terms with thy historian by itself is enough to prove that Livy fully accepted the new system.[131]   That Live dared to continue his history into the present shows that he could not have been in any active sense an opponent of the Augustan principate.[132]   One can understand the attitude. Like his contemporary authors, Livy was grateful for peace.[133]   He will have sympathized with many of Augustus' measures ;   the establishment of order and the end of popular politics,[134] the moral legislation,[135] and the religious revival which was concerned with just the elements that had figured so largely in Livy's romantic reconstruction of an earlier Rome,[136] the restoration of temples and the resumption of long-interrupted rites.   He had noted that the spirit of the old soldier-citizens had disappeared from the army and civil life, and is likely to have come to the conclusion that the size [137] of the Roman empire made a return to the old system impossible.   Thus he may well have seen in the principate a further stage in the inevitable evolution of government which is the theme of two speeches in his narrative of the struggle of the Orders.[138]   On the other hand, it is difficult to see how a man who gave so central a place to *libertas* [139] and to elected magistrates in his survey of Roman history, who ascribed Rome's greatness to a long succession of competent leaders rather than a few outstanding individuals,[140] and who in his account of the recent past had criticized Caesar and praised Pompey,[141] could have failed to recognize the true position of Augustus in 27 B.C.   At first, gratitude and a real hope of the regeneration [142] of the Roman people may have been his dominant emotions.   In the long run he can hardly have accepted the Principate as more than the inevitable solution to an intolerable situation.[143]

---

[127] As at 3, 20, 5 ; 4, 6, 12 ; 7, 2, 13 ; 7, 25, 9 ; note also 10, 40, 10 'iuvenis ante doctrinam deos spernentem natus '. (This last is in a far from philosophical context : an *exemplum* to show that a magistrate is justified in acting on the report of favourable auspices even when the report is false, cf. Latte, o.c. 201–2. This is a moral which Livy cannot have taken quite seriously, and this reflects on every element of the narrative. A different view : Walsh, *Livy* 51.)   Again cf. 43, 13, 11 ' non sum nescius ab eadem neglegentia qua nihil deos portendere vulgo nunc credant . . .' It has been noted that here Livy's pessimism exaggerates, cf. Latte, o.c. 289.

[128] 8, 11, 1 ' haec etsi omnis divini humanique moris memoria abolevit nova religvariaque omnia priscis ac patriis praeferendo, haud ab re duxi verbis quoque ipsis, ut tradita nuncupataque sunt, referre.'

[129] e.g. 1, 21, 4 (*fides*) ; 1, 24, 4–9 ; 1, 32, 5–14 (fetial procedure).

[130] See Walsh, *Livy* 10–19, also in T. A. Dorey (editor), *Latin Historians* 118–20; also H. J. Mette, *Gymn.* LXVIII (1961), 269–85 and W. Hoffmann, *Ant. u. Abld.* IV (1954), 170–86.

[131] Tac., *Ann.* 4, 34.   cf. his influence on the young Claudius : Suet., *Claud.* 41, 1

[132] R. Syme, *HSPh* LXIV (1959), 27–87.

[133] 1, 19, 3 (one of the remarkably few and widely separated compliments to Augustus. Others : 4, 20, 7 ; 28, 12, 12 ; *Per.* 59).

[134] cf. the numerous unfriendly references to tribunes.

[135] See the extraordinary puritanism of 30, 14, 5; cf. also 10, 23, 1–10 ; the account of Lucretia, 1, 57 ff. ; of Verginia, 3, 44–9 ; also 38, 24, on the wife of Orgiago.

[136] Syme, o.c. n. 132 above, 55–6, including the fetial ceremony. Latte, o.c. 294 ff.

[137] See P. Fraccaro, *Opuscula* I (1956), 81–102. Size of empire : *praef.* 4.

[138] 4, 4, 4 (Canuleius)—cf. Syme, o.c. n. 132, 74— and 10, 8, 9–12 (Decius Mus).

[139] 2, 1, 1—2, 5, 10 ; 2, 15, 3 ; 4, 15, 3 ; 6, 19, 6–7 ; 34, 49 ; 45, 17 ; 37, 54. The point, often a very sharp one, is directed against *regnum*, which Augustus had been careful to avoid. But *libertas* had been the slogan of Brutus and Cassius. The relevance to Augustus could hardly be missed.   Livy only qualifies his opposition to *regnum* by allowing it the task of training a people for liberty. 2, 1, 3–7 might justify a position like Augustus' for a limited period. 1, 49, 3–7 suggests what actions would make even such a position a tyranny.

[140] 9, 17, 5 ff. ; 18, 8 ff. (Alexander excursus). The point is also implicit in the strict annalistic form.

[141] Tac., *Ann.* 4, 34, 3.   Sen., *QN* 5, 184.

[142] In fact I know no passage suggesting the possibility of regeneration to balance the pessimism of passages cited in nn. 130–1 above, and some others in Fraccaro's paper (cited n. 137 above).

[143] No book dealing with Augustus' Principate seems to have been published in Augustus' lifetime. Strangely enough the last published book dealt with the proscriptions, cf. Syme, o.c. n. 132, 39, on superscription of *Per.* cxxi. H. Petersen, *TAPA* XLII (1961), 440–52, suggests that Liv. 1, 49, 1–7 on Tarquinius Superbus' relations with the Senate is an allusion to Augustus and hence advice and warning to the *princeps*.

II

Religion in the Panegyrici Latini

a) The character of the Panegyrici Latini

The twelve speeches contained in the collection of *panegyrici veteres*[1] were composed between the years 100–389 A. D. The earliest work is Pliny's speech in praise of Trajan. The later orators used this as a model which they adapted to fit their style and circumstances. Except for Pliny, all the orators were Gauls associated with the schools of Autun or Trier. No doubt the collection was formed to provide students about the turn of the fifth century with accessible examples of the best that had been achieved in the genre by speakers of their native land.[2]

The fact that the speeches belong to the same genre increases their usefulness. It is likely that differences in treatment between one speech and another are historically significant and not merely a result of the two orators following different conventions. Thus the *panegyrici* enable us to survey the evolution of the religion of Rome between the reigns of Trajan and Theodosius I, a period which spans the anarchy of the third century and which saw the conversion of Constantine to Christianity. It is true that a more detailed survey can be obtained from the imperial coinage,[3] but orations are more self-explanatory than coins.

The panegyrics were spoken at public festivals by men selected for their command of rhetoric, not for political insight or the fact that they represented important groups. As a rule it is the speaker's function to praise the emperor and the virtues he has displayed in his more recent achievements. The speech is to bring the festive assembly to a climax by uniting the audience in strong emotional approval of their ruler.[4] Thus the point of view of the speech is normally not personal but official. It may be that in this respect the Latin panegyrics differ from speeches delivered at similar functions in the Eastern half of the Empire. Certainly some of the speeches of Libanius[5] and Themistius[6] and the *de regno*[7] of Synesius show considerably more individuality.

It is of course impossible to prove that every detail of every speech represents the imperial point of view but where the matter can be tested it usually appears

---

[1] É. Galletier, Panégyriques Latins, t. 1–3, Paris 1949–55, has text, translation and valuable introductions and notes. I cite speeches in his numbering, and without indication of author. Pliny's panegyric is not included in this edition.

[2] Galletier, op. cit., t. 1, IX—XXIV.

[3] C. H. V. Sutherland and H. Mattingley, The Roman Imperial Coinage, t. I—IX, London 1923–62, cited R. I. C.

[4] J. A. Straub, Vom Herrscherideal der Spätantike, Stuttgart 1939, 146—59.

[5] Especially the Julianic orations XII and XIII.

[6] G. **Dagron**, L'empire au IVe siècle et les traditions politiques de l'hellénisme, Travaux et mémoires III, 1968, 1—235.

[7] C. Lacombrade, Le discours sur la royauté de Synésios de Cyrène, Paris 1951.

that the tendency of a speech corresponds to a known tendency of imperial propaganda or at least to the imperial interest of the moment.[1] The speeches of 313 and 321 in which Constantine is congratulated on double victory over Maxentius and over the Franks will serve as examples. A principal aim of the earlier speech is to justify Constantine's war; Maxentius is given all the traditional characteristics of a tyrant. Constantine made war — there is no suggestion that he was attacked — only in order to free Rome from tyranny.[2] The orator does not describe Constantine's actions at Rome after victory in any detail. The audience at Trier would not have been interested.[3] They were reassured by the statement that Constantine had not stripped the Rhine frontier of defenders when he marched against Maxentius.[4] The orator proclaims that Constantine 'returned to the senate its ancient authority'.[5] Other sources confirm that it was indeed Constantine's claim to have restored *libertas* to the state.[6]

A peculiar development is given to the fact that Maxentius' body was found and his head paraded round Rome.[7] We know that Constantine was so eager that the fact of his rival's death should be known that he had the head displayed in Africa.[8] The orator repeatedly and elaborately praises Constantine's clemency towards the soldiers of the defeated army.[9] Of course, the imperial virtue of clemency was much praised in the 4th century, as earlier; it was particularly relevant in the context of 313. About a year after the delivery of the speech Constantine invaded the territory of Licinius. No doubt Constantine was eager to be known for the clemency he showed the soldiers of past rivals in case Licinius' armies also might be induced to come over to his side.[10] Rivalry with Licinius is also behind the speech of 321. In that year Constantine nominated his two sons, Crispus and Constantine, for the consulate without obtaining the agreement of Licinius.[11] This action began the trend toward the second and decisive war between the two Augusti. But Constantine was nevertheless eager to show that he was not responsible for any war.[12] Accordingly the speaker of 321 not only blackens the character of Maxentius, he also devotes a good deal of space to showing how very reluctantly Constantine took up arms,[13] and that he only did so after Maxentius had refused a meeting for the discussion of terms which would have been generous, but are not stated.[14] Since the negotiations are mentioned by neither Zosimus nor Lactantius, nor the panegyric of 313, they are probably invented.

---

[1] In this the prose panegyrics resemble the verse panegyrics of Claudian which closely reflect the interest of Stilicho at the time of their composition. See A. Cameron, Claudian, Oxford 1970.

[2] Pan. IX, 3—4.

[3] Ibid. 20, contrast detail of X, 35 spoken at Rome.

[4] IX, 3.

[5] IX, 20.

[6] H. Dörries, Das Selbstzeugnis Kaiser Konstantins, Göttingen 1959, 217—8, 221—2. C. I. L. VI, 1145—6; 1132; VIII, 7005.

[7] IX, 17—18.

[8] X, 32, 6.

[9] IX, 11; 13; 19.

[10] As the armies of Severus and Galerius had deserted to Maxentius IX, 3, 4.

[11] E. Stein, Histoire du bas-empire, French edition by J.-R. Palanque, Paris 1959, t. 1, 104.

[12] Eusebius H. E. X, 8, 4; V. C. 1, 50 suggest the tendency of Constantine's propaganda.

[13] IX, 2, 1—2; 4 show that Constantine was in fact eager for war in 312.

[14] X, 8—11.

It is left to the audience to deduce the implications for the situation threatening in 321: once more a peace-loving Constantine is being driven to liberate oppressed Romans through war — but only because he has no alternative.

To sum up: both speeches show events as the emperor wishes them to be seen. It is of course possible that a speaker sometimes made individual comments or sought to represent the feelings of provincials. But as a rule this does not happen in the speeches of our collection.

What is true of the contents of the speeches as a whole is true of their treatment of religion: they represent an official point of view. Seen together, the panegyrics illustrate the development of state religion. Thus in the earliest speech Pliny leaves his audience in no doubt that Trajan owed the throne to Jupiter Optimus Maximus, the supreme god of the Roman state.[1] But if Trajan was a god-appointed emperor, he was nevertheless altogether a man and insisted, in deliberate contrast to Domitian, on receiving honour befitting a man, not a god.[2] When we turn to the panegyrics of the Later Empire, we notice a fundamental change.[3] The emperor, his family and everything associated with him, e. g. his edicts, his statues,[4] or his exchequer, are described with epithets otherwise applied only to gods. The phenomenon requires interpretation. Since religious veneration continues to surround the emperor even when he is a Christian,[5] it cannot imply that he was actually thought a supernatural being. In fact, the religious language makes a secular statement. It describes the replacement of the principate by full monarchy. The emperor is no longer merely the first among his peers, the senators, but he is raised by his office far above any subject. The change is, of course, reflected in the whole emphasis of the speeches. The orator no longer stresses the emperor's co-operation with the senators, the limelight is rather on the personal virtues which enable him to make the supreme decisions. Nevertheless, if the emperor is represented as a god among· men, it is not suggested that he is a god among gods — or with God.[6]

b) The imperial theology of the tetrarchy

While the use of religious language to describe the emperor and objects closely associated with him is a feature of all the panegyrics of the Later Empire, the speeches written in the reign of Diocletian have a character of their own. This is

[1] Pliny, Pan. 1, 5; 8, 1—4; 80, 3.

[2] Ibid., 52, 1—4, 6.

[3] The conservative tendency of Pliny's Panegyric — as of all public ceremony — obscures the gradualness of a development starting in the early principate. A. Alföldi, Die monarchische Repräsentation im römischen Kaiserreich, Darmstadt 1970, 29ff. traces the whole process.

[4] E.-Ch. Babut, L'adoration des empereurs et les origines de la persécution, Rev. Hist. CXXIII, 1916, 225—52.

[5] Examples from panegyrics addressed to Constantine: IX, 4, 5 divino consilio . . . hoc est tuo; ibid. 16, 5 sacris aedibus (palace); ibid. 25, 4 debebitur et divinitati simulacrum aureum; 26, 5 divina suboles tua. X, 2, 6 qui semper divina meditantur; ibid. 3, 3 divina virtus; 35, 3 divini principis monitis. Addressed to Theodosius I, XII, 3, 6 cui forma divina; 4, 5 deum dedit Hispania quem videmus; 8, 3 divino patre. Mr P. Wiseman reminds me that divinus expresses a very mild form of deification. See H. Merguet, Lexikon zu den Reden des Cicero, Hildesheim 1962, t. 2, 138—139.

[6] Distinction between gods and emperors is particularly clear in III, 6, cf. also II, 6, 4.

particularly marked in the orations of 289 and 291 which expound a consistent imperial theology. The Jovius title adopted by Diocletian and the Herculius title of Maximian imply — and the interpretation of the orator confirms — that the senior emperor was thought to be descended from Jupiter and the junior from Hercules. When in due course each Augustus selected a Caesar, these, by virtue of their rank, joined the divine dynasty of their respective Augustus.[1] There is a close parallel between the government of heaven and earth. Jovius and Herculius are the earthly representatives of the heavenly Jupiter and Hercules. As Hercules once rendered Jupiter the service of defeating the giants, so Maximian aided Diocletian by defeating barbarians.[2] All benefits enjoyed by man are owed to Jupiter, the ruler of heaven and to Hercules, the pacifier of earth. The relationship between the Augusti is the same. Diocletian initiates action. Maximian carries it out.[3]

The speech of 291 celebrates one of the joint birthdays of the Augusti.[4] It points out parallelisms between the behaviour of emperors and of gods. The emperors' tireless benevolent activity resembles that of the gods Jupiter and Hercules,[5] so does their division of duties.[6] Like the gods, the emperors can keep watch over parts of the empire from which they are physically absent.[7] The emperors' ability to meet in spite of all obstacles of geography and season implies a divine independence of the rulings of fate.[8] The radiance of the imperial presence is such as to draw their subjects to spontaneous worship.[9]

The speech of 297 is addressed not to Maximian but to the Caesar Constantius. In it one can already note a certain detachment from the 'Diocletianic' view of monarchy. Nevertheless it begins with a striking statement of the parallel organisation of the divine and the human orders. The speech delivered on the 1st March on the anniversary of Constantius' accession to the rank of Caesar is seen as part of the great natural process. As the world began in spring,[10] and each spring brings about its renewal, so the accession of Constantius has now assured the future of the world.[11] Moreover, the creation of Caesars has raised the number of emperors to four, a number which has a basic function in the construction of the universe: there are four elements, four seasons, four continents, etc.[12] The orator then

---

[1] W. Seston, Dioclétien et la tétrarchie, Paris 1946, 215ff.

[2] II, 4, 2.

[3] Ibid., 11, 5—6.

[4] Differing from Seston, op. cit. 222—3 I take the *geminus natalis* to be the true birthday of Maximian, not the day on which he took the Herculius title. III, 2, 2 and ibid. 19, 2 should refer to days of actual birth. It could be that by coincidence Maximian and Diocletian were born on same day of the year (in different years). More likely they were born on different days but shared the celebration of each birthday as they are said to have shared each other's different ages, III, 7, 7 and each other's honours, III, 11, 2. I imagine that the birthday of each emperor was celebrated with *vota* for both.

[5] II, 3, 108.

[6] Ibid. 3, 4—6.

[7] Ibid., 13, 5—14 passim.

[8] Ibid. 13. Cf. W. Ensslin, Zur Geschichtsschreibung des Ammianus Marcellinus, Klio, Beiheft XVI, 1923, 78.

[9] Ibid., 10, 4—5.

[10] A reminiscence of Virg. Georg. II, 336ff.

[11] IV, 2—3.

[12] Ibid. 4. H. Castritius, Studien zu Maximinus Daia, Frankfurter Althistorische Studien, Heft 2,

points out how the activity of Constantius confers benefits on mankind with more continuity than the sun.[1]

There is evidence for this theology apart from the panegyrics: for instance, some coins which combine portraits of Jupiter and Hercules each bearing significant symbols, seem to represent the heavenly counterpart to the imperial government of Diocletian and Maximian.[2] A sequence of mosaics in the villa of Amerina shows the deeds of Hercules culminating in representations of defeated giants and the crowning of Hercules by Jupiter. If, as is likely, the villa belonged to Maximian, this prominently-placed illustration of the Hercules myth illustrated the owner's constitutional position and function.[3]

What is the significance of this peculiar theology of tetrarchy? I have already argued on general grounds that it cannot signify that the emperors are thought to be actual gods.[4] This is confirmed by the course of the Great Persecution. The worship of a living man would have been extremely objectionable to Christians. Nevertheless, neither the apologetics of Arnobius and Lactantius, whom one might expect to explain why Christians cannot worship the emperor,[5] nor the events of the persecution [6] itself, suggest that worship of the emperors was an issue.

In the *De morte persecutorum* Lactantius comprehensively abuses the actions of the persecuting rulers. He does not castigate their delusion in claiming to be gods. In the imperial coinage legends describing emperors as gods disappear altogether.[7] Mamertinus, the orator of 291, confirms that the emperors were not gods when he praises their *felicitas*, the fact that they were lucky. Good luck is a highly desirable and mysterious quality but it is one which depends on supernatural favour. A god does not need it. Mamertinus attributes their *felicitas* to the emperors' 'good stars'.[8]

If then this theology does not mean that the emperors were in any real sense gods,[9] it does imply that they enjoyed close cooperation of the gods. The orators duly produce evidence of this. Fine weather aided the shipwrights who were building a fleet for Maximian but when water was needed for the launching, Jupiter sent rain.[10] The *felicitas* of the emperors was manifest in good travelling

---

1969, 26—29 argues that patron gods were now increased to four, Sol being assigned to Constantius and Mars to Galerius.

[1] IV, 4, 3. cf. ibid. 2, 2—3; this may be an allusion to Constantius' worship of Sol but the orator does not describe the sun as a divinity. This suggests that Sol was not part of the official theology of the tetrarchy but rather an object of the personal piety of Constantius.

[2] R. I. C. V, 2, index p. 631.

[3] H. P. L'Orange, Art forms and Civic Life in the late Roman Empire, Princeton 1965, 76ff. cf. II, 4, 2—3; III, 6—7.

[4] I follow N. Baynes, J. R. S. XXV, 1935, 83—4 = Byzantine Studies and Other Essays, London 1955, 343—5.

[5] Neither apologist explains this in spite of earlier precedents e. g. Tertullian, Apol. 34—35. Lactantius only criticises cult of *dead* emperors Inst. Div. II, 16.

[6] Cambridge Ancient History, t. XII, 659 (N. Baynes).

[7] R. I. C. V, 1, 397, ibid. V, 2,656 index a few coin legends under *deo*; ibid. VI, and VII index none. Baynes, op. cit., n. 43 above, p. 345.

[8] III, 19, 3.

[9] See also p. 391 note 6.

[10] II, 12, 5—8.

weather,[1] good crops, absence of disease,[2] and not least, numerous wars among the barbarian enemies of the empire.[3]

Close support is also proclaimed by the epithet *conservator* which is the one most frequently given to Jupiter on coins.[4] Patronage exercised by a rather less superior patron is suggested by the predicate *comes augusti* or *augustorum* which is frequently applied to Hercules.[5] Divine support is not limited to protection. Another aspect is granting to the emperor of peculiar powers of his divine patron. This was particularly true of Hercules. On coins legends recalling the *virtus* of the emperor or emperors are very frequently illustrated by engravings of Hercules. Finally, the theology implies that Jupiter and Hercules feel responsibility and concern for the actions of the *Augusti* who are their delegates and in a special sense their children.[6]

It would have been quite possible for Diocletian to claim divine support for his system without calling into existence a theology of the tetrarchy.[7] A possible explanation is that the imperial theology is intended to explain to the subjects of an empire an exceptionally complex form of monarchy and one that involved two *augusti* who were of equal rank but of whom Diocletian nevertheless had superior authority. The theology also shows in what spirit the tetrarchy, in particular the two *augusti*, must work the system if it is to survive. It is significant that the imperial virtue which the orator of 391 considered fundamental to the success of his god-descended emperors was *pietas*. In the context of the speech, this means essentially the ability to get on with one another.[8] But theology claims to do more than teach by parable. The theology of the tetrarchy attempts to support a potentially unstable system by showing that it is closely integrated into the government of the world. Whether or to what extent it achieved this aim, the evidence leaves obscure.

The 'imperial theology' of the tetrarchy is without parallel in the history of imperial Rome. Hercules and Jupiter had always been part of Roman religion, but the construction as a whole is un-Roman. It is obviously derived from Hellenistic theories of kingship[9] and related to the theological framework in which Eusebius was to place the Christian monarchy of Constantine.[10] One can go further.

---

[1] III, 9, 2.

[2] III, 15, 3–4.

[3] Ibid., 16, 2.

[4] R. I. C. VI, 701–2; VII, 741–2.

[5] Ibid. VI, 698–9. A. D. Nock, The emeror's divine *comes* J. R. S. XXXVII, 1947, = Essays on Religion and the Ancient World, Oxford 1972, t. 2, 653ff.

[6] E. g. R. I. C. VI, 163; 173; 351; 366 etc. The obvious qualities, and those appreciated by the soldiers paid with the coins, were those of a warrior but there was a tradition of longstanding which honoured Hercules for a much wider range of qualities including the ability to bestow immortality. See M. Simon, Hercule et le christianisme, Paris 1955. On divine parentage of emperors see references in Seston, op. cit., 215–16. On its significance cf. A. Wlosok, Die Gottesprädikation *pater et dominus* bei Laktanz; Gott in Analogie zum römischen *pater familias* in Laktanz und die philosophische Gnosis, Heidelberg 1960, 232–46.

[7] Roman emperors had always claimed the patronage of a particular god. At this time Constantius and Constantine claimed special protection of Sol, Licinius of Jupiter, both supreme gods. Galerius claimed special relation with Mars.

[8] III, 6, 3–7; 18, 5; 19, 3.

[9] Cf. Dio Chrys. I, 84.

[10] N. Baynes, Eusebius and the Christian Empire, Annuaire de l'Inst. de Philol. et d'Hist. Orient,

The imperial theology of the greatest of the persecutors had important features in common with the religion which they persecuted. Jupiter is the supreme god. His son, Hercules, acts as an executive and benefactor of man.[1] The resemblance to Christian theology is obvious. Of course, imperial theology makes use of this pattern a second time: Jupiter and Hercules are each represented on earth by a 'son'. It may be that the pagan state religion and Christianity were never closer in spirit than at the time of the Great Persecution.[2]

Related to the adoption of Hellenistic theories of kingship is an estrangement from certain traditional Roman features of the state religion. For Pliny and Trajan, Jupiter Optimus Maximus, or at any rate precisely the Jupiter whose temple stood on the Capitol, was the supreme god of Rome.[3] In the panegyrics of the tetrarchy, Jupiter is not given his ancient title and he is only defined as *capitolinus* in contexts involving the temple on the Capitol.[4] A parallel development is the gradual disappearance of all the traditional Roman gods except Jupiter, Hercules and Mars, from the coinage.[5] Since the court was now mobile and Rome had lost its position as the permanent capital of the Empire, and the Roman nobility was almost excluded from administration, the development is not surprising.[6] But it is important. It helps to explain the comparative ease with which the pagan gods, not least Jupiter, were eventually jettisoned. The fact that Roman cult was practised in many places far from temples and shrines of the city of Rome, deprived it of the strength derived from local emotional associations. This would to some extent reduce the gulf that separated the ancient national religion from its eastern rivals, most notably Christianity. The effect must have been increased by the fact that at this time the ruling circles of the Roman Empire, while very conscious of their Roman nationality, of literary and even of legal traditions,[7] were not at all interested in history.[8] It was in Roman historians, especially Livy, that the essential indivisibility of ancestral custom had been expounded. Towards the end of the century, interest in the history of Rome revived. By then it was too late for Roman paganism.[9]

II, 1934, 13—18 = Byzantine Studies, 168—72. F. Dvornik, Early Christian and Byzantine Political Philosophy, Washington 1966, 611—30.

[1] H. Mattingly, Jovius and Herculius, Harvard Theol. Rev., 1952, 131 sees a deliberate reshaping of paganism to make it acceptable to Christians. This goes too far.

[2] The religions are also brought closer by fact that Christianity was not yet so rigidly defined, cf. Lactantius' 'binitarianism' and the subordination of Jesus to God in Arnobius.

[3] Pliny, Pan. 1, 6; 8, 1; 52, 6; 94, 1.

[4] VI, 8, 7; VII, 15, 6; XII, 9, 5.

[5] Compare R. I. C. II (Vespasian to Hadrian) index 3 s. v. Apollo, Ceres, Diana, Fortuna, Janus, Minerva, Neptune, Venus, Vesta with R. I. C. VI (Diocletian to Maximinus) index 3. The old gods have become very rate or disappeared altogether.

[6] A. H. M. Jones, The Later Roman Empire, Oxford 1964, 366—7.

[7] On conservatism of Diocletian see W. Frend, Martyrdom and Persecution, Oxford 1965, 477—81 and W. Ensslin in R. E., 2. Reihe VII A2, s. v. Valerius (Diocletianus) cols. 2475—81. But religious revivals often include much innovation. That of Augustus had done so. J. Bayet, Histoire politique et psychologique de la religion romain, Paris 1969, 173—84.

[8] A. Momigliano (editor), The Conflict between Paganism and Christianity in the fourth century, Oxford 1963, 78—99 on Pagan and Christian Historiography in the 4th century A. D. by the editor.

[9] A. Cameron, The date and identity of Macrobius, J. R. S. LVI (1966), 25—38, esp. 36—8.

c) The neutral monotheism of the Christian Empire

In the speeches written after 306 and the end of the first tetrarchy, the religious atmosphere changed. It has been noticed that the orators reflect the religious development of Constantine.[1] It is also noticeable that, except in the speeches of 313 and 321, divine support recedes from the foreground. There is a return to the tradition of treating government as an essentially secular activity. Even the deistic version of Hellenistic-Eusebian theory of monarchy expounded by Themistius at Constantinople scarcely appears in our collection.

But if there is very little political theology all the speeches written after 312, including the speech addressed to Julian the Apostate,[2] reflect the situation created by the conversion of Constantine in that they are written in terms of a neutral monotheism which would be acceptable to Christians and pagans alike. This is also found in Ausonius' *Gratiarum actio ad Gratianum*, a speech of precisely the same type as our panegyrics.[3]

Usually the compromise religion of the panegyrics is simply ambiguous in that it can be understood in either a pagan or a Christian sense. There are striking examples of this in the speeches of 313[4] and 321.[5] But the convention also lets a Christian emperor be associated with pagan institutions. Ausonius praises the purity of the Christian emperor Gratian's private life. His bedroom is as sacred as the altar of Vesta. His bed is as chaste as that of a pontifex or flamen.[6] It is not surprising that a Christian emperor, or indeed any emperor, should be praised for chastity. The surprising thing is that pagan priests should be used as a pattern of purity. Evidently the same standard is thought to apply to priests of all denominations.

In the same spirit Ausonius compares his own election to the consulate with the procedure by which the college of *pontifices* had long ago co-opted new members 'since you the *pontifex maximus* (Gratian had not yet repudiated the office) in partnership with God held the election'.[7] Thus the Christian emperor's God is shown co-operating with him in the role of chief priest of the pagan religion.

Such passages imply that Christianity and paganism agree in worshipping the same God. Of course, Gratian soon after repudiated the title of *pontifex maximus*

---

[1] A. Batiffol, Les étapes de la conversion de Constantin. Bull. d'ancienne littérature et d'archéologie chrétienne, 1913, 178—187. J. Maurice, Les discours des panegyrici latini et l'évolution religieuse sous la règne de Constantin, C. R. Ac. Inscr. et B. Lettres, 1909, 165—79. Also J. Moreau, Scripta Minora, Heidelberg 1964, 76—91, sur la vision de Constantin = R.E.A. LV, 1953, 307—33.

[2] Or. XI addressed to Julian: 23, 2; 13, 2; 23, 2; 27, 2. 4; 28, 4; 32, 1.

[3] Ausonius, Gratiarum actio ad Gratianun, 1, 2 indulgentia divina, 7 consilium . . . ad deum uretli; 14 adorato dei numine; 18 aeterne omnium genitor.

[4] IX, 24 a prayer to supreme deity that might be taken in a traditional Roman, a philosophical or a Christian sense. In the speech Constantine's conviction that he has beaten Maxentius through the support of the Christian God is expounded — but translated into a neutral monotheism; ibid. 2, 5 may allude to the vision of Constantine, cf. Eusebius V. C. 1, 28.

[5] X, 7, 3—4; 12, 1; 13, 5; 14, 5; 15, 2—4; 16, 2 etc.

[6] Ausonius, Grat. Act. 14 operto conclavis tui non sanctior ara vestalis, non pontificis cubile cautius, nec pulvinar flaminis tam pudicum. On the literary convention, see A. Cameron, Claudian, 195.

[7] Grat. Act. 9.

and rejected the practical expression of compromise when he removed the Altar of Victory from the senate house and withdrew public support from the state cults of the city of Rome.[1] Nevertheless, in the conservative medium of the Latin panegyric, religious neutrality is maintained a little longer.

The last panegyric in the collection was addressed in 389 by the Gallic orator Pacatus to the pious Christian emperor Theodosius. The orator too appears to be a Christian. He relates that in worship (*divinis rebus operantes*) 'we' turn towards the rising sun. This was the Christian custom.[2] The pagan normally turned towards the cult image. Pacatus also draws an odd picture of the frates with writing-tablets sitting next to God and assisting his memory.[3] This looks like a translation into the traditional literary convention of the biblical concept of the angel who records the good and bad deeds of men in the Book of Life.[4] The image suggests familiarity with Christian writings. Nevertheless, the speech is written in the same neutral monotheism as its predecessors. It goes without saying that sacred epithets are applied to the emperor but the orator goes surprisingly far. The emperor's appearance, he writes, 'is fitting for one whom all nations adore, to whom all the world in a public or private capacity addresses prayers, from whom the sailor asks for fair weather, the traveller a safe return and the soldier favourable auspices.'[5] This passage, which seems to accept full worship of the emperor is an expansion of a traditional theme. Pliny described Trajan: cuius dicione nutuque maria terrae pax, bella regerentur.[6] Pacatus is just as far from implying that the Emperor had power over nature as Pliny was. Nevertheless, the passage is astonishing coming from a Christian.

The neutral monotheism of the panegyrics is, of course, a literary convention, but the convention reflects the fact that monotheism provided a wide area of common ground between Christians and pagans. This is a basic assumption of the apologetic writings of Arnobius[7] and Lactantius.[8] Constantine himself was a monotheist before he became a Christian.[9] The History of Ammianus is written from a monotheistic point of view.[10] Even Symmachus, in spite of the extreme conservatism of his attitude to ritual could write about the supernatural power in language very much like that of Ammianus or Constantine.[11] Again, what is known of the beliefs of Arnobius, Lactantius and Constantine show that Christianity,

---

[1] A. Cameron, Gratian's repudiation of the pontifical robe, J. R. S. LVIII, 1968, 96—102.
[2] XII, 3, 2.
[3] XII, 18, 4.
[4] Cf. Prudentius, Per. IV 169—171; X, 1121.
[5] XII, 6, 4. Galletier concludes that the author is pagan. Ed. t. 3, 50—1.
[6] Plin. Pan. 4, 4.
[7] Arnob. Adv. Gent. 1, 33.
[8] Lact. Div. Inst. 1, 3.
[9] Eusebius V. C. 1, 27.
[10] A. Demandt, Zeitkritik und Geschichtsbild im Werk Ammians, Bonn 1965, 81ff. P. M. Camus, Ammien Marcelin, Paris 1967, 133—148.
[11] Not only in the famous Rel. 3 but also Ep. 8, 13 ope divinitatis cf. 9, 12; 6, 30 summa divinitas; 8, 5 praesidii caelestis, 9, 72, caelestis nutus, 8, 47 caelestem potestatem. Such impersonal monotheism is found together with impersonal polytheism as in 6, 75 caelestes; 7, 1 numinum. See also J. Matthews on Symmachus in the forthcoming T. A. Dorey (editor) Studies in Latin Literature and its Influence: The Fourth Century, (Routledge, Kegan Paul — London).

of laymen, at any rate, was much more flexible than it later became.[1] In addition, caution in the face of persecution and desire to win educated converts, had induced Christians to find language to describe their religion in terms of traditional philosophical monotheism.[2]

The convention is a literary phenomenon but it was adopted in response to a particular historical situation. After his defeat of Maxentius, Constantine found himself the Christian emperor of a largely pagan empire. In the West, not only the rural population but the army and the nobility were largely pagan. Obviously, compromise was necessary. The traditional public rites at Rome were maintained. Pagan worship was on the whole permitted.[3] In the administration and army, Christians and pagans co-existed tolerantly. For public functions, a religiously neutral style was required. The men who were called on to praise Constantine after 312 had the task of demostrating that Constantine enjoyed divine support in language acceptable to all important subjects, irrespective of religion. They were successful and their solution became the accepted convention for the rest of the century.

But from around 380 the emperors Theodosius and Gratian rejected the Constantinian compromise.[4] Not content with being Christians who happened to be emperors, they insisted on being Christian emperors. The cults of Rome were disestablished. The suppression of paganism was begun. This also meant the end of the genre of the *panegyrici veteres*. The secular speaker is replaced by a bishop preaching, the panegyric by a sermon of the kind spoken by Ambrose on the deaths of the emperors Theodosius and Valentinian II.[5] The tradition of secular panegyric continued in the greater obscurity of learned verse.

---

[1] E. g. Arnobius allows existence of subordinate gods, Adv. Gent. 1, 28; ibid. 2, 14ff. soul potentially mortal. Lactantius ignored the Trinity. Constantine somehow identified his Christian God with Sol.

[2] Lact. Op. Div. 1, 20; 21, 1. See also J. Moreau, op. cit. 106—13, Zur Religionspolitik Konstantins des Großen = Annales Univ. Sarav. 1, 1952, 160—8.

[3] Constantius wanted to suppress paganism, C. T. XVI, 10, 2. 3. 4. 6. In the East an attempt was made to do so. E. g. Julian ep. 19; 21, 379 B; 36, 423 C (Wright) = 79; 60; 61 (Bidez-Cumont); mainly depending on local initiative Dagron, op. cit. 181—2. This would be rare in largely pagan areas.

[4] H. Bloch, A New Document of the Last Pagan Revival in the West, Harv. Theol. Rev. XXXVIII, 1945, 199—244 = Ein neues inschriftliches Zeugnis der letzten Erhebung des Heidentums, in Das frühe Christentum im Römischen Staat, ed. R. Klein, Darmstadt 1971.

[5] C. S. E. L. LXXIII, 329—404.

III

AMMIANUS, JULIAN AND DIVINATION[1]

It has often been suggested that the traditional religion of the Romans had lost creditibility long before the triumph of Christianity, and that the living elements of late paganism were provided by the 'mystery religions' of wich Mithraism was the most important.[2] But there is evidence favouring the view that the 'mystery religions', merely supplemented the ancestral ceremonies of Rome, and that these remained the heart of Roman paganism as long as paganism survived at all. In the present paper the continued strength of belief in traditional Roman divination, particulary as practised by the 'entrail-readers' (haruspices), is argued on the strength of a passage in **Ammianus.**

Ammianus gives a detailed account of the movements of Julian's army at the start of the Persian campaign in 363. He marched from Carrhae to Callinicum, and then along the Euphrates to Circesium. This brought him to the Abora (Khabur) river,[3] and the border of the Roman Empire.[4] The crossing of the river marked the beginning of the campaign proper. One feature of Ammianus' narrative has puzzeld historians: the crossing of the Abora river is related twice. According to XXIII 5,5-8, Julian crossed the river, advanced to Zaitha,[5] and on the Dura.[6] Then, XXIII 5,15 has a second account of the crossing. Finally, in XXIV 1,5, we are told for the second time that Julian reached the neighbourhood of Dura - after a march of two days. How is this seeming duplication to be explained?

Klein suggested that Ammianus has imperfectly combined two sources.[7] It is however **a priori** extremely unlikely that an author describing events in which he himself took part should have used sources in so mechanical a manner. E.A. Thompson argued that Ammianus had been confused by his own notetaking.[8] Thompson's analysis of Ammianus' source of information made an important contribution to the evaluation of that historian.[9] Nevertheless the 'mistake-theory' can only be accepted as a last resort, that is if it proves impossible to show that the duplication has been made deliberately, with a definite literary purpose.

An ingenious explanation has been proposed by W. Chalmers.[10] According to this the two reports of the crossing refer to the beginning and the end of that operation, while the earlier of the two arrivals in the neighbourhood of Dura was that of a high-level reconnaissance group led by Julian, in which Ammianus participated.[11] Chalmers suggests that while the army was crossing[12] Julian reconnoitred ahead. When the whole army had crossed, Julian addressed it, and then marched it off along the road which he had previously explored. I do not think that this theory can be altogether disproved.[13] Nevertheless it is not necessary. The apparent doublet can be explained in terms of literary composition: it has been produced by a resumption of the main narrative after an excursus.

This was first seen by Rosen[14] who pointed that the two accounts of the crossing are separated by a narrative which contains nothing but a succession of unfavourable omens.[15] These are given dramatic emphasis by being related at the fatal turning point in Julian's career, the moment when Julian crossed the Abora river to open his disatrous campaign. In order to build up an impressive list Ammianus has related the omens that happened near Zaitha and Dura ahead of their proper place in the chronology of the campaign. It is this which has produced the apparent duplication. I have no doubt that Rosen is right.[16] The second report of the crossing 'fracto igitur ut ante dictum est ponte, cunctis transgressis' (XXIII 5,15) tells us that the author is resuming the story after the digression on omens. Brok cites a number of other passages where ut ante dictum est is used in a similar way.[17] It is a feature of Ammianus' style that he sometimes interrupts the chronological progress of the narrative without making this explicit. To support his disordered notes theory Thompson cites a similar doublet in the account of Valens' departure on the campaign that ended disastrously at Adrianople. But there too the two notices are separated by an excursus which relates slightly earlier events, without notice of this departure from chronological order having been given.[18]

The excursus of omens is remarkable, not only for its position but also for its contents. It is written (admittedly in Latin) by a Greek, in a context of events in the East. In spite of this its religious character is almost entirely traditionally Roman. To examine the omens in turn:

a) Sallustius' letter announces that at Rome sacrifices had not yet obtained the **pax deorum**.[19]

b) **pontem avelli praecepit nequi militum ... revertendi fiducia maneret.** This is just the kind of action which according to traditional Roman belief might mysteriously cause the action which it prefigured, and would therefore have to be either rejected formally, or acepted.[20]

c) The army passes a corpse - an event of evil omen. It was perhaps made more sinister by the fact that the man concerned had been executed, and that by mistake. Constantius too had passed a corpse shortly before his death.[21] A Roman was traditionally particularly watchful for signs when starting on an enterprise, especially a journey.[22]

d) A lion charges some soldiers and is killed by them.[23] It was left to those traditional diviners of the Roman state, the **haruspices**, to provide the correct interpretation. They interpreted it as prohibitory for a ruler invading another's territory.[24]

e) A soldier called Jovianus was killed by lightning while leading two horses from the river.[25] Again it was interpreted by the **haruspices**, according to whom it forbade the expedition.[26]

We note that Julian was accompanied by traditional public diviners,[27] who acted in a traditional way. They were consulted at the beginning of a war.[28] They were experts on the signifiance of lightning.[29] They attached importance to the distinction between offensive and defensive wars.[30] and their role was restricted to warning or approval.[31]

Ammianus' treatment[32] of the ominous background to the start of the Persian campaign is unique and clearly deliberately so. He has not cited any of the oracles written in hexameter verses which have been preserved in the historical tradition concerning Julian's campaign,[33] even though he seems to have known at least one oracle, that Julian was fated to die in Phrygia.[34]

Ammianus' use of supernatural indications of the future is in the Roman tradition. He reports omens and prodigies of general warning rather than oracles.[35] Ammianus' practice resembles that of **Tacitus** rather than **Livy**, in that the signs are warnings of coming disasters without any implication that disaster might be avoided by correct ritual expiation.[36] The suggestion is that disaster could have been avoided by putting off the invasion of Persia.

The omens of XXIII 5,5-14 are only a few out of many ominous or portentous events described in Ammianus' account of Julian's stay at Antioch in winter 362-3 before the start of the campaign. Unfavourable omens may indeed be said to dominate the narrative. The start with the shrieks of women bewailing the death of Adonis at precisely the moment when Julian entered Antioch, and continue with the burning of the temple of Apollo at Daphne[37] (XXII 9,15; 13,1-5). There follows the mysterious failure of the attempt to rebuild the temple at Jerusalem, the sudden deaths of three prominent associates of Julian, an earthquake at Constantinople and a warning derived from the Sibylline books at Rome.[38] Even the description of Julian's desperate and exessive sacrifices suggests the behaviour of a man set upon forcing the gods to give him an assurance of support which the gods were refusing to give.[39] This interpretation is confirmed by the last minute letter of advice from the praetorian prefect of Gaul asking Julian to give up the campaign **'nondum pace numinum exorata'**.[40] The reader is left in no doubt that Julian could have avoided disaster if he had shown the traditional Roman sensitivity to religious warnings of the kind recognised by traditional state religion.

Ammianus' list of omens at the time of Julian's crossing of the Abora river is not found in other writers. Where did he get the information?[41] He is not likely to have invented it.[42] Presumably most of it derives from his own experiences or from conversations with men in the following of the emperor. Conduché has pointed out that the view that the gods were opposed to the Persian expedition might well have been held by pagan officers of the Gallic army who had made Julian emperor precisely so that they might not have to march to the East and against the Persians. The letter of the praetorian prefect Sallustius and the reports of the **haruspices** would have represented the point of view of these officers.[43] As a **protector** Ammianus must have been in close contact with many of these men during the campaign, and may have come to see the operations to some extent through their eyes.

Nevertheless, we ought not to assume that Ammianus' sources of information were necessarily military. After all the civilian **Libanius** was also among those who had favoured more negotiations with the Persians,[44] even if he was to praise the campaign in retrospect. Taking Ammianus' account of Julian as a whole, the point of view seems to be that of the imperial entourage, but not specifically of the military part of it. This becomes obvious when we compare Ammianus' attitude with that of Libanius. Both men admire Julian, but Libianus observes the emperor's reforms as they affect Antioch and the cities of the Empire, while Ammianus descibes their effect on the military and civilian officials at court. Libanius praises Julian for thinning out court and central administration since this relieved the tax payer and allowed greater play to local self-goverment. Ammianus commends him for putting an end to unedifying behaviour in the capital which 'infected the state with crooked passions', but he also mentions that Julian dismissed some men unjustly and thus caused unnecessary redundancies.[45] Again Libanius is highly commendatory of Julian's measures to strengthen the city councils where Ammianus is bitterly critical of the fact this means recalling to their curial duties well established civil servants or officers.[46] Civilian courtiers were surely Ammianus' source for the account of Julian's undignified reception of the philosopher **Maximus** during a session of the senate at Constantinople.[47]

Even if Ammianus' account is ultimately based on what was seen or said by soldiers and civilians in Julian's entourage, it remains likely that what was actually seen or said was developed and embellished in the thirty years or so that passed between Julian's campaign and the writing of Ammianus' History.[48] The death of Julian featured in religious polemic. Christian writers presented it as a divine judgment on the Apostate and his religious beliefs.[49] Ammianus' account, as we have seen, has a religious message too. Ammianus believed that the signs recognised by traditional Roman divination were indeed significant and his narrative upholds the validity of traditional Roman divination.[50] But for a pagan polemist, even as moderate a pagan as Ammianus, the failure of the ruler who tried to restore the worship of the gods posed a problem: why had the gods not supported their champion?

The difficulty was particularly severe in the area of divination, because Julian had been notoriously active in employing every conceivable from a pagan ritual for the purpose of reading the future. The whole of pagan divination was discredited by the fact that it had not warned Julian that his Persian War would end in catastrophe, quite the reverse according to the official version, the divine signs before the campaign had been favourable.[51]

Libanius, the pagan sophist and admirer of Julian in 365 wrote a biography of Julian in the form of a funeral oration.[52] He avoided the topic of Julian's conspicuously unsuccessful divination by omitting all reference to divine signs relating to the Persian campaign. The Christians, **Gregory** of Nazianzenus[53] and **John Chrysostom**[54] were of course only too eager to put together all failures and misfortunes of Julian's reign, and to interpret them as indications of divine condemnation of the pagan revival as a whole, or of particular actions undertaken in the course of it.[55] Subsequently pagan writers too drew attention to unfavourable oracles[56] or signs.[57] **Eunapius'** account unfortunately only survives in fragments and the abbreviated version of **Zosimus**,[58] so we can't be sure how he handled Julian's inability to benefit from information provided by pagan divination. It is possible that he simply left the question open.[59] Ammianus faced the question. We have seen that he maintained the validity of pagan divinatory science in general.[60] I would suggest that he rehabilitated it by drawing a distinction between divination as practised by Julian, and the traditional divination on the Roman people. Julian's procedures were incorrect: he sacrificed victims in exessive numbers, he allowed divination to be practised by the not properly qualified.[61] He was overzealous in his attempts to foretell the future. In short Julian was superstitious rather than properly religious: superstitiosus **magis quam sacrorum legitimus observator**.[62]

On the other hand Roman divination if correctly carried out remained valid. This Ammianus took particular care to establish with regard to the ancient science of the **haruspices**. The truth of haruspicy is in the first place asserted, against the rival claims of Neoplatonist philosophers, presumably Maximus and **Priscus**. The philosophers who were very 'persistent in matters with which they had little acquaintance' produced arguments for disregarding the signs or considering them favourable.[63] Julian followed the advice of the philosophers instead of that of the **haruspices** and continued his campaign. On two more occasions **haruspices** proved the value of their science.[64] Julian again disregarded their warnings, and proceeded to his doom.

The value of traditional divination was topical in the 380's after the Emperor Theodosius had published edicts making the pagan cult illegal. These also forbade divination from sacrificial animals, a speciality of the **haruspices**.[65] More specifically, in the controversy between **Symmachus** and **Ambrose** over the restoration of the Altar of Victory Julian and the **haruspices** were mentioned. The estates of the **haruspices** were among the endowments of Roman priesthoods that had been confiscated by imperial decree.[66] Symmachus, following in an old tradition of apologists of the Roman state religion, had defended the value of pagan rites pragmatically.[67] In reply Ambrose pointed out - among other things - that it was precisely the advice of the **haruspices** that had persuaded Julian to the disastrous of burning his fleet.[68] Thus it can be seen that Ammianus' account of the role of these diviners on campaign justifies a branch of divination that had been prominently challenged, but which might in the view of Ammianus still perform valuable service to the Roman state. It remained, to quote his words elsewhere, **doctrinae genus haud leve**.[69]

Ammianus' History as has been noted,[70] does not take sides in the larger controversy whether the Empire should be Christian or pagan. He does, however, in passing, comment on points of detail which were raised in the course of the dispute. It had been part of Symmachus' case that the state cult helped to ensure Rome's food supply.[71] Ammianus descibed a sacrifice made by an urban prefect to Castor and Pollux that did just that.[72] Ambrose had scorned the worldly display of the vestal virgins.[73] Ammianus pointed out the pomp and circumstance of the bishop and clergy of Rome.[74] Symmachus had praised the precedent set by the Emperor Constantius who, although he was a practising Christian himself, preserved the tempels and shrines of Rome. Ammianus describes how Constantius reconsecrated at Rome an Egyptian obelisk dedicated to the sun god, and bearing a religious inscription of which Ammianus provides a translation.[75] Ammianus' moderate and pragmatic defence of certain pagan positions is parallelled by similar criticism of certain aspects of Christianity.[76] The tendency can be summed up as a reminder that some pagan rites are useful, and that Christianity is not quite as beneficial as its protagonists maintained.

The attitude seems to belong to the period leading up to the usurpation of Eugenius,[77] when pagan senators made one more effort to have the Altar of Victory and the lost revenues restored. The attitude would also have been relevant during the period of the usurpation itself (392-4). Than the pagan senatorial supporters were able to restore some of the public cults of Rome with the acquiescence of the Christian usurper. In the revival **haruspices** played a prominend role.[78] But the defeat of Eugenius was also seen as a divine judgment against the religion of his most prominent followers, and the case for the limited usefulness of the pagan rites collapsed. It is no coincidence that the **Sciptores Historiae Augustae** mock haruspices along with long-term forecasting.[79] When **Prudentius** wrote his answer to Symmachus in 402 A.D. he no longer felt the need to refute Roman divinatory science.[80] In 402 **Claudian** wrote his last poem, the Gothic War, to Commemorate Stilicho's victory over Alaric. In this tradition-governed poem he precedes the narrative of the decisive battle by reports of portents frightening to the Romans, encouraging for the Goths. The outcome discredited both. Alaric confiding in the signs was defeated, Stilicho who ignored them, was victorious. The lesson Ammianus embodied in his narrative of Julian's invasion of Persia was reversed.[81] Even so beliefs in portents, and the Etruscan science of the **haruspices** had not been finally discredited. Christians did not claim that omens and the like were meaningless, but only insisted that they were sent by demons.[82] Animal sacrifice was prohibited, but men continued to note such signs as could be observed without it as late as the reign of Justinian and beyond.[83]

This paper has centred on the continued strength of belief in the science of the **haruspices**. It was not the only element of 'ancestral', as opposed to 'Graeco-Oriental' religion, to survive strongly in late paganism. By and large pagans continued to rely on the traditional Roman rites when the welfare of the state and society was the object of intercession. The army of Eugenius and Nicomchus Flavianus fought under the protection of Jupiter and Hercules.[84] In 408 when Alaric was besieging Rome the urban prefect Pompeianus - on Etruscan advice - proposed the revival of the old state cults. In the event the rites were not resumed, even though the revival is said to have received the consent of the Pope.[85] The race (but presumably not the sacrifice) of the Luperci was held as late as 495. Pope Gelasius was concerned at the attendance or participation of numerous Christians. It was thought that the rite would ward off disease.[86] This obstinate survival was so 'ancestral' that it was thought to be older than the city of Rome itself.[87]

NOTES

[1] I wish to thank John Matthews and his Late Empire Seminar for hearing and discussing a version of this paper, also Walter Chalmers for criticism of a later draft. Errors and omissions remain my own.

[2] See for instance A. Piganiol, L'Empire Chrétien, Paris [2]1972, 259; 'Depuis longtemps le paganisme romaine ne contentait plus les âmes vraiment religieuses, qui s'étaient tournées vers les cultes orientaux.'; ibid., 261; 'Les nobles romaine sont attachés à la religion traditionelle par patriotisme.' But religion and patriotism cannot be separated in this way. Patriotic pagans believed that the traditional religion secured divine support for their society.

[3] Amm. XXIII 3,1-9; 5,1-3 cf. R.T. Ridley, Notes on Julian's Persian Expedition (363), Historia 22, 1973, 317-30.

[4] L. Dilleman, La haute Mesopotamie et les pays adjacents, Paris 1962, 203-204.

[5] 60 stadia from Circesium (Zos. III 14). From Zaitha it is possible to see Gordian's tomb, which Eutropius IX locates 20 miles from Circesium. The site of Zaitha has not been identified: M.F.A. Brok, De Perzische Expeditie van Keizer Julianus volgens Ammianus Marcellinus, Groningen 1959; commentary on Amm. XXIII 5,7.

[6] This is the famous Dura Europus, then deserted, 45 miles from Circesium on the other side of the Euphrates. Between the second account of the crossing and the report of the arrival near Dura there is a speech of Julian and an excursus on the geography of the Persian Empire.

[7] W. Klein, Studien zu Ammianus Marcellinus, Klio Beiheft 13, 1914, repr. 1963, 42-44.

[8] E.A. Thompson, The Historical Work of Ammianus Marcellinus, London 1947, repr. Groningen 1969.

[9] Thompson has established that Ammianus, when writing the history of his own times, compiled his own narrative from what he had personally seen, heard or read, and he did not 'follow' any already existing account. So also G.A. Crump, Ammianus as a military historian, Historia Einzelschrift 27, Wiesbaden 1975, 23-31, and L. Dilleman, Ammien Marcellin et les pays de l'Euphrate et du Tigre, Syria 38, 1961, 87-158.

[10] W.R. Chalmers, An alleged doublet in Ammianus Marcellinus, RhM 102, 1959, 183-9.

[11] Amm. XXIII 5,17.

[12] Ibid., XXIV 1,3, the marching column stretches over ten miles.

[13] It requires the reading of an implied qualification into XXIII 5,5, Statimque transgressus, pontem avelli praecepit, namely that the bulk of

the army had not yet crossed and that the bridge should only be destroyed when it had. Ammianus' account is less complete than it seems to be. He does not mention that Dura lay on the bank of the river opposite to that on which the army was advancing. (Amm. XXIII 5,8 and XXIV 1,5). He omits that Julian travelled some way by boat, as we learn from Zosimus III 13 and, in a slightly different context, from Magnus of Carrhae, FHG IV, 5, cited from Malalas 328, 20ff.

[14]K. Rosen, Studien zur Darstellungskunst und Glaubwürdigkeit des Ammianus Marcellinus, Bonn 1970, 153, one of many perceptive passages in this book. See also Dilleman op. cit., note 11 above, 133-135.

[15]The passage is thus comparable to the long lists of frightening omens found in Livy at the beginning of the years of the battles of Lake Trasimene and Cannae. Signs are particularly significant because they happen at the very begining of an operation. Omens on the first day of the year (Ovid, Fasti I 72; 165; 178), or of a magistracy (Suetonius, Claudius 7), or during the first skirmish of a war (Livy XXI 29,4) are predictive of the outcome.

[16]There is one difficulty. The tumulus of Gordian which is mentioned out of chronological order (on Rosen's view) in XXIII 5,7 is nevertheless referred to as already seen in Julian's address to the army (XXIII 5,17 cuius monumentum nunc vidimus). This could be a mistake on Ammianus' part. A neater solution would be that the parade was held not on the east bank of the Abora, immediately after the crossing, but somewhere near Zaitha.

[17]Brok op. cit., note 5 above, 79-80, who takes the same view of the excursus as Rosen, cites as parallels that XV 5,35 refers back to 31; XVII 8,4 to 7,1; XVIII 6 to 7,4; XXIV 33 to 22,2; XX 3,9 to 2.

[18]E.A. Thompson op. cit., 30 on Amm. XXXI 11,1-2, 1.

[19]XXIII 5,4.

[20]Ibid., 5,6; cf. Julian's last words to the Antiochenes in XXIII 2,4. See Riess in RE s.v. omen, and Pease's commentary on Cicero, De Div. I 103 also Fraenkel on Aschylus, Agamemnon 1653.

[21]XXIII 5,6, cf. XXI 15,2 where Constantius passes a corpse shortly before his own death. Seneca, Ad Marc. IX 4 includes mention of bereavement (luctus) among words which might be taken in an ominous sense and diverted on to somebody else. Cf. also Servius In Aen. XI 2.

[22]Cf. Suetonius Aug.92.

[23]Amm. XXIII 5,8.

[24]Ibid., 5,10.

[25]Ibid., 5,12.

[26]Ibid., 5,13.

[27]In the text of XXIII 5,10, Etrusci tamen haruspices qui comitabantur gnaros prodigalium rerum ... gnaros is an emendation of Mommsen. Surely

gnari of some manuscripts is preferable. Ammianus is stating that the haruspices are the experts in these matters, just as in XXIII 5,13 he describes the haruspices as harum rerum interpretes. He contrasts these professionals with amateurs, the philosophers. Comitari used absolutely is quite common, if poetic, e.g. Virgil Aen. II 42; Amm. XIX 1,5; XX 1,8,2.

[28]Consultation of haruspices before war: Livy XXXI 5,7 (200 B.C., before Second Macedonian War); ibid., XXXVI 1,3 (191 B.C., before war against Antiochus); ibid., XLII 20; 30,8-10 (172 B.C., before war against Perseus). Manuals for active service (libri exercituales): Amm. XXIII 5,10.

[29]A. Piganiol, Sur le calendrier brontoscopique de Nigidius Figulus, in Studies in Roman Economic and Social History in Honor of Alan Chester Johnson, ed. P.R. Coleman-Norton, Princeton 1951, 79-87. This discusses a section of John Lydus' De Ostentis. See also Seneca, Quaest. Nat. II 31-41; Pliny, NH II 137-48.

[30]XXIII 5,11. See R.M. Ogilvie, A Commentary on Livy, Books 1-5, Oxford 1965, 110-12 and 127-9 on fetiales. The Romans were always concerned to show retrospectively that their wars were waged only because just restitution had been refused by their opponents. See Cicero De Offic. I 34-6. Marcus Aurelius revived the fetial ceremony (Dio LXXII 33,3), and justified wars as defensive (Pausanias VIII 43,6) cf. P. Brunt, JRS 64, 1974, 17. So it is likely that the books of haruspices listed signs from which the divine opinion of the justness or otherwise of an offensive war could be deduced. If, there were men who doubted the wisdom, and indeed justness, of Julian's expedition (Libanius Or XVIII 164; XVII 119) it would have been traditional Roman behaviour for them to observe divine signs confirming their opinions

[31]The dead lion was presumably a Greek sign interpreted in a Roman way.

[32]W. Seyffarth (Ed.) in a note on XXIII 5,9 points out that Cicero De Div. II 56 (113-6) probably provided Ammianus with his exempla of ambiguous oracles. If so Ammianus has omitted all trace of Cicero's scepticism. Of course the Athenian oracle (Herodotus VII 140) is not in the Cicero passage.

[33]Hexameter verses (one favourable, one ambiguous): Eunapius frgs. 26-27 in FHG IV, 25 = R.C. Blockley, The Fragmentary Classicising Historians of the Later Roman Empire II, Liverpool 1983, nos. 28,4; 28,6.

[34]XXV 3,9.

[35]Omens and oracles are alike in being ambiguous, but there is a science of interpreting prodigies: XXIII 5,8-10.

[36]W.Liebeschütz, Continuity and Change in Roman Religion, Oxford 1979, 56-8, 159-60.

[37]XXII 9,15; 13,1-5.

[38]XXIII 1,2-3; 5-7.

[39]XXII 12,6.

[40] XXIII 5,4.

[41] For a comprehensive analysis of Ammianus' sources see G.Sabbah, La méthode d'Ammien Marcellin, Paris 1978, 115-239.

[42] Cf. M. Meslin, Le merveilleux comme langue politique chez Ammien Marcellin, in: Mélanges William Seston, Paris 1974, 353-63.

[43] D. Conduché, Ammien Marcellin et la morte de Julien, Latomus 24, 1965, 359-80 treating the subject matter of this paper from a slightly different point of view.

[44] Libanius and many others had favoured negotiations with the Persians: Or XVIII 164; Amm. XXII 12,3-4. Ammianus has omitted both of Julian's refusals to negotiate (Libanius Or XVIII 164; 257-9).

[45] Libanius Or. XVIII 130ff.; Amm. XXII 4.

[46] Libanius Or. XVIII 154; Amm. XXII 9,12.

[47] XXII 7,3-4; XXIII 5,11; 14. Eunapius' biography of Maximus is also ambivalent cf. V.S. 473. Maximus prosecuted the man who later beame emperor Valentinian (Zos. IV 2).

[48] Indications of date in Julianic books: XXII 16,12 Serapeum still standing: burnt 391 A.D; XXI 10,6 Aurelius Victor praefectus urbi: 389 A.D. The date of the later books is still controversial. Thompson, op. cit., 18 and 117: scarcely before September 394. H.T. Rowell, Ammianus Marcellinus, soldier historian of the late Roman Empire, Cincinnati 1964, 28-29: after proclamation of Eugenius. A. Demandt, Zeitkritik und Geschichtsbild im Werk Ammians, Bonn 1965, 63-148: after death of Valentinian II. R. Syme, Ammianus and the Historia Augusta, Oxford 1968, 12-6: 395. K. Rosen, Ammianus Marcellinus, Darmstadt 1986, 31-35 between 395 and 397.

[49] N.H. Baynes, The Death of Julian the Apostate in a Christian Legend, JRS XXVII, 1937, 22-9 = Byzantine Studies and Other Essays, London 1955, 271-281. See also S.N.C. Lieu, op. cit., note 51 below.

[50] Ammianus asserts belief in divination: XIX 12,19, remarking that portents are ignored because they are no longer expiated. XXI 1,7-14: survey of means of divination. XXV 3,19 Julian foretold his violent end. In view of this I do not longer think it is sufficient, with Rosen, op.cit., note 14 above, 168ff., to explain the reports of prodigies simply as a device of 'tragic presentation'. Ammianus descibed prodigies etc. because he thought that they were a fact of the world as it is.

[51] Julian, Ep. 98. Presumably the finding of a new Apis bull (Amm. XXII 14,6) was a favourable sign. See also allusion to consultation of oracles before the war in Ephrem the Syrian, Hymns against Julian, in S.N.C. Lieu (ed.) The Emperor Julian, Panegyric and Polemic, Translated Texts for Historians, Greek Series I, Hymn III 13ff., cf. Hymn II 15-17; III 26: all pagan divination discredited.

[52] Libanius Or XVIII.

[53]Gregory Nazianzenus, Orationes IV-V (contra Julianum), PG XXXV 531-720 written some time after 363.

[54]John Chrysostom, De S. Babyla, C. Julianum et gentiles, PG L 533-571 written after 381 (PG L 534).

[55]Gregory Nazianzenus, PG XXXV 663B death of three followers of Julian, 669B failure to rebuild temple, 672A earthquake and floods.

[56]Libanius Or XXX 41 (written in 386).

[57]Zos. III 12 presumably derived from Eunapius.

[58]Photius Bibl. cod. 98, II 66, cf. R.C. Blockley, the Fragmentary Classicizing Historians of the Later Roman Empire, vol.I, Liverpool 1982, 2; Ilona Opelt, RLAC VI, 928-936, s.v. Eunapius.

[59]Zos III 12, (echoing Herodotus II 123; 171), cf. Eunapius fr. 26 = 28,6 R. Blockley.

[60]See above note 50.

[61]XXII 12,6-7. Contrast Libanius' praise of Julian's conversation with gods: Or XVIII 172-173, 180. Hence Libanius has no explanation of the god's failure to protect Julian, ibid., 281. Ammianus on the other hand could not convincingly reconcile his portrait of Julian as an ideal emperor with a narrative which showed him acting foolishly in matters of great importance. See J. Matthews, Ammianus' historical evolution, in: B. Croke and A.M. Emmett (eds.), History and Historians in Late Antiquity, Sydney 1983, 30-41.

[62]XXV 4,17.

[63]XXIII 5,11.

[64]XXIV 6,17; XXV 2,5-8.

[65]C.T. XVI 10,7 (381) East; a.O. 9 (386) East.

[66]Ambrose, Ep. XVIII 16.

[67]Symm., Rel, III 9,15-17.

[68]Burning of fleet: Ambrose Ep. XVIII 38. Amm. XXIV 7,4, admits Julian's mistake but says nothing of **haruspices**.

[69]XXI 1,7.

[70]See Demandt, op.cit., note 79, also R.C. Blockley, Ammianus Marcellinus, Collection Latomus 141, Brussels 1975, 123-136.

[71]Symmachus, Rel. III 15-17; Ambrose Ep. XVIII 17.

[72]Amm. XIX 10,4.

[73]Ambrose Ep. XVIII 11-12.

[74] Amm. XXVII 3,14.

[75] Symmachus, Rel. III 6; Ambrose, Ep. XVIII 32; Amm. XVII 4,6-23 esp. 13: Nihilque committere in religionem recte existimans si ablatum uno templo miraculum Romae sacraret, id est in templo mundi totius.

[76] L'Angliviel de la Beaumelle; Remarques sur l'attitude d'Ammien Marcellin à l'égard du Christianisme, in: Mélanges William Seston, Paris 1974, 15-23. In this section I am not arguing that Ammianus wrote in support of Symmachus' Relatio III. Alan Cameron in JRS 54, 1964, 15-25 has convincingly shown that no close link existed between Symmachus and Ammianus. Moreover Ammianus was writing a history and not a pamphlet. Nevertheless I do not think that over that dispute the views of the two men were far apart.

[77] See now J. Matthews, Ammianus and the eternity of Rome, in C. Holdsworth and T.P. Wiseman (eds.), The Inheritance of Historiography 350-90, Exeter 1986, 17-29, esp. 24-26.

[78] On Ammianus and Eugenius see A. Demandt, op.cit., note 48 above, 148-151.

[79] J. Matthews, The historical setting of the Carmen contra paganos, Historia 19, 1970, 464-479. On the senatorial embassy to Theodosius in 390-391 see F. Paschoud, Reflexions sur l'idéal religieux de Symmaque, Historia 14, 1965, 215-235 esp. 217. The main source is Ambrose, Ep. LVII 4 and, garbled in various ways, Paulinus, Vit.Ambr. 26; Pseudo Prosper, Prom. III 38,41. On employment of haruspices under Eugenius: Rufinus, HE XI 33; Carmen contra paganos 8; 30; 50. Flavianus was an expert in augury as well (Macr. Sat. I 24,17).

[80] SHA, Tac. 15; 16,4. Prob. 24,3. Syme, op. cit., note 48 above, 140. Long range forecasting: Augustine, civ.Dei XVIII 5,3.

[81] Christians could now afford to appreciate Symmachus as a litrary man (Prudentius, c.Symmachum 1,631), and Julian as a ruler:
    ductor fortissimus armis,
    conditor et legum, celeberrimus ore manuque,
    consultor patriae, sed non consultor habendae
    religionis, amans ter centum milia divum.
(Prudentius, Apotheosis, 449-53).

[82] Frightening signs: Bell.Get. 227-269. The wolf prodigy has some resemblance to Julian's experience with the lion. Divine voice encourages Alaric: ibid., 545ff. Disastrous result: ibid., 552. Claudian, like Ammianus was well acquainted with the traditional Roman practice regarding prodigia. In Eutropium 1,10ff. treats the consulate of the eunuch as a prodigium which must be appeased. Ibid., II 25ff. describe prodigia which signal the enormity of the consulate and demand appeasement. See C. Gnilka, Götter und Dämonen in den Gedichten des Claudians, A&A 17, 1973, 144-160.

[83] Portents reveal demons'callousness: Augustine, civ.Dei III 17,23; 31.

[84] John Lydus' De Ostentis presents some of the lore of haruspices to Justinianic society.

[85]Augustine, civ.Dei V 26; Thodoret H.E. V 24,4. The cults actually re-stored by Nicomachus Flavianus seem to have been those of Magna Mater and Attis, the Megalesian Games and the Floralia. All had long been part of the state cult of Rome, even if Attis and, earlier, Magna Mater were derived from the 'Orient'. See Carmen contra paganos, 103-109. A temple of Hercules was restored at Ostia, one of Venus at Rome, cf. -J.F. Matthews, op.cit., note 77 above, also Symmachus and the Oriental Cults, JRS 63, 1973, 175-195, esp. 189.

[86]Zos. V 41, cf. J.F. Matthews, Western Aristocracies and Imperial Court A.D. 364-425, Oxford 1975, 291-292.

[87]Gelasius, Ep. adversum Andromachum et ceteros Romanos qui lupercalia secundum morem pristinum colenda constituunt, 11ff; ibid., 16-17 show that the manner of celebration has been changed, 12 recalls that the original objective had been to cure sterility of women. For text, translation and notes see G. Pomarè's Gélase, 1re Lettre contre les lupercales et dix-huit masses du sacramentaire léonien, Paris, 1959.

[88]Dion. Hal, I 32,80; Liv. I 5.

IV

The Fall of John Chrysostom

The deposition of John Chrysostom, bishop of Constantinople is a surprising episode. Chrysostom was able and 'holy'. He had a large following among the population of his city. He received fervent support from senatorial ladies. He was careful to keep out of political controversy. It seemed that he was set for a long and successful episcopate. In fact he was deposed for the first time in the autumn of 403, in only his sixth year as bishop, and died in exile four years later. How was this possible?

The basic story is well known.[1] But in recent years our understanding of the background to these events has been greatly increased. F. van Ommeslaeghe's discovery that the *Life* of 'Martyrius' is a contemporary document has necessitated a relative revaluation of the principal sources. G. Dagron has greatly added to our knowledge of the governing élite, of the development of authority of the patriarch, and of the evolution of the monastic movement at Constantinople.[2] I have therefore thought it worthwhile to return to the history of the fall of John Chrysostom. In the present paper I have reconstructed the story in the hope that the sequence and chronology of events will suggest that the explanation must be more complex than that which has generally been accepted. In another paper I have examined the friends and enemies of John Chrysostom and suggested motives for the emnity.[3]

The sources for the deposition of Chrysostom are good, but have very definite limitations. The principal texts are more or less hagiographical, and tend to personalise the narrative. Chrysostom's opponents are represented as villains. Their motivation is seen in terms of human resentments and jealousies. The ecclesiastical historians, Socrates and Sozomen, in accordance with the rules of their genre, say very little about secular politics—even where secular considerations are likely to have influenced ecclesiastical affairs. While both Socrates and Sozomen sympathise with Chrysostom, Socrates is the more detached, and has included material which seems to be derived from the

---

[1] P. C. Baur, *Der heilige Johannes Chrysostomus and seine Zeit* (Munich, 1929-30, 2 vols), ii. 142-362. E. Demougeot, *De l'unité à la division de l'empire romain* (Paris, 1951), pp. 296-35, is better on the political background.

[2] For references to F. van Ommeslaeghe's work see below notes 4 and 8; and to G. Dagron's notes 20 and 82.

[3] 'Enemies and friends of John Chrysostom' in *Maistor, Classical and Byzantine Studies for Robert Browning* (Byzantina Australiensia, iv, Canberra 1984), pp. 85-111.

propaganda of Chrysostom's enemies. Sozomen wrote a little later than Socrates. His account is fuller, and in a number of places he seems to have tried to supplement or correct his predecessor.[4] Palladius wrote his *Dialogue on the Life of John Chrysostom* not long after the events, of some of which he had been an eye witness. He probably wrote in exile at Syene in Egypt.[5] Theophilus is the villain of his history. Like the ecclesiastical historians he has little about secular politics. In fact he has gone further, and tried as far as possible to keep the empress out of the story (although he was aware of her role).[6] It must also be borne in mind that Palladius has few dates and does not always indicate the passage of time.[7] It is also important to remember that the *Dialogue* is not a narrative in chronological order, but is composed of thematic as well as chronological sections. The reader who wants to reconstruct how things really happened must constantly turn back or forward from one section to another. Palladius' narrative is selective. Facts and events have been omitted from both apologetic and literary motives. An argument from Palladius' silence is often a weak one. F. van Ommeslaeghe has recently drawn attention to the value of a hitherto neglected source, the biography of John Chrysostom by his contemporary 'Martyrius'. The reassessment of Socrates, Sozomen and most of all Palladius which he has set in motion will only be completed when historians have studied and absorbed the edition of 'Martyrius' which he is preparing and which will shortly appear in print.[8]

According to the generally accepted view the explanation of the deposition was basically trivial: the empress Eudoxia was offended by one of John's sermons directed against the vanity of women. As a result she combined with some others who held grievances against the bishop of Constantinople, and together they succeeded in persuading the emperor. According to this view, Chrysostom's position was undermined by the intrigues of a handful of bishops and of aristocratic women, who resented the vigorous moral standards upheld by Chrysostom.[9]

---

[4] For criticism of versions of Socrates and Sozomen see articles by F. van Ommeslaeghe, 'Jean Chrysostome en conflit avec l'impératrice Eudoxie', *Analecta Bollandiana*, xcvii (1979), 132-59 and 'Jean Chrysostome et le peuple de Constantinople', *ibid*. xcix (1981), 329-49, esp. 332.
[5] Palladius, *Dialogue de vita S. Joannis Chrysostomi*, ed. P. R. Coleman-Norton (Cambridge, 1928); cf. E. D. Hunt, 'Palladius of Helenopolis, a party and its supporters in the church of the late 4th century', *Journal of Theological Studies*, xxiv (1973), 456-80.
[6] *Dial*. 30 (p. 51); Chrysostom is said to have called Eudoxia 'Jezebel'. But Palladius blames ladies of the court rather than Eudoxia: 16 (p. 25), 27 (p. 45).
[7] E.g. the death of Chrysostom is not dated.
[8] F. van Ommeslaeghe, 'La valeur historique de la Vie de S. Jean Chrysostome attribuée a Martyrius d'Antioch', *Studia Patristica*, xii (1975), 478-83. Also 'Que vaut le témoinage de Palladius sur le procès de Jean Chrysostome', *Anal. Boll*. xvc (1977), 389-414, and articles cited n. 8 above.
[9] Pall. *Dial*. 16-17 (p. 25).

This view is not altogether satisfactory. One would not expect that particular group of opponents to have had the weight and persistence which the enemies of Chrysostom were to display. Eudoxia no doubt was passionate and easily offended. But she had also been a great admirer of Chrysostom, and after his first exile her hostility ceased very rapidly.[10] One would not have expected her to show the steady hostility which ensured the second and final exiling of Chrysostom. There is also the fact that the persecution of John and his followers continued after her death. Again, two of the bishops who figure in the sources as the local leaders of the plot against Chrysostom, Severianus of Gabala and Antiochus of Ptolemais,[16] were preachers of skill and ambition but not otherwise impressive figures. Acacius of Beroea was a man of standing in the Syrian church and highly respected among ascetics[12] but he, like the others, had absented himself from his episcopal duties, and must have been vulnerable for that reason. I would argue that the facts of the long sequence of events are incompatible with a conspiratorial explanation of the deposition. What they suggest is that over the whole period there was a powerful body of opinion determined that Chrysostom should not be bishop of Constantinople.

The First Deposition

At the beginning of his episcopacy John's relations with the empress were extremely good. The christianisation of the Roman aristocracy in East and West offered new scope to aristocratic women who could employ their wealth, influence and personal qualities in the service of the Church and of charitable work.[13] Eudoxia was one of these religiously active women. When Chrysostom became bishop she was one of several who helped him in his work. Empress and archbishop cooperated in the struggle against Arianism at Constantinople.[14]

---

[10] Soz. viii. 18; not explicitly stated by Socrates or Palladius.

[11] On Severianus see Pauly-Wissowa-Kroll, *Real-Encyclopädie der klassischen Altertumswissenschaft*, iiA. 1930, s.v. Severianus 17. On Antiochus see *Dictionnaire d'histoire et de géographie ecclésiastique*, iii. 707, s.v. Antiochus 6.

[12] Provided Theodoret with information for *Historia Religiosa*, 1313C, 1324B, 1344D. Theodoret admired him: *Ecclesiastical History*, v. 27. This may be why Theodoret who admired Chrysostom as well has given little space to the account of his deposition. Acacius' hostility reflects the fact that in general 'the monks' were against Chrysostom. Evidence in Dagron *op. cit.* note 82 below.

[13] See chapter by Jill Harris in *Marriage and Property*, ed. E. M. Craik (Aberdeen, 1983).

[14] 'Hom. 2 cum imperatrix media nocte in magnam ecclesiam venisset', *Patrologia Graeca*, lxiii. 469; Socr. vi. 8, Soz. viii. 8.

The relationship was not, however, a stable one. In the autumn of 400 Chrysostom was not in a position to help Porphyry bishop of Gaza to obtain imperial authorisation to destroy the pagan temples in his diocese.[15] According to the 'Life' of Porphyry Chrysostom had lost favour because he had criticised the empress for coveting and seizing someone's private property.[16] If this is true, and the whole story,[17] we have purely a personal reason for Chrysostom's disgrace: fearless outspokenness on the part of the bishop, resentment of a deserved rebuke on the part of his imperial parishioners. But we must remember that this was the time when Gainas was leading his army of German mutineers through Thrace, and when Chrysostom himself spent a considerable period away from Constantinople negotiating with the German leader.[18] In the autumn of 400 Chrysostom — and also the emperor — were faced with plenty of problems of greater urgency than the destruction of the temples of Gaza. Nevertheless, there is likely to be some truth in Marc the Deacon's statement that Chrysostom had lost favour with the empress. It is, however, significant that John's disgrace was of only short duration. By the end of the year Chrysostom was again enjoying the full favour of the court. This is proved by his ability to intervene in the ecclesiastical affairs of Ephesus and of other churches of Asia and neighbouring provinces. Without full imperial backing this would have been quite impossible. The first estrangement between the empress and John Chrysostom was in many ways typical of their future relationship. The bishop employed little of the diplomacy which was usual when addressing members of the imperial family. The empress was explosively angry, but remained in awe of the bishop, and took him back into favour after a short

---

[15] H. Grégoire et M. A. Kugener, *Marc le diacre, 'Vie de Porphyre évêque de Gaza'* (Paris, 1930), c. 37. The date is Grégoire's, who concludes that something like five months must have passed between the arrival of the bishops and the birth of Theodusius II in spite of the 'in a few days' of c. 44.

[16] *Ibid*. c. 37, 15 with editor's note.

[17] Did Marc the Deacon know of an incident out of which the unhistorical-looking story of the vineyard of the widow of Theognostus might have developed? For the story as told by Theodor of Trimithus (c. 680 AD) and George of Alexandria (c. 700 AD) see their biographies of Chrysostom in F. Halkin, *Douze récits byzantins sur S. Jean Chrysostom* (Subsidia Hagiographica, lx, Brussels, 1977). That Eudoxia did have a reputation for greed, and that Chrysostom did sometimes rebuke her for it is suggested by 'Martyrius'. See F. van Ommeslaeghe, *Anal. Boll*. xciii (1979), 150. Eunapius Frg. 87 (*Fragmenta Historicorum Graecorum*, iv. 52-3) is a bitter attack on sale of office. In the text as we have it the accused is Pulcheria. R. A. Blockley, 'The ending of Eunapius' history', *Antichthon* xiv (1980), 170-9 argues that Eunapius in fact attacked Eudoxia.

[18] Chrys. 'Hom. cum Saturninus et Aurelius acti essent in exilium', *PG*, lii. 414-20. Theodoret, *HE*, v. 33; also a lost work summarised by Photius, *Bibliotheca*, 273. When the exiles returned they were bitter against Chrysostom: Zos. v. 23.

time. Eudoxia's anger might easily have triggered government measures against Chrysostom. But it could not have provided the sustained, unrelenting pressure which enemies of Chrysostom exerted on the government from Theophilus' first arrival at Constantinople to the day of Chrysostom's death and beyond. It is significant that the death of Eudoxia on 6 October 404 did nothing whatsoever to help John and his followers.

To resume the narrative, in the first quarter of 401[*][19] John's good relations with the imperial family had been restored and he proceeded to exercise patriarchal authority in the ecclesiastical province of Asia in a way which was unprecedented.[20] Since the council of Constantinople of 381 the bishop of Constantinople had enjoyed a 'seniority of honour' second only to that of the bishop of Rome,[21] but he had no unambiguously recognised regular jurisdiction even over the bishops of Thrace,[22] the diocese in which Constantinople was situated, never mind the diocese of Asia. The outcome was certainly dramatic. Invited to consecrate a new bishop of Ephesus, Chrysostom travelled to Ephesus, convoked a council of 70 bishops of the diocese of Asia, and faced with two rival candidates, appointed a third, his own deacon Heraclides. He then proceeded with the collaboration of the synod to replace at least six, perhaps as many as sixteen bishops.[23] He also expelled Novation and Quartodeciman sectarians from a number of their churches.[24] Finally on his way home he replaced the bishop of Nicomedia in the diocese of Pontus.[25] Chrysostom was establishing disciplinary supervision by the bishop of Constantinople over the bishops of neighbouring dioceses.[26] He did this with the full backing of the emperor, since he was able to offer deposed bishops the consolation of immunity from curial service.[27] Moreover only the emperor could have provided the armed force needed to enforce the

---

[19] For date of mission see Baur, *Johannes Chrysostomus*, ii. 127 n. 13. Chrysostom returned soon after Easter 401, having been away over 100 days: 'Oratio post reditum', *PG*, lii. 421.[*]
[20] G. Dagron, *Naissance d'une capitale: Constantinople et ses institutions de 330 à 451* (Paris, 1974), pp. 466-9.
[21] J. D. Mansi, *Sacrorum Conciliorum Collectio*, iii. 560.
[22] G. Dagron, *op. cit.*, pp. 458-9.
[23] Pall. *Dial.* 47 (p. 82). See also n. 26 below.
[24] Only reported by Socrates vi. ii, but he was particularly sympathetic towards Novatians, cf. i. 20 and iv. 28.
[25] Appointing Pansophius, tutor of Eudoxia: Soz. viii. 6.
[26] Pall. *Dial.* 47 (p. 83, 6) admits deposition of six bishops, all in Asia. He ignores Gerontius of Nicomedia in Pontus, who was certainly deposed. According to Sozomen viii. 6, thirteen bishops were deposed in Lycia, Phrygia and Asia as well as Gerontius of Nicomedia. Theophilus alleged deposition of 16 (*Dial*). 47, p. 82, 24).
[27] Pall. *Dial.* (p. 51, 16).
[*] For 401 read 402, see Alan Cameron, *Chiron* XVII (1987), 350-1.

decisions of Chrysostom's synod. Citizens resented the imposition of a new bishop. The Nicomedians wanted Gerontius back,[28] and there were riots against the newly appointed bishops of Ephesus.[29] In the long term the most important consequence of the synod of Ephesus was the deep worry which such empire-building on the part of the bishop of Constantinople produced in bishops of Asia and beyond. Where would it end? Many bishops did become hostile to Chrysostom. This did not matter as long as Chrysostom kept the favour of the emperor. It became disastrous as soon as he lost it: for it was the verdict of bishops sitting in synod that had the power to decide the future of an accused bishop.[30] For the time being the emperor was with Chrysostom, but perhaps not wholeheartedly: after all only a year earlier he had prevented Chrysostom from going to Ephesus to investigate its bishop.[31]

When Chrysostom returned to Constantinople some time after Easter 401[32]* he was an extremely controversial figure. Meanwhile at Constantinople things had not gone well. During John's absence his place at the head of the administration of the church of Constantinople had been taken by Serapion his archdeacon, while the role of principal preacher had been taken over by the visiting bishop Severianus of Gabala. The two men got on extremely badly. Eventually Serapion insulted Severianus by refusing to stand up as the bishop was passing. Whereupon Severianus burst out: 'If Serapion dies a clergyman, Christ was not incarnate'. He insisted that Serapion should be stripped of his office. It seems that John had the dispute examined by a synod of bishops, and that Severianus refused to accept the decision when it went against him. Chrysostom asked Severianus to leave Constantinople and return to Gabala.[33] But Severanius had won the favour of Eudoxia, and the emperor ordered John to let Severianus return and to be reconciled with him. John yielded the first point, but refused the second. Thereupon Eudoxia came to see Chrysostom in St Apostles carrying her son, and placing the baby on his knees begged the bishop to resume communion with

---

[28] Soz. viii. 6.

[29] Socr. vi. ii. There is an alternative version. See edition by W. Bright (Oxford, 1878), pp. 280-2. Heraclides was later accused of violence. He was a pupil of Evagrius Ponticus and a former monk of Scetis (Soz. viii. 6) and therefore close to the 'Tall Brothers'.

[30] *Mansi*, iii. 560-4. V. Grumel *Les regestes des actes du Patriarcat de Constantinople* (Paris 1932), i. 4, no. 5.

[31] Pall. *Dial*, 49 (p. 86, 22).

[32] Note 19 above. * For 401 read 402, see above p. 5.

[33] Socr. vi. 11; Socr. vi. 11 (alternative version); Soz. viii. 10 which looks like a more critical version of Socrates vi. 11. Only Socr. vi. 11 (alternative version) mentions the synod; cf. P. C. Baur, ii. 138-9.

Severianus. Chrysostom gave in.[34] He could hardly had done anything else. But Eudoxia must have remembered the humiliation. Moreover it is quite clear that as between Serapion and Severianus right had not all been on one side. Serapion was arrogant, and particularly unpopular with the clergy of Constantinople. It was said that he advised Chrysostom: 'You will never be able to govern these men, unless you drive them with a rod'.[35] Thus when Chrysostom sided with Serapion, he is likely to have alienated many of his own clergy.

Meanwhile a conflict was developing in which Chrysostom would need all the support he could possibly get, a conflict with Theophilus bishop of Alexandria, the 'pharaoh of Egypt', the most powerful prelate in the East. The conflict was probably sought by neither party but it was not the less dangerous for that. The dispute started as an internal matter of the Egyptian church. In a dispute between the majority of the monks of Egypt who insisted that God had human form, and a minority of intellectuals who held that God must be incorporeal as had been argued by Origen, Theophilus, bishop of Alexandria, thought it politic to take the side of the majority. With the support of an episcopal synod meeting at Alexandria, he condemned the Tall Brothers as followers of Origen. He then proceeded to organise an attack on their monasteries and to drive them out. The fugitives, 300 in all, first tried to settle in Palestine, but the authority of Theophilus was sufficient to have them expelled from there as well. The refugees, therefore, by now reduced to 50, sailed to Constantinople hoping that the emperor would arrange for their case to be tried.[36] At Constantinople everybody knew that to support the monks meant a conflict with the bishop of Alexandria, something not to be undertaken lightly. As a result the monks were received with sympathy but little more. Chrysostom allowed them to pray in churches of Constantinople but did not admit them to communion.[37] They managed to meet the empress while out driving in her carriage. She promised that she would cause a council to be convened before which Theophilus would be summoned.[38] But in fact no immediate action followed. The monks came to Constantinople in the autumn of 400.[39] The summons to Theophilus seems to have been issued in the summer of 402, nearly two years later.[40]

---

[34] Cf. 'Homilia de recipiendo Severiano', PG, lii. 426.

[35] Socr. vi. 4 (cf. 11), Soz. viii. 9.

[36] Pall. Dial. 22-24; Socr. vi. 7; ibid. 13. Soz. viii. 11-12, J. N. D. Kelly, Jerome (London 1975), pp. 243-5, 259-61. An edict of at least the prefect of Egypt authorised the expulsion; Pall. Dial. 24 (p. 39, 7) Jerome, Apologia adversus Rufinum, l. 12.

[37] Dial. 24-25, Socr. vi. 9; Soz. viii. 13.

[38] Dial. 26.

[39] K. Holl, Gesammelte Aufsätze (Tübingen, 1927-8), ii. 327; Jer. Epistulae, 90 reports that Tall Brothers have sailed to Constantinople.

[40] Jerome, Ep, 98, a translation of Theophilus' Easter letter of 402, has no reference to summons.

8

In the autumn of 400 of course, emperor and bishop had more urgent preoccupations than the injustice suffered by some Egyptian monks. This was the time when Gainas was operating in Thrace,[41] and when this threat had been eliminated Chrysostom was deeply involved in the ecclesiastical affairs of the diocese of Asia. But even after Chrysostom's return from Asia in the spring of 401 another year passed before Theophilus was summoned.

Meanwhile there was only diplomatic activity. Chrysostom wrote at least two letters to Theophilus in which he counselled conciliation.[42] He achieved the opposite. Theophilus had been misinformed that Chrysostom had taken sides with the monks.[43] In any case he resented the fact that the bishop of Constantinople was interfering in the affairs of the Egyptian church.[44] Theophilus sent monks trained in rhetoric to accuse the monks at Constantinople.[45] Chrysostom brought together the Tall Brothers and the monks whom Theophilus had sent to accuse them, and tried to persuade both to drop their charges and to end the matter. According to Palladius he only succeeded in annoying both parties, but nevertheless left the meeting under the impression that he would now be able to forget the whole business.[46] He was mistaken.

The Tall Brothers continued to press their grievances — not with immediate success. The pastoral circular sent out by Theophilus at Easter 402 and preserved in Jerome's translation[47] mentions that the Long Brothers are canvassing the powerful at Constantinople in order to get them to attack Theophilus. Theophilus himself was sufficiently worried to offer, in the vaguest terms, to forgive the monks.[48] There is no suggestion that the monks' efforts had met with any success so far.

Not so very long after, the Long Brothers succeeded in petitioning the empress while the imperial couple were attending a service in the church of St John the Baptist.[49] If this was on the occasion of the festival of the church's patron saint it was on 24 June.[50] The petition was successful. The imperial reply was that

---

[41] Zos. v. 19-22.
[42] Soz. viii. 13, Pall. *Dial*. 25 (p. 41, l. 20 and p. 42, l. 13).
[43] Soz. viii. 13.
[44] *Dial*. 25 (p. 42, l. 20).
[45] *Ibid*. p. 41, l. 24.
[46] *Ibid*. p. 43, l. 1. Palladius has probably played down Chrysostom's sympathy for the Tall Brothers.
[47] Jer. *Ep*. 98.
[48] *Ibid*. 98, 23.
[49] Pall. *Dial*. 26 (p. 43, l. 10).
[50] Baur, *Johannes Chrysostomus*, ii. 184.

Theophilus would be summoned to Constantinople to be tried by Chrysostom, while the accusers from Egypt would be required to substantiate their charges against the Tall Brothers before a secular court.[51]

One might ask why somebody decided to grasp the nettle at precisely that point. It may be that the evidence against Theophilus was overwhelming, and that his counter-charge of Origenism seemed absurd.[52] Furthermore, even if Chrysostom remained diplomatically neutral, men who had been closely associated with the Tall Brothers were prominent among his clergy and are likely to have been influential. At any rate the government took action. The accusers sent by Theophilus were put in court to prove their charges or to face punishment for false accusation.[53] They were eventually condemned.[54] An official was sent to fetch Theophilus to Constantinople where he was to face trial before John Chrysostom.[55] Theophilus was in no hurry; in fact he did not appear at Constantinople for another year.

But he did not waste the time. He was in a very serious situation, and fought ruthlessly and skillfully to get out of it. Theophilus could not attack the emperor who had ordered him to stand trial, but he could discredit the proposed judge, Chrysostom, and thus make it unlikely that the emperor would continue to support him through the forthcoming trial. So he proceeded to smear Chrysostom with the charge which he had brought against the monks whom Chrysostom seemed to be supporting, the charge of holding the heretical views of Origen. Chrysostom's links with so many former associates of the Tall Brothers made the charge more plausible. Theophilus had an ally in the very old and widely revered Epiphanius, bishop of Salamis in Cyprus, a virulent opponent of heresy who was motivated by obsessive hostility to the teachings of Origen. Theophilus had involved Epiphanius in the struggle against the Tall Brothers as soon as he heard that they were taking their complaints to Constantinople. He had induced him to hold a synod in Cyprus to condemn Origenism, and to publicise its decrees on the mainland of Asia Minor.[56] Now he urged Epiphanius to travel to Constantinople,

---

[51] *Dial.* 26 (p. 43, l. 14).

[52] E. D. Hunt, *Holy Land and Pilgrimage in the Later Roman Empire* (Oxford, 1982), pp. 194-5: John Cassian and Germanus at Constantinople itself, Heraclides bishop of Nicomedia, Palladius bishop of Helenopolis.

[53] *Dial.* 26 (p. 43, l. 15).

[54] *Ibid* p. 43, ll. 21 et seqq. Photius, *Bibl.* 59, 18a, 2nd charge, and 19th charge, 18b, petition of John the monk; 19a, 15th charge all accuse Chrysostom of having caused the imprisonment of the accusers.

[55] *Dial.* p. 43, l. 19.

[56] *Jer. Ep.* 90 of BD 400.

to proclaim the condemnation of Origen before an assembly of bishops and clergy, and to involve Chrysostom in the charges against the Tall Brothers whom he was said to be protecting. Epiphanius agreed. He travelled to Constantinople, and once there proceeded to boycott Chrysostom as if he was tainted with heresy. This is not the place to go into detail of Epiphanius' activities. The important point is that he won over neither the empress[57] nor the emperor. Eventually he abandoned his scheme. He may have realised that there was no substance in the charge against the Tall Brothers.[58] He died on the way back to Cyprus on 12 May.[59] It is evident that at this point the authorities were still backing John Chrysostom.

But this was about to change. Socrates and Sozomen link Chrysostom's loss of favour with a sermon he preached against the vices of women, shortly after the departure of Epiphanius.[60] This was widely understood as a veiled attack on the empress and was brought to her notice by enemies of the bishop. That audiences were in the habit of reading between the lines of sermons, we know from the fact that some of Chrysostom's very generalised criticism of the rich was understood as criticism of the behaviour of particular individuals, who recognised themselves in the bishop's description, and stayed away from church.[61] Since the text of the sermon has been lost we cannot now judge how provocative it was. As a rule John's sermons were diplomatic, but he was to deliver a sermon which was extremely provocative towards the empress on a later occasion.[62] When Chrysostom was angry and thought the other party in the wrong he could be very outspoken indeed. On this occasion he was believed to have been under the impression — probably mistakenly — that Eudoxia had stimulated Epiphanius' intrigues against himself.[63] If this was so, he may simply not have cared whether the empress would recognise herself in the sermon, or whether she would turn against him if she did. But whatever the character of the sermon, Socrates and Sozomen are agreed on its consequences. Eudoxia complained to the emperor that Chrysostom had deliberately attacked her, and requested that Theophilus should be summoned to hold a council to try John. According to Socrates and less explicitly Sozomen,[64] the emperor agreed to his wife's request. If they are right, it

---

[57] Soz. viii. 15.
[58] Soz. *ibid.* Socr. vi. 4 warning of possible riots.
[59] *RE*, vi. 193 s.v. Epiphanius 3.
[60] Socr. vi. 15; Soz. vii. 16.
[61] Pseudo Martyrius p. 480a-b cited by van Ommeslaeghe, *Anal. Boll.* xcvii (1979), 150. On the manuscript tradition of the letter, which has been transmitted among the works of Chrysostom, see van Ommeslaeghe, *Anal. Boll.* xcv (1977), 414.
[62] See below p. 18.
[63] Socr. vi. 15; Soz. viii. 16.
[64] Socr. vi. 15; Soz. viii. 16.

was at this point, that is soon after the departure of Epiphanius in May 403, that Chrysostom's fate was decided, and the sermon was the principal cause why the emperor made up his mind to back not John, but his enemies.

But Palladius' very much fuller and more circumstantial version suggests that the ecclesiastical historians have simplified the story. They are evidently right to state that the sermon was strongly resented. In fact it came to form the basis of a charge of treason.[65] But according to Palladius the emperor summoned Theophilus, and convoked a council, because he still intended Theophilus to be tried, and not because he had decided to put Chrysostom on trial. It was only after Theophilus had arrived at Constantinople and rallied Chrysostom's many enemies in the autumn of 403[66] that Arcadius turned against Chrysostom. I will argue that Palladius' version is the more accurate one. Palladius cites a letter of Chrysostom to Pope Innocent I in which Chrysostom relates that after the arrival of Theophilus at Constantinople, Arcadius had asked him to investigate the charges against the bishop of Alexandria. This Chrysostom had refused to do on the grounds that it was not proper for a bishop to be tried outside his province.[67] According to the letter it was only after that, that Theophilus won over the clergy of Constantinople, and began to draw up charges against Chrysostom.[68] The narrative of the letter is elaborated in Palladius' main narrative. First Theophilus and his supporters gained widespread support. Then they drew up a list of charges. Finally they petitioned the emperor to order Chrysostom to appear before Theophilus' synod.[69] Their petition was granted, for when Theophilus' synod of bishops met,[70] and summoned Chrysostom, the summons was brought by an imperial notary,[71] and its judgement was enforced by an *agens in rebus*.[72] Chrysostom had the support of 40 bishops,[73] but since the emperor supported the other side this was no use to him at all.

There are very strong reasons for preferring Palladius' version to that of Socrates and Sozomen. Palladius was an eye witness and he cites what at least

[65] Pall. *Dial.* 30 (p. 50, l. 25).
[66] Not precisely dated: Autumn 403 according to Baur, *op. cit.* ii. 202. Cf. n. 94 below.
[67] Pall. *Dial.* 9 (p. 9, ll. 16 et seqq).
[68] *Ibid.* p. 9, ll. 25 et seqq.
[69] *Ibid.* 27 (p. 44, l. 19 - p. 45 l. 25); cf. also van Ommeslaeghe's quotation from Ps. Martyrius in *Anal. Boll.* xvii (1979), 150-1.
[70] *Dial.* 29 (p. 48, l. 18: 36 bishops from Egypt. *Ibid.* 12, p. 16, ll. 15-17: 29 from Egypt, seven from elsewhere. Photius, *Bibl.* 59, 19b: 46 bishops.
[71] *Dial.* 29 (p. 49, l. 28).
[72] *Dial.* 9 (p. 11) the *curiosus* of the city.
[73] *Dial.* 29.

purports to be a letter of Chrysostom himself.[74] It is true that Palladius provides no single explanation of the imperial volte-face, but this is in his favour. Political decisions tend to have complex causes. The version of Socrates and Sozomen which accounts for the decision by reference to secret female intrigue, motivated by injured female vanity, seems to reflect the ambiguous attitude to women, prevalent in an ascetic age, a tendency to see women either as villains or saints. Palladius, John Chrysostom and perhaps even Chrysostom's modern biographer, the Benedictine monk J. C. Baur, shared this outlook.[75] But if we reject the version of Socrates and Sozomen, it becomes necessary to suggest an alternative, or at least supplementary, motive for the change of imperial policy.

I would suggest that the motive was provided by the widespread and powerful hostility to Chrysostom both at Constantinople and in the provinces of Asia.[76] Theophilus was extremely skillful at fanning and exploiting this latent hostility. He arranged to arrive at Constantinople in the autumn of 403, some time after the grain fleet from Alexandria,[77] so that he would find a crowd of Egyptian supporters in the city. He had travelled at least the last part of the journey from Lycia by land[78] rallying opponents of Chrysostom in Asia. When he reached Chalcedon he was already followed by many bishops.[79] Eventually he was to achieve a following of 36 (or 45) bishops at the Synod of the Oak.[80] At Constantinople he spent the next three weeks canvassing for further support and gathering material which could form the basis for formal accusations at the trial of Chrysostom. He joined forces with three provincial bishops, Severianus of Gabala, Antiochus of Ptolemais and Acacius of Beroea whom Chrysostom had antagonised and who seem to have resided almost permanently in the capital. Eugraphia, a great lady and friend of Eudoxia, offered her home for meetings of

---

[74] Baur and Coleman-Norton accept the letter as genuine. Palladius cites many documents and refers to more. See Coleman-Norton, *Ed.* liii-lvi.

[75] K. G. Holum, *Theodosian Empresses* (Berkeley, 1982), p. 69 et seqq., has again made Eudoxia principally responsible for the fall of Chrysostom. He has done this in the context of an argument which, to my mind, very much exaggerates the power and influence of the Augusta. See my forthcoming review in *Classical Review* 1985.

[76] See my 'Friends and enemies of John Chrysostom', cited n. 3 above.

[77] Soz. viii. 16. That the ships for which Theophilus had waited were *the* grain fleet is a generally accepted conjecture. Whether this is right or wrong, they surely were the ships carrying bishops from Egypt mentioned Soz. viii. 14.

[78] Soz. viii. 14, Baur *op. cit.* ii. 198, Pall. *Dial.* 29 (p. 49, l. 13): stay in Lycia,. According to 'Martyrius' Theophilus travelled by land all the way: F. van Ommeslaeghe, 'Le temoinage de Pallade sur le procès de Chrysostome', *Anal. Boll.* xcv (1977), 402.

[79] Soz. viii. 14, Socr. vi, 15.

[80] See Pall. *Dial.* 12, *ibid.* 28: 36 bishops: Photius, *Bibl.* 59; 45.

the faction. Two deacons whom Chrysostom had expelled from the church,[81] as well as Isaac, the revered leader of monks of Constantinople, furnished accusations.[82] They won over Chrysostom's archdeacon and through him a great part of the clergy of Constantinople. In his letter to Innocent Chrysostom even used the word 'all'.[83] Among the supporters of Theophilus were the two men who were to succeed John as bishop of Constantinople, Arsacius, brother of John's predecessor, and Atticus who was to be highly respected as bishop.[84] Support for Chrysostom's enemies was evidently growing like an avalanche. In the circumstances the very considerable support which Chrysostom retained among the episcopate,[85] and the general public of Constantinople could easily be overlooked. It might appear that Chrysostom was doomed. At the same time Theophilus managed to make his peace with the surviving Tall Brothers.[86] After this it would have been extremely difficult to bring charges against Theophilus. In these circumstances I would suggest that his counsellors advised Arcadius to abandon the case against Theophilus, and to support proceedings aimed at deposing Chrysostom. His own clergy was against him. He had not shown respect for the imperial dignity. In spite of his holiness and his eloquence it seemed sensible to drop him.[87]

The trial itself was a farce. Chrysostom refused to appear before the hostile judges. The charges as we read them in Photius' summary of the proceedings were largely trivial. That John would be condemned and deposed was a foregone conclusion. The detail of the proceedings is still far from clear.[88] The difficulty is that Palladius who was an eyewitness of the events has written a narrative which is very detailed in some points, and passes over others entirely. He has written an impressive and vivid account of how Chrysostom sat with the bishops who still supported him in the refectory of the bishop's residence and waited for the

---

[81] Pall. *Dial*. 27, see also 21.

[82] *Dial*. 21 (p. 34, l. 6). On Isaac's hostility see G. Dagron, 'Les moines et la ville', *Travaux et Mémoires*, iv (1970), 229-76, esp. 262 et seqq. and my article cited above n. 76. Photius, *Bibl*. lists Isaac's charges.

[83] *Dial*. 9 (p. 9, 27).

[84] Photius, *Bibl*. 59, 19a.

[85] See above n. 73.

[86] Soz. viii. 16 shows that the agreement was reached *before* the trial of John. Socr. vi. 16 states that Theophilus took communion with the monks immediately after the deposition.

[87] The councillors I would imagine to have been the principal office holders, above all the praetorian prefect of the East and the men who are mentioned as playing a role in the second part of the story. See below n. 137 and my paper cited note 76 above.

[88] van Ommeslaeghe, 'Le témoinage de Pallade sur le procès de Chrysostom', pp. 389-413, esp. 403.

summons,[89] and has given the seemingly misleading impression that the whole affair was completed within one day.[90] One can see both literary and polemical motives for this treatment. Palladius has written a moving and dramatic narrative. On the other hand he has also given a quite inadequate impression of the weight of opinion ranged against Chrysostom. There is no explanation of the hostility of Isaac, the revered leader of the monks of Constantinople, just as earlier there had been little about the hostility of the 'rich' emphasised so strongly by 'Martyrius',[91] or of the suspicion left by the events of the mutiny of German mercenaries under Gainas.[92] In accordance with rhetorical technique Palladius has magnified the hero of his biography by trivialising those opposing him. But by doing this he has given an excessive importance in the events to conspiracy.

The Second Deposition of John Chrysostom

That the emperor's decision to back Theophilus against Chrysostom was not simply based on a successful intrigue and a chance combination of circumstances was shown by the sequel: Chrysostom's first exile was extremely short and ended with the archbishop's triumphant return to Constantinople.[93] He seemed to have won a complete victory over his enemies. But appearances were deceptive. The forces that insisted on his deposition were as strong as ever and by Christmas 403 Arcadius was once more persuaded to drop Chrysostom.[94]

Events after Chrysostom had been deposed by the Synod of the Oak and departed into exile undoubtedly showed that Arcadius and his advisers had enormously underestimated the strength of Chrysostom's popular support, as well as the awe which his holiness inspired in themselves. According to Socrates the news of Chrysostom's deposition immediately produced mass demonstrations

---

[89] *Dial.* 27-30.

[90] Contrast Photius *Bibl.* 59 and 'Martyrius' summarised by van Ommeslaeghe, *op. cit.* 410-11.

[91] van Ommeslaeghe, *op. cit.* p. 396 on 'Martyrius' p. 491b-495b; 499a-b; property owners objected to establishment of a leper-hospital in the outskirts of Constantinople. One suspects that this too is one-sided. Perhaps Chrysostom's use of the property of Olympias and other wealthy ladies also gave offence. See Dagron, *Naissance d'une capitale*, pp. 501-6.

[92] van Ommeslaeghe, *op. cit.* p. 403 on 'Martyrius', p. 483a-486b.

[93] Socr. vi. 16; Soz. viii. 18; Pall. 2 (10).

[94] The chronology is uncertain because we have no precise date for the Synod of the Oak. According to Palladius 32 (p. 54, 27) the intrigues against Chrysostom filled nine or ten months. He has not defined the end-point of the intrigues, but he presumably meant John's final departure on 20 June 404. This would put the first exile and hence the Synod of the Oak around the end of September 403. See Baur, ii. 204, n. 6. After two months his opponents launched a new offensive (Pall. 9 (30)) towards December, and by Christmas the emperor refused communion with John (Socr. vi. 18; Soz. viii, 20).

which for three days made it impossible for the emperor's officer to take Chrysostom into exile.[95] The incident is not mentioned by Palladius, neither in Chrysostom's letter to Pope Innocent, nor in Palladius' own narrative.[96] But this need not mean that the ecclesiastical historians are mistaken. Neither passage in the *Dialogue* sets out to tell the whole story, and Palladius was careful to avoid any suggestion that the partisans of John ever ceased to be law-abiding citizens, and therefore was careful to minimise clashes between John's party and the authorities. 'Martyrius' does not mention the three days of rioting either. His motive is likely to have been the same as that of Palladius. Socrates and Sozomen on the other hand give circumstantial accounts of popular disturbances. They should be accepted. Fragments of a sermon suggest that Chrysostom considered the possibility of resisting the imperial order and facing martyrdom.[97]

Next, on the very next day after the departure of Chrysostom some accident (Θραῦσις) happened in the imperial bedroom. In all likelihood Eudoxia had a miscarriage.[98] The imperial couple were shaken, and recognised a sign of divine anger at the way they had treated their bishop. They decided to recall him[99] and Brison, the *cubicularius* of the empress, who had worked with John when they organised orthodox processions to counter those of the Arians, was sent to fetch

---

[95] Socr. viii. 18; Soz. vi. 15.

[96] I would argue that Palladius has simply omitted the two days when the crowd prevented the arrest of Chrysostom. Otherwise van Ommeslaeghe, Jean Chrysostome et le peuple de Constantinople' (above p. 2 n. 4), pp. 229-49, who argues that Socrates and Sozomen are wrong. The reference to noon as the time of Chrysostom's giving himself up without attracting notice (Socrates and Sozomen) is compatible with the statement in the letter to Pope Innocent (Pall. 10) that Chrysostom was trailed by a crowd while being dragged through the city by an *agens in rebus* towards evening, if Chrysostom surrendered at noon but was only taken down to the harbour and embarked in the evening.

[97] The status of the sermon, or fragments of sermons, 'Homilia ante Exilium' (*PG*, lii. 428-30) and 'Cum iret in exilium' (*ibid*. 435-38), is uncertain. See J. A. Aldama, *Repertorium Pseudochrysostomicum* (Paris, 1965), nos. 422 and 528. But the study of the *spuria* of Chrysostom has scarcely begun, cf. S. J. Voicu, 'Le corpus pseudo-Chrysostomien, questiones préliminaires et état des recherches'. *Studia Patristica*, xvii (1982), iii. 1198-1205. It could be that the two sermons are fragments of rhetorical exercises by writers who set themselves to invent a sermon which Chrysostom might have held in his besieged cathedral. More likely they represent faulty and overlapping reports of a single sermon held by Chrysostom in the besieged church, influenced by words of Ambrose at Milan in 385 in comparable circumstances: cf. *PG*, lii, 437-8 with Ambrose, *Ep.* 20.

[98] Pall. *Dial*. 30 (p. 51). That the Θραῦσις was a miscarriage seems to be confirmed by 'Martyrius'. See van Ommeslaeghe, p. 337.

[99] So Palladius and 'Martyrius', but Socrates vi. 16 and Sozomen viii. 18 give rioting as the cause of the recall.

him.[100] This at least is the version of Socrates and Sozomen. According to Palladius a 'domestic notary' was given the mission.[101] John returned by boat as far as Anaplus, a property which belonged to the empress.[102] He then remained for some time at Marianae.[103] He refused to enter Constantinople, insisting that as he had been deposed by a synod he could only be reinstated by one.[104] Meanwhile the question of his recall became the object of bitter disputes, and even fighting, between his opponents and supporters. The monk, whose leader Isaac was one of the bitterest opponents of Chrysostom, invaded the churches and tried to compel the congregations to anathematize John.[105] They were driven out by a combination of people and soldiers. In order to forestall further trouble,[106] the emperor now asked Chrysostom to return to the city and to his church at once. Chrysostom agreed. He was welcomed by 30 bishops.[107] Against his will he was induced to preach a sermon.[108]

Chrysostom obtained an assurance from the emperor that he would call a synod to review the verdict of the Synod of the Oak, and presumably to overturn it.[109] According to Sozomen something like this actually happened: sixty bishops

---

[100] J. R. Martindale, *Prosopography of the Later Roman Empire* (Cambridge, 1970-80, 2 vols, in progress), ii, s.v. Brison.

[101] *Dial.* 30. Perhaps the *cubicularius* fetched John from Praenetum, while the notary accompanied him into the cities several days—or weeks—later. This suggestion is corroborated by Pall., *Dial*, 31 (p. 54, l. 4).

[102] Soz. viii. 18.

[103] Socr. vi. 16. The location of neither Anaplus nor Marianae is known. Marianae is described as a 'suburb' i.e. an estate situated on the edge of the city. On the delay and its causes see Van Ommeslaeghe, 'Jean Chrystostome et le peuple de Constantinople,' *Anal. Boll.* (xcix 1981), 335 et seqq.

[104] Pall. *Dial.* 30, omits this.

[105] See the important article of T. E. Gregory, 'Zosimus, v. 23 and the people of Constantinople', *Byzantion*, xliii (1973), 63-81.

[106] Soz. viii. 18; Socr. vi. 16.

[107] Pall. *Dial.* 10 (letter to Innocent).

[108] Is '*Post reditum*', PG, lii. 445-8, that speech? Sozomen (viii. 18) saw this speech, or one very like it, since he mentions the comparison of Theophilus to the pharaoh who tried to take away Abraham's wife, and also details of the letter Eudoxia is said to have sent to Chrysostom the day after his exile. Since T. E. Gregory (see note 105) has explained that blood could well have been spilt in the baptistery in riots before John's return, there is little in the sermon irreconcilable with known circumstances. But one still wonders that Eudoxia should have had to send parties to search for John in all directions only one day after he had been sent into exile, surely with some official escort. Could this be rhetorical exaggeration, or does it after all show the sermon to have been a fake? Theodoret *H*, v. 34 refers to a succession of messengers.

[109] Pall. *Dial.* 10 (letter to Innocent).

assembled at Constantinople, annulled the decrees of the Synod of the Oak, and confirmed that Chrysostom was entitled to perform all duties of a bishop.[110] If this is true Chrysostom's triumph was indeed complete, but at the same time the tactics with which his enemies so soon resumed their attack become inexplicable. In fact neither Socrates nor Palladius mention the decision of sixty bishops. If there really had been such a decision this would be surprising, since the question whether Chrysostom had returned to his see with proper authority was central to the controversy over his second expulsion. Chrysostom's opponents insisted that Chrysostom had returned without proper ecclesiastical authority and that he could therefore be deposed without any further judicial procedure. The vote of sixty bishops, if it had really taken place, would have provided the authority, and destroyed the opponents' case. My conclusion is that Sozomen's synod of sixty bishops never took place. The story is likely to be a Joannite invention which Sozomen found among his sources.[111] In fact it seems to have been a genuine weakness in the position of Chrysostom that a significant body of opinion believed that the return from exile had been contrary to ecclesiastical law.

Nevertheless, Chrysostom was for the moment secure, because the emperor and the empress supported him once more. In addition, the strength of his popularity at Constantinople had been revealed. Clearly it would not be possible to remove the bishop without considerable trouble. Of his opponents some had been expelled from the city.[112] Others remained and the campaign to depose him was resumed at once.

In the first encounter Chrysostom's popular support won him a complete victory. Not daring just then to attack Chrysostom directly, Theophilus who was still at Constantinople accused Heraclides, whom Chrysostom had consecrated bishop of Ephesus, of acts of violence.[113] Riots resulted in which Theophilus and his Egyptian supporters fought with citizens of Constantinople in the streets. As might have been expected the locals won. After this Severianus of Gabala and other bishops hostile to Chrysostom no longer felt safe in the city. A little later, 'early in winter', Theophilus departed as well, and with him Isaac the leader of the monks.[114] It must have been around this time that Chrysostom persuaded the

---

[110] Soz. viii. 19.

[111] It is significant that in Soz. viii. 20 Chrysostom justifies his return not by reference to a vote of sixty bishops but to 'the vote' of the bishops who had communicated with him since his return, in other words, he relied on *de facto* recognition, not on a formal vote of recall.

[112] Pall. *Dial.* 10 (letter to Innocent).

[113] Soz. viii. 19; Socr. vi. 17; Pall. *Dial.* 10.

[114] Soz. viii. 19 (*PG*, lxxii, 1565a).

emperor to call a synod of bishops so that he could be formally cleared and reinstated.[115] Letters of summons were sent,[116] and bishops began to arrive in Constantinople.

We have seen[117] that it is extremely unlikely that any assembly of bishops ever formally voted to confirm John's reinstatement as bishop of Constantinople. It is however possible to suggest how this error got into the tradition. When the bishops began to arrive around Christmas 404[118] many of them took communion with John.[119] Because of this John could maintain that the fact that 65 bishops had held communion with him constituted *de facto* recognition.[120] Subsequently some Joannite apologist will have turned *de facto* recognition into a formal vote of reinstatement. The bishops did eventually meet and debated John's case. But when they did so, the issue was no longer the reinstatement of Chrysostom, but whether it would be possible to treat him as deposed without further judicial process.

This was several weeks later. Before that meeting, and still before Christmas, Chrysostom had once more proved his own worst enemy. Simplicius, the prefect of the city, had erected a silver statue of the empress Eudoxia close to the cathedral of St Sophia.[121] The occasion was of some public importance, since copies of the statue were distributed over the provinces.[122] It was celebrated with performances by mimes and dancers, and all the noise of popular festivity. The services in the cathedral were disturbed. John Chrysostom, therefore, had some justification to be annoyed. Socrates thought that the right course would have been to organise a petition against the offensive games.[123] Chrysostom was more aggressive. He attacked the games in a sermon, and when the empress took the sermon personally and threatened John with another council, Chrysostom

---

[115] Pall. *Dial.* 10 (letter to Innocent).

[116] Pall. *loc. cit.* See also *Corpus Scriptorum Ecclesiasticorum Latinorum*, xxxv. 87, 19. Pall. *Dial.* 31 (p. 52, l. 16) implies that John's opponents summoned the bishops of the East, but only the emperor was entitled to issue invitations to a general council. See J. Gaudemet, *L'église dans l'empire romain* (Paris, 1958), pp. 456-60. The fact is that in 30.1 Pall. has omitted all mention of the original purpose of the council.

[117] See above p. 16.

[118] Soz. vii. 20 (*PG*, lxvii. 1568b-c).

[119] Pall. *Dial.* 31 (p. 52, l. 21).

[120] Socr. vi. 18; Soz. viii. 20.

[121] Socr. vi. 18; Soz. viii. 20; Marcellinus comes, *Chronicle*, a 403, *MGH, AA*, xi, 67, cf. K. Holum, *Theodosian Empresses*, p. 76.

[122] *Collectio Avellana*, 38, 1 (*CSEL, xxxv, 85*) shows that this was controversial. K. Holum, *op. cit.* esp. pp. 34 et seqq. on statues of Flaccilla Augusta in provinces.

[123] Socr. vi. 18.

escalated his attack with a second sermon starting: 'Again Herodias raves, again she is troubled. She dances again, and again desires to receive John's head on a charger'.[124]

In this way Chrysostom practically recreated the situation that existed before the Synod of the Oak. Emperor and empress once more ceased to back him, and began to listen to the bishops and others who insisted that Chrysostom would have to go. Once again one might ask whether the sermon and the implied slighting of the imperial majesty was the principle cause of the imperial decision, or whether it was the last straw which turned the balance. The fact remains that by Christmas the emperor's mind seems to have been made up for he announced that he would not take communion with Chrysostom until he had cleared himself of the charges.[125] In other words he assumed that Chrysostom was guilty, unless he could prove himself innocent. There is no evidence that he ever again moved from this position. The declaration was a very strong indication of disfavour. There might have been a hope that Chrysostom would take the hint and thus save the authorities a lot of trouble by resigning as Gregory Nazianzius had done. But John did not resign.[126]

The tremendous popularity of Chrysostom made the prospect of deposing him an uninviting one. Soon after Christmas it became clear that people were as ready to demonstrate on behalf of John as they had been after the Synod of the Oak. On 29 January a law was issued threatening officials of the central administration with dismissal and confiscation of property if they engaged in riotous conventions.[127] A new trial would give Chrysostom a chance to state his case and would almost certainly produce worse disturbances. Then some bishops proposed a way out. According to the fourth canon of the Council of Antioch of 341 a bishop who returned without formal reinstatement to a see from which he had been expelled by a synod forfeited the right to a second trial, and must be considered deposed. In accordance with this canon Chrysostom could be expelled without further judicial process.[128] This scheme was proposed at a meeting of

---

[124] Soz. viii. 20. A text purporting to be that of second sermon survives (*PG*, lix, 485). It is not thought genuine. See Baur, *Johannes Chrysostomus*, ii. 237 n. 8.

[125] Soz. viii. 20; Socr. vi. 18.

[126] Eudoxia is said to have asked Chrysostom to resign. She would take full responsibility. Chrysostom replied that she could no more take responsibility for his resignation than Adam could shelter behind Eve, cf. 'Jean Chrysostome en conflit avec l'impératrice Eudoxia' (above p. 2 n. 4), p. 153 on 'Mart.' 506b-507a.

[127] *CT*, xvi. 4, 4.

[128] Pall. *Dial*. 30-31. According to Palladius the idea came from Theophilus, who this time stayed in Egypt.

bishops, including supporters of Chrysostom, in the presence of the emperor. A number of bishops argued that the canon had been adopted by a heretical council, and was therefore invalid. No formal decision could be taken. This was soon after Christmas 403.[129] The result was deadlock. John's opponents continued to insist that John had ceased to be bishop since the Synod of the Oak. The emperor continued to behave as if he accepted their judgement, but Chrysostom was not treated as excommunicated. He continued to live in his palace, and to meet the 42 bishops who supported him. Above all he continued to hold services and to preach.[130]

Just before Easter 404[131] things came to a head. John had a meeting with the bishops opposing him, and demanded a formal trial. The hostile bishops categorically rejected this, and formally voted that Chrysostom had been deposed. Presumably the vote was taken at a meeting of the hostile bishops only. The forty or so bishops who supported Chrysostom were ignored. It is not known how many voted against him. In any case it would not have mattered whether they were a majority or not, since the court was on their side.

With this decision to back them up a delegation of bishops asked Arcadius to order the expulsion of Chrysostom. The emperor agreed. He was even now hoping that the bishop would resigned voluntarily. This John refused to do. So in the end Chrysostom was escorted from his church and placed under house arrest in his residence. This was to bring the division of the churches of Constantinople into the open. A considerable number of clergy and of bishops continued to recognise Chrysostom as the bishop of Constantinople, and to hold services in his name, even in the cathedral of St Sophia. Chrysostom's lay followers refused to recognise the clergy that had excommunicated John.[132]

This state of affairs inevitably led to further escalation of the conflict: with the authorisation of the *magister officiorum* troops were used to break up the

---

[129] Pall. *Dial.* 32. This meeting is described only by Palladius, but Sozomen viii. 20 (1568C) and Socrates vi. 18 (717C-720A) suggest that the use of the 4th canon was brought up *after* the emperor had refused communion with John, i.e. after Christmas.

[130] Pall. *Dial.* 32. The period, when John met with his 42 bishops and the people continued to enjoy his teaching, must lie between the meeting just described and Easter 404 — when Chrysostom was forbidden to take services.

[131] Socrates vi. 18 (720A): 'just before Easter'. Soz. viii. 20 might suggest soon after Christmas, but *ibid.* 21 shows that he too dates the deposition to just before Easter. Both Socrates and Sozomen have conflated the deposition meeting before Easter with the abortive discussions after Christmas described in Pall. *Dial.* 31-2. Palladius has not described the second meeting at which John was deposed.

[132] Pall. *Dial.* 32.

services of the followers of Chrysostom, first on the night before Easter Sunday in the cathedral,[133] the following morning in the Baths of Constans, and finally in an improvised stadium for chariot races known as the Pempton.[134] According to Palladius the initiative was taken by the bishops Antiochus, Severianus and Acacius, who asked the *magister* (presumably the *magister officiorum*) to put an officer and troops at their disposal, and then made the decision to engage the troops to break up the service by force, without further consultation.[135] This is most unlikely. That the troops were supplied by the *magister officiorum* is presumably correct, since the troops involved seem to have belonged to a *schola scutariorum*,[136] and the *scholae* were for administrative purposes at least under the *magister officiorum*'s command.[137] But the use of soldiers against civilians was not at all usual in the cities of the Eastern empire. It is very hard to believe that a tribune of the *scutarii* would have been prepared to order his men to use force against civilians at the request of a group of bishops — unless the request of the bishops had been explicitly confirmed by the emperor, or at least by the *magister officiorum* acting as his representative. Some kind of imperial order to engage the troops had surely been provided. As elsewhere, Palladius has omitted facts so as to exonerate the emperor and to put all the blame on the bishops.[138] It is quite

---

[133] Soz. viii. 21; Pall. *Dial*. 11 (letter to Innocent), 'Martyrius' in van Ommeslaeghe, 'Jean Chrysostome et le peuple de Constantinople', pp. 341. Palladius 33 and Socrates vi. 18 locate the services disrupted on the eve of Easter Sunday in the baths of Constans.

[134] Pall. *Dial*. 11; Soz. viii. 21.

[135] *Dial*. 33.

[136] *Ibid*, p. 57, 7 τοῦ ἀριθμοῦ τῶν ὁπλοφόρων. Did he describe the troops as 'Thracians' because Thracians had a classical reputation for savagery (cf. Thucydides vii. 29)? In 404 genuine Thracians could have been recruited not far from the capital! It is likely that Lucius' troops were Goths, or some other kind of German.

[137] A. H. M. Jones, *Later Roman Empire* (Oxford, 1967, 3 vols), i. 369. Anthemius, soon to be the virtual regent of the Empire, held the office in Spring 404 (See Martindale, *Prosopography*, ii, s.v. Anthemius 1) — not a man easily persuaded to act against his own judgement.

[138] A peculiar feature of Palladius' account is his motivation of the attack. The bishops, noticing that while the service in the baths was crowded, the cathedral was empty, feared that if the emperor saw the empty cathedral he would recognise Chrysostom's popularity, and turn on the bishops who had been accusing him. So they obtained the dispatch of an officer and troops to persuade the people to leave the baths and to reassemble in the cathedral. When persuasion failed the bishops induced the officer to use force to disperse the congregation. This is an unlikely story. The popularity of Chrysostom was known to the emperor. The prospect that a congregation compelled to abandon the service of its chosen priests would obligingly transfer to that of the clergy they had rejected was surely negligible. The operation is unlikely to have been attempted. Palladius seems to have combined the operations of the night before Easter and of Easter day into one.

clear that the government had adopted a policy of suppressing the Joannites by breaking up meetings, imprisoning clergy and expelling prominent laymen. The policy was a failure.

The surprising thing is that even now Chrysostom was allowed to stay in the city to meet the bishops, now reduced to around 25, who continued to support him,[139] and to engage in ecclesiastical diplomacy. Perhaps the authorities hoped that the Joannites would eventually return to the recognised clergy, if it was made impossible for them to attend separate services conducted by clergy loyal to Chrysostom. In fact the schism continued and spread to churches in the provinces. In some places the clergy was divided from the bishop on the question of recognition of Chrysostom. In others the laity was divided.[140] At this time[141] Chrysostom appealed to Pope Innocent and other bishops in the West.[142] Powerful laymen became involved on John's side[143] and eventually, though only a year or so later,[144] Honorius wrote three letters altogether.[146] We do not know the date of the first, so we cannot be sure at what stage the ecclesiastical schism became closely involved with the rivalries of the Eastern and Western governments. But we can be sure that much earlier still, namely as soon as the letter of Chrysostom and successive refugees from Constantinople began to win the active support of the pope, the growing sense of independence of the Eastern governing class will have opposed consessions to John and his followers.

Meanwhile, at Constantinople, John continued to reside in his palace accompanied by a band of loyal bishops, and in contact with sympathisers in the city itself, in the Eastern provinces[147] and in the West. A large crowd of people took turns to guard John in his palace night and day.[148] From the government's point of view this was an impossible situation. According to Palladius, it was once more left to bishops, namely to Acacius, Antiochus, Severianus and Cyrinus to induce the emperor to complete the deposition by exiling Chrysostom, and arranging for the election of a successor.[149] It is likely that Arcadius and his

---

[139] Pall. *Dial*. 13 (p. 12, l. 14).
[140] *Ibid*. p. 14, ll. 15 et seqq.
[141] *Dial*. 11, Letter written before John's second exile.
[142] *Ibid*. 12, Venerius of Milan and Chromatius of Aquileia.
[143] See P. Brown, *Religion and Society in the Age of Augustine* (London, 1972), pp. 214 et seqq. and my paper cited n. 76 above.
[144] See below p. 29.
[146] Pall. *Dial*. 15, l. 146. See below p.
[147] Shown by the wide range of his correspondents in exile.
[148] Soz. viii. 22.
[149] Pall. *Dial*. 34; the date: 5 days after Whitsun.

advisers did not need much pushing. On 20 June Chrysostom was ordered to go into exile, and on 26 June Arsacius was elected to succeed him,[150] a man — according to Palladius — with less power of speech than a fish and of action than a frog.[151]

Needless to say the schism continued. The followers of Chrysostom, clerical and lay, refused communion with Arsacius, and held services in various parts of the city. Troops were once more called in to disperse them. The most prominent and zealous were imprisoned.[152] In the provinces, too — as far away as Egypt — Joannites refused communion with the recognised clery and held separate meetings. An imperial edict went out ordering governors to suppress such assemblies.[153] Meanwhile Joannite bishops and clergy found their way to Rome in a steady stream, bringing with them copies of the imperial edicts that had caused their exile: if a bishop is not in communion with Theophilus and Arsacius and Porphyrius he is to be deposed from office; if he has property that is to be confiscated.[154] A little later it was decreed that the house of anyone who gave shelter to a bishop or priest in communion with John was to be confiscated.[155]

That the state should use force to end division in the church was a tradition going back to Constantine.[156] In the case of the Joannite schism there was added a public order issue. Before Chrysostom's exile a large crowd was on permanent watch outside the bishop's palace. The exiling itself was accompanied by public disorder, and an outbreak of fire which destroyed the cathedral of St Sophia and the senate house. Naturally this produced immediate widespread arrests, especially of bishops, and eventually a formal investigation into the causes of the fire.[157]

Our sources have simplified their accounts of these events with a view to producing an impression of straightforward religious persecution. Only one 'persecutor' is named, the urban prefect Optatus,[158] although a second prefect, Studius, is mentioned among the officials who received the church treasure after

---

[150] O. Seeck, *Regesten der Kaiser und Päpste* (Stuttgart, 1919), p. 307; Socr. vi. 18: Chrysostom had been under house arrest for two months.
[151] Pall. *Dial.* 36.
[152] Soc. viii. 23.
[153] *Codex Theodosianus*, xvi. 4, 6 (18.11.404).
[154] Pall. *Dial.* 13.
[155] *Ibid.*
[156] Jones, *Later Roman Empire*, pp. 94-5.
[157] Pall. *Dial.* 36; Zos. v. 24; Soz. viii. 23; Socr. vi. 18.
[158] Socr. vi. 21; Pall. *Dial.* 14.

the burning of the cathedral.[159] In fact three prefects seem to have held office successively in the months following the exiling of Chrysostom. Soon after the exiling, Paianius became prefect of Constantinople.[160] To judge by the letters John wrote to him, Paianius sympathised strongly with the cause of the deposed bishop. Not surprisingly he was very quickly replaced. The next prefect was Studius[161] who received the church treasures after the burning of the cathedral,[162] and conducted an investigation into the causes of the fire. Two bishops (Cyriacus and Eulysius) and other clergy were put on trial but accquitted.[163] Nothing is said of torture at this stage. At the end of August Studius announced through an imperial edict that the incendiaries had not been found, and that the arrested clergy, both local and foreign, would be released.[164] Studius seems to have tried to be just. One of his laws orders that all foreign clergy found at Constantinople are to be shipped home and that houses used to harbour foreign bishops or clerics are to be confiscated.[165] Clearly Studius had decided that public order in the capital was threatened by the activities of all foreign clerics irrespective of ecclesiastical party. The foreigners, of course, included the clerical leaders of the agitation against Chrysostom as well as some of his followers. That the authorities were still observing moderation in their suppression of the Joannites is also suggested by the fact that the lady Olympias could still hope to influence the authorities to allow Chrysostom a more agreeable exile than Cucusus.[166] It looks as if she had not yet been attacked.

But in the autumn of 404, between the 9 September and 24 November,[167] Optatus became prefect of the city. He is the man who has gone down to history as the persecutor of the Joannites, and there is reason to think that a new and more violent phase of persecution started with his appointment. Socrates, the less well-informed of the two principal ecclesiastical historians, states that Optatus, a pagan,[168] put many of John's friends to death because of the fire.[169] Palladius

---

[159] Phall. *Dial*. 13.

[160] John Chrys. *Ep*. 220, written in exile, congratulates Paianius on his office. *Ep*. 204 shows him in office. *Epp*. 95 and 193 are written to a friend. See also Martindale, *Prosopography*, ii, s.v. Paianius. Since the letters have not been dated precisely it remains possible that Paianius did not precede but followed Studius.

[161] See Martindale, *Prosopography*, ii, s.v. Studius 1.

[162] Pall. *Dial*. 13.

[163] *Ibid*. 36.

[164] *CT*, xvi. 2, 37 (29.8.404).

[165] *CT*, xvi. 4, 5 (11.9.404).

[166] Joh. Chrys. *Ep*, 13, the first letter from Cucusus, where he arrived around 12 or 14 September, according to *Ep*. 234. On Olympias' attempts to help see also *Ep*. 14. 1; 193.

[167] The year is O. Seeck's; *Regesten*, p. 405.

[168] On the supposed paganism of certain prefects of Constantinople see Dagron, *Naissance d'une capitale*, p. 291-4. Optatus was surely a Christian, cf. Martindale, *Prosopography*, i, s.v.

relates that women of the upper class were brought before him and compelled either to communicate with Arsacius, or to pay a very heavy fine of two hundred pounds of gold to the treasury. Anchorites and virgins, presumably of humbler status, were tortured. News of these atrocites was carried to Rome by one Domitius.[170] He was the last of a succession of refugees who brought news of the measures taken against John and his followers at Constantinople. The fact that Domitius appears to have been the first to report torture and the coercion of upper class women suggests that they had not been employed before, and that Optatus had intensified pressure on the Joannites. Sozomen — without naming Optatus — gives examples of the application of the measures reported by Domitius. He describes a court hearing in which the 'prefect' first asked Olympias why she had set fire to the cathedral, and later attacked her for refusing communion with Arsacius. At a subsequent hearing he fined her heavily.[171] Sozomen also tells of a presbyter Tigris, who was severly tortured 'about the same time'. Later Tigris was banished to Mesopotamia.[172] Both Sozomen and Palladius mention the case of Eutropius, a deacon and singer, who was tortured so severely that he subsequently died.[173]

Optatus' brutal methods did not end the schism. The Joannites continued as separate communities at Constantinople and many cities in the East. They remained a challenge to the government, whose response was to exile bishops and clergy to remote parts of the empire. Palladius lists bishops, priests and other followers from Constantinople who were forced to live in exile at the time of writing, in all thirty three names. They do not include Constantinopolitans who had gone into hiding. Palladius seems to have had no information about provincial clergy other than bishops.[174]

Optatus 1.

[169] Socr. vi. 21.

[170] *Dial.* 14 (p. 29, 9).

[171] Soz. viii. 24; Olympias must have been examined many months after the burning of the cathedral. Joh. Chrys. *Epp.* 234 (after 12 or 14 September) and 13 (6 in *Jean Chrysostom, lettres à Olympias*, ed. A.-M. Malingrey) show her still in a position of influence. A later letter mentions violent persecution, but not yet of Olympias herself (*Ep.* 1, vii, ed. AMM). In *Ep.* 14 (AMM, ix) Olympias's attempts to improve Chrysostom's exile have failed but she could still protect Bishop Maruthas, and influence the election of a bishop for the Goths in the Crimea. By now the sailing season was over. *Ep.* 5 (AMM, xi), 6 (AMM, xii), 7 (AMM, xiii), 16 (AMM, xiv) successive letters dated early in 405 mention the attack on Olympias. In 5 and 16 she is still at Constantinople, in 7 and 16 in exile.

[72] Soz. viii. 24; Pall. *Dial.* 72. In August 404 (*Ep.* 12) Tigrinus was still free while others were in prison.

[73] Soz. viii. 24; Pall. *Dial.* 72. Not dated. According to the Roman martyrology his anniversary was 12 January (Baur, *Johannes Chrysostom,* ii 265).

[74] *Dial.* 71-3. CT, xvi, 2, 35 (42, 405), cited by Baur, *op. cit.* ii. 276, is Western and not relevant.

Palladius' list is without dates, so we cannot tell when the policy of dispersing the leadership of at least the Constantinopolitan community of Joannites was begun. There is some reason to believe that the policy was not introduced immediately but only in late autumn 403 or later still.[175]

It should be noted that the period of intense persecution of the Joannites only began around the time of the death of the empress Eudoxia (4 October 404).[176] This is difficult to reconcile with the view that she was the principal cause of the attacks on John Chrysostom. About a year later (11 November 405) there occurred the death of Arsacius, John's successor as bishop of Constantinople.[177] This created an opportunity for restoring Chrysostom without deposing anyone else. There is no evidence that this possibility was considered, thought is is an interesting fact that four months passed before Atticus was chosen to succeed him.[178] In fact the policy of suppression was still being maintained around 408 when Palladius wrote his *Dialogue*.

Atticus was maintained by the 'establishment' and indeed came to be widely respected.[179] But at least in the first years of his administration he met with strong opposition from Joannite laymen at Constantinople and from bishops of eastern cities. The emperor issued edicts to strengthen his position'. If any bishop does not communicate with Theophilus, Porphyrius and Atticus let him be expelled from the church and his property confiscated'. Laymen, too, were threatened if they refused to communicate with the authorised bishops: officials are to lose their positions, soldiers are to be discharged from the service and ordinary people fined and banished.[180]

One can see a number of reasons for the persistence of the policy of suppression. The Joannite group did not disappear.[181] Even in exile John remained in contact with clergy and laymen all over the East.[182] He received

---

[175] According to *Ep.* 14 (AMM, ix) of later in the autumn of 404, Bishop Hilarius was still at Constantinople working for John. Later he was beaten and exiled to Pontus (Pall. *Dial.* 71). *Ep.* 14 mentions Heraclides as at Constantinople under pressure; later he was imprisoned at Nicomedia (*Dial.* 71).

[176] Socr. vi 19, 6 October according to Seeck, *Regesten*, pp. 307-9.

[177] Baur, *Johannes Chrysostom*, ii. 300, on Pall. Dial. 36; Socr, vi. 20; vii. 2; vii. 25; Soz. viii. 27.

[178] Soz. viii. 27.

[179] Soz. viii. 27 relates that in youth Atticus had been a monk of the Macedonian sect. This will have brought him close to the monks of Constantinople whose traditions too seem to have been Macedonian. For the character and reputation of Atticus see Socr. vii. 2-4.

[180] Pall. *Dial.* 37 (not in the *Codes*).

[181] At Constantinople petitions that John should not be recalled were circulated for signature ('Martyrius' 521b-522a cited by van Ommeslaeghe).

[182] Soz. vii. 27. He had plenty of financial resources and ransomed prisoners taken by the Isaurians.

visitors, he wrote letters. He inspired a missionary campaign for the conversation of pagans in Phoenicia.[183] The letters show that Chrysostom was a dynamic force even in exile, and that his following continued to offer a threat to his successors Arsacius and Atticus, as well as to the bishops whom Chrysostom had once deposed and who were now reinstated.[184] As a result they were all afraid to tolerate the Joannites. Atticus personally was not a fanatic. At least he was more tolerant towards the Novatians than Chrysostom had been.[185] The emperor and his advisers naturally supported the bishops whom they had appointed at least indirectly, by suppressing their opponents.

There was, moreover, one circumstance which must have strengthened the authorities' determination to intervene against the Joannites. This was the fact that John's case had been taken up strongly by the pope and emperor in the West.

Chrysostom wrote to Pope Innocent for help soon after Easter 404 when he had been deposed and forbidden to hold services, and was staying in his residence under a kind of house arrest. This letter was supported by another letter, signed by forty bishops, and a third one from John's clergy.[186] While Innocent had already received a letter from Theophilus,[187] it is clear that he favoured John from the first, and replied to both parties that a council should be summoned consisting of bishops from East and West to review the case of Chrysostom.[188] In the course of the summer news of successive developments at Constantinople came to Rome, and confirmed Innocent in the view he had taken at first.[189]

In the autumn Innocent wrote letters to Chrysostom, and to his Constantinopolitan clergy. The letter of John is sympathetic but counsels patience. In the letter to the clergy the pope unambiguously stated that in his view John had been deposed unjustly. He explicitly condemned, as passed by a heretical council, the fourth canon of Antioch, which had provided the legal justification for Chrysostom's second deposition.[190] A letter stating the opinion of the bishop of the old capital might well be expected to have a considerable effect on public opinion. Eventually, it was the knowledge that the bishop of Antioch had restored the name of Chrysostom to the diptychs of his church that produced

---

[183] *Epp.* 51, 53, 54, 55. See T. auf der Mauer, *Mönchtum und Glaubensverkündung in den Schriften des Hl. Johannes Chrysostom* (Beiträge zur Geschichte der altchristlichen Literatur und Theologie, xiv, Freiburg, Switzerland, 1959).
[184] Pall. *Dial.* 51.
[185] Socr. vii. 25.
[186] Pall. *Dial.* 7-8 arrival of letter, 8-12 text of letter.
[187] Pall. *Dial.* 8: Theophilus' first letter. *Ibid.* 12 a second letter with minutes of the Council of the Oak.
[188] Pall. *Dial.* 12.
[189] Pall. *Dial.* 12-14.
[190] Soz. viii. 26. The letters were written around the time of the extraordinary hailstorm, just before the death of Eudoxia.

an irresistible demand at Constantinople that Atticus should restore Chrysostom's name at Constantinople as well.[191] But in 405 the letter which Innocent had written to the clergy and people of Constantinople had no effect on the authorities. Innocent can never have expected that an even more outspoken letter addressed to Theophilus would persuade that formidable enemy of Chrysostom to change his mind.[192] In fact the pope's letter of the autumn of 404 seems to have received no acknowledgement at all. If there was any response it was intensification of the pressure on the Joannites. A law of 18 November instructs provincial governors to prevent meetings of persons who, while holding the correct beliefs, despise the holy church and seek to hold meetings elsewhere. All who do not recognise communion with Arsacius, Theophilus and Porphyrius are to be excommunicated.[193]

It was around this time that Optatus was appointed prefect of Constantinople and resumed the investigation into the burning of the cathedral using torture and also began to exert severe pressure to compel Chrysostom's most prominent followers to accept communion with Arsacius.[194] It seems that the Eastern government saw Western support for Chrysostom simply as a symptom of the West's aggressive attitude towards the East. This was the time when Stilicho, commander in chief and principal minister of the West, was preparing to win eastern Illyricum from the Eastern government. He probably hoped to gain access to the recruits provided by that territory. The military pressure was to be provided by the Goths of Alaric.[195] In fact the attack on Eastern Illyricum was forestalled by the invasion of Radagaisus in 405.[196] Stilicho did not, however, give up his project. It is therefore not at all surprising that the Eastern government remained extremely suspicious of any Western diplomacy.

The Western initiative which Pope Innocent had announced in his letters developed slowly. Innocent induced the emperor Honorius to assemble a Western council of bishops to discuss the affair of John Chrysostom, and the Western bishops eventually assembled.[197] Palladius gives no indication of the passage of time between the coming of the news of the persecution of Optatus in late autumn 404[198] and the assembly of the synod. But the interval must have been long enough

[191] See below n. 219.
[192] P. Jaffé, *Regesta Pontificum Romanorum* (2nd ed., Leipzig, 1885-88, 2 vols), i. 287, 288; Pall. *Dial.* 12.
[193] *CT*, xvi. 4, 6.
[194] See above nn. 167-73.
[195] Zos. v. 26, 2 for date; J. F. Matthews, 'Olympiodorus of Thebes and the History of the West (A.D. 407-425)', *Journal of Roman Studies*, lx (1970), 87.
[196] J. F. Matthews, *Western Aristocracies and Imperial Court AD 364-425* (Oxford, 1975), pp. 274-5.
[197] Pall. *Dial.* 15.
[198] *Ibid.* 14.

for the invitations to reach the bishops and for the bishops to travel to Rome. We have an indirect indication of the date. When the ambassadors who carried the recommendations of the synod came to Constantinople they learnt that Atticus had 'leaped' on to the episcopal throne.[199] This cannot have been much earlier than April 406.[200] In that case the synod itself cannot have been much earlier than the summer of 405.

The embassy carried among other documents a letter from the Emperor Honorius to his brother Arcadius, which is quoted by Palladius. Honorius writes that this is his third letter and that he had not received any answer to the first two.[201] When did he write the earlier letters? We have what purports to be one of them.[202] Since it contains no reference to Arcadius having failed to answer a previous communication on this subject, it would seem that this was the first letter. This letter already alludes to the decisions of the synod.[203] So it would appear that Honorius only began to correspond with his brother about the case of John after the Western bishops had met. It is also clear that this letter, if indeed it is genuine, was more of a propaganda broadsheet than a diplomatic document. The letter recalls sharp criticism of the sending out of images of Eudoxia and of the devastated condition of the prefecture of Illyricum.[204] It then goes on to describe the breaking up of the Joannite congregations which is condemned in language very close to that used by Joannite writers.[205]

The synod decided that Chrysostom's case ought to be reviewed by a joint council of Western and Eastern bishops which was to meet at Thessalonica. Chrysostom should be restored to his church and to communion before the council, so that he could attend as bishop.[206] Thessalonica was not simply a meeting place equally convenient for bishops from East and West. Thessalonica was a see where the pope was trying to establish his ecclesiastical influence, just as Stilicho was hoping to establish political control of Illyricum.[207] Secular and ecclesiastical ambitions were parallel, if not coordinated. The recommendation of

---

[199] *Ibid.* 16: four months after death of his predecessor, Soz. VIII. 27.

[200] Sea closed approximately from 8-15 October to April (*CT*, xiii, 9, 3 (AD 380) cited by Jones, *Later Roman Empire*, ii. 843 n. 45.

[201] Pall. *Dial.* 15.

[202] *Corpus Scriptorum Ecclesiasticorum Latinorum*, xxxv. 85-88, an older text: *PG*, lii. 539-42.

[203] *Ibid.* 87, 28 Namque ii, quorum exspectabatur auctoritas (i.e. the Western council) ... sanciendam concordiam censuerunt, nec quemquam putarunt ante iudicium consortio repellendum.

[204] Quamvis super imagine muliebri, novo exemplo per provincias circumlata ... literis aliis commonuerim ... quamvis etiam super excidio pereuntis Illyrici pio apud vos prodiderimus effectu ....

[205] Cf. Pall. *Dial.* 11 (letter to Innocent) and 33.

[206] Pall. *Dial.* 15.

[207] Jones, *Later Roman Empire*, i. 211, 888-9; E. Caspar, *Geschichte des Papsttums* (Leipzig, 1931, 2 vols), i. 308.

the synod strengthened by a supporting letter of the Emperor Honorius to his brother Arcadius were taken to Constantinople by an embassy consisting of five bishops, two priests and a deacon.[208] This was probably in the spring or summer of 406.[209] It may well be that no attempt to have the deposition of Chrysostom reviewed could have succeeded, but the way in which this particular embassy was received suggests that their mission was seen simply as an unwarranted attempt by the West to intervene in affairs of the East. The ambassadors reached Athens but were prevented from sailing on to Thessalonica. Instead they were rushed on to two boats, and taken to the neighbourhood of Constantinople. There they were interned and the letter of Honorius taken from them by force. They were offered a large sum of money (3,000 solidi) if they would communicate with Atticus, the new bishop of Constantinople. When they refused, the Western bishops were sent back to Italy.[210] The Eastern bishops who had accompanied them were arrested and deported to remote towns, Cyriacus to Palmyra, Eulysius to Bostra, Demetrius to the Egyptian desert.[211] The persecution of other followers of John was intensified.[212] The embassy was treated purely and simply as an insult to the emperor. The depth of resentment at Western interference can be judged from the fact that a monk called Stephen was beaten and imprisoned for ten months for no other reason than that he had brought letters from the church of Rome to Constantinople.[213]

Since a Western attack on eastern Illyricum had only been prevented by the fact that the West was preoccupied first by the Radagaisus' invasion of Italy (AD 405 to August 406), and then by the overrunning of the Rhine frontier on the last day of 406,[214] any intervention on the part of the Western church or state on behalf of Chrysostom was bound to be counterproductive. John's powerful sympathisers in the West could not prevent, but more probably helped to provoke, his transfer to a more remote place of exile at Pityus on the edge of the Caucasus. Although he was an invalid he was made to go on foot (the journey lasted three months), and if Palladius is to be trusted, the officials of the praetorian prefect who escorted him made conditions as unpleasant as they could. Chrysostom died on the way on 12 September 407.[217] His party remained. 'Martyrius' ends his biography with an

---

[208] Pall. *Dial.* 15; Soz. viii. 28.

[209] See above p. 29 n. 200.

[210] Pall. *Dial.* 16.

[211] *Dial.* 71 (p. 126, ll. 10-21), 72 (p. 129, l. 15-131, l. 10).

[212] *Ibid.* 71-72 but we cannot tell how many of the men listed suffered persecution at precisely this time. Some, or most, may have been punished earlier.

[213] *Ibid.* 71 (p. 128, ll.13-16).

[214] Zos. v. 26. Jones, *Later Roman Empire*, pp. 184-5; Martindale, *Prosopography*, ii, s.v. Radagaisus, dates Radagaisus' invasion 405-6, and gives the last day of 406 for the breaching of the Rhine frontier. N. H. Baynes, *Byzantine Studies* (London, 1959), pp. 338-40 argued for dates a year earlier than the generally accepted ones.

[217] Socr. vi, 21.

appeal to the followers of the dead bishop not communicate with his opponents. The death of Nabob has not justified Jezebel.[218]

It was only in 416 that Atticus rehabilitated the memory of Chrysostom by allowing his name to be restored to the diptychs of the cathedral of Constantinople, so that henceforth his name would be read out during the service, together with other bishops, martyrs and distinguished persons associated with the church of Constantinople. The decisive factor was not the pressure of the Western Emperor, or of the pope, who refused communion with Constantinople as long as Chrysostom had not been rehabilitated, but the fact that the people of Constantinople knew that Chrysostom had been restored to the diptychs of Antioch and insisted that the same should happen at Constantinople. Only then did Atticus consult the emperor, that is in practice the regent Pulcheria or the praetorian prefect, and with his or her consent restored the name of Chrysostom to the diptychs of Constantinople.[219]

It may be significant that when Chrysostom's name was restored to the diptychs neither Anthemius nor Aurelian was any longer in power. A new generation of officials had taken over.[220] Monaxius the praetorian prefect of the East belonged to this generation.[221] Other powerful laymen who had participated in the deposition of Chrysostom were either dead, like Arcadius and Eudoxia, or at any rate retired from public life like Eutychianus, Optatus and John. The Western empire had received a tremendous battering at the hands of the Germanic invaders, and the threat which it had represented under the guidance of Stilicho had gone—never to return.

---

[218] Cited by van Ommeslaeghe, 'Jean Chrysostome en conflict avec l'impératrice Eudoxie' (above p.2 n. 4), p. 155.

[219] Socr. vii. 25, Theodoret, *HE*, v, 34, *Ep. ad Cyril.* 75, (*PG*, lxvii, 348-49). See Baur, *Johannes Chrysostomusm*, ii. 376.

[220] K. Holum argues that the replacement of Anthemius in 414 was a result of the Augusta Pulcheria's becoming *de facto* regent for her young brother, Theodosius II, and that this marks a significant break in policy *Theodosian Empresses*, pp. 97 et seqq.

[221] Martindale, *Prosopography*, ii, s.v. Monaxius.

Note

G. Albert, *Goten in Konstantinopel, Untersuchungen zur oströmischen Geschichte um das Jahr 400 n. Chr.* (Studien zur Geschichte und Kultur des Altertums, Neue Folge 2, Paderborn (1984) appeared too late to be used by me.

V

Friends and Enemies of John Chrysostom

John Chrysostom was consecrated bishop of Constantinople on the 26th February 398. He started with the favour of the court, particularly of the empress Eudoxia. His pulpit eloquence soon won him a mass following. His sermons were full of social concern, but he did not attack individuals by name, and kept out of political controversy. So he seemed set for a long and successful episcopacy. Yet in his sixth year as bishop he was summoned to appear before the so-called Synod of the Oak in order to answer a long list of charges. He refused to appear and was formally deposed. This was in autumn 403. The first exile was brief. He was recalled after only one day. He did not enter the city and resume his duties as bishop immediately, but after a not very long interval he agreed to do both. His opponents however remained as determined as ever and soon resumed their attacks. By Christmas 403 the emperor again refused to take communion with him. Just before Easter 404 Chrysostom was forbidden to officiate at services and on 20th June 404 he was escorted into exile. This time there was no recall. He died on 14th September 407, while he was being moved to an even more remote place of exile at Pityus on the Black Sea.[1] How can this disastrous conclusion after so promising beginning be explained?

The sequence of events which led to the deposition of John Chrysostom is long and complicated. But one fact stands out: from the time, just before the Synod of the Oak, when the emperor Arcadius turned against him to the end of his life Chrysostom was faced by powerful and determined opposition which first brought about his deposition and exile, and then made sure that he would not be recalled and that those who continued to recognise him would be persecuted.[2]

Modern scholarship has, on the whole, followed the ancient sources[3] in explaining the fall of John Chrysostom by a conspiracy

---

1. The standard biography: P.C. Baur, *Der heilige Johannes Chrysostomus und seine Zeit* (Munich, 1929-30).
2. See my article "The deposition of John Chrysostomus" in *NMS* (forthcoming).
3. The principal sources are: Socrates, *Ecclesiastical History* (hereafter Socr.); Sozomen, *Ecclesiastical History* (hereafter Soz.) with deliberate corrections of Socrates; Palladius, *Dialogue Concerning the Life of St John Chrysostomus* (hereafter Pall., *Dial.*), page references in brackets are to the edition of P.R.

theory. The empress Eudoxia was offended by one of John's sermons directed against the vanity of women. As a result she combined with some bishops and others who held grievances against the bishop of Constantinople, and together they succeeded in persuading the emperor Arcadius to use his authority against John. Chrysostom's position was undermined by the intrigues of a handful of bishops and a few aristocratic women, who resented the vigorous moral standards upheld by Chrysostom.[4]

The view is not altogether satisfactory. One would not expect that particular group of opponents to have had the weight and persistence which the enemies of Chrysostom were to display. Eudoxia no doubt was passionate and easily offended. But she had also been a great admirer of Chrysostom, and after his first exile at least her hostility ceased very rapidly. One would not have expected her to have maintained the steady and persistent hostility, which ensured the second and final exiling of Chrysostom. There is also the fact that the attack on the Joannites did not in the least slacken after Eudoxia's death in October 404. Again, two of the bishops who figure in the sources as the local leaders of the plot against Chrysostom, Severianus of Gabala[5] and Antiochus of Ptolemais[6] were effective preachers, but otherwise men of the second rank. Acacius of Beroea had made a reputation by resisting

---

Coleman-Norton, *Palladius, Dialogus de vita S. Ioannis Chrysostomi* (Cambridge, 1928); finally the unpublished "Life" of "Martyrius", the subject of important articles by F. van Ommeslaeghe who is editing it.

4. The most compact statement of the "conspiracy theory" is Pall., *Dial.*, 16-17 (p. 25). Palladius, however, has very little about the part played by the empress Eudoxia – it would seem deliberately. In this he follows the line taken by John himself in his letter to Innocent I (Pall., *Dial.*, 8-12). For him Theophilus of Alexandria was the principal conspirator. The role of Eudoxia is high-lighted by Socrates and Sozomen, but she was already a principal villain for "Martyrius".

5. K.G. Holum, *Theodosian Empresses* (Berkeley, 1982), 70-78, argues that there was a deep and permanent motive for Eudoxia's hostility to Chrysostom in the bishop's opposition to women in positions of authority, and in particular his "challenge to Eudoxia's *basileia*". This is interesting but debatable. It is doubtful whether Eudoxia was a "ruling Augusta" in the way her daughter Pulcheria was to be a few years later. There is also little evidence that Chrysostom challenged her position, except defensively when he felt under attack himself. "Hom. cum iret in exsilium", PG, 52 cols. 435-38, esp. 437 cited by Holum, p. 77, is directed at women in authority but like its companion "Hom. ante exsilium", PG, 52, cols. 427-32, it may well not be genuine. The study of pseudo-Chrysostomic works has scarcely begun.

6. See *RE*, IIA, col. 1930, *s.v.* Severianus 17.

FRIENDS AND ENEMIES OF JOHN CHRYSOSTOM

Arianism in Syria, and he was highly respected among ascetics,[7] but he, like the others, had absented himself from the duties of his see and must for that reason have been vulnerable.[8] Theophilus, the patriarch of Alexandria, was of course a formidable figure.[9] But while he was a determined and persistent enemy of Chrysostom he returned to Alexandria soon after John's return from his first exile[10] and was never again in Constantinople when the important decisions were taken.

One can see that the bishops with access to court through the empress had the potential to form a pressure group, but if their demands were to carry enough weight to overthrow a bishop with considerable personal following, they surely required backing from a powerful body of opinion in the Church or the imperial administration, or both. Roman emperors reached decisions after consulting their consistory,[11] and normally the praetorian prefect of the East was the chief adviser of the Eastern emperor. Admittedly in matters concerned with the Church, emperors since Constantine consulted synods of bishops.[12] But in this case the bishops were divided and the emperor had to decide between them. Moreover, the case involved a charge of disrespect for the empress and whatever was decided would have implications for public order. In this situation, surely, the praetorian prefect and other eminent laymen are likely to have been consulted. The action against Chrysostom was not taken on impulse. The gradualness with which the attack on Chrysostom gathered weight after the first exile suggests that Arcadius and his advisers were by then well aware how risky it would be to use force to depose the bishop of Constantinople, but that they were unable to withstand the sustained pressure of those who insisted that he must go. It is the purpose of this paper to

---

7.   See *DHGE*, III, 707, *s.v.* Antiochus 6.
8.   Earlier Chrysostom had sent him on a diplomatic mission to the pope at Rome, Pall., *Dial.*, 18; Soz., VIII, 3.   He was admired by Theodoret and contributed information for the *Historia Relig- iosa*.   See A.J. Festugière, *Antioche païenne et chrétienne*, (Paris 1959), index, *s.v.* Acace.   Palladius, *Dial.*, 21, gives a trivial motive for his hostility.   In fact his attitude probably reflects that of the monks who were generally against Chrysostom. See below, 90-94.
9.   Theophilus had consecrated Chrysostom as bishop under pressure from court.   Pall. *Dial.*, 19-20, Soz. VIII, 2, Socr. VI, 2.
10.   Pall. *Dial.*, 10 (Letter to Innocent), 30.   Admittedly he continued to participate by letter: Pall. *Dial.*, 30, also 8 and 13; *ibid.*, 15 (p. 22, 5) shows that the emperor Honorius thought Theophilus the cause of all "these evils".
11.   A.H.M. Jones, *The Later Roman Empire 284-602*, 3 vols. (Oxford, 1964) (hereafter *LRE*), 333-38.
12.   F. Millar, *The Emperor in the Roman World* (London, 1977), chap. 9.

argue that the "conspiracy" against John Chrysostom was indeed
backed by a powerful body of opinion among both clergy and high
officials, and that the victory of Chrysostom's enemies was made
possible by this support.

After so many generations of readers have felt sympathy and
admiration for the personality and character of John Chrysostom, it
is difficult to believe that he was disliked by many of his
contemporaries, and not only the wicked, jealous or ambitious. But
there is plenty of evidence of hostility among the clergy of
Constantinople and neighbouring provinces. These were the people
whom the four dissident bishops could most easily organise into a
pressure group against their bishop. The charges brought up
against Chrysostom at the Synod of the Oak show that his ecclesiastical administration had been extremely contentious. He had - so it
was claimed - unjustly dismissed a deacon for striking a servant.[13]
He had been abusive of some of his clergy, describing them as
dishonourable, corrupt, capable of anything, and not worth three
obols.[14] He had written a slanderous pamphlet bringing his clergy
into disrepute.[15] He had allowed clerics to be tried in public
courts and to die in prison.[16] A number of charges concern his
financial administration.[17] To us most of the charges seem
trivial, as they did to contemporaries at Rome.[18] But this does
not mean that they seemed trivial to the clergy of Constantinople:
in fact one can be sure that Theophilus and the other bishops
masterminding the trial would not have accepted (or perhaps helped
to compile)[19] this particular charge-sheet, unless they had thought
that it would win them support, and do damage to Chrysostom. It is
clear even from the sympathetic accounts of the ecclesiastical
historians and Palladius that Chrysostom's government of the church
of Constantinople left many people discontented. He was a strict
disciplinarian. He expelled a considerable number of clerics from
the church. He appointed the stern and unpopular deacon Serapion
as his second in command.[20] He tried to prevent the clergy from
living under the same roof with their housekeepers, usually
dedicated virgins of good family.[21] This arrangement was wide-

---

13. Photius, *Bibliotheca*, 59, charge 1 (18a, 1).
14. *Ibid.*, charge 5 (18a, 24).
15. *Ibid.*, charge 8 (18a, 13).
16. *Ibid.*, charge 19 (18a, 31), also charge 2 (18a, 2) Isaac's
charge 15 (19a, 22). These were the envoys sent by Theophilus to
accuse the Tall Brothers (Pall., *Dial.*, 26). Palladius shows that
they had been sent to prison by a secular official.
17. *Ibid.*, charges 3, 4, 16, 17.
18. Pall., *Dial.*, 12 (pp. 16, 18).
19. *Ibid.*, 27 (p. 45). Many of the charges lie in what today
would be called "personnel management".
20. Socr., VI, 4.
21. Pall., *Dial.*, 20. The two surviving pamphlets on this problem

FRIENDS AND ENEMIES OF JOHN CHRYSOSTOM

spread and seems to have been traditional at Constantinople. It has been suggested that it reflected an ideal of chastity that sought to abolish the distinction between the sexes.[22] The attempt to suppress the custom caused widespread indignation.[23]

Chrysostom had overhauled the finances of the church of Constantinople in a way that was resented. He personally intervened regularly in the way the funds of the church were spent.[24] He checked the extent to which clergy kept the offerings of the faithful. There is no evidence to assess how far he was trying to subordinate the minor churches to the Great Church of Constantinople - if such was his aim at all.[25] He certainly cut expenditure in the bishop's household, and transferred the money saved to the upkeep of a hospital. Presumably this caused redundancies among the household staff, as the men dismissed from the household were not necessarily the same as the doctors, cooks and celibate workers whom he appointed to the hospital.[26] He abolished episcopal banquets, which had provided perquisites for the church's stewards (οἰκονόμοι).[27] Chrysostom gave very high priority to helping the poor. He refused to use marble which his predecessors had bought for the decoration of St Apostles, and sold it.[28] He also sold many valuable items from the treasury of the church.[29] The men who had looked after finance under his predecessor considered this irresponsible and improvident - or worse. At any rate both items figured among the charges at the Synod of the Oak, and Arsacius, brother of the late bishop Nectarius, gave evidence against John on the sale of valuables charge.[30] Chrysostom was accused of having sold an inheritance left to the church by a lady called Thecla,[31] and also of failing to produce accounts for his

(PG, 47, cols. 496 ff.; more recent edition by J. Dumortier, *Les cohabitations suspectes, comment observer la virginité* [Paris, 1955]) seem to have been written at Antioch. I, 1 suggests that John was not yet bishop. See Baur, *Johannes Chrysostomus*, I, 141 note 62.

22. G. Dagron, *Naissance d'une capitale: Constantinople et ses institutions de 330 à 451* (Paris, 1974), 514 note 2.

23. Pall., *Dial.*, 19 (p. 31). Dagron, *loc. cit.*, suggests that charge 8 (Photius, *Bibl.*, 59 [18a, 13]) refers to a pamphlet criticising clergy on account of these *virgines subintroductae*.

24. Charge 17, Photius, *Bibl.*, 59 (18a, 28).

25. G. Dagron, *op. cit.*, 498.

26. Pall., *Dial.*, 20 (p. 32, 9 ff.).

27. *Ibid.*, 40 (p. 70, 5).

28. Charge 4 (Photius, *Bibl.*, 59 [18a, 5]).

29. Charge 3 (*ibid.*, 18a, 4). Church treasures were checked by civil authorities after John's second exile (Pall., *Dial.*, 13).

30. *Ibid.*, 19a, 34.

31. Charge 16 (*ibid.*, 18a, 27).

expenditure of ecclesiastical revenues.[32] It is obvious that there was great dissatisfaction with the financial side of Chrysostom's administration.

Discontent with John Chrysostom was by no means restricted to members of his clergy. There is evidence that the monks of Constantinople were to a large extent against him. We have no satisfactory account of the origin of this antagonism, because the fact of it was as embarrassing to Palladius as an apologist for Chrysostom, as it was to the biographers of the monks Isaac and Hypatius, who wrote after John had been rehabilitated.[33] Nevertheless, there can be no question about the basically hostile attitude of the Constantinopolitan monks.[34]

Palladius describes Isaac as the leader of false monks, who spent all his time abusing bishops and as one of the principal conspirators against John.[35] The rhetorical abuse obscures the fact that one principal antagonist of Palladius' hero was generally regarded as a holy man and as the founder and unofficial leader of the monks of Constantinople.[36] In fact Isaac was very unlikely to represent only himself when he took so prominent a part in the attack on John Chrysostom. At the trial Isaac produced his own list of seventeen charges,[37] and he was one of the men who brought the final summons for John to appear before the Synod.[38] One of the charges was that Chrysostom had caused a lot of unpleasantness to Isaac personally.[39] Sozomen explains the cause of this hostility. "John had several disputes with many of the monks, particularly with Isaac. He highly commended those who remained in quietude in the monasteries and practised philosophy there...but

---

32. Charge 17 (*Ibid.*, 18a, 20).
33. See below, note 36.
34. See the important article by G. Dagron, "Les moines et la ville: Le monachisme à Constantinople jusqu'au concile de Chalcédoine (A.D. 451)," *TM*, 4 (1970), 229-76, esp. 263.
35. Pall., *Dial.*, 21.
36. G. Karo and other pupils of F. Buecheler in their edition of Callinicus, *Vita S. Hypatii* (Leipzig, 1895), xiii-xv, proved that Isaac the enemy of Chrysostom is identical with the father of monasticism at Constantinople. A.D. 383, which according to the *Vita Isaacii*, AASS May, VII, 258 d, was the year of Isaac's death, was in fact the date when Dalmatius, his successor, first entered the monastery. That the date should have been mistaken and Isaac killed off early, is a measure of the embarrassment caused by this conflict of two saints. When Dalmatius succeeded Isaac he was consecrated by Atticus bishop of Constantinople. This cannot have been before 406. Isaac was buried in the "martyrium" of St Stephen (*Vita Isaacii, loc. cit.*).
37. Photius, *Bibl.*, 59 (18b, 33 ff.).
38. Pall., *Dial.*, 40.
39. Photius, *Bibl.*, 59 (19a, 28).

FRIENDS AND ENEMIES OF JOHN CHRYSOSTOM

the monks who went out of doors and made their appearance in the city he reproached and regarded as insulting philosophy. For these causes he incurred the hatred of the clergy and of many of the monks, who called him a hard, passionate, morose and arrogant man. They therefore attempted to bring his life into disrepute, by stating confidently that he would eat with no-one, and that he refused every invitation to a meal".[40]

It is significant that while our sources mention Isaac as leader of the false monks they do not mention any corresponding leader of the good monks. The ascetics belonging to John's party, that is Olympias and her home of dedicated virgins,[41] the Gothic monks living on the property that had belonged to Promotus,[42] and the Tall Brothers and their sympathisers,[43] were none of them typical Constantinopolitan monks. There were no mass demonstrations by monks in favour of Chrysostom to compare with the violent rioting of monks to prevent his return from his first exile. It is also significant that one of Chrysostom's principal enemies among the bishops was Acacius of Beroea, a Syrian like Isaac, and an ex-monk highly respected by the monks of his native province. When Chrysostom was on his way into exile, he was actually attacked by monks as he was staying at Caesarea in Cappadocia. There is every reason to believe that "the monks" were against Chrysostom.[44]

Unfortunately we have no account written from the monks' point of view. Most of the monks were probably illiterate, and if literate, were not concerned with writing. The oldest hagiographic source, Callinicus' *Life of Hypatius*, written *ca* 447-50,[45] i.e. after the rehabilitation of Chrysostom, is carefully neutral between Isaac and Chrysostom. Each is given a paragraph of praise. Not a word is said of the conflict between them, or of any part Hypatius himself might have played in those troubles.[46] In his Constantinopolitan writings Chrysostom occasionally mentions monks with approval. But the references are not to urban monks.

---

40. Soz. VIII, 9, translation by C.D. Hartrauft in vol. 2 of the Postnicene Fathers series.

41. A.M. Malingrey, ed., Jean Chrysostom, *Lettres à Olympias et la Vie anonyme d'Olympias* (Paris, 1968), 418 ff.

42. Joh. Chrys., *Ep.*, 14, 5 and 207.

43. Soz., VIII, 11 ff.; Socr., VI, 7. Pall., *Dial.*, 23 ff. Bibliography in article by Dagron (above, note 34), 259 note 152. A. Guillaumont, *"Les Képhalaia Gnostica" d'Évagre le Pontique et l'histoire de l'origènisme chez les Grecs et chez les Syriens*, Patristica Sorbonensia, 5 (Paris, 1962).

44. T. Gregory, "Zosimus 5. 23 and the people of Constantinople," *Byzantion*, 43 (1973), 61-83; Joh. Chrys., *Ep.* 14,2.

45. G.J.M. Bartelink, *Callinicos. Vie d'Hypatios*, SC, 177 (Paris, 1971), 11-12. The early part of the "Life" illustrates the informality of monasticism around Constantinople around A.D. 400.

46. *Ibid.*, § 11, praise of Chrysostom seems slightly artificial,

The monks are described as "those of the hills"[47] or the "brothers of the hills".[48] "Those who dwell in the mountains",[49] those "who have embraced life in the desert".[50] The passages look like nostalgic memories of the hermits of the hills on the desert edge around Antioch.[51] He says nothing either in praise or blame that might be applicable to monks roaming the streets of the capital.

So the history of the conflicts between Chrysostom and the monks of Constantinople has to rely heavily on the passages of Sozomen already cited and some inferences, based on odd scraps of evidence bearing on the nature of monasticism at Constantinople. Dagron has pointed out that monasticism at Constantinople was started by Eleusius and Marathonius, assistants of the semi-Arian bishop Macedonius, and was strongly influenced by the ideas of Eustathius of Sebaste. It had features which some contemporaries, and certainly the leaders of the more disciplined and controlled monasticism of later years, found discreditable. The theology might be semi-Arian. Some monasteries contained both men and women. There was little discipline. Monks moved in and out of monasteries, changed monasteries, retired from monastic life almost as it pleased themselves, certainly without reference to any ecclesiastical authority. They wandered among the urban population. They had a strong social conscience. While the founders and financial supporters of monasteries belonged to the official class the bulk of the monks were ordinary people, who shared with much of the population of the city the fact that they were recent arrivals from the provinces.[52]

One can see that the monks might be considered a threat to public order - indeed they were. They also offered a challenge to any bishop who took a monarchical view of the government of his church. After all they were largely outside his jurisdiction. Sozomen suggests that this was precisely the point where they clashed with Chrysostom. The behaviour of the monks at Constantinople did not correspond to what Chrysostom thought proper. He tried to confine monks to monasteries and to subject them to the control of their bishop. This provoked resentment. Dagron goes as far as to interpret Chrysostom's charitable foundations as an attempt to transfer welfare work from monks to the episcopal church.[53] There is no evidence for this motive. That the monks of

---

and the balance between Isaac and John is surely quite deliberate.

47. *Hom.* 7, in *Act.*, 4.

48. *Hom.* 13, in *Act.*, 4.

49. *Hom.* 10 in *Hebr.*, 7.

50. *Hom.* 34, in *Hebr.*, 8.

51. But Isaac, the urban monk, was a Syrian by origin and so were the bishops Antiochus, Severianus and Acacius who led the attack on Chrysostom.

52. See Dagron, "Les moines et la ville" (above, note 34).

53. *Ibid.*, 264.

FRIENDS AND ENEMIES OF JOHN CHRYSOSTOM

Constantinople maintained hospitals or other social institutiions is an inference from what is known of the monks of Eustathius of Sebaste. But Chrysostom's own passionate interest in helping the poor went back to his Antioch days, and was certainly not simply a reaction to the charitable works of the monks of Constantinople.[54]

It is difficult to estimate the importance of Chrysostom's conflict with the monks since we know so little about their numbers and influence. According to Callinicus there existed crowds of monasteries in and around Constantinople, each with around 150 monks at the turn of the century.[55] If this was so, a conflict between monks and bishops would cause endless disturbances of a kind which would seriously worry the administration. We know that the opposition of the monks of Constantinople was to contribute significantly to the fall of Nestorius thirty years later.[56] We simply lack the evidence to assert that the monks' contribution to the fall of Chrysostom was comparable. But it is likely.

The disaffected monks certainly were natural allies of Theophilus, and therefore made his task of building up opposition to Chrysostom much easier. Just as Chrysostom was the natural protector of the Long Brothers, the intellectual monks of Egypt, so Theophilus was the natural ally of the ordinary monks of Constantinople. After all he seems to have quite deliberately chosen to side with the unsophisticated.[57]

It is certainly not a coincidence that two of the most prominent laymen among the opponents of John Chrysostom, the general Saturninus,[58] and Aurelian[59] twice praetorian prefect, had close links with the monk Isaac. Saturninus had given him the land for his first cell, and indeed built the cell itself.[60] Aurelian arranged for Isaac to be buried in the Martyrium of Stephen which he had built.[61] Was this before the finding of the bones of Stephen at Caphargamal in Palestine in December 415?[62] The ability of monks to combine with ordinary people to make an extremely

---

54. Baur, *Johannes Chrysostomus*, I, 312-16.

55. *Vita Hypatii*, 11, 1.

56. See T. Gregory, *Vox populi, Violence and Popular Involvement in the Religious Controversies of the Fifth Century A.D.* (Columbus, 1979), 129-43.

57. Soz., VIII, 11.

58. A.H.M. Jones, J.R. Martindale *et al., Prosopography of the Later Roman Empire* (Cambridge, 1971-) (hereafter *PLRE*), I, *s.v.* Saturninus 10; when Saturninus died his widow continued the enmity.

59. *Ibid., s.v.* Aurelianus 3.

60. *V. Isaacii*, IV, 14.

61. *Ibid.*, IV, 18.

62. *Ep. Luciani*, PL, 41, cols. 807 ff. See E.D. Hunt, *Holy Land Pilgrimage in the Later Roman Empire* (Oxford, 1982), 211 ff. St Stephen had a Novatian church at Constantinople before his relics were found, Soz., VIII, 24.

powerful pressure group had already been demonstrated in the events leading to the abdication from the see of Constantinople of Gregory of Nazianzus.[63]   In antagonizing the monks Chrysostom had made formidable enemies.

Chrysostom's enemies were unfortunately not restricted to Constantinople and its immediate environments.   In the first quarter of 401[64*] John travelled to Ephesus in answer to an invitation by the local clergy, and proceeded to exercise patriarchal authority in the ecclesiastical province of Asia in a way which was unprecedented, and extremely controversial.[65]   Since the council of Constantinople of 381, the bishop of Constantinople had enjoyed a "seniority of honour" second only to that of the bishop of Rome,[66] but he had no unambiguously recognised regular jurisdiction even over the bishops of cities of his diocese in which Constantinople was situated, Thrace,[67] never mind the bishop of the diocese of Asia.   The outcome was certainly dramatic. Invited to consecrate a new bishop of Ephesus, Chrysostom travelled to Ephesus, convoked a council of 70 bishops of the diocese of Asia, and faced with two rival candidates, appointed a third, his own deacon Heraclides.   He then proceeded with the collaboration of the synod, to replace at least six, perhaps sixteen, bishops.[68]   He also expelled Novatian and Quartodeciman sectarians from a number of churches.[69]   Finally on his way home, he replaced the bishop of Nicomedia in the diocese of Pontus.[70]   Chrysostom was asserting the disciplinary authority of the bishop of Constantinople over the bishops of neighbouring dioceses.[71]   It is clear that he did this with the full consent and backing of the emperor.   For he was able to offer deposed bishops the consolation that they would probably

---

63. Dagron, "Les moines et la ville," 262, citing Gregory of Nazianzus, *Ep.* 77, 1.

64. For date of mission see Baur, *op. cit.*, II, 127 note 13. Chrysostom returned soon after Easter 401, having been away over 100 days: "Oratio post reditum," PG, 52, 421.*

65. Dagron, *Naissance d'une capitale* (above, note 22), 466-69.

66. Mansi, III, 560.

67. Dagron, *op. cit.*, 458-59.

68. Pall., *Dial.*, 47 (p. 82), 16 bishops deposed; Soz. VIII, 6, 13 bishops; Pall., *Dial.*, 47 (p. 83, 6), 6 bishops.

69. Only reported by Socrates VI, 11, but he was particularly interested in Novatians.

70. Appointing Pansophius, former tutor of Eudoxia: Soz. VIII, 6.

71. Pall., *Dial.*, 47 (p. 83, 6), admits deposition of six bishops all in Asia.   He ignores Gerontius of Nicomedia in Pontus who was certainly deposed.   According to Soz. VIII, 6, thirteen bishops were deposed in Lycia, Phrygia and Asia as well as Gerontius of Nicomedia. Theophilus alleged deposition of sixteen (*Dial.*, 47 [p. 82, 24]).

*   For 401 read 402, see Alan Cameron, Chiron XVII (1987), 350-1.

receive immunity from curial service,[72] a privilege which would require the imperial signature. Moreover only the emperor could provide any armed force needed to enforce the decisions of Chrysostom's synod. The depositions and consecrations decided at Ephesus angered and worried very many people. Citizens naturally resented the imposition of a bishop. The Nicomedians wanted Gerontius back[73] and there were riots against the newly appointed bishop of Ephesus.[74] Bishops must have been deeply worried by such empire-building on the part of the bishop of Constantinople. Where would it end? Events showed that many bishops did become hostile to Chrysostom. For the time being the emperor was with Chrysostom, but perhaps not wholeheartedly: after all a year earlier he had prevented Chrysostom from going to Ephesus to depose its bishop.[75] But if Chrysostom ever was to lose imperial support his unpopularity with many bishops would be extremely serious. After all the future of an accused bishop would be decided by his fellow bishops sitting in synod.[76]

Chrysostom thus did antagonise many people. Moreover his way of life did not help to reconcile those he had alienated. He preferred solitude to sociability. He evidently made a habit of dining alone.[77] His motives were admirable: to spend the church's money on any other object than the poor was sacrilege.[78] He was of course very busy. In addition to carrying out his duties as an administrator and preacher with extreme conscientiousness he was also a prolific writer. No doubt he thought he had better uses for his time than communal dining. Furthermore as a result of prolonged asceticism in his youth he had acquired a weak stomach which could not stand elaborate food. The fact remains that his dining habits made it much more difficult for people, whether clergy or laymen, to meet him. This was bound to cause resentment. People expected to be able to meet their bishop in order to call on his assistance and patronage.[79] Patronage was required of a bishop. Furthermore conversation over a meal has always been a good way of

---

72. Pall., *Dial.*, 51 (p. 51, 16).
73. Soz. VIII, 6.
74. Socr., VI, 11 (alternative version). Heraclides was later accused of violence. He was a pupil of Evagrius Ponticus and a former monk of Scetis, Soz. VIII, 6, and was therefore close to the "Tall Brothers".
75. Pall., *Dial.*, 49 (p. 86, 22).
76. Mansi, III, 560-64. V. Grumel, *Les Regestes des Actes du Patriarcat de Constantinople* (Istanbul, 1932-), I, 4, no. 5.
77. Charge 25, Photius, *Bibl.*, 59 (18b); Pall., *Dial.*, 39-45, is a lengthy defence.
78. Pall., *Dial.*, 40 (p. 70, 4).
79. Jones, *LRE*, 915. On the importance of meals and other forms of social intercourse in patron-client relations see Libanius, *Orr.* 51 and 52.

discussing contentious situations, and calming passions aroused by them. Chrysostom's zeal produced lots of such situations, but his way of life made it more difficult to discuss them with the people involved. Chrysostom's aversion to sociability was listed among the accusations of the Synod of the Oak, and Palladius felt obliged to include a very long defence of it in his *Dialogue*.[80] The solitary habits of Chrysostom made it easier for the visiting bishops and Theophilus to isolate him, and to organise a strong pressure group for his deposition, and indeed to turn a large part of the clergy of Constantinople against him.[81]

Now the existence of a large body of ecclesiastical opinion including a significant number of bishops was something the imperial government would take into account. In accordance with a tradition going back to Constantine, Christian emperors felt responsibility for the discipline and unity of the church, but preferred to base their policy on the advice of ecclesiastics, and especially of councils of bishops.[82] If it happened that the church spoke with two voices, it was left to the emperor to decide which to support and enforce. This was the situation in the case of Chrysostom. The church was divided. The bishop of Constantinople had fervent supporters, as well as determined opponents. The emperor had to make up his mind between them. In a situation like this the emperor would consult with his officials, especially those who would be concerned with the enforcement of any decision.[83] If a synod was subsequently held its composition,[84] usually decided by the emperor, would ensure that it reached a decision corresponding to the views of the emperor. In situations of this kind the opinions of the great secular officials were obviously of very great importance.

It is on the face of it, likely that an important group of officials threw its influence on the side of Chrysostom's opponents. Only so can it be explained that the opponents were strong enough not only to get the case for Chrysostom rejected, but before his second exile, to prevent it from being heard at all. It is a consequence of the fact that our principal sources are ecclesiastical that we are comparatively badly informed about the attitudes of laymen. There is, however, some evidence that a number of highly influential men were hostile.

I hope to argue elsewhere that the foreign and military policies pursued by the Eastern government during the reign of Arcadius show a remarkable degree of continuity. This continuity

---

80. See note 77 above.
81. Pall., *Dial.*, 9 (p. 8, 27), in Letter to Innocent I.
82. See note 12 above; also J. Gaudemet, *L'église dans l'empire romain* (Paris, 1958), 457-60.
83. Jones, *LRE*, 361.
84. At the Synod of the Oak 40 bishops present at Constantinople and supporting Chrysostom were simply ignored (Pall., *Dial.*, 29).

FRIENDS AND ENEMIES OF JOHN CHRYSOSTOM

is extremely unlikely to have been a result of the abiding influence of a very young, inexperienced, and, as far as we can tell,
undistinguished emperor. It is even more unlikely to have been due
to the advice of the even younger, less experienced, and volatile
empress Eudoxia. The continuity in policy seems to be grounded in
the fact that the principal office of state, the praetorian prefecture of the East, was held in alternation by a small group of men,
who might be described as the "Arcadian establishment".[85] Three of
these men were descendants of great *novi homines* of the court
of Constantine and Constantius. Two others of similar background
are mentioned as holding the prefecture of Constantinople.[86] All
appear to have taken sides against John Chrysostom.

In the case of Aurelian we have explicit evidence of positive
hostility to Chrysostom. He, together with the general Saturninus
and the *comes* John had been handed over to Gainas, and sent into
exile by that German general. According to Zosimus it was after
the return of the exiles to Constantinople that Eudoxia's hostility
to Chrysostom became manifest.[87]

Presumably these men bore a grudge against the archbishop who
had been influential during the time of their exile. It is likely
enough that they believed that Chrysostom could have prevented
their disgrace and danger - if not the whole Gainas crisis, and
that on returning to Constantinople they were intent on revenge.

We do not know what precise role Aurelian played in the controversies over John Chrysostom. As a former prefect of the city,
and praetorian prefect of the East, he is likely to have held an
influential position in the consistory of Arcadius. He did not
hold office in these years, and had to wait until 414 for his
second praetorian prefecture. But he was rich and highly respected.
As praetorian prefect in 414 he decorated the newly rebuilt senate
house with busts of Arcadius, Honorius and Pulcheria. In 415 he
added one of Theodosius II. He also received one himself. A
district of Constantinople came to be known after him - presumably
the district where his mansion had been situated.[88] He is likely

---

85. *Prefecture* of the East: 395-97 Caesarius 6.   397-99
Eutychianus 5. 399 (autumn) Aurelianus 3. 399 Dec. - 400 (autumn)
Eutychianus 5.   400 Dec. - 403 June Caesarius 6.   404-405
Eutychianus 5. 405-414 Anthemius 1. 414-416 Aurelianus 3. See
Fasti, in *PLRE*, II, 1250.
86. Eutychianus 5 and Aurelian 3 were sons of Taurus 3 (cos. 361).
Anthemius was a grandson of Philippus 7 (cos. 348). Caesarius 6
seems to have been a *novus homo*. Others of similar background:
Simplicius 4 (*PLRE*, II) *praef. urb. Cpl*. 403, brother or cousin
of Anthemius 1.   Optatus 1 (*PLRE*, I) *praef. urb Cpl*. 403-404,
nephew of Optatus 3 cos. 334.
87. Zos. V, 23; *PLRE*, I, *s.v.* Saturninus 10; *PLRE*, II, Joannes 1.
88. *PLRE*, I, *s.v.* Aurelianus 3; R. Janin, *Constantinople
byzantine* (Paris, 1964), 155-56.

to have been a man of influence, and a dangerous enemy even when not in office.[89] Of the other two exiles, Saturninus seems to have died soon after his return from exile, but his widow is reported to have been a prominent opponent of Chrysostom.[90] We have seen that both Aurelian and Saturninus had links with the monk Isaac.[91]

The *comes* John, the third of the exiles, had a particular grievance against Chrysostom. At the Synod of the Oak Chrysostom was charged with having informed against him during the "mutiny of the soldiers".[92] In all probability the "mutiny" refers to the occasion when the troops under Gainas demanded the surrender of the later exiles. John was a dangerous enemy since already at the time of his exile, early in 400, he enjoyed the confidence of both emperor and empress, and was even rumoured to have been the father of the little Theodosius II.[93] At the time of the Synod of the Oak he held the title of *comes*, and after the final exile of Chrysostom he was one of a number of magistrates who witnessed the receipt of valuables belonging to the church of Constantinople from the clergy of the exiled archbishop.[94]

One would expect the grievances of the "exiles" to have been shared by others who had suffered at that time. In fact pseudo-Martyrius states that his enemies charged John with having been ready to betray the church and state to Gainas.[95] There is evidence that Chrysostom was active and influential in the days when Gainas and his Goths were in occupation of Constantinople.[96] The fact that John went on a diplomatic mission to Gainas after the massacre of the Goths in the city also suggests that he was thought to be on good terms with him.[97] Our sources give great prominence to the courage with which Chrysostom opposed Gainas when the latter demanded a church for the services of his Arian soldiers.[98] It may

---

89. See the extremely flattering *Ep.* 34 of Synesius, written when Aurelian was not in office; also *Ep.* 31.
90. Pall., *Dial.*, 17.
91. See above, p. 93.
92. Charge 11, Photius, *Bibl.*, 59 (17b, 19).
93. Theodosius II was born on 10 April 401 and cannot have been conceived before June 400. For John to have been the father he must have been at Constantinople then, only a few weeks before the Goths in Constantinople were destroyed (12 July 400). This is not impossible but would contradict Soz., VIII, 8; Socr., VII, 6; Zos., V, 18, who agree that the three exiles were handed over before the Goths entered Constantinople, i.e. towards the end of 399.
94. Pall., *Dial.*, 13.
95. F. van Ommeslaeghe, *Anal Boll*, 97 (1979), 152.
96. Synesius, *De Providentia*, PG, 66, col. 1267 B, on the council in the bishop's palace after the destruction of the Goths.
97. Theodoret, *Historia Ecclesiastica*, V, 33; "Hom. cum Saturninus et Aurelianus acti essent in exsilium," PG, 52 cols. 413-20.
98. Socr., VI, 6; Soz., VIII, 4; Theodoret, *HE*, V, 30.

FRIENDS AND ENEMIES OF JOHN CHRYSOSTOM

be that this represents an attempt to counter John's reputation of having been excessively pro-Gainas. The Gainas episode must have left behind it much bitterness and resentment. But others who had collaborated with Gainas were forgiven. Eudoxia herself had been proclaimed Augusta during the period of Gainas' greatest influence.[99] Eutychianus the praetorian prefect at that time and an "establishment figure" if any, was again prefect when Chrysostom was exiled for the second time.[100] Together with the *comes* Joannes and others he signed the receipt of church valuables deposited with magistrates investigating the charges against Chrysostom's financial administration.[101] As praetorian prefect of the East Eutychianus was the principal adviser of Arcadius, one might almost say his first minister. He must have agreed with the attack on Chrysostom, more than likely he advised it.

We know the names of a few others who took part in the suppression of Chrysostom's followers. Of these the most important was Anthemius.[102] His name is not mentioned, but it is practically certain that he was "the *magister*"[103] (i.e. presumably *magister officiorum*)[104] who gave orders to Lucius, commander of the *schola scutariorum* to break up congregations of Joannites on the night before Easter Sunday 404. Anthemius' record of public service, especially of the nine years during which he practically governed the empire, does not suggest that he was the kind of man to be duped by three fairly obscure bishops. Troops were not normally used against civilians at Constantinople or in other cities of the East,[105] and an able and responsible official is unlikely to have

---

99. 9 January 400 according to *Chron.*, II, p. 66, cited by O. Seeck, *Regesten der Kaiser und Päpste* (Stuttgart, 1919), 301. Holum, *Theodosian Empresses*, 67: "She may have arranged her own promotion in order that she might resist more effectively the revolt of Gainas and Eutychianus". There is no evidence whatsoever that such was her intention.

100. See above, note 85. His return to the prefecture of the East is proof that at that time he was not thought to have conspired together with Gainas.

101. Pall., *Dial.*, 13.

102. *PLRE*, II, *s.v.* Anthemius 1. He was *magister officiorum* in spring 404. John Chrysostom, *Ep.*, 147, congratulates him on becoming praetorian prefect, a diplomatic gesture, not an indication of friendship.

103. Pall., *Dial.*, 33 (p. 57, 5 ff.).

104. "The *magister*" is usually the *magister officiorum*, and the *scholae* were for administrative purposes at least under the *magister officiorum*'s command. See Jones, *LRE*, 613. Anthemius will have been one of the "two or three courtiers" who aided Theophilus' group with a military force (Pall., *Dial.*, 16 [p. 25, 6]).

105. See my *Antioch* (Oxford, 1972), 117-118, 125.

V

given the order to engage troops inadvertently. If Anthemius gave the order we can conclude that at this time at least he favoured the suppression of the Joannites. This deduction receives some confirmation from the fact that when Anthemius became praetorian prefect he did not recall the exiled bishop. On the contrary he made the conditions of exile more severe. Chrysostom was first moved to Arabissus – this was probably on account of Isaurian raids – but he was then moved to Pityus on the edge of the Caucasus, to make it more difficult for followers to visit him.[106] Anthemius made no attempt whatsoever to reconcile Chrysostom and his enemies. It is also significant that when Chrysostom was posthumously rehabilitated in 416[107] Anthemius was no longer praetorian prefect.

Soon after Chrysostom had returned from his final exile Simplicius, the urban prefect, put up a silver statue of Eudoxia in the immediate neighbourhood of Saint Sophia and provoked Chrysostom into two disastrously tactless sermons.[108] What actually caused the bishop's wrath was a noisy festival that disturbed the service inside the cathedral. One wonders whether the provocation might have been deliberate. Simplicius was a kinsman of Anthemius, probably a brother or a cousin. If Simplicius had deliberately set out to sow discord between Eudoxia and John, we have another case of a member of the new aristocracy of Constantinople who was hostile to the bishop.[109]

Among the officials who persecuted the followers of John Chrysostom, the urban prefect Optatus has come down with the most lurid reputation. In fact of the three urban prefects known to have held office during the relevant period he alone seems to have displayed vindictiveness towards the Joannites.

The turn-over of officials was high during this troubled period. Paianius was appointed during the first month or so of Chrysostom's exile.[110] Chrysostom clearly considered him a friend.[111] He must have started the investigations into the cause of the fire that destroyed St Sophia and the senate house. Perhaps he did not show sufficient ruthlessness. At any rate he was very quickly replaced by Studius,[112] who received laws on the 29th August and 11th September. He continued in charge of the investigation into the fire, and discovered nothing. One of the laws

---

106. Pall., *Dial.*, 37–38; Baur, *Johannes Chrysostomus*, II,313 ff., 352 ff.
107. Socr., VII, 25; Theodoret, *HE*, V, 34; *Ep. ad Cyril.*, 75 (PG, 77, cols. 348–49). Baur, *op. cit.*, 373–77.
108. *PLRE*, II, *s.v.*, Simplicius 4.
109. Both were descendants of Philippus 7, see *PLRE*, I, 696–97.
110. *PLRE*, II, *s.v.* Paianius; Joh. Chrys., *Ep.* 220, congratulates him on appointment in 404. The office is not named but the urban prefecture is by far the more likely.
111. See Joh. Chrys., *Epp.*, 95, 193, 204, 220, 14. 1.
112. *PLRE*, II, *s.v.* Studius 1.

instructs him to release imprisoned clerics, since the sought-for fire-raisers had not been found.[113] The law will have been issued in the usual way at the suggestion of the official to which it is addressed. Studius may have shown too much sympathy for the Joannites.[114] At any rate by 24 November at the latest he too had lost his office, and was replaced by Optatus who was to hold office at least until 12 June 405.[115]

While Paianius and Studius are likely to have been well disposed towards Chrysostom, Optatus is represented as a persecutor who employed heavy fines and torture, to compel dedicated virgins, including Olympias and ladies like her, and also some hermits to abandon Chrysostom and take communion with his successor.[116] We know nothing of the family backgrounds of Paianius and Studius. This may suggest that their ancestors were not particularly distinguished. But Optatus was a senior senator and nephew of the consul of 334.[117] In other words he had the same kind of background as Eutychianus, Anthemius, Aurelianus and Simplicius. He was a member of the new establishment. Socrates calls him a pagan, but as Dagron has pointed out urban prefects were liable to this allegation, particularly if, like Optatus, they had "intervened" in an ecclesiastical dispute.[118]

The list of men who for different reasons may be thought to have been opponents of Chrysostom, Aurelian, John, Anthemius, Eutychianus, Simplicius and Optatus, is an impressive one. They represent the core of the new senatorial aristocracy of Constantinople.

The question next arises why precisely the "establishment" should have decided that Chrysostom was impossible. We have seen that the Gainas episode aroused the hostility of several important figures, including the highly respected Aurelian. It is also worth noting that two political interventions which were to be praised by our historical sources evidently aroused considerable criticism among some sections of opinion at the time when they happened. Both Chrysostom's behaviour towards the fallen eunuch Eutropius, and his successful resistance to Gainas' demand for a church in which his soldiers could hold Arian services, were to furnish material for hostile propaganda by his enemies.[119]

But there was one aspect of Chrysostom's behaviour which directly affected the families who were seeking to build up great senatorial fortunes: his successful efforts to mobilise the property of wealthy women into the service of the church. Palladius

---

113. *Cod. Theod.*, XVI, 2, 37.

114. Note the impartiality of *Cod. Theod.*, XVI, 2, 37; see also Joh. Chrys., *Ep.*, 197.

115. *PLRE*, I, *s.v.* Optatus 1.

116. Pall., *Dial.*, 14; Soc. VI, 18; Soz., VIII, 23.

117. *PLRE*, I, *s.v.* Optatus 3.

118. Dagron, *Naissance d'une capitale*, 291-94.

119. Socr., VI, 5; Soz., VIII, 4.

V

thought it necessary to defend at length John's relationship with
Olympias which evidently had aroused a great deal of criticism.[120]
We know quite a lot about this relationship not only because
of Palladius' account of it but also through a number of letters
which Chrysostom sent to Olympias from exile.[121] It is clear that
their relationship was one of deep personal friendship, without any
trace of a physical relationship. Indeed, sexual scandal was not
even alleged by Chrysostom's opponents. The scandal was not sexual
but financial, the way in which Olympias was guided by Chrysostom
in the use of her property for ecclesiastical ends.[122]

Olympias is one of a number of women, who played a prominent
part in ecclesiastical affairs around the end of the fourth
century. The condition which made their prominence possible was a
conjunction of the now ancient rights of Roman women, and new scope
given to their exercise by Christianity. The traditional rights
were the ability to own and inherit property as well as having a
relatively unrestricted social life.[123] Christianity offered an
opportunity of using the property and freedom to support the poor
and the sick, clergy and bishops. They might also be used to found
monasteries or nunneries. These opportunities were widely taken
up. We are especially well informed about senatorial women at
Rome,[124] of whom the best known are the two Melanias. The
biography of the Younger Melania still allows us to sense her
motivation including a deep reaction against her role as a passive
instrument of family continuity through arranged marriages and
childbearing, a positive dislike not only of sex but also of
cleanliness, in short a need to defy the older generation. We can
also see Melania's passionate desire to dedicate herself to God, to
fulfil the commandment to sell all property to give to the poor,
together with the consciousness that she is performing a vital
role, as supporter of the church and maintainer of holy men.[125]
The church, as represented by clergy and bishops, was very glad to

---

120. Pall., *Dial.*, 55 ff.; a reply to a specific attack by
Theophilus, 60-61.

121. Jean Chrysostom: *Lettres à Olympias*, ed. A.M. Malingrey, avec
le texte grec et la *Vie anonyme d'Olympias*, SC, 13 bis (Paris,
1968).

122. See *Vie d'Olympias*, 5-7 and on it Dagron, *Naissance d'une
capitale*, 503-506.

123. There is no good book on women at Rome. On social life: S.B.
Pommeroy, *Goddesses, Whores, Wives and Slaves* (London, 1975),
176-89. On control of property: J.A. Crook, *Law and Life at
Rome* (London, 1967), 113-15.

124. Thanks to the correspondence of St Jerome. See J.N.D. Kelly,
Jerome (London, 1975), *passim*. E.A. Clark, *Jerome, Chrysostom and
Friends, Essays and translations*, Studies in Women and Religion,
I (New York, 1979).

125. D. Gorce, ed., *Vie de sainte Mélanie*, SC, 90 (Paris, 1962).

FRIENDS AND ENEMIES OF JOHN CHRYSOSTOM

let the women play the new role.[126] These dedicated and unmarried or widowed women were used to exemplify the high valuation the church placed on the control of animal passions by reason and self discipline, the predominance of man's better nature. They also provided economic resources for charitable work and for the maintenance of the clergy.[127]

The role of these women was not restricted to charity and munificence. They came to play an extremely important part in ecclesiastical diplomacy. One might suggest two reasons why this was so. Firstly, hospitality and wealth which the great ladies of the capital cities could place at the disposal of their preferred ecclesiastics enabled the latter to travel to the capital, to stay there for as long as they thought necessary, and to have the means with which to publicise their views and to influence people.[128] Secondly, the ladies had social connections which the ecclesiastics lacked. Bishops were probably most often sons of curial families, but at this time rarely belonged to the senatorial aristocracy. If they were going to attain their ends, whatever these might be, in the capital, they needed contacts, and for ecclesiastics contact was easier to make with the pious womenfolk of the aristocracy than with the more indifferent (perhaps even only recently converted)[129] men. Thus the ladies were in a position to mediate between the ecclesiastical and secular hierarchies.

The story of Chrysostom introduces us to quite a number of ladies of this kind. Outstandingly the most important was of course the empress Eudoxia.[130] A number of ladies of the court used their resources and influence on behalf of Chrysostom's opponents.[131] Other ladies favoured Chrysostom and of these

---

126. E.g. Jean Chrysostom: *La virginité*, ed. J.H. Musurillo and B. Grillet, SC, 125 (Paris, 1966). *Idem, À une jeune veuve. Sur le marriage unique*, ed. B. Grillet and G.H. Ettlinger, SC 138 (Paris, 1968).

127. Hunt, *Holy Land Pilgrimage* (above, note 62), chaps. 7-9.

128. Olympias financed not only John Chrysostom but also for a time at least his opponents Theophilus of Alexandria and the three Syrian bishops. See *V. Olymp.*, 14; Pall., *Dial.*, 58. See also P. Brown, "The patrons of Pelagius," *JThS*, 21 (1970), 56-72.

129. P. Brown, "Aspects of the Christianisation of the Roman aristocracy," *JRS*, 51 (1961), 1-11, = *Religion and Society in the Age of Augustine*, 161-82.

130. Eudoxia evidently acted as patron of Chrysostom's enemies, the visiting Syrian bishops Severianus of Gabala and Antiochus of Ptolemais (Soz., VIII, 10). But she had also given crucial support to the Tall Brothers (Pall., *Dial.* 26, cf. Soz., VIII, 13 and 5). The fact that Eudoxia received and offered support to ecclesiastics does not mean that she was equally involved and equally powerful in secular matters.

131. Marsa (*PLRE*, II, 728), widow of the general Promotus (*PLRE*,

Olympias, whom I mentioned earlier, was the most important. She
was the granddaughter of Ablabius, for eight years praetorian
prefect of Constantine. In other words she belonged to the new
"establishment" of Constantinople, like Aurelian and Eutychianus
and Anthemius. She was also the heiress to very great wealth, with
estates in Thrace, Galatia, Cappadocia, Bithynia, and several
mansions in Constantinople and its suburbs.[132] Married when still
young she had soon been widowed. It was said that she had never
ceased to be a virgin. The emperor Theodosius wished to marry her
to his kinsman Helpidius, hoping in this way to give Helpidius
entrée into the aristocracy of Constantinople, as well as the use
of her vast wealth. Olympias refused to be used in this way, and
turned down the match. Evidently she justified her stand with the
precept, preached in so many sermons at the time, that it was
better for a Christian widow not to remarry. Theodosius was angry.
He not only put her property under guardianship, but also forbade
her to meet any bishops. But after his victory over the usurper
Maximus, Theodosius gave back to Olympias the disposition over her
property,[133] and, in defiance of the law which forbade the
consecration of widows less than 60 years old,[134] Nectarius bishop
of Constantinople ordained her as a deaconess. Olympias proceeded
to give money to the poor, and to keep open house for travelling
bishops and clergy. Among those who benefited from her hospitality
were the bishops Antiochus, Acacius and Severianus who were to
become the core of opposition to Chrysostom. She rarely visited
the baths, and then only for her health. She did not take off her
chemise even in the water.[135] When Chrysostom became bishop in 398
he immediately attended to the morals of the "order" of widows. To
those who were not living chastely he counselled a course of
asceticism, consisting of fasting and abstinence from baths and
attractive clothes. If they were not up to this they were to
hasten into a second marriage.[136] Olympias was advised to use her
property more discriminately.[137] She obeyed and became a close
friend. She looked after him and paid most of his living expenses,
so that he cost the church nothing.[138] In addition she gave vast

---

I, 750). The empress Eudoxia had been brought up in the house of
one of Promotus' sons. Also Castricia (*PLRE*, II, 271), widow of the
general Saturninus 10 (*PLRE*, I, 807), and Eugraphia (*PLRE*, II, 417)
who was the most fanatical opponent (Pall., *Dial.*,17) and offered
her house as a meeting place to Chrysostom's opponents (*Dial.*, 27).
132. *V. Olymp.*, 5, 21–33.
133. Pall., *Dial.*, 61; *V. Olymp.*, 5–6 and comments of Dagron,
Naissance d'une capitale, 503–506.
134. *Cod. Theod.*, XVI, 1, 27.
135. Pall., *Dial.*, 61.
136. *Ibid.*, 20.
137. Soz., VIII, 9.
138. Pall., *Dial.*, 61.

FRIENDS AND ENEMIES OF JOHN CHRYSOSTOM

donations to the church of Constantinople.[139]

Now one of the reasons why this relationship became controversial, to the extent that Olympias even suffered persecution after Chrysostom's exile, was the fact that she remained one of his most prominent and dedicated supporters, firmly refusing to take communion with his successor, Arsacius.[140] Another reason has been suggested by Dagron. Outlining the vast resources which under the influence of Chrysostom Olympias put at the disposal of the church of Constantinople, he argues that the opponents of Chrysostom, notably the empress Eudoxia were seriously concerned at the rapid growth of the economic resources of the church when compared with those of the state.[141] But this is to look at the situation anachronistically. Rapidly as the church's wealth was growing it was still very small in comparison with the enormous resources of the empire, and there is no evidence that its economic power was regarded as a threat to the state.[142] It is true that there was legislation to prevent the wealth of wealthy ladies passing to members of the clergy, either through the ladies' wills or intestacy.[143] But what worried the legislators was the fact that the influence of clerics over pious ladies was depriving heirs of property to which they were entitled, not that the church was becoming too rich. In other words the point of view is that of the great families whose social position depended on inherited wealth.[144]

We obtain an idea of how the great families resented the pious donations of some of the womenfolk when we consider the indignation displayed by the senatorial kinsmen of Melania the Younger when she and her husband Pinianus sold their estates and gave the proceeds

---

139. *V. Olymp.*, 5-6.

140. Soz., VIII, 24.

141. Dagron, *Naissance d'une capitale*, 501 ff.

142. Gregory of Nazianzus, *De Vita Sua*, lines 1475-78: wealth of the church of Constantinople. Yet Chrysostom only found one hospital belonging to the church and proceeded to establish others (Pall., *Dial.*, 20). In sermons at Constantinople Chrysostom did not complain that the clergy had to spend time on administration of property as he had done at Antioch. Clearly he accepted the fact that the church of Constantinople had to administer property. But the development was still in its beginnings (R. Brandle, *Matth. 24, 31-46 im Werk des Johannes Chrysostomus* (Tübingen, 1979), 114-21.

143. *Cod. Theod.*, XVI, 2, 20 (A.D. 370, West), *ibid.*, 27 and 28 (A.D. 390, East).

144. See Jill Harries, in *Marriage and Property*, ed. E.M. Craik, (Aberdeen, 1983). Cf. Ausonius, *Ep.* 27, 115: ne sparsam raptamque domum, lacerataque centum per dominos veteris Paulini regna fleamus, mourns the prospective dispersal of ancestral senatorial property.

to the poor or the church.[145] There is no reason to believe that
the senatorial families of Constantinople felt differently about
Olympias. Such feelings will have been strongest among families
that were seeking to build up an economic and social position to
rival that of the great senatorial homes of Rome, in other words
among precisely members of the new "establishment" of Constantinople.

Chrysostom antagonised some very wealthy and powerful persons,
and no doubt others who were simply rich. According to "Martyrius"
at least some of the wealthy claimed that they dared not go to
church because when Chrysostom preached about the misdeeds of the
rich all the congregation looked at them. Others complained that
by words and deeds Chrysostom was preventing them from making money
in their customary way.[146] There is no reason to doubt that Chrysostom's outspoken attempts to awaken the social conscience of the
well-to-do caused irritation and annoyance. "Martyrius" further
gives the impression that the poor and the sick were behind Chrysostom. This is likely enough. After all Chrysostom had constantly
called on those who had money to spare to give it to those in need,
and had preached one virtue more frequently than any other, readiness to make sacrifices in order to help the destitute. "Martyrius"
was able to contrast the behaviour of Chrysostom helping the poor
with that of Theophilus who intrigued with the rich.[147] He
describes how land-owners opposed Chrysostom's efforts to establish
a leper hospital in their neighbourhood and notes that they managed
to get this project stopped even before Chrysostom went into
exile.[148]

But if Chrysostom aroused the hostility of some of the rich,
he was certainly not without wealthy followers. When the Joannite
congregations were broken up at Easter 404, some "honestiores"
- or even "honorati" - were expelled from the city or imprisoned.[149] Their wives were robbed of jewellery.[150] The crowds that
demonstrated on Chrysostom's behalf were not composed of beggars.
The law of January 404 forbids staff of the imperial civil service
departments from attending tumultuous meetings. They were threatened with dismissal and confiscation of their property if they ignor-

---

145. Palladius, *Lausiac History* (hereafter *Hist. Laus.*), 54, 5;
V. Melaniae, 8-14; Ambrose, *Ep.*, 58, 3. See J. Matthews,
Western Aristocracies and Imperial Court (Oxford, 1975), 152.
146. F. Van Ommeslaeghe, *AnalBoll*, 97 (1978), 150, cites p. 480a-b.
147. *Idem, AnalBoll*, 99 (1981), 347.
148. *Idem, AnalBoll*, 97 (1979), 151, cites pp. 491b-495a.
149. Pall., *Dial.*, 34: οἱ δὲ ἀξιωματικοὶ τοῦ λαοῦ A later edict
was directed against officials, soldiers and ordinary people
(Pall., *Dial.*, 37).
150. Soz., VIII, 23, cf. also the wealthy wife of Eleutherus
(Pall., *Dial.*, 34), and Nicarete (Soz., VIII, 23).

FRIENDS AND ENEMIES OF JOHN CHRYSOSTOM

ed the prohibition.[151] The law of September 404 threatens masters who let their slave take part in "tumultuous conventicles". The fine is three pounds of gold per slave found taking part in such a meeting. Guilds were held responsible for the behaviour of their members, and threatened with a fine of no less than 50 pounds of gold if one of them was to take part in a "tumultuous conventicle". One guild is specially named: the money lenders.[152] There is some evidence that demonstrations were organised purposefully. At any rate when the verdict of the Synod of the Oak was announced a crowd gathered and demanded that the case ought to be tried again by a larger synod. This was precisely what John and his followers were demanding, and continued to demand to the end.[153]

Chrysostom had wealthy supporters, both at Constantinople and in the provinces. In exile he received offers of help from numerous wealthy people. One Arabius offered the use of a villa at Sebaste in Armenia.[154] Seleucia, wife of Rufinus of Caesarea in Cappadocia, invited Chrysostom to her villa. She also offered him the use of a fortified tower and the protection of her peasants and tenants against the attacks of monks. It was only when threatened by the bishop of Caesarea that she abandoned Chrysostom.[155] Other persons who showed friendship were Dioscurus, a landowner of Cucucus,[156] Sopater *praeses* of Armenia Secunda,[157] and in the capital itself the *comes* Theophilus and the lady Carteria.[158] These examples show that it is far from true that the "rich" as such were against Chrysostom. If he was afraid of any one class of people at the time of his exile, it was bishops.[159]

We hear of other sympathisers who were officials or had close links with the official classes. There was Paianius who briefly held the office of prefect of the city immediately after John's exile.[160] Brison, *cubicularius* of Eudoxia, not a senator but no less influential for that, received two friendly letters from the exiled bishop[161] and one Theodotus, "ex-consularibus" sent him presents.[162] Anatolius, described as ἐπαρχικός (*praefectianus*) continued to work for the exiled bishop at Constantinople.[163] To

---

151. *Cod. Theod.*, XVI, 4, 4.
152. *Cod. Theod.*, XVI, 4, 5.
153. Socr., VI, 15; Soz., VIII, 18.
154. Joh. Chrys., *Ep.* 121.
155. *Ep.* 14 = 9,2,68, ed. A.M. Malingrey.
156. *Ep.* 13, 1b = 6,1,23, ed. A.M. Malingrey.
157. *Ep.* 64, cf. *PLRE*, II, *s.v.* Sopater 1.
158. *Ep.* 4, cf. *PLRE*, II, *s.v.* Theophilus 2; for Carteria see *ep.* 232.
159. *Ep.* 14, 4 = 9,4,26 - even Isaurians are to be feared less.
160. See above, p. 100.
161. *PLRE*, II, *s.v.* Brison; *Epp.*, 190 and 234.
162. *Epp.* 61 and 141.
163. *Ep.* 205; *PLRE*, II, *s.v.* Anatolius 5.

this rather ramshackle list of high ranking sympathisers must be added a number of senatorial wives and widows. Before leaving Constantinople for ever Chrysostom said farewell to four pious and extremely aristocratic ladies: Olympias, Salvina, Pentadia and Procle.[164] Nothing is known of the background of Procle, but we have information about the others, which suggests that all three had connections with the West.

Olympias belonged to the new Eastern aristocracy,[165] but she was a widow of Nebridius 2,[166] a kinsman of Flacilla, the Spanish wife of Theodosius I. Olympias' charity was inspired by that of the Elder Melania, a great senatorial lady of Rome,[167] whose granddaughter the "Younger Melania",[168] was to support Palladius and other followers of John Chrysostom when they sought refuge and diplomatic assistance at Rome after the deposition of their bishop.[169] Salvina was a daughter of the North African chieftain and *comes et magister militiae per Africam*, Gildo. She was a widow of Nebridius 3, nephew of the empress Flacilla and stepson of Olympias.[170] Pentadia was the widow of Timasius, a general of Theodosius I and victim of the eunuch Eutropius.[171] That their son was called Syagrius suggests that the mother came from a great family of Gaul.[172]

It is difficult to estimate the significance of the fact that some of Chrysostom's most important supporters had western links.[173] They did indeed belong to the group that had governed

---

164. Pall., *Dial.*, 35.

165. *PLRE*, I, *s.v.* Olympias 1.

166. *PLRE*, I, *s.v.* Nebridius 2.

167. Pall., *Hist. Laus.*, 56. See also E.D. Hunt, *JThS*, 24 (1973), 477. *PLRE*, I, *s.v.* Melania 1.

168. *PLRE*, I, *s.v.* Melania 2.

169. Pall., *Hist. Laus.*, 41, 5; 61, 7; cf. above.

170. *PLRE*, I, *s.v.* Salvina.

171. *PLRE*, I, *s.v.* Timasius.

172. *PLRE*, I, *s.v.* Syagrius 1.

173. Ch. Petri, "L'aristocratie chrétienne entre Jean de Constantinople et Augustin d'Hippone 282-305," in Ch. Kannengiesser, ed., *Jean Chrysostom et Augustin* (Paris, 1975). Chrysostom had shown an interest in relations with the West from the first. One of his first acts was to send Acacius of Beroea to Rome to obtain the pope's recognition of Flavian of Antioch and to end the Antiochene schism - successfully. (Baur, *Johannes Chrysostomus*, II, 20-23. An extremely doubtful link with the West depends on the identification of Chrysostom's friend Evagrius, who according to Socr. VI, 3, ordained him, with Evagrius the friend of Jerome (*PLRE*, I, *s.v.* Evagrius 3) who had been influential at the Western court in the 370's. But Socrates' account is confused. According to Pall. *Dial.*, 19, Chrysostom was ordained by Flavianus. Chrysostom's friend may well not be identical with Jerome's.

the united empire for Theodosius I. His leading opponents on the
other hand belonged to the new ruling class of the Roman Empire of
the East. They were conscious of the Greek roots of its civilisation and extremely jealous of its political independence. It would
be tempting to interpret the deposition of John Chrysostom as one
aspect of the emancipation of the Eastern Empire. It might be suggested that the Eastern "establishment" opposed Chrysostom because
he was too Western, and that it was for precisely the same reason
that Chrysostom was to receive wholehearted support from the pope
and Western emperor. In fact there is little evidence of this.
What was more important was that the Joannites had a particular
advantage in appealing for sympathy to the West in the fact that
the attack on Chrysostom was originally linked with the persecution
of the Origenist monks of Egypt and their cosmopolitan imitators.
When the Tall Brothers and their admirers, who included Palladius
the biographer and John Cassian and Germanus,[174] found patronage[175]
and shelter with John Chrysostom at Constantinople, he gained the
potential support of the monks' powerful patrons in Italy, notably
the ladies and senatorial menfolk of the family of the Elder
Melania and of the ecclesiastics associated with them.[176] It was
clearly not a coincidence that Palladius, Germanus and Cassianus
came to Rome to report the persecution of the Joannites,[177] or that
John's envoys lodged with Melania the Younger,[178] or that the
leader of the unlucky Western embassy to Constantinople was
Aemilius bishop of Beneventum, a city of which Publicola, a son of
Melania the Elder, was *patronus ex origine*.[179] It is likely
that it was through Melania and her friends that Chrysostom gained
the support of two ladies of the great Anician family, Proba widow
of Claudius Petronius Probus,[180] four times praetorian prefect, and
Iuliana[181] perhaps her daughter-in-law and wife of the consul of
395, and also of Italica.[182].

---

174. See E.D. Hunt, "Palladius of Helenopolis, a party and its
supporters," *JThS*, 24 (1973), 456-80; *idem*, "Saint Silvia of
Aquitaine, the role of a Theodosian pilgrim in the society of East
and West," *JThS*, 23 (1972), 357-73.
175. John Cassian had been ordained by Chrysostom (*De incarnatione
Christi*, 7, 31 [PL, 1, 269]); Germanus: Pall., *Dial.*, 9; 13; 28;
his biography in *DCB*, *s.v.* Germanus 32.
176. P. Brown, "The patrons of Pelagius," *JThS*, 21 (1970), 56-72,
esp. 58-68 = *Religion and Society in the Age of Saint Augustine*,
208-226, esp. 210-15.
177. Pall., *Dial.*, 13.
178. Pall., *Hist. Laus.*, 61.
179. *CIL*, IX, 1591.
180. *PLRE*, I, *s.v.* Anicia Fultonia Proba 3; Joh. Chrys., *Ep.* 169.
181. Joh. Chrys. *Ep.* 169; cf. *PLRE*, I, *s.v.* Anicia Juliana 2.
182. *Ep.* 170, probably *PLRE*, II, *s.v.* Anicia Italica 2, but cf.
P. Brown, "The Christianization of the Roman aristocracy," *JRS*,

V

Such connections gained for Chrysostom the support of Western
bishops, pope and emperor, but this did not help him at all with
the authorities of the East. Quite the reverse. The strength of
Western support, at a time when Stilicho was threatening the East
with war for the sake of the control of Illyricum,[183] certainly
stiffened the determination of his enemies at Constantinople. It
may well account for the harshness of some of the measures taken
against the Joannites.

To sum up. John Chrysostom was unpopular with many of his
clergy at Constantinople. His interventions in the affairs of
neighbouring sees caused anxiety among bishops and resentment among
the citizens whose bishops John had deposed. He attempted to
discipline the monks living in or near Constantinople and in this
way made enemies of a formidable body of men. For the monks were
influential with ordinary people as well as with some of the
leaders of society. They could riot themselves and could induce
the people to riot. In fact they had already once before allied
with the bishop of Alexandria to bring down a bishop of Constantinople. At the same time Chrysostom's way of life tended to isolate
him. This itself caused resentment. It also helped the intrigues
of his opponents. It is clear that these circumstances made
Chrysostom vulnerable when a group of bishops and laymen began to
work for his deposition. The clique that worked for his overthrow
included two powerful figures, the empress Eudoxia and Theophilus
the bishop of Alexandria. Eudoxia was volatile and changeable,
moreover she died soon after the second and final exiling of
Chrysostom, but Theophilus continued to be associated with the
attack, though he did not again leave Egypt. That this group
nevertheless succeeded in keeping the imperial government favourable to its objectives for thirteen years was due to the fact that
they won the support of the ministers Eutychianus, Aurelianus and
Anthemius who dominated public life between A.D. 394 and 416. How
and why they won it is not altogether clear, but some relevant factors can be identified. Chrysostom had incurred bitter hostility
of the "exiles" Aurelian, Saturninus and John during the Gainas
affair. Moreover Aurelian and Saturninus were closely associated
with Isaac, the leader of the monks whose enmity Chrysostom had
aroused. We can conjecture that men like Aurelian and Anthemius,
members of recently enriched families that were now dominating the
political and social life of Constantinople, resented the activities of a bishop who was successfully urging senatorial women to

---

51 (1961), 1-11, esp. 5-6 - *Religion and Society in the Age of
Saint Augustine*, 171. The letters to the noble ladies seem to
form part of a group of letters sent to bishops who were going to
attend the synod called by the Western emperor (*Epp.* 160-170).
183. E. Demougeot, *De l'unité à la division de l'empire romain,
395-410* (Paris, 1951), 366 ff; Matthews, *Western Aristocracies*
(above, note 145), 274-75.

disperse the property on which the power of senatorial houses depended.   Finally as Western support for Chrysostom developed these men are likely to have seen the conflict with John and his followers as part of their struggle to maintain Eastern independence, and particularly Eastern control of Illyricum, in the face of the pressure of the Western government directed by Stilicho.

VI

Pelagian Evidence on the Last Period
of Roman Britain? [1]

It is well known that Pelagianism gained a considerable hold in Britain in the early fifth century [2]. As a considerable volume of Pelagian literature has survived it is a reasonable hypothesis that some of this literature might be found to contain references to Britain and thus to throw light on a very badly documented period of British history. Recently it has been suggested [3] that there are such references in the pseudo-Augustinian *De Vita Christiana*, notably in a passage concerning the deaths of certain judges [4]. In the present note it will be argued that the evidence is insufficient to establish the connection with Britain and that the passage is more likely to be concerned with events in the Mediterranean world.

The precise authorship [5] of the *De Vita Christiana* was already

---

(1) I wish to thank Dr. A. K. B. Evans, Mr. P. R. L. Brown and Mr. A. Cameron for suggestions and corrections.

G. DE PLINVAL, *Pélage, ses écrits, sa vie et sa réforme*, Lausanne, 1943, cited as DE PLINVAL, *Pélage*, has been used throughout. The works indubitably by Pelagius, or assigned to him by de Plinval, are listed *ibid.*, p. 26, 44-5. The 'Caspari' documents and the *Commentary on the Epistles of St. Paul* together with some fragments are now printed in *P.L. Suppl.* I, 1101 ff., the former also of course in C. P. CASPARI, *Briefe Abhandlungen und Predigten*, Christiana, 1890.

(2) Mission of S. Germanus, PROSPER, *Chron.*, Ann. 429 ; IDEM, *Contra Collatorem*, 21, *P.L.*, 51, 271. Cf. G. DE PLINVAL, Pélage, p. 382. N. K. CHADWICK, *Poetry and Letters in Early Gaul*, 1955, p. 248 ff. On Pelagian survival in areas troubled by invasion : DE PLINVAL, *op. cit.*, p. 380 ff. ; N. K. CHADWICK, *The Age of the Saints in the Early Celtic Church*, London, 1961, 15-17.

(3) John MORRIS, *Pelagian Literature* in *Journal of Theological Studies*, N.S., 1965, p. 26-60. See also *Dark Age Dates* in *Britain and Rome*, ed. M. G. JARRETT and B. DOBSON, 1965, p. 148-9.

(4) *P.L.*, 40, 1031-46 ; esp. 1035.

(5) Learned discussion summed up by R. F. EVANS, *Pelagius, Fastidius and the Pseudo-Augustinian' De Vita Christiana'* in *Journal of Theological Studies*, N.S., 13, 1962, 72-98. The evidence for the British bishop Fastidius : (1) One manuscript has the usual impossible

uncertain in Pelagius' life time. The same ([1]) passage from the pamphlet is found in St. Jerome's Dialogue against the Pelagians ([2]) and in St. Augustine's Latin translation of the Acts of the Council of Diospolis of 415 ([3]). Jerome and the bishops at Diospolis thought the pamphlet was by Pelagius himself. So did a number of monks known to Augustine who had acquired the pamphlet nearly four years earlier ([4]). But Pelagius denied authorship.

In modern times de Plinval has argued that the *De Vita Christiana* together with a considerable number of other pamphlets was the work of Pelagius himself ([5]). His argument has not gained universal assent ([6]). But there is no doubt that all the works assigned by him to Pelagius, whether they are actually by the same author or not, represent a homogeneous literary genre. An outstanding feature of the group is the occurrence of closely related passages in several pamphlets ([7]).

These pamphlets and letters contain relatively little detail bea-

---

attribution to St. Augustine corrected to Fastidius ; (2) GENNADIUS, 57 : *Fastidius Britannorum episcopus scripsit ad Fatalem quemdam de uita christiana librum et alium de uiduitate seruanda, sana et deo digna doctrina.* But against the identification, our *Vita C.* is one book not two, and unlike the books mentioned by Gennadius it was addressed to a woman, is not concerned specifically with the *preservation* of the widowed state, and was considered unorthodox soon after its appearance. Moreover the position of Gennadius' entry suggests that he thought Fastidius' pamphlets were later than the trial of Diospolis (415 AD). So the identification is extremely questionable. But it is difficult to imagine what evidence other than Gennadius the XIth Century writer who changed the attribution of the one manuscript from Augustine to Fastidius could have had. In any case the evidence in favour of the British bishop remains very much weaker than that which suggests an origin in the Central Mediterranean world among the men surrounding Pelagius himself. — See notes 1-4 below.

(1) *Post orationem domini et saluatoris nostri* (*Gest. Pel.* VI, 16) is not found in *De Vita Christiana* or in JEROME, *Dial.* III, 14. R. F. EVANS, *op. cit.*, p. 87 explains it as a derogatory interjection of Augustine's, taking *post* concessively. This makes sense, but one would like a parallel to this usage.

(2) Jerome, *Dial.* III, 14.

(3) *Gest. Pel.*, VI, 16.

(4) *Ibid.*, VI, 19.

(5) G. DE PLINVAL, *Pélage*, p. 26 f. ; IDEM, *Recherches sur l'œuvre littéraire de Pélage* in *R. Ph.*, 60, 1934, p. 10-42.

(6) Cf. J. MORRIS, *op. cit.* ; R. F. EVANS, *op. cit.*

(7) C. P. CASPARI, *Briefe, Abhandlungen und Predigten aus den zwei letzten Jahrhunderten des kirchlichen Altertums*, Christiana, 1890, p. 278-329, esp. 304 ff. ; G. DE PLINVAL, *Pélage*, p. 32-40.

ring on their place of origin. But such detail as has been noticed points to the senatorial world of Rome and the central Mediterranean area ([1]). The author or authors are engaged in the same task as St. Jerome a decade or two earlier : to preach the new ascetic ideal to high society, especially well-born virgins or widows, at Rome ([2]). After the sack of Rome by the Goths some members of society fled to Sicily or North Africa ([3]) and Pelagius followed them ([4]). We know that the teaching was received in a much wider circle ; for instance, eighteen bishops of small Italien towns eventually refused to sign the condemnation of Pelagianism ([5]). But not one of the pamphlets can be shown to have been directed at, say, the bishop of a small Italian city.

A single document, Caspari *Ep.* I, has been shown to have been addressed beyond the central Mediterranean area ([6]), quite probably to Britain ([7]). A young man travelling to the Holy Places in the East in the company of a monk came to Sicily. There he met a woman of senatorial rank, whose piety, faith and knowledge were known not only to laymen but also to many clerics. She gave him a

(1) *Ad Demetriadem, P.L.*, 30, 13-45 ; *Ad Marcellam, ibid.*, 50-55 ; *Ad Celantiam, P.L.*, 22, 12011-12 ; *De Lege Diuina, P.L.*, 30, 55-60 : c. 6 addressed to a senator ; The Gerontius whose daughters are addressed in *P.L.*, 30, 45-50, could have been the British general of the usurper Constantine, cf. J. N. L. MYRES in *J.R.S.*, 50, 1960, p. 34. But there is only the not uncommon name, and nothing in the letter to suggest this. See also below the Appendix on the public of the Caspari tracts and the *Laus Virginitatis*.

(2) D. GORDINI, *Origine e sviluppo del monachesimo a Roma* in *Gregorianum* 37, 1956, p. 220-260 ; P. R. L. BROWN, *Aspects of the Christianization of the Roman Aristocracy* in *J.R.S.*, 51 1961, p. 1-11 ; DE PLINVAL, *Pélage*, p. 210 ff.

(3) J. DILL, *Roman Society in the Last Century of the Western Empire*, 1921, p. 307-9 ; E. DEMOUGEOT, *De l'unité à la division de l'empire romain*, Paris, 1951, p. 483-4.

(4) *Gest. Pel.*, XXII, 46.

(5) MERCATOR, *Commonuit., P.L.*, 48, 945.
AUGUSTINE, *Con. II Ep. Pel.*, 1, 3, *P.L.*, 44, 551.

(6) Now *P.L. Suppl.* I, 1687, (*Honorificentiae tuae...*). G. DE PLINVAL, *Pélage*, p. 30, takes it for a later compilation. The autobiographical detail makes Pelagius' authorship impossible. Leaving aside the authorship it could be an early Pelagian pamphlet. J. MORRIS, *op. cit.*, p. 37, rightly stresses the youthful enthusiasm. It is unique in its tone of personal experience, almost calling for a novellistic interpretation.

(7) The long journey, including a sea voyage, *P.L. Suppl.* I, 1692 (5), the author's knowledge that in *Francia, Saxonia et omni barbaria* there were no Christians (*ibid.*, 1687 (11), suggest that Gaul or Britain was his home. Religious travel became characteristic of Britons. But at this time the habit also exited in Gaul ; N. K. CHADWICK, *Poetry and Letters in Early Christina Gaul*, p. 16-17.

new religious outlook ([1]), and he decided to remain with her in Sicily though at some future date he might go in her following to Rome ([2]). In the letter he explains the reasons for his absence to an elderly and anxious relative and uses the opportunity to preach a sermon on standard Pelagian themes.

The writer was a provincial, but there is nothing provincial about the sermon-letter. Its character is precisely the same as that of the other pamphlets assigned by de Plinval to Pelagius ([3]). This is not surprising. After all the young Briton had 'caught' Pelagianism in precisely the environment at which the other pamphlets seem to be directed.

A feature that Pelagianism shared with the Roman ascetic movement as a whole was that its preachers were not native Romans ([4]). Pelagius was a Briton. Some of his leading followers may have been ([5]). But this did not make Pelagianism a British movement ([6]). Even if it can be proved that one or more of the pamphlets was written by a Briton other than Pelagius it does not follow that circumstantial references contained in them are to Britain. As far as our group of Pelagian documents is concerned, the burden of proof lies very much on the man who wants to assert a remote provincial origin or a specific provincial reference for any one of them ([7]).

In the case of the *De Vita Christiana*, no conclusions can be drawn from the authorship which, as we have seen ([8]), has been in dispute almost since the time of writing. It is, however, more likely that a pamphlet which was known in Africa and in Palestine was written in the central Mediterranean area than that it should have been of

---

(1) *P.L. Suppl.* I, 1692 (5).

(2) *Ibid.* 1693 (5).

(3) See C. P. CASPARI, *op. cit.*, p. 238 f. ; 279 f.

(4) D. GORDINI, *op. cit.* ; cf. N. K. CHADWICK, *The Age of the Saints in the Early Celtic Church*, p. 30-1.

(5) See J. MORRIS, *op. cit.*, p. 40 f. ; but also G. DE PLINVAL, *Pélage*, p. 212. The argument for the British origin of Caelestius is refuted by C. P. CASPARI, *op. cit.*, p. 348, n. 2. He had been an *auditorialis scholasticus* (MERCATOR, *Praef.*, 4).

(6) PROSPER, *Chron.*, Ann. 429 ; IDEM, *Contra Collatorem*, 21, confirm that it was *introduced* there.

(7) One must also consider the author's attitude to historical events ; cf. *De Castitate*, 12, 2, three periods of history : ... *ante legem, aliud legis, et quod nunc gratiae tertium est.* Thus history has stopped. This view was not specifically Pelagian. Nevertheless they appear more profoundly indifferent to the calamities of their age than Augustine or Jerome.

(8) See above p. 437.

British origin. The addressee — a widow of standing — throws no light on the destination of the pamphlet. Moreover, it is likely that the bulk of the pamphlet was written without any consideration of the eventual recipient ([1]). The main body of the treatise is lacking in identifiable local detail. It is largely an argument that Christianity is an empty name unless accompanied by 'works' ([2]) — 'works' being understood, as in other Pelagian pamphlets, as the fulfilment in the literal sense of the New Testament commandments. The argument for or against the British reference is, therefore, entirely dependent on the interpretation of the sensational passage about the killing of the judges ([3]).

" For we have before us examples of numerous persons from which we can see that wicked and unjust men, once they have made up the total of their sins, are judged even here and now, and are deprived of their present life no less than of the life hereafter.

The truth of this can be seen more clearly by anyone who for various lenghths of time has been waiting for the downfall of various judges, acting in an unjust and wicked manner.

Of judges the shamelessness in wrong doing grows in proportion to the power and leads them to think that nothing is forbidden them that it is possible for them to do, and as long as these judges of others are not afraid that they will themselves be judged by someone else, they rush headlong into sin. Thus it happens that men who in their wrong doing are not afraid of the judgment of any man come to feel God as a judge and avenger. Of these some, who had frequently shed the blood of others, felt the wrath of God to such effect that they were compelled at last to shed their own —these men who had been so free with the blood of others. Others who had committed similar deeds were so completely overthrown by the wrath of God that their bodies lay unburied and became food for the beasts and birds of the air. Yet others who had unjustly destroyed a countless multitude of men have been torn to pieces limb by limb, piece by piece — so that the division of their limbs was no less than the number of punished victims they had killed. And of those men by whose judgment many women were made widows, after the execution of their husbands, many children left orphans, after the killing of their fathers, suffering beggary and nakedness as well as bereavement — now of those same men the widowed wives and orphaned children are daily in need of strangers' bread ".

---

(1) Only the first and last chapters refer to the widow. In the central piece the addresses to the reader are neither feminine nor in the flowery style of the introduction, eg. *P.L.*, 40, 1034 (2) : *O stulte, O irreuerens et ingrate, qui...* ; *ibid.*, 1036 (11) : *Tu ergo quomodo christianus diceris, in quo...* ; *ibid.*, 1041 (10) : *et fratrem persequeris, qui...*

(2) Cf. *Ep. of James*, 2, 14-26.

(3) *P.L.*, 40, 1035 (3).

The function of this passage is to give urgency to the moral of the treatise by showing that sinners will be punished not only after death but in this life too ([1]). The choice of judge ([2]) as an example for this lesson is particularly appropriate because the duties of his office involve a judge in actions that are diametrically opposite to that imitation of Christ which is the theme of all Pelagian writings ([3]). Pelagian missionary work, at Rome at any rate, was directed at men and women in whose families the holding of public office at some time of life was normal ([4]). The office of judge — or high civil official — therefore provided a perfect type of the worldly life which Pelagian audiences are required to renounce. The lesson would be all the more impressive if some prominent judges had recently met with well-deserved doom. It is therefore extremely likely that the author of De Vita Christiana is thinking of some recent and conspicuous example of the downfall of prominent officials.

In order to narrow down the range of officials that might be covered by this passage, it is not, in my opinion, admissible to deduce from dum alterius iudicium non timent that the author is thinking of officials who have no superior, not even the emperor. In this particular section he is not writing of any particular office but of the position of judge as such — even to the extent of noting that the position of some is higher than that of others ([5]). Moreover the sentence is little more than a factual statement of the position of a Roman governor, at any period of imperial history, as it would appear to a private individual suffering from his malpractice. Thus it would seem that on constitutional grounds there is scarcely any limit to the range of possible candidates — all civil officials of or above the rank of provincial governor could fall under the description. But for reasons which I have put forward earlier, it is extremely likely that the stories of these men were well known in the central Mediterranean area — at Rome and perhaps in Sicily or North Africa. The deaths may have

---

(1) Ibid. : Nos enim plurimorum exempla uidemus, per quae probare sufficimus, sceleratos et impios, et hoc etiam tempore iudicari, et praesentem eis uitam negari non minus quam futuram. I take hoc etiam tempore to be equivalent to in praesenti in two earlier sentences in c. 3 and to mean here and now in this life, as opposed to the time of the last judgment.

(2) Judge = government official. De Diu., 6, 2 ; P.L. Suppl. I, 1386 ; H. Heumann-E. Seckel, Handlexikon zu den Quellen des römischen Rechts, 10, ed., 1958, p. 291 f.

(3) De Diu. 6, P.L. Suppl. I, 1384-7.

(4) G. De Plinval, Pélage, p. 210-16.

(5) P.L. 40, 1035 : quo potestas sublimior est, eo ad peccandum maior audacia.

occurred more peripherally. But in that case the victims are likely to have been extremely prominent.

Even so, in a higly disturbed period violent deaths of officials must have been numerous and many are likely to have left no trace in the records (¹). The most sensational episode was the lynching of the principal officials of the Western Empire at Ticinum, followed by the arrest and execution of Stilicho (²) and the confiscation of the property of Stilicho and his followers (³). These events certainly represented a scene of the kind which the « judges-passage » forces us to envisage if we understand its plurals literally. But the plurals are likely to be rhetorical. Moreover there is an objection to the identification of the victims of Ticinum with our « judges » in the fact that the most prominent victim, Stilicho, who had followed a purely military career, could hardly be described as a judge. Moreover, while he was certainly charged with abusing his position to enrich himself (⁴), judicial murder for the sake of gain has, as far as I know, not been urged against him (⁵) or the other officials killed in 408 (⁶). There is also no record of Stilicho having been torn to pieces.

A closer approximation to the fate of the last and worst of the judges in the *De Vita Christiana* is provided by the circumstances of the death in 395 of the praetorian prefect, Rufinus. He was an Eastern official but his fate was celebrated at Rome by the poet Claudian. We are told that he was enormously rapacious (⁷), that he killed

---

(1) But recorded violent deaths of officials are only numerous between 408-13. 408, death of Stilicho and his officials ; 409, Pompeianus, prefect of Rome lynched ; 413, execution of comes Heraclianus (on his rapacity, JEROME, Ep. 130) and his followers, Marcellinus, a notary, Apringius proconsul of Africa, Olympius, the former magister officiorum ; also three Gallic nobles after the unsuccessful usurpation of one of them. See J. SUNDWALL, *Weströmische Studien*, Berlin, 1915.

(2) ZOSIMUS, V, 32 ; E. DEMOUGEOT, *De l'unité à la division de l'empire romain*, Paris, 1951, p. 414-29.

(3) *C.T.*, 9, 42, 20-21.

(4) ZOSIMUS, V, 1, 2 ibid. 12. BURY, *Later Roman Empire*, 107, n. 3 notes that Zosimus becomes much more favourable when he follows Olympiodorus.

(5) For accusations see E. DEMOUGEOT, *op. cit.*, p. 414-5, n. 308-15.

(6) In their careers men like the praetorian prefects Limenius (J. SUNDWALL, *Weströmische Studien*, 1915, p. 96) and Longinianus (*ibid.*, p. 96-7 ; A. CHASTAGNOL, *Les fastes de la préfecture de Rome au Bas-Empire* 1962, p. 257) must have had opportunities for judicial murder and extortion. The charges may not have come down to us.

(7) CLAUDIAN, 1, *In Ruf.*, 220 f.

thousands ([1]) and when he was killed, his body was torn to pieces ([2]), and the widows and orphans he had made frolicked over his body ([3]). His property was confiscated ([4]) and his remains were left unburied ([5]). I would suggest that he is likely to be the man referred to in the Pelagian pamphlet.

The others are more difficult to identify. Keeping to the same period we might suggest Gildo, the rebellious *Comes Africae* who died, probably by execution, in 398. If so, his body may well have been left unburied ([6]). Of him too, Claudian reports large scale judicial killing motivated by rapacity ([7]). On the other hand, his command was, strictly speaking, a military one, so the term *iudex* might not be altogether applicable to him.

A third « judge » who came to a bad end about this period was the pagan praetorian prefect, Nicomachus Flavianus, who was killed during the Eugenius rebellion. Flavianus had held a succession of high civil posts ([8]), but in spite of the fact that his energetic leadership of the pagan reaction under Eugenius gained him the bitter hostility of Christians ([9]) he seems not to have been charged with rapacity or judicial killing ([10]).

---

(1) CLAUDIAN, 2, *In Ruf.*, 423 ; cf. 1. *in Ruf.*, 230 f.

(2) 2, *In Ruf.*, 407 f. ; cf. also *Vita Christiana : non minor fuerit concisura membrorum quam quos interimi fecerant* with 2, *in Ruf.*, 424-6.

(3) *Ibid.*, 429-30.

(4) *C.T.*, IX, 42, 14 ; SYMMACHUS, *Ep.*, VI, 14.

(5) 2, *in Ruf.* 451.

(6) Execution : CLAUDIANUS, *Cons. Stil. II*, 258 ; OROSIUS, VII, 36, 11 ; 12 ; *Chron. Minor.* I, 528 ; 1214. Suicide : ZOSIMUS, V, 11. Cf. E. DEMOUGEOT, *op. cit.*, 186. Men executed for treason were usually denied burial. *Dig.* 48, 24, 1, cf. 3. See F. VITTINGHOFF, *Der Staatsfeind in der römischen Kaiserzeit*, Berlin, 1936, p. 43 f. ; Th. MOMMSEN, *Strafrecht*, p. 987 ; PLATNER and ASHBY, *Topographical Dictionary of Ancient Rome*, 1929, *s.v. scalae gemoniae*. In 1st cent. suicide might safeguard burial : TACITUS, *Ann.* 6, 29.

(7) *B. Gild.*, 155 f., 169 f. ; property confiscated : *C.T.*, VII, 8, 7 ; *Not. Dig. Occ.*, XII 5.

(8) Even if prefecture of 383 is eliminated, cf. *C.T.*, VII, 18, 8 and IX, 29, 2 and E. DEMOUGEOT, *op. cit.*, p. 120, n. 6 ; A. H. M. JONES in *J.R.S.*, 54, 1964, p. 89 ; J. GUEY in *R.E.A.*, 52, 1950, p. 77-89.

(9) *Poet. Lat. Min.*, 3, 286-92 referred by Th. MOMMSEN in *Hermes*, 1870, p. 350-63 = *G.S.*, VII, p. 484-98, to Flavianus. Otherwise : G. MANGANARO in *G.I.F.*, 13, 1960, p. 210-214. But Mommsen's view upheld by A. CHASTAGNOL, *op. cit.*, p. 266 and H. BLOCH, *The Pagan Revival in the West at the End of the Fourth Century* in *Paganism and Christianity*, ed. A. MOMIGLIANO, 1960, esp. p. 217.

(10) Earlier AMMIANUS, XXVIII, 6, 28, had praised his justice

444

While the identification of Gildo and Flavianus taken in isolation from that of Rufinus must appear, uncertain, I would suggest that the identification of Rufinus is likely. There cannot have been many officials of whom it could be said, even with heavy rhetorical exaggeration, that they had killed thousands and who ended by being torn to pieces. If this identification is — at least provisionally — accepted, there follows a comparatively early date for the pamphlet : around 400 A.D. Since at this period the movement is likely to have been less extensive than it later became, the identification might be evidence in favour of de Plinval's view that the *De Vita Christiana* was written by Pelagius himself ([1]). But this problem can be solved, if as all, only by close examination of texts of the kind promised by F. R. Evans : an examination of Pelagius' general reliability at Diospolis and a detailed comparison of the contents of the *Vita* with Pelagius' assured writings now extant ([2]).

But whoever the author may be there is very little reason to suppose that the pamphlet has any bearing on Britain. But the problem of British — and Gallic — Pelagianism remains an interesting one. It is likely that the last word has not yet been written on the subject.

APPENDIX THE PUBLIC OF THE CASPARI TRACTS
AND THE LAUS VIRGINITATIS

Ep. I. *Honorificentiae tuae...*, CASPARI, 1-3, *P.L. Suppl.* I, 1687.
Written by a Gaul or a Briton from Sicily to an older relative at home. See above. As such it is unique.

Ep. II. *Humanae referunt litterae...*, CASPARI, 14-21, *P. L. Suppl.* I, 1375.
This may be by the *same writer* as Caspari, *ep.* I. But while the first letter is addressed to a relative, the second is addressed to a stranger, *ibid.* 1375.

It is extremely unlikely that the conclusion, *uolo te semper Deo uiuere et perpetui consulatus honore gaudere*, refers to an actual secular office. For a Pelagian to live for God and to enjoy seular office were not compatible ; cf. from same letter, *P. L. Suppl.* I, 1379 (5) : *non licet... in terrenis honoribus aut facultatibus gloriari, cui... ignominia magis quam nobilitas conuenit. Turpe est... et uelle se temporalem diuitem dici cui perpetuae diuitiae promittuntur.*

The 'perpetual' consulship must be a development of the metaphor of treasure in heaven (LUKE 12, 33). Cf. *Ad. Demet.* 11, 14, *P.L.* 30, 27 ; 28-9. *Ad. Marcel.* 8, *P. L.* 30, 54 ; *Ad. Ger. Fil.* 3, *P. L.* 30, 47.

---

(1) G. DE PLINVAL, *Pélage*, p. 37.
(2) R. F. EVANS, *op. cit.*, p. 98.

It is implied that the addressee belongs to a noble family and is asked to renounce his prospect of a consulate of a year for a perpetual one — in heaven. See also the forthcoming article of A. CAMERON in *Journal of Theological Studies* on Prudentius, *Peristephanon* II, 549-60. But cf. J. MORRIS, *op. cit.*

III *De Diuitiis*, CASPARI 25-67, *P. L. Suppl.* I, 1380-18.

(a) c. 6. The outstanding abuse of riches lies in the acquisition of governorships.

(b) c. 19.4. A trader's stay at *Rome* chosen as an example.

(c) c. 20, 1. Reference to estates scattered over every part of the world ; cf. A. H. M. JONES, *Later Roman Empire*, 782, on estates of senatorial order.

(d) The teachings known in Sicily in 414 : AUGUSTINE, *Ep.* 156-7 ; also to Proba grandmother of Demetrias : AUGUSTINE, *Ep.* 130. The pamphlet was clearly addressed to members of the senatorial order, certainly in Sicily, perhaps also in N. Africa and Rome.

IV *De Malis Doctoribus*, CASPARI 67-113, *P. L. Suppl.* I, 1418-157.

C. 1 and 17, 2 show that the letter was written to a man of standing at a time when Pelagianism was under heavy attack. Prominent themes are that faith is not enough without works, c. 4 f., and that idolatry is not the only unforgivable sin, c. 9-11. It may be possible to establish a stage in the controversy, when these were central issues ; but cf. G. DE PLINVAL, *Pélage*, p. 117-20, 223-4. CASPARI, *op. cit.*, 34, deduces from c. 1 and 17, 2 that the pamphlet was written after 418, the year of the imperial rescript and the papal *tractoria*. C. 11, 4 might be directed against Jerome's type of religious polemic.

V *De possibilitate non peccandi*, CASPARI 114-22, *P. L. Suppl.* I, 1457-64.

(a) c. 1. The addressee is not in the same place as the writer. He is a man of standing. He has been interested in a public career.

(b) c. 2. The author has been under attack and is defending himself. The defence is against the charge of teaching the possibility of sinlessness which was made against Pelagius and Caelestius, after Augustine's *De Remissione* in 412-13, cf. DE PLINVAL, *Pélage*, p. 261 f. ; CASPARI, 349-50.

(c) The addressee knows the writer and is convinced of his goodness but seems to have doubts about his rightness on this particular issue, c. 2, 3.

The anonymous author must be one of the men attacked by name for doctrines thought to be his. This would fit Pelagius himself or perhaps Caelestius rather than an anonymous pamphleteer.

VI *De Castitate*, CASPARI, 122-67 ; *P. L. Suppl.* I, 1464-1504.

(a) c. 4, 11 pagan features in Christian marriages, including *augurium* and *auspicium*.

(b) c. 10, 8 ; 16 ; References to the Roman heretic Jovinianus. The author's attitude, opposed to Jovinianus but also critical of Jerome is the same as that of Pelagius in 392-3 ; cf. G. DE PLINVAL, *Pélage*, p. 150 on JEROME, *Ep.* 49 ; 50.

(c) At the time of writing Jovinianus seems to have been dead ; c. 10 *Iouiniani quondam haeretici*. Jovinianus died before 406. JEROME, *Adv. Vigilant.* I ;

cf. F. HOMES DUDDEN, *The Life and Times of St. Ambrose,* 1935, p. 395. Since in c. 10-11 highwaymen, poisoning, execution by Imperial edict are mentioned as causes of early death, but not barbarian invasion, we might conclude that the pamphlet was written before the invasion of Radagaisus late in 405.

(d) c. 17, 1. The letter is addressed to a very rich man. The last sentences show that he is both rich and prominent. His sisters are choosing a life of virginity. He is exhorted : Inpleatur in te illa sententia ; beatus qui habet in Sion semen, non in *senatu,* et domesticos in Hierusalem non in urbe *Roma,* Babyloniae suis sceleribus conparata (CASPARI, 161).

The passage was surely addressed to a Roman of senatorial rank.
Virginitatis Laus, P. L. 30, 163-176.

c. 16 *unde pulchre Romana Ecclesia, apostolico sine dubio cuius sedem obtinet spiritu animata, tam seueram nuper de huiusmodi sententiam statuit,* suggests that this letter too was written from Rome.

But Gildas, *De Excidio,* 38, quotes as written by a countryman, *quidam nostrum* (cf. *ibid.,* 62) *non agitur de qualitate peccati sed de transgressione mandati,* which occurs word for word in *Virginitatis Laus,* c. 6. From this it may be deduced, as Morris has done in *op. cit.,* p. 37, that the *Virginitatis Laus* was written by a Briton, that a copy was preserved in Britain and perhaps also that it was originally written in Britain.

But this conclusion is not inevitable. First, our *Virginitatis Laus* is anonymous and this seems to have been true of many of the early Pelagian pamphlets ; cf. AUGUSTINE, *Gest. Pel.,* VI, 16-17, 19. ; JEROME, *Contr. Pelag.* III, 16.

Secondly, the idea expressed in the quotation is one that occurs repeatedly in the pamphlets, cf. *De Diu. Leg.* 5 ; *ad Cel.* 6 ; *Ep.* I, CASPARI 6-7 ; Julian of AECLANUM in AUGUSTINE, *Op. Imperf. Adu. Iul,* VI, 23. Indeed in *De Malis Doctoribus* 13 the phrase recurs differing only in that *actum est* replaces *agitur.* The phrase is likely to have occurred in pamphlets now lost. In any case its slogan form would give it life independently of its context. I would suggest that Gildas saw the phrase in a pamphlet which unlike our *Virginitatis Laus* bore the name of an identifiable British author, or again unlike our *Virginitatis Laus,* contained internal evidence pointing, not to a Roman, but to a British origin. Gildas' citation need therefore not be regarded as establishing a British origin for our *Virginitatis Laus,* a Roman origin remains more likely.

CONCLUSION

The Caspari pamphlets show astonishingly little trace of the catastrophical events that were happening in the years during which they were written. But a few passages in pamphlets II, III, VI are directly addressed to a Roman senatorial audience. I originated in the following of a Sicilian senatorial lady, even if it was sent out to the northern provinces. These passages suggest that we are dealing with missionary work directed at the highest social class. The deduction is based on few sentences in only some of the pamphlets, but it gains force from the fact that nothing in the remaining pamphlets is incompatible with such an audience. Indeed the extremely polite tone of the prefaces of IV and V suggests that these too were addressed to men of very high rank. V could well be addressed by Pelagius himself to one of his former Roman acquaintances. I would conclude that the Caspari documents express the views of a movement whose missionary activities were concentrated on the highest classes in Italy especially the senatorial order.

The *Virginitatis Laus* may well have a different author from some or all the Caspari documents — as it has a different history of transmission. But the relationship of all the writings is so close that once we abandon de Plinval's view that all — except ep. I — were written by Pelagius himself, the task of establishing the authorship of individual pamphlets becomes extremely difficult. But whoever was the author of the *Virginitatis Laus*, I would suggest that he was addressing the same audience as the author or authors of the Caspari documents.

The object of the writer, or more likely writers, of all these pamphlets appears to have been to persuade men and women of the highest society, especially Roman senatorial society, to opt out of their privileges and to live a life like that of the members of the first Christian communities.

VII

DID THE PELAGIAN MOVEMENT HAVE SOCIAL AIMS?

Explanations of heretical movements in terms of social or political conflicts have been put forward by several modern historians of the Later Roman Empire. E. Stein and G. Ostrogorsky have seen in the powerful hold of the monophysite heresy on the populations of Syria and Egypt an expression of the political separatist tendencies of these provinces. W. H. C. Frend has suggested that Numidian Berber antagonism to the Roman Empire and its civilization lay at the root of the Donatist Movement.[1]

Recently there has been an interesting attempt to understand the Pelagian Movement as a reaction to corrupt practices and particularly to the granting of unjust favours by Imperial officials.[2] In the present essay an attempt is made to define more comprehensively the scope of "Gratia," both in 4th Century society and in the teachings of the Pelagians, and to examine the place occupied by criticism of abuse of power in the surviving Pelagian writings. For the first part of the investigation, much of the evidence has been taken from the writings of the Antiochene Sophist, Libanius.

[1] G. Ostrogorsky, "History of the Byzantine State," translated J. Hussey, 1956, p. 55. "Monophysitism served as an outlet for the political separatist tendencies of Egypt and Syria; it was the rallying cry of the Copts and Syrians in their opposition to Byzantine rule." E. Stein, "Histoire du bas-empire", (Paris 1949), p. 34. "Les aspirations d'ordre national et social aux quelles le monophysisme servait de paravent ..." Cf. ibid., pp. 164 and 174ff.

Donatism, an expression of Numidian Berber antagonism to the Roman Empire and its civilisation: W. H. C. Frend, "The Donatist Church, a movement of protest in Roman North Africa." (Oxford 1952).

A criticism of social and political explanations of heresies: A. H. M. Jones, "Were the ancient heresies national or social movements in disguise ?" Journal of Theological Studies, new series X, 2, 1959, pp. 280–95. This also contains references to the works where the social and political explanations are most fully argued, notably E. L. Woodward, "Christianity and Nationalism in the Later Roman Empire," London 1916. J. Maspero, "Histoire des patriarches d'Alexandrie depuis la mort de l'empereur Anastase jusqu'a la réconciliation des églises jacobites" (518–616), Paris 1923. E. R. Hardy, "The Patriarchate of Alexandria: a Study in National Christianity," Church History, XV, 1946, pp. 81–100. By the same author, Christian Egypt: Church and People (New York, 1952).

R. Devréesse, Le Patriarcat d'Antioche (Paris 1945). The discussion is summarised by P. R. L. Brown; "Religious Dissent in the Later Roman Empire," History, 46, 1961, pp. 83–101.

[2] J. N. L. Myres, "Pelagius and the end of Roman Rule in Britain" J. R. S. 1960, pp. 21–36.

The writings of Libanius[3] are exceptionally valuable, because they reveal not only the opinions and behaviour of Libanius himself, but also throw a great deal of light on the attitudes of his numerous acquaintances and correspondents. Libanius was extraordinarily well-connected. Well-placed relatives and school-friends provided the earliest links in a widely spread network of influential connections, which for the rest of his life Libanius strove to enlarge. In this he was very successful. Well-situated families from over a wide area of the Near East sent their children to Libanius' school at Antioch and Libanius was careful to cultivate the friendship both of the parents and of the children, particularly if the latter made successful careers. In addition, Libanius' fame as the leading exponent of rhetorics of his time was such that men in high positions, whether just passing through Antioch or holding for a limited period a place in the administration there, usually sought out his acquaintance. These acquaintances also he cultivated carefully, by means of diplomatically written letters. The reward of so much diplomacy was that Libanius at most times had connections in important positions, and was in an excellent position to obtain favours from the administration.[4]

The surviving letters of Libanius' correspondence reveal how wide was the range of favour which an influential man might ask officials. He might merely ask for help for a traveller, but he might also seek to influence the verdict of a judge in a criminal case in favour of the accused.[5] Official aid might be sought to help a man in private business,[6] or to obtain his appointment to a public post.[7] Often the post was one from which the candidate was legally disqualified.[8] Libanius very frequently sent such letters to provincial governors with whom he happened to be acquainted. Occasionally, he made use of his connections at Constantinople to obtain a favourable decision at court.[9] He made quite the same kind of request orally to the officials resident in his native Antioch. Indeed, whenever he happened to be on particularly good terms with these officials, the making of requests occupied a considerable part of his time.[10]

[3] Libanius, opera, ed. R. Foerster, Vols. 1–4 and 10–11. For use with Libanius: P. Petit, "Libanius et la vie municipale à Antioche au 4 ème siècle ap. J. C.," Paris 1956. For use with Libanius' letters: O. Seeck, "Die Briefe des Libanius zeitlich geordnet," Leipzig, 1906.

[4] The connections through which Libanius gained his pupils, well described by P. Petit, "Les étudiants de Libanius," Paris 1956, pp. 95–135, summaries pp. 135 and 165.

[5] To judges: 56, 83, 105, 110, 151, 163, 394, 400 (oral request).

[6] e. g. eps. 108, 1438.   [7] eps. 1449, 545, 1260, 1224, 841.

[8] E.g. Letters written to help curiales to offices giving curial immunity, brought together in R. Pack "Curiales in the correspondence of Libanius," T.A.P.A. 1951, p. 182.

[9] e.g. eps. 864–8 and 850–2, written to prominent men at Constantinople in support of an Antiochene embassy or eps. 904–9 for his assistant Eusebius to help him regain immunity from curial service. eps. 922–30 help his friend Thalassius IV into Senate at Constantinople.   [10] ep. 589 (357), 351 (359–60). ep. 1437 (363).

Did the Pelagian Movement have Social Aims?

Libanius was well aware that official favour-giving might open the way to terrible abuses. Indeed, his speeches reveal and attack a formidable number of evils directly resulting from official favours. The influence of powerful patrons with decurions, and incidentally at court, enabled other decurions to escape from the service of their local Councils.[11] The influence of patrons who were themselves high officials or ex-officials enabled peasants to avoid paying taxes[12] and to resist their masters.[13] The informal influence of these same officials and ex-officials was gradually replacing the voice of the Council as the representative of the city in the councils of the governors.[14] Patrons used their influence to turn the force at the disposal of the administration against men who stood in their way,[15] to strengthen their control over their own clients,[16] and to enlarge their estates.[17] As a favour, powerful men were allowed to compel peasants to carry out of the city the rubble produced in their private building schemes.[18] Influence of ex-officials and others on the verdicts of governors acting as judges made a mockery of justice. As Libanius was led to argue in the course of a forceful attack on the evil effects of the governor's private audiences, there is little profit in the defeat of foreign enemies if injustice rules the law courts of the victors.[19]

But if Libanius saw the evils brought about by official favour-giving, he did not, as we have seen, for that reason give up asking favours. Indeed, his writings show quite clearly that a man of his position could not just stand aside from the traffic in favours. He had numerous clients: relatives less successful than himself or otherwise in need of help,[20] clients of his family,[21] various unfortunate men who came to him for protection.[22] He felt obliged to look after the interests of all exponents of rhetoric.[23] He exercised a special patronage on behalf of the bakers.[24] The moral obligations of the patron-client

[11] Or. 49c. 14–15; Or. 48c 19 and c. 37–8.   [12] Or. 47c. 7–10.   [13] Or. 37c. 11ff.

[14] Or. 35c. 6 and c. 8. on respect in which the powerful are held by officials, in contrast to the disrespect felt for councillors. Also Or. 52, c. 11. On this class of patrons and their differences from the prefeudal nobility of West see Petit, Libanius, pp. 370ff.

[15] Or. 14c. 10–11 (a "potens"), Or. 55, c. 11 (an influential sophist).

[16] Or. 39 cs. 10–11 (farmers), Or. 52 c. 16ff. (shopkeepers).

[17] Or. 39c. 11.   [18] Or. 50 favour element discussed c. 18.

[19] Or. 51. cs. 2–3.   [20] eps. 544, 217–19. helping cousin with liturgy.

[21] e. g. ep. 152 clients taken over from uncle. Family of Zenobius clients of L.'s for several generations, eps. 101–2 (359–60); for one relative of Zenobius, ep. 118–9 (357), and 532 (356) for another relative, the elder Boethus. ep. 931 and 955-6 (of 390) for younger Boethus of same family.

[22] ep. 1033 for orphans. ep. 567 for female slave of his. ep. 244 official to be given easier work on account of age. ep. 1339 for debtor to creditor. ep. 1041 for peasant who accidentally set fire to home of a neighbour. ep. 1253 for Manichaeans. Or. 45 on condition of prisoner.   [23] eps. 312, 382, 1517, 1047, 816-7, 796, 996-7, 175.

[24] The bakers at Antioch regularly came under pressure from the governors in time of famine to which their collective reaction was flight, or threat of flight. Or. 29.5ff. At such

relationship were old and strong.[25] Clients could not just be neglected. We are reminded that the notorious Probus was "forced" to take public office to be in a position to satisfy the demands of his numerous clients.[26] In Libanius' case there was the further motive that the eagerness of parents to send their children to his school depended to a considerable extent on his success in finding former pupils good positions in the administration,[27] or on his making smooth their way by other means, for instance, by obtaining for them the favourable notice of the governor, when they were beginning to practise as advocates in the courts.[28] Besides, the fourth century was an age of insecurity. A prominent man was always liable to attack by his enemies, particularly when he was for some reason without official protection. The best protection was to have close relations with a prominent official of the administration and to have this fact publicised as widely as possible.[29] The strongest evidence of the existence of such close relations was ability to obtain favours for third parties.[30] Thus, there was every motive for prominent men to ask favours of members of the administration and to receive requests for favours with sympathy, if, as was likely to happen, they should come for longer or shorter periods to hold public office themselves.

Libanius' observation of the evils of favour-giving, together with his need to make full use of the opportunities the system offered, led him into striking contradictions. He attacked the abuses of the private audiences of governors,[31] yet he also attacked a governor for not granting enough of them.[32] He realised that a "favour in accordance with the law" is a contradiction in terms. But he expected to receive favours nevertheless.[33] As a schoolmaster he prepared his charges for official careers, reminding them that governors should not grant

times Libanius acted as patron of individual bakers or of the bakers as a whole. Or. 1. c. 226, Or. 29. Cf. bakers at Ephesus, W. H. Buckler, ,,Labour Disputes in the Province of Asia," in Anatolian Studies presented to Sir William Mitchell Ramsay, p. 30. The edict is also printed in B.C.H. t 7, 1883, p. 504. A baker's guild at Thyatria, C. I. G. 3495.

[25] Fustel de Coulanges, "Histoire des institutions politiques de l'ancienne France: les origines du système féodal," ed. 5, p. 224, "La clientèle n'était pas dans les lois — mais elle régnait dans la société".   [26] Ammianus 27, 11, 3. Cf. notes 67 and 83.

[27] Libanius Or. 2. Criticised as a good orator but a bad teacher, L. defends himself by naming the officials that have come from his school, and explains that conditions of the time put rhetorically trained men at a disadvantage in the competition for official posts.

[28] Ep. 838 (363), Or. 51 cs. 13–17. Teachers spend much time making requests to governors, this causes number of their pupils to increase.

[29] L's influence and standing in city are increased when he has received letters from great men. e.g. Ep. 1004 (391) Symmachus, ep. 1173 (364) Datian, ep. 963 (390) Siburius, ep. 940 (390) Proculus.

[30] ep. 284 and 293 L. wants to be known to be able to help.   [31] Or. 51 and 52.

[32] Or. 56, c. 2–3. Similarly against another official who had not received Libanius and his son in the way Libanius had anticipated Or. 54, c. 4–6, and ibid, c. 9.

[33] Cf. Or. 51, c. 26 and Or. 57, c. 21.

favours but rule with ἀκρίβεια. Yet, more than once, he saw himself obliged on some later occasion to ask a former pupil in an official position not to apply this strictness to himself.[34]

Libanius was to some extent conscious of the contradictions between his teaching and practice. In his letters to judges he sometimes included such arguments as that it would not be disgrace for a judge anxious to help the right to listen to another person speaking in the cause of justice,[35] or that to help an accused man would only be wrong if to be accused and to be guilty were the same.[36] But any doubts Libanius may have had about the propriety of his behaviour did not prevent him from feeling profoundly hurt if his requests were not granted.[37] And when Libanius encountered a governor who ruled with ἀκρίβεια he had arguments ready to persuade him to take a more flexible view. He might urge him not to erase the Graces from the number of the gods,[38] or that τὸ δὲ ὅλως ἐκβαλεῖν τὰς Χάριτας οὐχ Ἑλληνι-κόν,[39] or that a man who does not grant just favours attacks Athena who maintains the Graces in her porch.[40] He argues, in other words, that it is traditional for men of education to give favours to their friends. He is appealing to the tradition of Greek politics.

This tradition of city state politics is discussed by Plutarch in the little treatise 'praecepta reipublicae gerendae'. Plutarch suggests that a civic politician would be justified in letting his friends reap some benefit from his position. He might, for instance, help a friend to some civic magistracy or arrange for him to be chosen a member of an embassy, sent with a decree of honour to the Emperor, with a message of good will and friendship. He might also help a friend to make money, either by helping him to some profitable briefs as an advocate in a court case or to a lucrative contract or lease. Lastly, a friend might be given favours which would result in his being praised by third persons. In other words, the politician is to listen to requests made by friends on behalf of others.[41]

This was the spirit in which Libanius wrote his letters and made his personal intercessions and this was the spirit in which the officials received them. The conscientious official would insist that a judge should always act impartially. But it was not always easy to draw rigid division between the decisions of an official acting as a judge and those made in other capacities. A governor's office was known as δικαστήριον, whatever he was doing. Thus the distinction

---

[34] ep. 696 reminds a pupil, taught not to give favours, that Pericles once asked Athenians to transgress a law he had himself made, in order to confer Athenian citizenship on his son by Aspasia.   [35] ep. 56.   [36] ep. 105.

[37] See the whole of Or. 54. The fact that L. made a speech of his grievances proves that he could expect others to sympathise with his disappointment.

[38] ep. 221.   [39] ep. 217. Cf. ep. 357.   [40] ep. 673.

[41] Plutarch, Praecepta gerendae reipublicae 806ff.

between a "strict" official and a less "strict" one was perhaps mainly a question of where favour-giving stopped.[42]

The lack of firm ethical rules of conduct to guide officials is illustrated by an exchange of letters between the official Macedonius and St. Augustine.[43] Macedonius challenged Augustine to justify his practice of interceding on behalf of condemned criminals, on religious grounds. He argues that a patron who tries to save a guilty man from punishment thereby comes to share in his guilt, and that the practice of intercession is particularly harmful in cases where the condemned man is still clinging to the gains for the sake of which he committed the crime. By present day standards this is a strong argument. Nevertheless, Macedonius appears to have put it forward only as a debating point on which he wished to learn Augustine's opinion, and he seems to have granted Augustine's request even before he had received Augustine's letter of justification.[44]

It is clear that so flexible an attitude to favour-giving on the part of judges and public opinion must lead to acts of injustice and hence to widespread discontent, particularly among those groups which could neither gain favours themselves nor have them obtained for them by influential and generous patrons. In view of the evidence of discontent among the subjects of the later Roman Empire,[45] one might expect the development of a movement of opinion directed to the eradication of injustice through a root and branch attack on favour-giving of all kinds. That this did indeed happen is the theme of J. N. L.

---

[42] In ep. 1249. Libanius advocates the striking of a balance between strict enforcement of the law and favour-giving, further idealised as φιλανθρωπία.

The same letter shows that some judges were really strict. Such a one was Ecdicius consular of Galatia. 360–1: ep. 308.

Eps. 1168–9, 1237–8, 1249 show how by sheer persistence Libanius persuaded a governor to discharge his pupil Dionysius who had committed rape.

[43] C.S.E.L.t. 44, p. 393, ep. 152. Macedonius' inquiry; ibid. p. 395, ep. 153. Augustine's answer; ibid., eps. 154 and 155, further letters of Macedonius and Augustine respectively. For Myres view of these letters see article cited above note 2 p. 29/30.

[44] ibid., ep. 152, p. 393, l. 8. Itaque sine mora, quod optabat obtinuit. I take this to be the request which he asks Augustine to justify retrospectively.

See also ibid., p. 395, l. 4. "Ceterum mihi hoc propositum est, ut intercessoribus praesertim talis meriti qualis tu es etiam gratias agam. Pleraque enim, quae sponte facere videri nolo, ne remissio severitatis alios armet in crimina, opto bonis intercessoribus relaxare, ut, quod libens concedo, salva severitate iudicii, alterius merito videatur indultum." I imagine that Augustine's attitude to intercession was usual among bishops. Comparable on a grander scale are the interventions of Ambrose with the Emperor Theodosius. That "intercessio" of long standing, C. Serdica c. 5. (343).

[45] On discontent see for instance E. A. Thompson on the Bagaudae in Gaul in "Zosimus and the end of Roman Britain," Antiquity 1956, p. 165, and "Peasant revolts in Roman Gaul and Spain," Past and Present 2, 1952, pp. 11–23. W. H. C. Frend," The Donatist Church," Oxford 1952, especially p. 72.

Myres' re-interpretation of the Pelagian Movement in the article mentioned earlier.[46]

Pelagius,[47] a Briton and man of education, probably with some legal training and experience,[48] began about 394 A.D. to win a considerable following among law students and well-to-do families at Rome.[49] The movement spread to Sicily and Africa. It soon met with opposition in which St. Jerome and particularly St. Augustine played leading parts. It was largely due to the efforts of the latter that Pelagius' teachings were in turn condemned by councils of African bishops and by the Pope. The ecclesiastical decisions were given sanctions by Imperial edicts in 418, 419 and 421 but the movement was not finished. In 425 the bishops of Gaul were ordered to forswear Pelagianism. In 429 St. Germanus, Bishop of Auxerre, was sent to Britain to combat Pelagianism there.[50] In 431 it was condemned at the council of Ephesus. But for long after Pelagian doctrine continued to influence theological writing in Gaul.[51]

[46] J. N. L. Myres, Pelagius and the end of Roman Rule in Britain, J. R. S. 1960, pp. 21–36.

[47] On Pelagius and the Pelagian writings. See G. de Plinval "Pélage, sa vie, ses écrits et sa réforme," Lausanne 1943, cited "Pélage." Also by de Plinval "Essai sur le style et la langue de Pélage, suivi du traité, inédit, De induratione cordis pharaonis," Fribourg en Suisse, 1947, cited "Style". More recently, J. Ferguson "Pelagius," Cambridge, 1956.

[48] De Plinval (Pélage p. 66) deduces legal training from lawyer-like arguments favoured by Pelagius. Eg. insistence that God requires only what is possible, for instance in, "De possibilitate non peccandi" c. III, can be compared with Dig. (Celsus), 4, 17, impossibilium nulla obligatio.

Both de Plinval (Pélage p. 53) and Ferguson (Pelagius p. 77) argue that Jerome's ep. 50 refers to Pelagius ... "Liberatus est mundus de periculo et hereditariae vel centumvivales causae de barathro, quod hic (i.e. Pelagius?) forum negligens se ad ecclesiam transtulit."

[49] This can be deduced from references in many Pelagian pamphlets to the wealth and rank of the readers. e.g. Virginitatis Laus c. 13, P. L. 30, col. 173, addressed to girl of noble family; similarly ep. ad Celantiam c. 21, C.S.E.L.t. 56; also ep. 2 Caspari p. 21, Haslehurst p. 28; opto te semper Deo vivere et perpetui consulatus honore gaudere, written to someone for whom consulship was thinkable. Ep. ad filias Gerontii, addressed to daughters of a wealthy man P.L. 30 col. 47/8, De Divina Lege, P.L. 30, col. 111, turpe est inter parentes senatores atque grammaticos, scholasticum, pro Christo voluntaria humilitate deiectum, verbis simplicibus esse contentum; Ep. 3 ad Marcellam P.L. 30 col. 51 vidimus te in tempore illo, quo domum tuam regalis affinitas ambiebat.

De Castitate c. 17 Haslehurst p. 273 addressed to a rich man. Augustine on two followers C.S.E.L. 44, p. 692 ep. 179 quidam ex discipulis honestissime nati et institutis liberalibus eruditi. See also de Plinval, "Pélage," pp. 211–6.

[50] The edict of 418. Mansi, Collectio Conciliorum 4 col. 444, expulsion of leaders, with trial, confiscation of property and deportation of followers. In fact, 18 bishops were expelled from Italy. In 419 further edict Augustine ep. 201, Mansi, 4, col. 446. In 421 Celestius banished from Rome, Mansi, 4, col. 448. That this last edict was needed shows that previous ones were not effective or at least only for a short period. In 425 bishops of Gaul ordered to forswear Pelagianism. P.L. 48 col. 409.

[51] N. K. Chadwick, "Poetry and Letters in Early Christian Gaul," pp. 170–221.

Now their opponents often described the followers of Pelagius as the "inimici gratiae."[52] This epithet has always been understood to refer to the movement's attitude to the theological doctrine of Grace. But Myres, after examining the use of the word "gratia" in the Theodosian Code, points out that in legal and indeed in ordinary usage the word "gratia" was a euphemism for "judicial corruption in the courts, or for official hanky panky of all kinds in public life," — in fact that it had exactly the meaning which we have found to be that of Χάρις in the writings of Libanuis. Myres proceeds to suggest that the Pelagian Movement was directed against all manifestations of "Gratia" in secular administration as well as in theology,[53] and that it was the social implications of the doctrine that gained the movement both its widespread support and such passionate opposition.

This suggestion receives further support from passages from Pelagian writing which show that their author, whether Pelagius himself or a disciple,[54] was deeply moved by the cruelty, callousness and favouritism of some judges:

"Under your eyes the bodies of men, sharers in your own nature, are beaten with leaden scourges, broken with cudgels, crushed under the claw, or burnt in the flames ... And your Christian compassion allows you to gaze at this; ... To gaze at it is horrible enough, what can I say of him who orders it ... ? Any Christian after this feels such pity that he cannot even sleep till he has performed the offices of mercy upon him, whom you

[52] The title "inimici gratiae Christi," e.g. C.S.E.L. 44, p. 664. Ep. 176 (of African bishops to Pope); ibid., p. 669, ep. 177.

[53] In article cited in note 46, J.R.S. 1960 pp. 25–6. Myres also notes that the laws directed against "gratia" in the Theodosian Code cease after 419, i.e. in the year after the official suppression of Pelagianism. He suggests that after the elimination of the Pelagian pressure-group the officials, following their personal interest, gave up the fight against "Gratia" in the administration.

But perhaps the disappearance of the word "gratia" from laws after 419 is more a question of fashion in drafting, and the same abuses continued to be attacked under other names.

[54] Only two complete works certainly by Pelagius survive, the commentary on the Letters of St. Paul, edited by A. Souter t. IX in "Text and Studies," Cambridge, 1926, and the letter to Demetrias P.L. 30 col. 15ff. (De Plinval, Pélage, p. 26).

De Plinval has however established a much longer list comprising in the first place texts edited by C. Caspari in „Briefe, Abhandlungen und Predigten aus den zwei letzten Jahrhunderten des Kirchlichen Altertums und dem Anfang des Mittelalters", Christiana 1890. (These have been reprinted and translated by R. S. T. Haslehurst. "The works of Fastidius," London 1927). Also included in de Plinval's list are a number of treatises which have come down among the writing of St. Jerome (especially in P.L. 30) and of St. Augustine. Pelagius' authorship of all these pamphlets has not been universally accepted as proved. See for instance A. Souter on de Plinval's "Style" in Journal of Theological Studies, 1949, t. 50, p. 227 or Myres in J.R.S. 1960, p. 27. But the resemblance in the moral and theological teaching of the pamphlets is striking. Ferguson has noticed (Pelagius p. 121) that the use of bible texts in the commentaries of St. Paul, which are undoubtedly by Pelagius, corresponds to that found by de Plinval throughout the writings.

have commanded to be tortured so often ... You sometimes thrust even the innocent into prison, urged by motives of gratitude to others or of a feeling of personal wrong ... (quia aut gratiarum aut iniuriarum pulsaris adfectibus). But you upholder of wealth and trafficker in offices after these cruelties recline at ease, lolling on piled up embroideries; you entertain your guests with the story, saying how you tortured and mangled the man in the sight of the people, and with what manner of death you killed him ... "[55]

Moreover, affirmations of the justice of God, particularly of the teaching "God is no respecter of persons"[56] feature prominently in Pelagian theology.[57] The Pelagian authors repeatedly insist that God judges men, without showing favours to individuals, strictly according to their achievement or failure in obeying the divine law.[58] In some impressive passages they deny that the observation of divine ordinances is impossible. For to punish men for faults they could not help but commit would be contrary to every notion of justice.[59] If men sin, it is because they have been given full freedom of will to choose either good or evil.[60] Any other condition would imply divine favouritism, favouring some in helping them to obey the law and dooming others to punishment.[61] But while God's power would allow him to act in such a way, his justice and "pietas" would not.[62]

[55] Passage quoted part of De divitiis c. 6, 2, Haslehurst, p. 42. translation is Haslehurst's.
Incidentally, cf. et tu ... securus, sublimibus fultus tapetibus, recubas ... with ... qui forte tapetibus altis exstructus toto proflabat pectore somnum, ... Vergil Aeneid. 9, 325-6.
Other passages with reference to abuse of power and official positions:
De castitate c. 10–11, Caspari pp. 146–7, Haslehurst, p. 246, De vita christiana c. 3, P.L. 40 col. 1035, and ibid., c. 11–12 P.L. 40 col. 1041–2. On this material cf. Myres in J.R.S. 1960 pp. 27–8.   [56] Acts. 10, 34.
[57] De induratione Pharaonis c. 20 and 31.
De Plinval, Style, p. 159 and 171. De Castitate c. 13, Caspari p. 152, Haslehurst p. 256.
[58] Description of trial in De malis doctoribus et operibus fidei c. 18ff., Caspari 102–11, Haslehurst p. 168ff. Discussed by Myres in J.R.S. 1960, p. 28. Also Expl. Rom. XI, 20, ed. Souter p. 89, tu autem fide stas, non quo personam tuam deus acceperit et illos sine causa proiecerit.
[59] De possibilitate non peccandi c. 2, Haslehurst, p. 192. Conveniat sane Deo aliquid impossibile praecepisse, si vel homini convenit; aut, si etiam humana conditio iniquum putat contra possibilitatem cuiquam aliquid imperare, quae perversitas est, haec vel sentiri de Deo, quod nec mortalium quidem natura suscipiat.
[60] Ad Demetriadem c. 2, P.L. 30, col. 17. ... quem tamen iustitiae exsecutorem Dominus voluntarium esse voluit non coactum. Ideo ... posuit ante eum vitam et mortem, bonum et malum: et quod placuerit ei dabitur illi. ibid., c. 4, col. 19. Est enim, inquam, in animis nostris naturalis quaedam (ut ita dixerim) sanctitas; quae par velut in arce animi praesidens, exercet mali bonique ... iudicium ...
[61] e.g. Ad. Demetriadem c. 8, P.L. 30, col. 25. Non enim a iusto Deo aut ille puniri meruisset, aut hic eligi, nisi uterque utrumque potuisset.
[62] God's power restrained by his justice: De induratione cordis Pharaonis c. 22, De Plinval "Style," p. 161. In quo, licet sit tanta potestas ut omnia quae voluerit faciat, ... tamen est in eo ratio et iustitia simul et pietas, quae contradicunt potentiae, ne quid tale fiat, quod eius bonitati inconveniens sit aut diabolus reprehendat.

Now the principles governing divine justice are certainly applicable to human justice. Indeed it is a reasonable assumption that Pelagius' theology was the outcome of reflections on his own experience of profane legal theory and practice, and represents a transfer into the sphere of theology of Pelagius' own passionate hatred of every kind of favouritism on the part of human judges. One would expect a man filled with so strong a sense of justice, to make his moral theology the basis of a radical criticism of the courts and administration of the Roman Empire. But in fact the surviving pamphlets do not at all suggest that he did so.

To begin with, the Pelagian attitude to "Gratia" is never stated as explicitly as, for instance, the doctrine of the power of the free will. In numerous passages in the commentary on the epistles of St. Paul, Pelagius appears to be simply endorsing the words of the apostle at their face meaning. Sometimes he adds a rider suggesting that he would define Grace rather broadly, as something that can be deserved or that includes the gift of the scriptures and the example of Jesus.[63] He was evidently very careful not to appear to contradict the words of St. Paul. The full logical implication of the Pelagian doctrines of free will and divine justice only emerged in the course of the ensuing controversy. Pelagius' opponents, led by St. Augustine, drew attention to the implications of Pelagian doctrines which appeared to contradict accepted views of the relationship of God and man, and expressed this contradiction in slogan form by branding the Pelagians as "enemies of grace."[64] The Pelagian movement did not therefore start as protest against "Gratia" as such.

[63] On the problem of Pelagian doctrine of Grace, A. von Harnack, "Dogmengeschichte" t III, p. 179ff. Also J. Ferguson 'Pelagius,' p. 132ff. with references. A full endorsement of Pauline doctrine: Argumentum omnium epistularum, ed. Souter, p. 4, l. 22. "Romanorum namque plerique tam rudes erant ut non intellegerent, dei se gratia non suis meritis esse salvatos." Cf. In Rom. V, 1; ibid. I, 7; in Gal. I, 4.

"Grace deserved": In 2, Cor. III, 6 "Gratia vero etiam impium iustificat convertentem." Cf. in Rom. I, 3, and VIII, 17. "multi filii gratia ..." with "qui meretur esse filius."

"Grace" understood as the scriptures and example of Jesus, In Rom. 3, 21.

[64] See for instance how in his de Gratia Christi c. 22, P.L. 44, col. 371, St. Augustine selected a quite subordinate sentence of Pelagius's "Ad Demetriadem" to support his charge that Pelagius denied the necessity of divine Grace. The sentence "Ad Demetriadem" c. 25, P.L. 30, col. 40: "Ostendit quo modo resistere debeamus diabolo, si utique simus subditi deo, eiusque faciendo voluntatem ut divinam etiam mereamur gratiam."

In his "De bono viduitatis" cs. 26–8, P.L. 40, col. 442–4, Augustine calls Pelagius an enemy of Grace and justifies this by arguments based on "Ad Demetriadem" c. 2ff. (the power of free will as basis of moral action) and c XI "spirituales vero divitias nullus tibi, praeter te conferre poterit." But in doing this Augustine did not so much criticise the teachings of Pelagius actually found in the letter as draw implications from them which Pelagius need not by any means have intended. A very similar attack on "Ad Demetriadem" in ep. 188, P. L. 33, col. 848–54.

In their argument Augustine and Pelagius appear indeed to have been for much of the time at cross purposes. This was not because Augustine "could not afford to argue with

Then, the theme of all the surviving Pelagian writings is not so much a simple, rather pathetic claim to social justice, as a call to individual Christians to realise in their lives as fully as possible the letter and spirit of New Testament ethics. Accepting the authority of the New Testament in its literal sense, the Pelagians contrasted with its terms a variety of aspects of Roman upper class life. These ranged from the ostentation, luxury[65] and ruthless competition[66] in the lives of individual private citizens to the numberless acts of oppression committed by officials of the character of the Praetorian Prefect, Petronius Probus,—that husband, father-in-law and grandfather of pious Christian women.[67] On the positive side, keeping the precepts general and close to the New Testament wording, the Pelagians call for moral reform.

"We are bidden not to lie, or curse, or perjure ourselves, or even to swear truthfully, to render no man evil for good, to love our enemies, to pray even for our persecutors and slanderers; we are not allowed to recover things stolen from us, or appeal to wordly tribunals, not to return wrong to those that have wronged us. We are forbidden to eat with fornicators, drunkards, swearers or extortioners, we must not even utter an idle word."[68]

When we examine the theological teaching about Grace and free will and divine justice in their contexts, we find that they were always used to support such moral teaching. Pelagius began his letter to Demetrias with a statement of his doctrine of the power to do good of the free will. His aim, as he himself explained, was to show that the moral lessons he was about to give could really be carried out.[69] On the other hand, the fact that favours were not to be

Pelagius in terms of social reform" (Myres, J.R.S. 1960, p. 29) as that he was not prepared to argue in the terms of a man whose moral and religious experience was obviously diametrically opposed to his own.

[65] e. g. De divitiis c. 14., Haslehurst, p. 76. De castitate c. 17., Haslehurst, p. 282.

[66] De malis doctoribus, c. XI, Haslehurst p. 142. "Nemo, proximum superiorem quam se dici patitur, nemo meliorem. Ad suum enim unusquisque odium amorem proficere veretur alterius, suam vituperationem putat proximi laudem ... etc.

[67] The wrongs of officials, see references note 55. Cf. the characteristic of Sextus Petronius Probus, Ammianus 27, 11, 2–6 and 30, 5, 4–10.

On his wife Proba, his daughter-in-law Juliana, his granddaughter Demetrias, see biographies in P. W., I, article Anicii.

[68] De divitiis c. 19. (Caspari p. 60, Haslehurst p. 96. Also De castitate, c. 10, Caspari p. 144, Haslehurst p. 240. Virginitatis laus, c. 6, P.L. 30, col. 167. Cf. De vita christiana, c. 14, P.L. 40, col. 1044.

[69] Ad Demetriadum c. 2. "Quoties mihi de institutione morum et sanctae vitae conversatione dicendum est, soleo prius humanae naturae vim qualitatemque monstrare et quid efficere possit, ostendere ... ne nihil prosit ad ea vocari, quae forte sibi impossibilia esse praesumpserit. Nequaquam enim virtutum viam valemus ingredi, nisi spe ducamur comite."

On the other hand opponents of Pelagian teachings are said to want to retain an excuse for continuing sinful lives, e.g. De induratione Pharaonis c. 2. de Plinval "Style," p. 139. De possibilitate non peccandi, c. 3, Haslehurst p. 194. "Ergo hominem non peccare possibile est? Dura haec re vera et amara peccantibus vox est" etc.

expected from God, makes strict observance of his ordinance all the more urgent.[70] But the Pelagian theological principles were never used to support collective action, social aims, or the reform of institutions.

The moral teaching too is always directed at individuals. Even the passages condemning the wickedness of judges do not stand in contexts concerned with the proper behaviour of a Christian who happens to be a judge. They are rather put forward as types of wickedness to illustrate an argument that is not directly concerned with jurisdiction at all, that the possession of riches puts men into a position in which they are likely to commit terrible sins,[71] or that God will not listen to prayers of wicked men,[72] or that it is no merit to give away extorted wealth in deeds of charity,[73] or that sinners will be punished in the end,[74] or that in a world where men are frequently unjustly executed it would be wiser to prepare for after-life than for marriage.[75] Certainly, the fact that the Pelagians chose evil officials as types of wickedness is in itself noteworthy. But reformers who were primarily concerned with the fairer functioning of the courts would have approached the problem more directly.

In fact, the Pelagian writings suggest a comparative indifference to society and its institutions. The Pelagians were vehement upholders of celibacy and viewed the eventual end of the human race with equanimity.[76] As we have seen, they urged Christians not to take oaths nor to go to court.[77] Quite apart from the criticism of the behaviour of sinful individuals in the position of judges, the writings suggest distrust of the very role of a man set up to judge his fellows, where Jesus submitted to be judged.

"Quid est Christiane? Quid est Christi discipule? Non haec tui est forma doctrinae. Ille ante tribunal humilis stetit. Tu in tribunali, super elatione enixus, super stantes sedes iudicaturus."[78]

---

[70] The writings insist on the reality of the punishment. E.g. De malis doctoribus et operibus fidei, c. 13 and 15. Haslehurst p. 148 and 156. Terror of Last judgment, De divina lege, c. 7. P.L. 30. col. 113. Cf. de Plinval, "Pélage," pp. 184–88.

[71] De divitiis, c. 6, Caspari pp. 31–2, Haslehurst pp. 40–2.

[72] De vita christiana, c. 11, Haslehurst p. 310.

[73] De vita christiana, c. 12, Haslehurst p. 312, P.L. 40, col. 1041–2.

[74] De vita christiana, c. 3. Haslehurst p. 301, P.L. 40, col. 1035.

[75] De castitate c. 10–11. Haslehurst p. 246, Caspari pp. 246–7.

[76] De castitate c. 13, Caspari p. 154, Haslehurst p. 256. In favouring separation of married couples, Pelagius went beyond St. Paul. See Expl. 1, Cor. VII, 5, ed. Souter, pp. 161–2. De Plinval "Pélage," pp. 158–62.

[77] See references in note 68. Also Ep. Ad Gerontii filias c. 2, P.L. 30, col. 46.

It was of course traditional that Christians should settle disputes among themselves, especially by submitting them to clergy. I Cor. 6. As far as civil disputes were concerned, provided both partners accepted the bishop's arbitration, the state upheld the practice. C.T. 1, 27, 1 (318), ibid. 2 (408). Ed. Sirm. I (333) even makes consent of one party unnecessary. Cf. A. Piganiol, "L'empire chrétien," p. 369.

[78] De divitiis, c. 6, 2, Haslehurst p. 40.

The nearest the Pelagian writers came to a social programme is on the distribution of property. The admonition "sell all thou hast and give to the poor," is accepted in its literal sense, and the rich are urged to give away their wealth.[79] The criticism that there will be nobody to give alms when the rich have given away their property is answered: "tolle divitem et pauperem non invenies. Nemo plus quam necessarium est possideat, et quantum necessarium est omnes habebunt."[80] But these striking sentences are only one argument in a long treatise. The treatise as a whole aims at the moral good of the soul of the rich man, rather than the raising of the standard of living of the poor.

When we compare the passages in the Pelagian writings which touch on social matters with the writings of Libanius, we find ourselves in different worlds. In Libanius' writings the problems of human society are important for their own sake. Libanius' descriptions of the evils of favour-giving are as outspoken as the Pelagian writings, and considerably more comprehensive, even if they lack the moral fervour and urgency. But Libanius, like every man of standing, was himself so deeply involved in the network of favour-giving and favour-taking that he could not escape from it. To the complex problems facing a man in Libanius' position, the Pelagian writings offer no solution and do not even attempt to do so. It is very unlikely that men who were to any considerable extent concerned with the eradication of "Gratia" from secular institutions would make so few concrete or relevant suggestions in their pamphlets.

But if the contents of the Pelagian writings do not allow us to see Pelagianism as a movement of social reform, they fit very well into the background of the ascetic movement of the late 4th Century, which found its most eloquent expression in the letters of St. Jerome.[81] Of course, the Pelagian writings have marked characteristics of their own, but their ascetic aims are quite comparable

---

[79] See whole of De divitiis, Haslehurst p. 3off. Note argument for equality of property, ibid. c. 8. God's gifts, air, warmth, rain, light, the sacraments, shared equally among all. Inequality only found in goods whose distribution left to man.

Also argument against validity of property rights, ep. Ad Gerontii filias P.L. 30, c. 2, col. 46: since goods of this world are in themselves worthless and since nature does not recognise individual ownership, there cannot be any true justice about their distribution: "ibique iudicia vera non esse ubi sint mentita negotia."

[80] De divitiis c. 12. The Pelagian arguments seem to have met with some success. See letter of Hilarius, bishop of Syracuse asking Augustine's opinion on whether the rich must really sell all their goods even though they were using them charitably. C.S.E.L. 44, p. 448, ep. 156. Augustine's reply, ibid., p. 472, ep. 157. See also Augustine's reassuring remarks to Proba, ibid. ep. 130, p. 41. Cf. de Plinval, "Pélage." p. 188ff. and 221ff.

[81] A brief survey of ascetic movement in the West characterised by the life of St. Jerome and of some of the great ladies whose spiritual adviser he was in A. Piganiol's "L'empire chrétien," pp. 230–9.

De Plinval "Pélage," p. 113ff. Also the very interesting article of P. R. L. Brown, "Aspects of the Christianization of the Roman Aristocracy," J.R.S. 1961, pp. 1–11.

to those of St. Jerome. Moreover, both men appear to have addressed the same upper class public, including women of the highest aristocracy.[82] So it came about that when young Demetrias, of the great Anician family, the grand-daughter of the notorious Petronius Probus, took a vow of virginity, she received letters of advice both from St. Jerome and Pelagius.[83] Pelagius may well have been right to think that Jerome's opposition to himself was motivated by envy.[84] There appears to have existed at Rome a widespread feeling, that the official recognition of Christianity after the conversion of Constantine, and the rapid expansion of the Church that followed, had resulted in a relaxation of standards, and that a return to a stricter way of life was necessary.[85] This feeling was expressed in their different ways by both St. Jerome and Pelagius.

This is not to deny that the most characteristic features of Pelagius' teaching, his insistence on individual responsibility, his emphasis on God's justice and impartiality, grew out of Pelagius' legal knowledge and experience of court procedure, nor that they express dissatisfaction with the kind of justice handed out by many judges of his time. But it is necessary to insist that his experience of legal theory and practice induced him to lead an ascetic movement, not a movement of social reform. In this he showed himself a characteristic representative of an age which saw much creative thought in theology amid rapid decay of social institutions. One might compare Pelagius with that anonymous follower of his, the author of the Carmen de Providentia, who sought consolation for defeat and captivity by turning his mind from the contemplation of the devastation around him to the defeat of evil in his own soul.[86]

There remains the consideration that a theology which placed so much emphasis on the power of the free will must inevitably act as a stimulus to independent thought and action, and thus provide the emotional and spiritual force necessary to make the repudiation of an old and corrupt regime possible.[87] This is a very much wider issue and its discussion lies outside the scope of the present paper.

[82] Cf. note 49.

[83] The differences and similarities in the approach of Pelagius and his opponents stand out most clearly in the writings addressed to Demetrias, her mother and grandmother.

Pelagius ad Demetriadem P.L. 30, col. 15ff.

St. Jerome ep. 130, P.L. 22, col. 1107.

St. Augustine wrote "De bono viduitatis" to Demetrias' mother about the same time. P.L. 40 col. 429. C. 21 is a reply to Pelagius' argument about the power of the human will in his letter to Demetrias.

Also a direct reply to Pelagius letter is Augustine's ep. 188, P.L. 33, col. 848.

Augustine's ep. 150 C.S.E.L. 44, p. 380, congratulates Proba, grandmother of Deme-trias and widow of Sextus Petronius Probus, on her daughter's vow.

[84] Augustine, Contra Julianum II, 36.   [85] De Plinval, "Pélage," pp. 115–20.

[86] Carmen de providentia P.L. 51, col. 617ff. Cf. Myres in J.R.S. 1960 p. 31.

[87] See Myres, ibid., p. 31 and following pages, for a view of the stimulating effect of

As for the problem of "Gratia," we must remember that the bureaucracy of the Roman Empire administered a very large area, under, by modern standards, primitive economic conditions. Communications were extremely slow. The state could only afford a low basic salary to so large a clerical civil service.[88] The standards of public life suited a city state rather than a large territorial empire. Under these conditions the prevalence of "Gratia" was inevitable.

Pelagianism in Britain. For an opinion of the more general problem of human psychology, see R. G. Collingwood and J. N. L. Myres, "Roman Britain and the English Settlements," [1st volume in the Oxford History of England] p. 309.

[88] A. H. M. Jones, "The Roman Civil Service, Clerical and Subclerical Grades," J.R.S. 1949, p. 51.

The clerks lived on fees rather than on wages. "Roman Inflation," Economic History Review, 1952/3, p. 307.

VIII

EPIGRAPHIC EVIDENCE
ON THE CHRISTIANISATION OF SYRIA

That inscriptions can be used to illustrate the religious transformation as a result of which Christianity became the religion of the Roman Empire has been recently shown by G.Alföldy's study of the area of Aquincum.[1] I have worked through the inscriptions conveniently collected in the volumes of IGLS with the intention of doing something similar for Syria. Of course the nature of the inscriptions, especially the comparative scarcity of inscriptions put up by the Roman army or civil administration, means that the Syrian study cannot illustrate the same aspects of the transformation as the Pannonian one. There is far less evidence about the later forms of paganism and far more about the process of Christianisation.

The Early Empire is most fully represented in the inscriptions of the famous sanctuary of Baalbek (Heliopolis) which was settled as a veteran colony probably as early as 15 BC.[2] The inscriptions enable us to study the religious impact of veteran settlement on the native cults of the site and of the territory around it. We can observe the

Romanisation of the great Semitic sanctuary,[3] to which
Baalbek still owes its name, after it had been dedicated to
Jupiter Optimus Maximus Helipolitanus and become the centre
of the public cult of the Roman community.[4] Rural sanctuaries too were Romanised, or partly Romanised, and adopted
by the settlers.[5] Baalbek was very conscious of its Roman
status and it is probably no accident that so far few
indications have been found of the worship of living emperors.[6]
The same is true of the 'mystery cults' also.[7]

Religious inscriptions of Baalbek survive in largest
numbers from the Severan[8] period and then cease. The latest
pagan inscription which can be reliably dated is a dedication
made on behalf of the Emperor Gordian (238-44).[9] One might
be tempted to conclude that at Baalbek paganism died in the
second quarter of the 3rd century.[10]

But this conclusion would be altogether mistaken. There
is abundant evidence for the lasting strength of paganism
at Baalbek. Constantine prohibited ritual prostitution
practised in honour of a goddess identified with Venus. He
destroyed her temple and replaced it by a church.[11] During
the brief reign of Julian the Apostate popular resentment
was vented on the Christians.[12] Around the end of the 4th
century Baalbek still retained a reputation as a 'city of
demons',[13] whose citizens would not suffer the name of
Christ to be pronounced.[14] Theodosius I is said to have
destroyed the temple of Jupiter and to have established a
church in its vicinity.[15] Existing remains of the basilica

in the great sanctuary date from the 5th or 6th century.[16]
As late as the reign of Justinian among a number of pagan
priests arrested at Constantinople two were natives of
Baalbek.[17] Thus it is clear that at Baalbek it cannot have
been a decline in worship of the pagan gods that produced
the drying up of pagan inscriptions. There must be some
other cause.

The ending of pagan inscriptions cannot be separated
from the general decline in inscriptional commemoration.
Baalbek has produced six dated inscriptions up to Trajan,
five Severan inscriptions and no dated inscriptions at all
between 213 and 313. Then we have one dated inscription of
the fourth century, two from the fifth, one from the sixth
and two from the seventh century.[18] The number of securely
dated inscriptions is increased if we include those that
refer to a ruling emperor. In this way we obtain 22
inscriptions up to and including the reign of Commodus,
12 Severan inscriptions,[19] 1 dedication - offered on behalf
of Gordian[20] and then a long gap. The tetrarchy of Diocletian has left 5 inscriptions.[21] The few inscriptions later
than that have no references to emperor or imperial institutions.[22] We see that there was a dramatic decline after the
Severan period. There was some recovery under the tetrarchy
but it was brief. The old habits were not restored. The
decline in religious inscriptions is only part of the wider
pattern.

How can the trend be explained? I think it can reasonably

be asserted that in the classical city when men put up an inscribed monument their motives were usually political or at least social: they sought to publicise something or some-body to the citizen body.[23] This is obvious in the case of inscriptions which publish laws, decrees or privileges. But even inscriptions commemorating individuals performed a political role. Normally they proclaimed somebody's services to the city or to the empire, and were a means by which leading men advertised themselves and each other to the imperial authorities, their peers and the mass of fellow citizens.[24] At Baalbek there was an additional motive: the city was a Roman colony set in the midst of a Greek or Aramaic speaking population. Its citizens were part of the imperial people and their official language, maintained up to the early 4th century, was Latin. Needless to say they proclaimed their privileged status and association with the government of the empire on monuments inscribed in the Latin language.[25]

Many of the social motives for putting up secular monuments are relevant to religious monuments also. A large proportion of religious inscriptions at Baalbek and elsewhere seek divine support for the emperor and at the same time proclaim that the dedicant is a loyal subject.[26] Of course there are many purely private dedications. At Baalbek these were usually undated and offered on behalf of the dedicant's family.[27] But here too the dedicant's motives are likely to have included personal publicity.

That inscriptional commemoration should almost cease
around 240 AD is not surprising. These years saw the
beginning of great instability in Syria which started with
civil war between rival emperors and culminated in destructive Persian invasions and the rise and fall of the empire of
Palmyra.[28] Baalbek itself was not directly harmed, as far
as we know, but it was natural that in the prevailing uncertainty people should cease to put up expensive monuments.
What is significant is that even when the empire had been
restored by Diocletian the old type of commemoration did not
return, or at least returned only very temporarily. In the
East there can have been no question of permanent impoverishment. The cause must be a profound change in the way men
wished to be remembered, for what kind of actions and by
whom.

Underlying the change in fashion is a permanent change of
attitude among the wealthy monuments building classes towards
the political competition in their cities and perhaps to the
empire as such.[29] There is no logical reason why loss of
pride in the empire and Roman citizenship or increasing
indifference to personal publicity among all who could read,
should prevent men from putting up monuments to express
gratitude to the gods. But this nevertheless seems to have
happened. Once monuments ceased to be fashionable in
secular situations they were also no longer employed to
express religious gratitude.

In the case of religious inscriptions there was of course

an additional reason why there could be no lasting recovery.
The restored empire soon became Christian and new pagan
monuments might attract Christian vandalism, even in a
predominantly pagan community.[30] In the circumstances it is
understandable that pagans chose to become a 'silent
majority'.

In contrast to Baalbek, and indeed many of the most highly
urbanised or militarised parts of the empire, large areas of
Syria have produced very many late inscriptions. Indeed the
late inscriptions are very much more numerous than the early
ones. This paradoxical situation is due to the fact that
the inscriptions are of a different type from those that
almost ceased to be carved since the third century: the late
inscriptions of Syria are on the whole concerned with neither
city nor empire.

These late inscriptions come largely from areas of eastern
Syria situated between the Orontes and the desert. This was
a region of substantial villages rather than cities. That
so many inscriptions have been preserved is due to the fact
that the area was much more densely populated in late
antiquity than in more recent times. As a result ancient
buildings have not been demolished for building material
and survive to heights unusual for ancient remains. That
inscriptions were carved at all appears to have been due to
two causes, Christianity and economic development.

Christianity produced a new motive for epigraphy; a desire
to mark buildings with Christian symbols, at the very least

a cross, but often a biblical or liturgical text as well.
This was done almost universally in Syria, less widely in
Egypt and to an even lesser extent in Asia.[31] Syrian Christians felt it necessary to mark not only churches and tombs
but their dwellings also. The inscription was usually placed
on the lintel over a doorway and very often dated. The date
was perhaps normally that of the day on which the lintel had
been put into position.[32] One suspects that there was a
ceremony in which the new house was formally blessed, but I
know of no Syrian evidence to that effect.[33] The inscription
was a proclamation of faith, but it was no doubt also
intended to secure divine protection for the house. To
Christians, as to Jews, the Bible provided a large armoury
of powerful divinely inspired words of a kind not available
to pagans whose religion lacked sacred books.[34] The decorated
and dated lintels begin towards the end of the 3rd century
and are overwhelmingly, though not a hundred percent,
Christian.[35]

The other factor that furthered the putting up of
inscriptions was rural economic development. This has been
studied in detail only in the limestone hills east of
Antioch.[36] There the architecture of buildings, and inscriptions mainly on tombs and sanctuaries, establish that the area
was settled from at least the 2nd century AD. But the 4th,
5th and 6th centuries saw a steady increase in the area of
land utilised and of the population maintained by it.[37]
In the limestone hills economic expansion was based on olive

plantations. The olive is not likely to have played so
decisive a role further east in the area of the 'limes of
Chalcis' or further south. Nevertheless there is reason to
believe that economic development took place here too, even
though at present the explanation of the development of the
frontier areas of Syria, Arabia and Palestine in the Later
Empire is far from clear.[38] Meanwhile the fact of the development makes it more difficult to use the inscriptions as
evidence for Christianisation. The appearance of Christian
inscriptions in a particular area may simply be due to the
economic development of a previously empty or 'backward'
area and not to the conversion of pagans to Christianity.

As has been mentioned earlier, the most thoroughly explored
zone is the limestone plateau east of Antioch. In the Roman
period this region was divided between the rural territories
of Antioch and Apamea. In the Antiochene area the earliest
(probably) Christian inscription dates from 272/3.[39] But the
tide of Christian inscriptions only began to flow after
Constantine had defeated Licinius and taken over the government of the East in 324.[40] We then have Christain inscriptions
from 335, 336/7, 341/2, 349, 349/50, 351.[41] Christian inscriptions quickly became the majority. Out of 33 inscriptions
between 326 and 376 AD 23 are Christian; out of 38 inscriptions between 377 and 427 AD the Christian stones number 33.[42]
The year 367 saw the last recorded restoration of a pagan
temple.[43] After this date the strength of paganism has to be
deduced - as at Baalbek - from the absence of positive

indications of Christianity. From around 380 inscriptions suggest an intensification of Christianisation and of the building of churches.[44] This was of course the time when Theodosius began to issue anti-pagan legislation and when the monks of Syria waged a campaign against rural temples.

The area of the Antiochene Christian inscriptions lies on both sides of the Antioch - Beroea (Alepo) road.[45] Communications from villages on each side of the road converge on the plain of Dana. It is certainly no coincidence that the hill sides surrounding the plain were frequented by hermits and that some of the earliest monastic communities in N.Syria were founded here.[46] Christianity was enormously strengthened first by the accession of a Christian emperor in Constantine, and by the fact that henceforth emperors, with one exception, were Christians. It is possible that the limestone area enjoyed a special imperial connection through the existence in the area of imperial estates.[47] But in these rural areas the influence of hermits and monks was more immediate than that of emperors. It was they who provided both inspiration and coercion[48] to complete conversion and to intensify the building of churches.

The Antiochene area of the limestone plateau had long been inhabited and included major rural sanctuaries. The Christian inscriptions therefore certainly mark Christianisation. But the area was also undergoing economic and social transformation. The rural population was growing, extensive areas suitable for no other crop were being planted with olive trees,

and a class of free peasants working on a small scale was
coming into existence.[49] It remains an open question whether
religious and economic change were related. It is conceivable
that conversion to Christainity discouraged infanticide, and
by enlarging the population furthered economic development as
well as migration and monasticism.[50]

Christianisation of the Apamean part of the limestone
plateau to the west of the modern Ma'aret En Noman[51] seems to
have taken place in basically the same conditions as in the
area further north. This too was land of old settlement, with
ancient pagan sanctuaries, in the process of economic expansion based on olive plantations. The position of the earliest
Christian inscription in relation to the Beroea (Alepo) -
Chalcis - Apamea road[52] suggests that here too the source
of Christianity lay to the east of the hills and in the
Alepo-Chalcis area rather than the Orontes valley and the
city of Apamea in the west.[53] Christianity came to these
Apamean villages somewhat later. The earliest inscription
dates from 364. The period 326-76 produced only 4 Christian
inscriptions; the following fifty years produced 23 Christian
inscriptions out of a total of 34 inscriptions of all kinds.[54]
By the end of that period dated inscriptions were extremely
numerous, approaching one per year and the overwhelming
majority were Christian. The later date of Christianity in
the territory of Apamea suggested by epigraphic evidence is
confirmed by literary sources. The bishop of Apamea set out
to destroy temples in his see with the aid of gladiators

only to be finally slain by angry pagans when attempting to destroy the temple of Aulon.[55]

Further south, in the area studied by J.Lassus, Christianity was later still. At the same time there is also less evidence of Early Empire settlement of any kind. Lassus found only 5 inscriptions dated before 300. Even the 4th century has produced only 2 (or perhaps 4) inscriptions. 12 of Lassus' inscriptions were set up between 400 and 500 and no less than 29 after 500.[56] This is an area where it is difficult to be certain whether the lateness of Christian inscriptions was due to the lateness of conversion to Christianity or simply to absence earlier of an inscription-writing population. But taking the evidence at its face value, and bearing in mind that generally speaking the Christianisation of the Syrian countryside progressed from north to south,[57] one would conclude that large parts of the region noth of Epiphania (Hama) were converted to Christianity only in the second half of the 5th century, and some regions, especially the basalt hills of the Gebel Ala, only in the 6th century.[58] Similarly late expansion of Christianity during the second half of the 5th century is suggested by inscriptions of the 'limes of Chalcis'.[59]

South of Epiphania (Hama)[60] a particular type of inscription seems to have been particularly popular: the dated tombstone.[66] Tombstones inscribed with the day of the month and the year of the deceased's death (most often dated according to the Seleucid area) have been found in small

numbers in scattered parts of Syria: in what was sometime
the province of Euphratensis, in the 'limes of Chalcis',[62]
among the limestone villages of Apamea[63] and at Apamea
itself.[64] But the greatest concentration of such inscriptions
has been found between Emesa (Homs) and Epiphania (Hama),[65]
south of Emesa[66] and especially at Emesa itself.[67] These
inscriptions begin in the late 1st century AD. The majority
are of 2nd century origin. A few date from the third
century or later.[68] Thus they are nearly all pre-Christian.[69]
In fact it looks as if Syrian Christians for some reason
very rarely commemorated their dead in this way,[70] and it is
likely that the occasional stones of the 4th and 5th centuries were still put up by pagans.[71] The usefulness of such
dated tombstones to the historian lies in the fact that they
give unambiguous evidence that an area was inhabited by
sophisticated or at least Greek-writing inhabitants. In
such an area lack of explicitly Christian inscriptions cannot
be a result of absence of inhabitants, but reflects a
shortage of Christians.

Many dated tombstones have been found in the wide Orontes
plain south of Hama. In this area there are also a few
positive indications of third and even fourth century
paganism, and a considerable number of 4th century and
even 5th century inscriptions without any religious indication. Christian inscriptions are less numerous and date
from the second half of the 5th and from the 6th centuries.[72]
This was, and is, fertile land in which were situated four

other cities besides Epiphania viz. Salamias, Arethusa, Raphanea and Mariamme.[73]

It looks as if this area remained strongly pagan to the late 4th century and beyond. The cities had Christian communities and bishops[74] but Christianity did not make anything like the same progress as it did further north. It was not chance that Arethusa saw a violent pagan reaction under Julian.[75] It is also significant that Raphanea and Mariamme were linked by Phoenician origin and history with Aradus on the coast. The territory of Aradus too was an area where paganism continued to be strong for a long time and where Christian inscriptions are few.[76]

Further south along the Orontes was Emesa (Homs), a city with a strong Christian community, a bishop and a centre of monasteries.[77] But it also had a famous temple of the sun god.[78] South of the city we observe the same phenomenon as around Epiphania: a lot of dated tombstones of the Early Empire and a few late, or very late, Christian inscriptions.[79] Many sites that have produced dated tombstones have no Christian inscriptions at all.[80] The evidence is compatible with the view that the land in the neighbourhood of Emesa was owned by a local aristocracy which remained essentially pagan.

Further south still along the Beqa valley was Heliopolis (Baalbek) the starting point of this paper. Here there are comparatively very few Christian inscriptions, although enough to show that Christianity had eventually prevailed since they come from the great sanctuary itself,[81] as well as from sites in the neighbourhood of the city.[82]

It seems to be a general rule that the pagans in S.Syria, along the Palestinian coast and in the province of Arabia, maintained their religion more strongly than those further north. In the late 5th century Severus, who was to become patriarch of Antioch, found plenty of pagan activity among the students at Berytus.[83] Further south at Caesarea the population became Christian under pressure of legislation rather than by conviction. At least this was the view of the 6th century historian Procopius, a native of the place.[84] Further south still we have a detailed account how the bishop of Gaza around 400 needed and obtained imperial permission and military backing to destroy the chief temples at Gaza.[85]

There was resistance to the destruction of temples in the Arabian provinces too,[86] and here paganism seems to have maintained itself longest of all. Roman Arabia certainly has impressive Christian sites, but not only did the carving of pagan inscriptions continue longer than elsewhere but even by the 6th century Christian inscriptions had not achieved the predominance which in N.Syria they gained in the second half of the 4th century.[87]

The success achieved by Islam in Syria after the Arab invasions is easier to understand if we bear in mind that over large parts of rural Syria the population had become Christian within the last 150 years or less.

1. 1963: 109

2. Rey Coquais, 1967, 34-5.

3. Wiegand, 1921-5. Ward-Perkins, 1970: 418-20.

4. Eg 2723 and many others. The temple, like the Roman Capitol, was dedicated to a triad, but to Jupiter, Venus and Mercury instead of Jupiter, Juno and Minerva. On the combination of Roman with Syrian features see P.Collart and P.Coupel, 1951, 134-41.

5. Eg.2909, 2923, 2926, 2925 Iovio Optimo Beelsedi, 2743 ex responso dei Conari, 2929-38 dedications at sanctuary of Dea Syria Nihatena.

6. 2791, 2762, 2761 to imperial divi. There is no inscription to a deified living emperor.

7. No reference to Isis, or Mithras. It is just possible that 2731: Διὶ μεγίστῳ Ἐλιοπολείτῃ καὶ θεῷ Ἐγυπτίῳ is a reference to Sarapis. More likely both epithets refer to Zeus.

8. 5 inscriptions all of a public nature.

9. 2715.

10. J.Geffken, 1929: 120-6.

11. Eusebius VC III,58; Praep.Evang.IV, 16, 22; Theophania II, 14 ed. H.Gressmann in Gr.Christl. Schriftsteller XI, 2, (1904) 85; Sozomen HE. V,10; Cassiodorus Hist.Trip.VI, 12, 6.

12. Theodoret HE III, 3; Chron.Paschale, ed.Bonn I, 546; Cassidorus loc.cit.

13. Theodoret Hist.Rel. 9, PG LXXXII, 1384.

14. Theodoret HE IV, 22 Ephraim Vita S.Juliani transl. G.Vossius in Acta Sanctorum Jun. II p.174.

15. Malalas XIII, 344; Chron.Paschale ed. Bonn.1 p.561. According to Michael Syr. IX, 33, the temple was destroyed by heavenly fire under Justinian.

16. IGLS VI p.44.

17. Michael Syr. IX, 33.

18. See table in IGLS VI p.266.

19. 2958, 2765-7, 2918, 2744, 2771-2, 2713, 2918, 2899, 2746 and perhaps 2770, 2745.

20. 2716.

21. 2927, 2771-2, 2900, 2963.

22. There are 13 Christian inscriptions out of a total 306 inscriptions in IGLS VI.

23. Mocsy, 1970: 199-212.

24. Honorary inscriptions: 2761-98.

25. The last inscription 'ex decreto decurionum' honours the Caesar Galerius (296-306).

26. Eg 2711-7, 2723, 2727.

27. Such are the Greek dedications in the great sanctuary 2728-31, 2751, 2755 and at rural sanctuaries 2905-6, 2916, 2921, 2930.

28. Downey, 1961: 246-69.

29. Brown, 1971: 40.

30. Eg Theodoret HE III, 3; Chron.Paschale,ed.Bonn I.p.546.

31. See the article 'Citations bibliques dans l'épigraphie Grecque', DACL III, 1731-56. by L.Jalabert.

32. 18, 1633, 2001.

33. Mohlberg, 1960, 224-7 (LXXV-VI, 1556-65).

34. Prentice, 1906: 137-50. One suspects Deuteronomy 6,9 and also 6,1 was behind the custom. It seems to be agreed that Syrian and Mesopotamian Christianity was strongly influenced by Judaism, eg.Segal, 1970: 120; S.Jerome Vir.Illust.3, on Nazaraeans at Beroea; and G.Bardy: Saint Jerome et l'évangile selon les Hébreux, Mélanges de science religieuse III (1946) 5 ff.

35. 476 of 236 AD with a religiously neutral inscription is the earliest dated lintel from Antiochene territory. 393-5 of 272/3 are the earliest Christian door-inscriptions. 1545 of 325 is the earliest Apamean lintel inscription and simply records the builders, as does 1908 of 344.

36. Tchalenko, 1953-8.

37. See the production of dated inscriptions in successive half-centuries in the neighbourhoods of Antioch, Apamea and Chalcis:

	Antioch	Apamea	Chalcis
200 - 250	9	8	2
251 - 300	2	5	2
301 - 350	13	6	2
351 - 400	33	18	2
401 - 450	28	29	2
451 - 500	31	25	2
501 - 550	18	42	6
551 - 600	15	52	4
7th Century	2	3	2

38. Tchalenko, 1950: 389-97.

39. 393.

40. 594 (326/7)

41. 600, 443, 518, 596, 396, 542-3.

42. See table of date inscriptions IGLS IV p.375-8.

43. 652.

44. The oldest epigraphically dated church is at Fafertin, IGLS 389 of 372. Butler, 1929:25ff would date some churches as early as the mid 4th century stylistically. Tchalenko, 1953-8, Vol.1: 332 places Qirqbize, which seems to have originated as a chapel attached to a villa, in the first third of the 4th century, ibid. vol.3:34-6, inscr. No.39 (Has);No 39a (Herbet Muqa),- Theodosian.

45. G.Tchalenko, 1953-8, vol.2: Pl.CCIV.

46. The earliest monastery was Gindarus to west of limestone hills: Theodoret HR 2, 1313 BC.
In or near plain of Dana: Teleda 1: HR IV, 1340 D, this had many daughter houses:ibid 1352 A.
Teleda 2: HR XXV, 1368A
Telanisus: Syr.Life of S.Symeon,ed.Hilgenfeld -Lietzmann, 25.
Monastery of Bassus;Theodoret HR.1469D.
On monasticism in this area see Festugière,1969: 312-13 and Tchalenko 19 1953-8, Vol.1.

47. The property of the Persian prince Hormisdas was probably a gift from the emperor to whom it eventually returned. For its location see IGLS 528,2.

48. Libanius Or XXX.

49. Tchalenko, 1953-8, Vol.1: 404-21.

50. Vast number of monasteries: ibid 151-4.

51. See ibid vol.3, 57 for border of Antiochene territory. Tchalenko has not examined the Apamean villages as thoroughly as those of Antioch.

52. Eg at Frikya: 1415 (364); Kerratin: 1625 (368) Hass: 1509 (372) 1523 (376) 1507 (378).

53. Hermits and monasteries at Chalcis: Theodoret HR 1328, 1337. If Nikertai (Theodoret HR 1325) was the decisive influence one would look for the monastery at Naqira near Kafartab (Dussaud, 1927:184) rather than at Qarrutiye (Tchalenko 1953-8. vol.3:101). But Theodoret Ep.119, PG LXXXIII, 1329, placing it three miles from Apamea, favours Qarrutiye.

54. Table IGLS IV.

55. Sozomen VII, 15: militant pagans from Lebanon called in to defend the temples of Apamea and its neighbour-hood.

56. Lassus, 1935: 230-1.

57. cf below.
However the area also included a region of 'late development' in the basalt region of the Gebel Ala. But there Christianisation and 'development' i.e. the building of houses sufficiently monumental to have inscribed lintels, may well have happened at the same time.

58. See in IGLS IV inscriptions of Seyh Ali Kasoun, Tamak, Esfin, Nawa, Oumm et Tin.

59. Particularly at and around Anasartha: Mouterde and Poidebard, 1945: 193-7, IGLS II,281-301.

60. Inscriptions in IGLS V.

61. Dated tombstones must be distinguished from inscribed and dated entrances to monumental tombs, underground chambers or rock cut tombs.

62. Mouterde and Poidebard, op.cit.210 No.40-1 (Hierapolis)
213 No.48 (Memele) 214 No.50 (Kalkoum).

63. Eg IGLS 1498. There are very few from the limestone
plateau. The bulk of the dated tombstone of IGLS IV
comes from further south. Antioch has so far produced
very few dated tombstones like 755 of 166 AD.

64. 1378, 1389, 1355, 1367, 1370.

65. 1996, 1848, 1974, 1928, 1871-2, 1530, 2505, 2509, 2547.

66. See IGLS V p.247-313 with dated tombstones at Bab Omar
Zaidal, Feirouzi, Meskene Borg Qattine,Koufr Abde etc.
Between Epiphania (Hama) and Emesa (Homs):2015, 2085,
(5/6 AD), 2095, 2096-7, 2104, 2132,2148/9, 2163, 2165,
2170 (432), 2177, 2184 (303), 2185, 2190-2, 2195-6,
2198.

67. At least 62 stones between 78/9 and 385/6 AD. They
include the stones of the princely family of
Samsigeramus.

68. 2693 (425), 2577 (313), 2586 (309-10).

69. 2659 (479-80) is a dated Christian tombstone, but unlike
Christian dated lintels over entrances to tombs, these
are extremely rare.

70. Lefebure, 1902 shows that Christians sometimes used
dated tombstones in Egypt. But (a) the vast majority
of tombstones are undated. (b) the dated tombstones
are nearly all from Alexandria, the most Hellenised
part of Egypt, or very late.

71. Eg 2349 (335/6) or (perhaps) 2693, 3079.

72. See Fig. 2.

73. On cities see A.H.M.Jones,1971: 260-8.

74. See Devréesse, 1945: 181 ff.

75. Soz. HE V,10 (194 B).

76. See Rey Coquais,(IGLS VII)especially the inscriptions
of the great sanctuary of Baetocaeca. As at Baalbek,
the resiliences of paganism and the relative weakness of
Christianity is shown by the scarcity of Christian
inscriptions rather than the presence of pagan ones:
cf Rey Coquais, 1975: 256-8.

77. Devréesse, 1945: 203-4.

78. Temple of sun god: Pagan reaction under Julian:
    Theodoret HE III,7, 5; Chron.Pasch.PG XCII, 741.

79. See Fig.3.

80. Deir Balba, Ferouzi, Bab Omar, Qatine, Kefr Adi,
    Shinshar, etc.

81. 2832-5.

82. IGLS VI,has about 15 Christian inscriptions out of a
    total of 306 inscriptions from city and neighbourhood.

83. Zach. Vit.Sev.(ed.Kugener) p. 57 ff.

84. Procopius, Anecdota XI,26. Precariousness of Christians
    in Palestine in the 6th cent: Cyril of Scyth.V.Sabae,62.

85. Marc the Deacon V.Porph. Popular attacks on monks sent
    to destroy temples in Phoenicia: John Chrysostomus,
    Ep.51,123, 126; Theodoret HE V, 29.

86. Soz HE VII, 15.

87. See dated inscriptions in E.Littmann, R.Magie and
    R.Stuart,Syria, III A.

Alföldy,G. 1963. Geschichte des religiösen Lebens in
Aquincum, Acta Archaeol.Acad.Sc.Hung.XIII:109 ff.

Brown,P. 1971. The World of Late Antiquity. London:Thames
and Hudson.

Butler,H.C. 1929. Early Churches in Syria.Princeton:U.P.

Collart,P. and Coupel,P. 1951.L'autel monumental de Baalbek.
Paris: Geuthner.

Devréesse,R.1945. Le patriarcat d'Antioche.Paris:Libr.
Lecoffre.

Downey,G.1961. A History of Antioch in Syria.Princeton:U.P.

Dussaud,R.1927 Topographie historique de la Syrie antique
et médiévale.Paris,Geuthner.

Festugière,A.J.1969. Antioche paienne et Chrétienne.Paris:
Boccard.

Geffken,J.1929. Der Ausgang des griechisch - römischen
Heidentums. Heidelberg: Winter.

Jalabert,L. and Mouterde,R.and others.1929ff. Inscriptions Grecques et Latines de la Syrie,(IGLS) Vols.1-VII.Paris: Geuthner.

Jones,A.H.M.1971. Cities of the Eastern Provinces of the Roman Empire (2nd ed.).Oxford:U.P.

Lassus,J.1935 Inventaire archéologique.Beirut:Imprimerie Catholique.

Lefebure,G.1902, Recueil des inscriptions grecques chrétiennes d'Égypte.Cairo: Service des Antiquités de l'Égypte.

Littmann,E., Magie R.,and Stuart,R.1921. Syria:Publications of the Princeton University Archaeological Expedition to Syria. Vol.IIIA. Leyden: Brill.

Mocsy,Y.A.,1970, Gesellschaft und Romanisation in der romischen Provinz Moesia Superior. Amsterdam: Hakkert.

Mohlberg,L.C.1960. Sacramentarium Gelasianum. Rome: Herder.

Mouterde,R. and Poidebard,A. 1945. Le limes de Chalcis. Paris: Geuthner.

Prentice,W.K.1906. Magical formulae on lintels of the Christian period in Syria; A.J.A.,X.

Rey-Coquais,J.P. 1975 Arados et sa pérée aux epoques grecque, romaine et byzantine. Beirut: Inst.Franç.d'archéol. 1967. Baalbek et Beqa: Inscriptions Grecques et Latines de la Syrie (IGLS).Vol.6. Paris:Geuthner. Inscriptions d'Arados IGLS . Vol.7. Paris: Geuthner.

Segal,J.B. 1970. Edessa. Oxford:U.P.

Tchalenko G.1950. La Syrie du nord: étude économique: Actes du VI e Congrès International des études byzantines. Paris. 1953-8 Villages antiques de la Syrie du nord. 3 vols. Paris: Geuthner.

Ward-Perkins,J.B. and A.Boethius,1970.Etruscan and Roman Architecture. London,Penguin.

Wiegand,T.1921-5. Baalbek. Berlin and Leipzig.

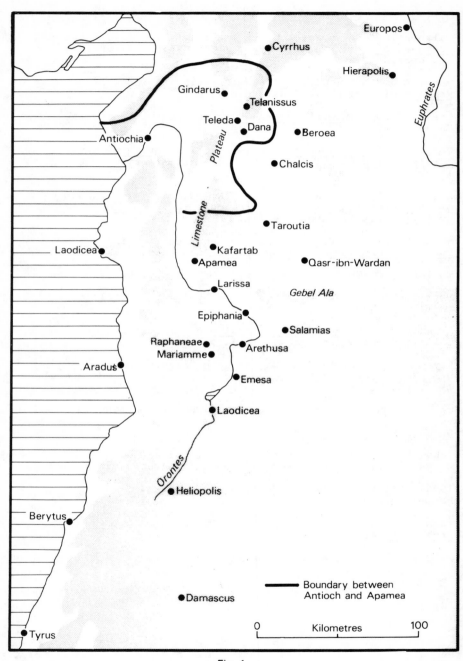

Fig. 1

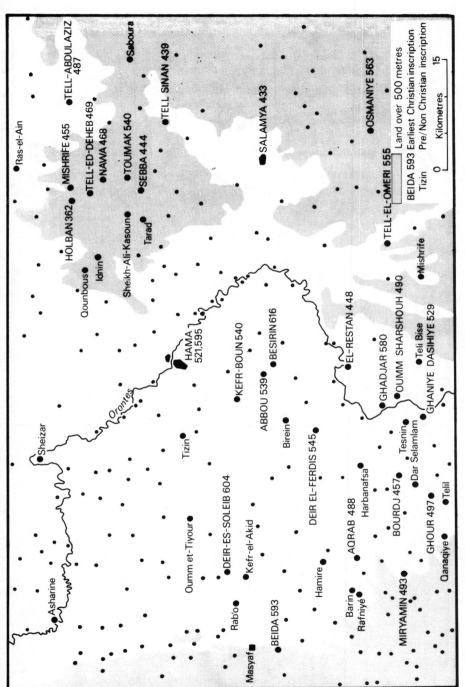

Fig. 2

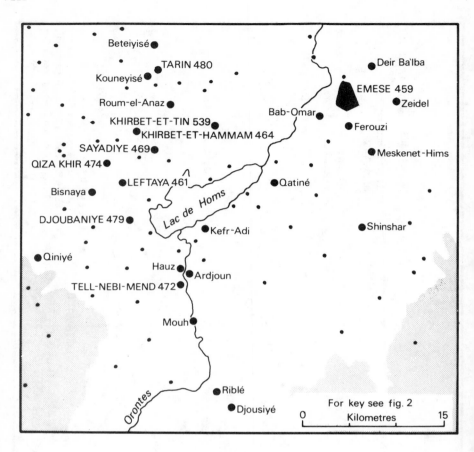

Fig. 3

IX

PROBLEMS ARISING FROM
THE CONVERSION OF SYRIA

IT is the aim of this paper to ask questions rather than to
answer them. The area with which I am concerned is a strip of
central Syria extending from the Euphrates in the north to
Baalbek (ancient Heliopolis) in the south. This region has a large number
of village-remains from late antiquity, some of them exceptionally
well preserved. These remains have yielded a large number of inscriptions, of which a significant proportion bears a date. They are being
collected in the volumes of the *Inscriptions grecques et latines de la Syrie*.
Seven volumes have appeared.[1]

The inscriptions start in the early empire and continue to the end of
the sixth century. They thus start in pagan times and cover the whole
development of Syrian Christianity.[2] Only a few of the Christian
inscriptions come from the great cities of Syria, for example Antioch,
Aleppo [Beroea], the ancient Apamea, or Homs [Emesa]. They do
not therefore throw light on the development of urban Christianity,
which at Antioch especially was of great importance, and of long
standing. The development reflected by the inscriptions is the
conversion of the countryside.

The first conclusion suggested by this material is that there was very
little rural Christianity in this area before Constantine. In the territory
of Antioch the flow of Christian inscriptions starts, with only a few
isolated exceptions,[3] after 324, the year Constantine gained control of
the east.[4] Contrary to the opinion of Harnack[5] it would seem that

---

[1] *IGLS.*

[2] See list of dated inscriptions *IGLS* 4, pp 375–8.

[3] Isolated early Christian inscriptions from territory of Antioch: *IGLS* nos 393–5
(272/3), from Aradus: *ibid* no 4042 (287).

[4] Start of the Christian series after Constantine's conquest: *IGLS* nos 594 (326), 600 (335),
443 (336/7), 518 (341/2), 596 (349), 396 (349/50), 542–3 (351). The series continues
without break until c600.

[5] In my opinion the negative evidence of inscriptions outweighs the plausible inferences
from a few literary passages on the basis of which A. von Harnack concluded that
rural Christianity was significant even before Constantine. See *Mission und Ausbreitung
des Christentums*, 2 (Leipzig 1906) p 279.

pre-Constantinian Christianity in Syria was largely an urban phenomenon.[6] We are once again reminded of the importance of the conversion of the emperor for the expansion of Christianity in the Roman
empire.[7]

The evidence of inscriptions suggests that Christianity spread from
north to south. Christianisation of the territory of Apamea was fifty
years or so behind that of the territory of Antioch. Further south, in
the territories of Hama [Epiphania], Homs [Emesa] and Baalbek
[Heliopolis] conversion to Christianity would appear to have been
later still, as late as the middle, or even the end, of the fifth century.
Eventually Christianity prevailed everywhere, but when the
Mohammedan Arabs broke into Syria in 634 many Syrian villages
would have been Christian for one hundred and fifty years or less.[8]
The Arabs conquered an area in which Christianity was not yet deeply
rooted.[9]

The inscriptions do not tell us how Christianity was spread, but
they do suggest that there was a relationship—at least in northern
Syria—between the settlement of hermits and monks and the expansion of Christianity in the countryside. The main area of early
Christian inscriptions in the territory of Antioch lies on both sides of
the Antioch-Aleppo [Beroea] road. Communications from villages
on each side of the road converge on the plain of Dana. It is surely
not a coincidence that the hillsides surrounding that plain were
thronged by hermits, and that some of the earliest monasteries of
Syria were founded there. This is the region where saint Symeon
Stylites was to spend some forty two years (417–59) on the top of pillars,
and where his memory has been preserved by a great monastery and
pilgrimage centre whose remains are impressive even today.[10] That
monks played an essential part in the conversion of Syria is confirmed

[6] Some evidence on urban Christianity in R. Devréese, *Le patriarcat de Antioche depuis la paix de l'église jusqu'à la conquête Arabe* (Paris 1945) caps 8, 11.
[7] A. H. M. Jones, *Constantine and the Conversion of Europe* (London 1949) pp 237–9.
[8] For the evidence see my paper 'Epigraphic Evidence [on the Christianisation of Syria'], *Akten des XI internationalen LimesKongresses, Székesfehérvar*, ed J. Fitz (Budapest 1978) pp 485–505.
[9] Paradoxically the Maronites seem to have been comparatively late arrivals in the territory in which they have maintained their identity so vigorously ever since. Their early history is still very obscure. See article 'Maron', *DACL* 10, cols 2188–202; S. Vailhé, 'Les origines religieuses des Maronites,' *EO* 4 (Paris 1900) pp 96–103, 154–62; K. S. Salibi, 'The Maronites of Lebanon under Frankish and Mamluk Rule (1099–1516)', *Arabica* (Leiden 1957) pp 288–303.
[10] A. J. Festugière, *Antioche païenne et chrétienne* (Paris 1959) pp 311–13. [G.] Tchalenko, *Villages [antiques de la Syrie du nord]*, 3 vols (Paris 1953–8) I, pp 145–82.

Problems arising from the conversion of Syria

by the contemporary testimony of the Antiochene orator Libanius writing around 380,[11] and of Sozomen, the ecclesiastical historian, a native of Gaza, writing after 440.[12]

In the territory of Apamea, and in areas further south, the history of monasticism is much more obscure. The location of the famous monastery of Nicerta is being currently sought by archaeologists.[13] There is however no reason to doubt that the monks played an important role there also.

The preceding paragraphs summarise the conclusions of an earlier paper of mine where more detailed references to the inscriptional evidence can be found.[14] Some problems arise from it. First there is a problem of method: is the approach valid? If this question is answered affirmatively, there arises the further question of how far the method can profitably be applied to other parts of the empire.[15] There are very few areas where so large a proportion of inscriptions bear a date, or where they have been so conveniently collected. On the other hand other areas have produced more extensive literary evidence to provide a check on the conclusions derived from epigraphy. North Africa and Asia Minor [16] are areas which have produced large numbers of early Christian inscriptions.

The Christianisation of Syria touches on a wider historical problem: that of the interrelation of religious and economic change. It is a fact that the area of northern Syria where Christianisation started was undergoing economic development. G. Tchalenko has examined the remains of villages on the limestone plateau between Antioch and Aleppo and traced the development of a prosperous rural society, whose livelihood depended on steadily expanding olive plantations.[17]

---

[11] Libanius, Or. 30, Pro Templis. See also G. Fowden, 'Bishops and Temples in the Eastern Empire,' JTS 29 (1978) pp 53–78.

[12] Sozomen, HE 6, 34.

[13] [P. H. E.] Voûte, ['Chronique de fouilles et prospections en Syrie de 1965 à 1970'], Anatolica 14 (Istanbul 1971–2) pp 83–137, relevant pp 92–3.

[14] For references see my 'Epigraphic Evidence'.

[15] D. I. Pallas, 'Investigation sur les monuments chrétiens de Grèce avant Constantin,' Cahiers Archéologiques 24 (Paris 1975) pp 1–19. The pre-Constantinian evidence is very thin. M. Leglay, Saturne Africain (Paris 1966) is very informative on the epigraphic evidence for the last stages of paganism and the beginnings of Christianity.

[16] F. Cumon, Les inscriptions chrétiennes de l'Asie Mineure (Rome 1895). [W. M.] Calder, 'Early Christian Epitaphs from Phrygia,' Anatolian Studies 5 (London 1955) pp 27–38; Calder, 'Philadelphia and Montanism,' BJRL 8 (1923) pp 309–54.

[17] Tchalenko, Villages I, esp pp 404–21. D. Bowder, The Age of Constantine and Julian (London 1978) p 144 stresses that the economy of the plateau involved its population in close contact with the Christian population of Antioch.

It is a plausible hypothesis that the dissolution of an older order, dominated by large landowners, favoured conversion to Christianity.[18] The areas further south, which were converted later were also undergoing economic development. They too have provided extensive late-ancient remains[19] but the period of rural building like that of conversion was delayed. South of the limestone plateau expansion was presumably not based on monoculture of olive trees. Perhaps there was a settlement of previously nomadic tribesmen, and an advance of agriculture at the expense of nomadism.[20] Village development was in fact a characteristic of many frontier areas in late antiquity. It can be observed in Syria, Palestine,[21] Arabia,[22] Cyrene, Tripolitania and perhaps even Egypt.[23] It is a phenomenon the scale of which has not been fully taken into account in A. H. M. Jones's gloomy portrayal of the condition of the late-Roman peasantry.[24] It has still to be fully explained.

It is conceivable that Christianisation favoured village development. As we have seen Christianity was spread by monks. The process of conversion was preceded and accompanied by the settlement of hermits, and later by the foundation of an enormous number of monasteries. Hermits and abbots were men of authority. They were influential locally, and they were also heard with respect by members of the imperial administration.[25] I would suggest that by their presence in villages these men changed the balance of power between city and countryside. They were effective patrons, who could protect men

[18] In North Africa too rural conversion took place in combination with economic development based on the production of olive oil. Both happened earlier in Africa. See W. H. C. Frend, *The Donatist Church* (Oxford 1952) pp 42–8.

[19] J. Lassus, *Inventaire archéologique de la région au nord-est de Hama* (Beirut 1935).

[20] H. Seyrig, 'Caractère de l'histoire d'Émèse, *Syria* 36 (Paris 1959) pp 184–92. R. Sullivan, 'The dynasty of Emesa,' in H. Temporini, *Aufstieg und Niedergang der römischen Welt*, 2, pt 8 (Berlin 1978) pp 198–219 is pure political and military history but cites literature.

[21] M. Avi Yonah, 'The Economics of Byzantine Palestine,' *Israel Exploration Journal* 8 (Jerusalem 1958) pp 39–51. S. A. M. Gichon, 'Roman Frontier Cities in the Negev,' *Acts of the 6th International Congress of Limes Studies* (Zagreb 1961) pp 195–207. R. Paret, 'Les villes de Syrie du sud et les routes commerciales d'Arabie à la fin du VIe siècle,' *Akten des XI internationalen Byzantinisten Kongresses* (Munich 1960) pp 438–44.

[22] G. M. Harper, 'Village Administration in the Roman Province of Syria,' *Yale Classical Studies* 1 (1928) pp 103–68.

[23] R. Goodchild, *Libyan Studies* (London 1977) pp 8–9, 92, 255–6. A. C. Johnson and L. C. West, *Byzantine Egypt: Economic Studies* (Princeton 1949) p 32 concluded that Egypt was prosperous.

[24] A. H. M. Jones, *The Later Roman Empire* (Oxford 1964) 2, p 823.

[25] P. Brown, 'The Rise and Function of the Holy Man in Late Antiquity,' *JRS* 61 (1971) pp 80–101. Interference with tax collection: Theodoret *Hist Rel* 17 PG 82 (1864) col 1413.

Problems arising from the conversion of Syria

from the demands of landlords, creditors or tax collectors. They were in a position to mitigate the effect of debt, that perpetual threat to the existence, or at least freedom, of small peasants. They could settle disputes between villagers. Henceforth there would be less need to visit the city for the sake of justice. Again, wealthy villagers might leave legacies to a local monastery or church,[26] with the result that the countryside retained resources which in earlier times might have been diverted to conspicuous public expenditure in the city. It is at least arguable that such development contributed both to the flourishing condition of villages and to the decline of cities which happened in the east no less than in the west, even if the decline of the eastern cities was considerably delayed.[27]

I would like to mention now some problems of narrower scope. According to Tchalenko there is a distinction between the layout of monasteries in the territory of Apamea and those in the territory of Antioch. Antiochene monasteries seem to be open to the world, Apamean ones shut-off. The distinction is particularly obvious in the planning of churches. In the territory of Antioch we find large separate churches which seem to have been open to the villagers. Around Apamea, monasteries have small chapels, tightly tied into the layout of the rest of the buildings.[28] Tchalenko's book is based on a more thorough study of Antiochene than of Apamean remains.[29] If his observation is nevertheless valid it raises the question: how can we account for the coexistence of two plans in adjacent areas? In the monophysite schism Syria I, the province of which Antioch was the capital, was largely monophysite while Syria II, the province of Apamea, was on the whole Chalcedonian.[30] While the religious division did not correspond precisely to the administrative one we are left with the possibility that the planning of the monasteries reflects the religious allegiance of their monks.[31]

---

[26] E. Wipsycka, *Les resources et les activités économiques des églises en Égypte du IVe au VIIIe siècle* (Brussels 1972) p 37.

[27] D. Claude, *Die byzantinische Stadt* (Munich 1969). E. Kirsten, *Die byzantinische Stadt, Berichte zum XI internationalen Byzantinisten Kongress 1958* (Munich 1958).

[28] Tchalenko, *Villages* 1, p 178; 2, plate 51.

[29] He is extending his survey year by year though the material has not yet been published. See Voûte p 85.

[30] W. H. C. Frend, *The Rise of the Monophysite Movement* (Cambridge 1972) pp 223-9 and map on pp 250-1. In the city of Antioch itself monophysites were never a majority. See G. Downey, *A History of Antioch in Syria* (Princeton 1961) p 510.

[31] Passages like Theophanes, *sa* 6003, pp 153.29–154.2; Evagrius, *HE* 3, 32; Mansi, 8, pp 425-9, 1130-8; *Collectio Avellana* (*CSEL* 35) esp p 139; Michael the Syrian, 1,

A final problem. Among the Christian inscriptions of Syria there are a large number bearing the formula εἷς θεός 'One God' or 'God is unique', or longer phrases including this formula.[32] The inscriptions derive from tombs, churches and private houses. The majority come from the lintels of doorways. One is inevitably reminded of *Deut* 6, 14: 'Hear O Israel, the Lord is our God, the Lord is one. And these words which I command you this day you shall write them on the doorposts and on your gates.' Jews have of course always obeyed this commandment literally.[33] Inevitably one asks whether the Christianity of the Syrian countryside was strongly influenced by Jewish Christianity. One thinks of the Nazaraeans of Beroea [Aleppo], among whom Jerome claimed to have seen a gospel according to saint Matthew written in Hebrew.[34] One also recalls that the Christianity of Edessa is said to have been strongly influenced by Judaism.[35]

The εἷς θεός inscriptions are not evenly distributed over Syria. The area south of the limestone plateau, that is most of Syria II, has produced very few of them.[36] In the Arabian and Palestinian provinces it seems to be restricted to particular areas, and even there the number of inscriptions is small. A few come from the territory around Damascus.[37] Some more have been found in the Hauran and Batanaea around Bostra.[38] This is another region where Jewish-Christians emigrated at the time of the sack of Jerusalem.[39] Some

---

cols 270–4 show that the monasteries of Syria II acting collectively were Chalcedonian. But Tchalenko, *Villages* 2, plate 153 shows that at least some of the monasteries on the Apamean side of the limestone plateau were monophysite.

[32] A mass of εἷς θεός material, mainly Christian, but also pagan and Jewish, has been assembled in [E.] Peterson, ΕΙΣ ΘΕΟΣ, *Forschungen zur Religion und Literatur des alten und neuen Testaments*, NF 24 (Göttingen 1926). See also the indices of the volumes of *IGLS*.

[33] W. O. E. Oesterley and G. E. Box, *The Religion and Worship of the Synagogue* (London 1911) pp 447–9, 454 *seq*. On the Shema prayer see *ibid* pp 364 *seq*, 432, 477 *seq*.

[34] Jerome *Vir Illustr* 3; J. N. D. Kelly, *Jerome His Life Writings and Controversies* (London 1975) p 65.

[35] J. B. Segal, *Edessa, the Blessed City* (Oxford 1970) p 100; H. J. W. Drijvers, 'Edessa und das jüdische Christentum,' *Vigiliae Christianae* 24 (Amsterdam 1970) pp 4–33.

[36] *IGLS* 4 (regions of Apamea and Laodicca) has twenty-five inscriptions; *IGLS* 5 (Hama and Homs) has six. *IGLS* 6 (Baalbek) has none; *IGLS* 7 (Aradus) has one.

[37] Peterson p 27 nos 70–1, no 72 is in the Golan.

[38] *Ibid* pp 28–37, nos 74–85.

[39] For the date see W. H. C. Frend, *Martyrdom and Persecution in the Early Church* (Oxford 1965) p 177 n 116. Eusebius *HE* 3, 5. Epiphanius *Haer.* 18, 1; 29.7. Origen debated the pre-existence and independent hypostasis of the Son with bishops at Bostra: Eusebius, *HE* 6, 33. See J. E. Coulton and H. Chadwick, *Alexandrine Christianity*, (London 1954) p 430.

Problems arising from the conversion of Syria

inscriptions derive from the neighbourhood of Jerusalem itself.[40] The oldest of the 'Syrian' inscriptions come from Dura Europos on the Euphrates, and must therefore be earlier than 256.[41] The bulk of the inscriptions date from the fourth and first half of the fifth century. They fade out in the second half of the century, and almost cease in the sixth.[42]

The second large group of εἷς θεός inscriptions has been found in middle and upper Egypt. Over a hundred are known. The great majority of them are on tombstones. In Egypt the forumula has not been found on lintels and surprisingly, on only one papyrus.[43] Most of the inscriptions are undated or only dated with reference to the indiction, which does not provide an absolute date. But the tombstones continue into the period of Arab rule.[44] In addition to the Greek inscriptions there are numerous Coptic ones bearing the formula.[45] It would therefore seem that the phrase continued to be popular in Egypt, or at least in parts of Egypt, long after it had ceased to be so in Syria. A few isolated inscriptions have been found outside Syria (using the term in its widest sense) and Egypt. But it looks as if Syria and Egypt were the areas where the formula had special importance for Christians.[46]

The εἷς θεός inscriptions raise many problems. How did this slightly adapted[47] Jewish formula come to be used almost as a proclamation of religious identity[48] by so many Christian villagers? Why was the popularity of the phraise limited to some areas only? Why did the use of the phrase fade out in Syria when it did? Did the

---

[40] Peterson, pp 37–40, nos 86–91.

[41] C. H. Kraeling, *Dura Europos: Final Report*, 8, pt 2 (Yale 1956) p 95; P. V. C. Baur, M. I. Rostovtzeff, A. R. Bellinger, *Dura Europos: Preliminary Report* 4 (Yale 1923) p 150 nos 291–2.

[42] Peterson has only two sixth century inscriptions from the Syrian area: nos 6 and 30.

[43] Peterson p 275.

[44] G. L. Lefebure, *Recueil des inscriptions grècques chrétiennes d'Égypte* (Cairo 1907).

[45] Peterson p 76.

[46] Peterson has also assembled a good deal of non epigraphic material including evidence bearing on the Jewish and pagan use of the formula.

[47] The formula was used in popular acclamations against bishop Ibas at Edessa: J. Flemming, *Akten der ephesinischen Synode vom Jahre 449*, *AAWG*, PhK, ns 15 (1917) pp 15, 17, 41. It was used by bishops in acclamation at the council of Constantinople: Mansi 8, pp 49a, 1083; also at Chalcedon: *ibid* 7 pp 49, 1087, 1091.

[48] [M.] Simon, [*Verus Israel*] (Paris 1948) p 357, n 2 cites Epiphanius, *Haer* 1, 30, 12 where the defeat of Jewish magic by the name of Jesus and the sign of the cross is acclaimed: εἷς θεὸς ὁ βοηθῶν τοῖς Χριστιανοῖς
On the use of the formula in apocryphal Acts of apostles and in hagiography to acclaim the marvellous divine power revealed by a miracle see Peterson pp 183–8.

use of the phrase derive from Jewish Christianity or did it perhaps arise in the course of the continuous competition between Judaism and Christianity in Syria?[49] Should the rise and fall of the formula be linked with that of the Antiochene theology? Or is it perhaps part of the prehistory of so-called monophysitism? Thanks to Peterson we have a great deal of material—and some interesting suggestions.[50] But the answers still have to be worked out.

[49] See Simon pp 220, 356–93.

[50] See also his interesting suggestions in εἷς θεός in der sepulkralen Epigraphik,' *Zeitschrift für Katholische Theologie* 58 (Vienna 1934) pp 400–2 and 'Jüdisches und christliches Morgengebeet in Syrien,' *ibid* pp 110–43. The latter, based on a passage in the Acts of the martyr Romanus, ed H. Delehaye, *An Bol* 50 (1932) pp 241 *seq*, see esp p 256, suggests that our formula was part of a morning prayer in use in Syria.

X

GOVERNMENT
AND ADMINISTRATION
IN THE LATE EMPIRE
(TO AD 476)

When Diocletian and Constantine rebuilt the structure of the Empire shattered by the events of the third century they were faced with many problems that had not existed during the Principate (Rostovtzeff, 1957; Cook, Adcock *et al.*, 1939; Walser and Pekáry, 1962; Alföldy, 1979, 139–64). The Empire was now under more or less continuous attack, often at more than one frontier at a time. The needs of defence impelled the government to make much greater and inevitably more unpopular demands on the manpower and resources of the Empire than ever before. At the same time it had lost cohesion. The army, once the great romanizer, had become regionalized, and the soldiers' concern for their native province, and often their attachment to particular generals had become stronger than their loyalty to the Empire as a whole. The economic ties linking frontier areas with the central provinces had grown weaker as the provinces had become self-sufficient in many of the items that they had previously imported from Mediterranean areas. There was thus less need for traders and shippers. The need had been further reduced by the fact that armies and civil servants had come to be paid in produce, raised and distributed by compulsory transport duties (MacMullen, 1976, 173ff.; Hopkins, 1980, 106 and 123–5). As the economy had become more localized the Roman way of life had lost some of its appeal. Even under the most favourable conditions romanization ceased to advance; in the north-western provinces it went into retreat.

From the point of view of administration the most harmful aspect was the weakening of city organization in Britain and parts of Spain and Gaul as well as the Balkan provinces. By leaving most administrative tasks to city authorities the Empire had been able to manage with a very small staff of officials of its own. This would no longer be possible after the third century. Another damaging development was that the patriotic pride of the ruling and privileged Roman nation which had once held together the empire had been diluted out of existence with the conferment of citizenship on all free inhabitants of the empire by Caracalla (AD 212). More damaging still, privilege of citizenship had been progressively replaced by privilege of class, the division of the inhabitants of the empire into *honestiores* (soldiers, decurions, equestrians and senators) and *humiliores* (everybody else, including the peasants), with the inevitable long term result that those without privilege became completely alienated from the Empire (Garnsey, 1970; de Ste Croix, 1981, 474ff.).

The circumstances required a thorough reform of the administration. Diocletian, a very great emperor, seems to have grasped the scale of the problem quite early in his reign, and the reforms introduced by him and carried further in some important respects by Constantine, succeeded in giving the Empire a second lease of life. Diocletian saw that the Empire would henceforth require more than one emperor, and that the administration would have to become much more active at provincial level. He therefore established a tetrarchy of two senior emperors (*Augusti*) and two junior partners (*Caesars*), and he subdivided almost all the provinces of the Empire, doubling their number to around a hundred. The doubling of provincial governors caused a problem of supervision, which he solved by creating an intermediate unit of administration between court and province: the diocese. The system may have been established by 293 (Barnes, 1982, 203–5, 224–5; cf also Jones, 1954 otherwise Noetlichs, 1982). The three-tiered structure of administration remained intact until the end of the Roman Empire in the West, and in the East into the seventh century.

The tetrarchic system did not last, but from the reign of Diocletian to the deposition of the last western emperor in 476 there were relatively few years when there was only one emperor. After the death of Constantine there were normally two or three. When Theodosius I died in 395 he was for practical purposes the sole ruler, but then the Empire was divided between his sons Arcadius and Honorius, never again to be united under a single monarch. Nevertheless in law, all emperors (*Augusti* and any Caesars) continued to form a college which jointly ruled an undivided Empire. Imperial constitutions were issued in the names of all emperors. One coinage circulated over the whole Empire. The inhabitants enjoyed one citizenship. For most of the fourth century there was one elite which provided officials for all the Empire. Nevertheless east and west were growing apart. The development accelerated as Constantinople grew into a second Rome, and the real capital of the east (Dagron, 1974). After 395 east and west were for practical purposes separate realms, linked but also divided by their past history.

A new feature of the fully developed system of the Late Empire was the separation of military (Part 3, Chapter 7) and civil administration. Under the Principate a senator was thought equally capable of civil government and military command, and the governorships of important provinces combined both types of administration. Not so under the Late Empire, although the transition was gradual. We hear of a number of dukes in charge of parts of frontier armies under Diocletian, but in many frontier provinces the governor was still in command of the troops (Seston, 1946, 313–19). The praetorian prefect continued to act as commander-in-chief (under the emperor), and a vicar might deputize for the prefect in his military as well as his civil capacity. The separation was completed at the earliest by Constantine. He created a permanent mobile field army commanded by a master of the infantry (*magister peditum*) and a master of the cavalry (*magister equitum*). It was probably also in his reign that the frontier units still under the control of governors were placed under dukes (van Berchem, 1952, 100–5). By the 360s the masters of the soldiers had become the superiors of the dukes of the frontier armies. The praetorian prefects had lost all military authority and the two hierarchies were united only in the person of the emperor. The two branches of the administration grew entirely distinct. The commanders had purely military careers, the governors no military experience whatsoever. Besides a growing proportion of the generals and of their troops was of barbarian origin (Demandt, 1980), with the result that some of the most important positions came to be held by men born outside the Empire. The new system had advantages. Armies were commanded by experts. A general had no authority over the departments that paid and supplied his troops, and this made rebellion more difficult. But the division also involved risk of conflict between the civil and military branches of government.

The structure of the developed system was something like this. The emperor was head of state and source of all authority. His unique position was proclaimed by increasingly elaborate protocol and ceremony. For much of the fourth century emperors travelled from crisis-spot to crisis-spot, and spent longer periods of time at large cities with easy access to frontier areas, Antioch, Nicomedia, Naissus, Serdica, Sirmium, Trier. Court and central administration travelled with the emperor. Eventually this proved intolerably inconvenient, and there was a return to a permanent capital. By 395 Constantinople was the permanent imperial residence in the east. In the west this development was never completed, but Trier, Milan and especially Ravenna came near to becoming capitals at different times.

The court (*comitatus*) consisted of the officials and attendants of the emperor's household (*sacrum cubiculum*), his advisers (*consistorium*), the confidential shorthand writers who took down the discussions and decisions of the *consistorium*, and might be sent out to see their enforcement in the provinces (*notarii*), and last but not least the principal officers of state with their office staffs. Chief of these was the praetorial prefect. Although he had lost his military command he remained responsible for the feeding and supplying of the army, and since troops, like all other imperial employees, were paid most of their wages in kind, he was in fact the principal finance-officer of the Empire. He was also the superior of all provincial governors, and had great influence over appointments. A wide range of laws concerning provincial government was addressed to him, often because the laws had been promulgated in response to the prefect's request. As deputy of the emperor the praetorian prefect exercised appellate jurisdiction over the whole

Empire. The prefect might fairly be described as the premier-minister of his part of the Empire.

Second in importance among the great officers was the *magister officiorum*, an office which was split from the praetorian prefecture by Constantine. The creation of this post was a consequence of the great numerical growth of the central administration for he was the principal administrative official – as it were the registrar – of the court. The master of the offices was head of the secretarial departments (*scrinia*) which had developed out of the offices staffed by freedmen under the early principate. He was also responsible for the public post, which he supervised by means of his own corps of inspectors the *agentes in rebus*. Through the same *agentes*, whose activities were far from secret, he received information from all over the Empire. Since *agentes in rebus* finished their career as head of the offices (*officia*) of praetorian prefects and other important officers, the *magister officiorum* was able to obtain information how these officers conducted their administration, and to pass on his knowledge to the emperor. The *magister officiorum* was in at least administrative command of the palace guards (*scholae palatinae*). The *magister officiorum* was also concerned with the reception of ambassadors, and from time to time might be sent on an embassy himself. He was often the official chosen to represent the emperor at church councils. The nature of his responsibilities made it essential that the *magister officiorum* should be a man whom the emperor, or whoever else directed policy, could trust absolutely. They were often 'new men'.

Two other officers of the *comitatus*, the *comes sacrarum largitionum*, and the *comes rei privatae*, were concerned with finance. The former was responsible for gold and silver mines, mints, and taxes levied in precious metals. In other words his sphere was the collection, production and expenditure of money. Owing to the extent of the state natural economy, controlled by the praetorian prefect, he did not have the importance of a modern chancellor of the exchequer but the *stipendium*, paid in money, and above all the donatives given on imperial anniversaries still played an essential part in maintaining morale and loyalty of the army. By depriving his Caesar Julian of a *comes sacrarum largitionum*, Constantius, the senior emperor, hoped to prevent the development of dangerously close ties between Julian and his troops. The *comes rei privatae* was responsible for the administration of the emperor's estates. His officials collected rents, and claimed properties forfeited to the emperor, as for instance the estates of men found guilty of treason. The emperor's private estates were extensive, and their income enabled an emperor to reward members of the *comitatus* and others with the generosity that was expected of him. The last of the great civil officers was the *quaestor*. He was the direct superior of the secretarial departments (*scrinia*) who were responsible for dealing with the vast mass of petitions, consultations and appeals addressed to the emperor. The *quaestor* was also responsible for the drafting of imperial constitutions. In addition to the civilian officials there were the military members of the *comitatus*, above all the *magistri militum praesentales* commanding the field army units accompanying the emperor, and the two *comites domesticorum* who were in charge of the corps of officer cadets, the *domestici et protectores*.

The great civil officers of the *comitatus* represented each of the principal concerns of a Roman emperor: the raising and spending of taxes to supply and pay army and civil service, the making of law and the administration of justice, and the answering of a vast mass of miscellaneous requests for assistance by individuals, corporations, cities and provinces. The military officers represented the fact that for most of the fourth, but not the fifth century, the emperor was active commander in chief of fighting armies and that even when he ceased to be that he had to maintain a special relationship with the officer corps, symbolized by the ceremony of the adoration of the sacred purple. Towards the end of the fourth century the total civilian strength of the court was around 3,000. The palace guards (*scholae*) amounted to as many men again. The total of 6,000 does not of course include the units of the field army attached to the emperor (*palatini*).

At diocesan level the administration was represented by vicars (the diocese of Oriens being governed by a *comes*, and Egypt by a *praefectus Augustalis*). These had at their disposal an office staff of around 300, divided between judicial and financial departments. Originally, the deputy praetorial 'prefects' might have some military function too, but from the reign of Constantine onwards their main duties were the distribution of levies and the hearing of appeals. The departments of the *sacra largitio* and the *res privata* also had officials at diocesan level. Up to a point vicars were the superiors of the provincial governors, but orders were often passed directly to governors from the *comitatus*. Provincial governors and citizens of the provinces in their turn often by-passed the vicar, to communicate with the *comitatus* directly.

The governors of eventually about 119 provinces, (de Ste Croix, 1981, 491) had *officia* around 100 strong (the proconsuls had a larger staff), of basically the same structure as those of the higher officials, being made up of three sections: judicial, financial and sub-clerical. The first two represented a governor's principal activities: jurisdiction and taxation. The governor's court had replaced local courts for most kinds of case, civil or criminal. The governor spent much of his time travelling from assizes to assizes, and much of the rest supervising the collection of taxes. He would normally take a very active role in the administration of cities. He was a busy man, and access to him was likely to be slow and expensive. Constantine authorized an alternative source of jurisdiction in civil disputes: the court of the Christian bishop (Waldstein, 1976).

The total number of active civil servants in the Late Empire has been estimated at around 30,000 (Jones, 1964, 1057). This is a very modest figure for the administration of so vast an Empire. It must however be remembered that in addition to the salaried civil service there was a large number of unpaid but nevertheless privileged supernumeraries and honorary office holders. The creation of this large army of active and inactive civil servants certainly made a very great change compared with the administration of the principate, and one which would have far-reaching consequences.

X

Members of administration all belonged to the legally privileged class of *honestiores* and all but the humblest had the rank of soldiers. Their service was known as *militia*. They wore the military belt (*cingulum militiae*), and like soldiers they were paid in rations (*annonae*). The military organization of the civil service (MacMullen, 1963, 162ff.) was partly a consequence of the filling of civilian office staffs with men seconded from the army (Jones, 1949), partly of the fact that civil administration as a career service for citizens had not existed during the Republic and early Empire. As it gradually came into existence it was shaped on the only available model, the army. Under the early emperors the office work of the Empire was done by imperial freedmen. In the course of time these were replaced from the top downwards by knights (*equites*) and humbler freeborn citizens. Nevertheless as late as the reign of Diocletian freedmen still seem to have played a significant role. It was left to Constantine to grant military privileges and status to departments still staffed by freedmen. In the emperor's private household freedmen of course continued to be employed, and the chamberlains (*cubicularii*), eunuchs who had originated as slaves bought in Persia, might exercise great influence without corresponding responsibility.

The administration of the Late Empire was still far from being manned entirely with career civil servants. In fact all the executive posts, magistracies and governorships of the old type as well as the headships of the central departments continued to be filled by amateurs, of high social status who in the course of their lives normally held only a small number of posts, and those only for a relatively short time (p. 461 below). But these holders of high office were assisted and served by departments staffed entirely by professionals, who were employed by the state until they formally retired like soldiers (*honesta missio*), after spending their working lives advancing slowly from grade to grade. The successful functioning of the service depended on the professional knowledge and experience of the more senior of these men. John Lydus, an official of the praetorian prefecture of the east in the reign of Justinian, has preserved the outlook of such a man in his book on the magistrates of the Roman people (*De Magistratibus Populi Romani*), which has been analysed and translated in Carney (1971). While career civil servants often found themselves in positions of power *vis-à-vis* the public, they were poorly paid, on average around 4 *solidi* a year (or its equivalent in kind) or less. In wages most of them were probably worse off than private soldiers. But there was a very wide gap between the average salary and the salaries of the highest paid heads of the various offices. Roman civil servants (particularly the senior men) were however in a position greatly to increase their earnings by charging the public for services such as access to the governor, completion of legal documents, enforcement of the orders of a court, or even the paper used in making court records. Tax collectors had to be paid fees. Earnings were highest in the central departments. Not only were the litigants that used the courts of the capital wealthy, and the amounts at stake large, but officials were also in a position to charge for imperial benefits such as commissions in the army, codicils of real or honorary rank, privileges, immunities, or laws favouring special interests which poured out from the *comitatus*. Fees (*sportulae*) were so much part of the accepted emolument that the government produced tables of the amounts that might be legally charged, and were no doubt regularly exceeded. In his first year of service in the prefecture of the east John Lydus earned 1,000 *solidi* in fees, more than thirty times his salary.

Salaries of officials were supplemented by privilege of status. As *honestiores* all holders of *militia* were immune from the more savage punishments. Members of the central departments were exempt from normal jurisdiction, and could claim to have their cases tried by their head of department (*praescriptio fori*). This privilege might also be claimed by sinecure holders of official positions. The eastern government in the fifth century attempted to limit the abuse. In ceremonial precedence even the humblest officials, the office staff of provincial governors (*cohortalini*) were at least the equals, often the superiors, of city-councillors, and they were of course exempt from the expensive and troublesome duties which city-councillors were obliged to perform. As a result service in even a provincial office might seem attractive to a decurion – if he had reason to believe that he might be able to circumvent the legislation which tied him and his children to the service of his local *curia*. Nevertheless the *cohortalini* were the humblest of officials, and their low pay and slow promotion to the posts of high pay and perquisites, and not least the expensive transport duty (*primipili pastus*) which was required of the officials who retired with the rank of *primipilaris*, made service in a provincial office unpopular with those who saw prospects of entering central departments. The government responded characteristically by making service compulsory and hereditary.

As has been shown earlier the clerks and accountants of the career civil service continued to be directed by heads of department who were amateurs as far as departmental work was concerned. These holders of *dignitates* or *honores* were appointed with codicils issued by the *primicerius notariorum*. The average term of office was less than two years, and most men only held one or two such posts in their lives. A majority seem to have been content with just one post. A small number of individuals, ambitious to reach top posts like that of praetorian prefect or master of the offices held a succession of posts. It is clear that there was tremendous pressure to obtain *honores*. It was perhaps partly a matter of pay. The fifty *annonae* and fifty *capitus* of the Augustan prefect of Egypt in the reign of Justinian will have amounted to 100 times the wages of his humble clerks, while the 100 lbs of gold of the praetorian prefect of Africa must have amounted to something like 1,800 times as much. Even so Justinian's prefect of Africa earned less than half the salary of the proconsul of Africa under the principate (1,000,000 *sesterces* = 220 lbs of gold). Salaries would of course be supplemented by perquisites of office. Not all of this was pure profit. The holder of the dignity will have paid a very large sum for it either to a patron for his support (*suffragium*), or later to the emperor himself or to another official to whom the emperor had turned over the right to make the appointment. Perhaps the greatest attraction of imperial *honores* was the rank conferred by them, which raised the ex-official above his former peers in civic society and which might, with a little luck, provide a means of avoiding curial duties not only for the man himself but also for his descendants. During the fourth century rank suffered from inflation comparable to that of the currency. More and more posts came to entitle their holder first to simple senatorial rank (*clarissimus*) and then to its higher grades (*spectabilis, illustris*). Senatorial rank also came to be awarded honorifically to men retiring from leading places in palatine offices, or to private individuals in return for miscellaneous services, or just because they had influential patrons, or because they had paid for the honour. No doubt the elaborate rules of precedence and seniority helped to oil the working of the administrative machinery. Not the least important function of rank was to integrate the otherwise completely separate hierarchies of military and civil administration. Another effect was to demonstrate on public occasions that position derived from proximity to the emperor excelled all other sources of social distinction.

The most important function of the bureaucracy was to supervise the collection of the taxes out of which soldiers and civil servants themselves were paid. The exercise through which the annual list of demands (*indictio*) was prepared was a bureaucratic operation of a size without parallel in the early Empire. Annual returns from the various departments, military and civilian, were passed up the hierarchy to the praetorian prefecture where the officials would calculate how much corn, or clothing, or whatever would be required by government employees in different areas, and would then proceed to distribute the burden as equally as practicable between dioceses and provinces. At provincial level the burden was divided between cities who were told not only how much they would have to provide but also where to transport it. In the city, administration passed out of the hands of paid civil servants into those of city councillors, who were not only unpaid, but also held collective liability for deficits, and who might be required to transport the supplies for great distances at their own cost (e.g. in Egypt from Hermopolis to Syene, 370 miles by river). Supervision of the magazines where the product of taxation was stored and the making of payments to imperial employees, whether in kind or in money equivalents, were also curial duties. The operation might be profitable, particularly if the decurions were men of influence, but it also involved the risk of extremely unpleasant consequences. A decurion who failed to collect the amount due might suffer savage corporal punishment. Alternatively – or even additionally – he might be compelled to sell his property to make up the deficit (Jones, 1964, 951–62).

Assessment of taxes was based on an empire-wide census of land and population which was revised every twelve years. According to Jones's view (Jones, 1957) the taxable value of land over most of the Empire was assessed in *iuga*. The *iugum* was a notional unit, like our rateable value, which in some provinces, e.g. Syria, took into account the quality of land and the use to which it was put, but more often did not. The corresponding unit for assessing the tax on population was the 'head' (*caput*). The total value for tax purposes of a piece of land was obtained by adding *iuga* and *capita* together. The annual tax liability was then stated as so much of each item per *iugum* or *caput*. Empire-wide uniformity was not achieved. In Asia (unlike Syria) the *iugum* took into account use – but not quality of land. In Italy the unit was the *millena*, and in Africa the *centuria*, both simple units of area. In Gaul, confusingly, a unit called *caput* seems to have been used to assess liability for land tax. The value of the *caput* too seems to have varied regionally. Some of this confusing variety of terms may be due to the coexistence of imperial units, used by the central administration, and local units used in the provinces. It may be that the annual indiction was announced in standard *iuga* and *capita* by the prefecture but that this was translated into local units when the burden was distributed at diocesan or provincial level. The above account based on Jones is almost certainly oversimplified. It has been shown that Jones's account of a single *iugatio-capitatio* tax seems to apply fully only to the diocese of Asia. In most areas a poll tax charged per head of the male population seems to have been quite separate from the land-tax (MacMullen, 1976, 129–52; Chastagnol, 1979; also 1982, 364ff.; Cerati, 1975).

The principal tax after being collected in kind, was paid out in salaries also assessed in kind, namely in rations (*annonae*) and fodder allowances (*capitus*). For employees whose salaries exceeded what they needed for immediate subsistence this system was intolerably clumsy. There is no doubt that from the beginning salary earners bargained with the curial storekeepers to draw their emolument in money rather than kind. Officials and soldiers abused their position to extort favourable prices. This led to a succession of laws forbidding or regulating commutation (*adaeratio*) in particular circumstances. But while this did not prevent a great deal of commutation, the principle that the main revenue (*annona*) should be both collected and paid out in kind remained intact for a long time. The conversion of tax payments into payments in gold was only completed in 424 in the west. In the east it was left to Anastasius to convert the bulk of the land tax (except for supplies needed to feed the army) into gold. Salaries continued to be stated (if not paid) in *annonae* and *capitus* for much longer. The fact that *adaeratio* was completed earlier in the economically weaker west shows that the natural economy of the state was maintained not because of economic weakness but because it was in the interest of the administration and its officials: the stronger administration maintained it longer.

But even while its principal revenue was in produce the government needed an income in precious metal. This was provided in part by the 'voluntary' contributions of *curiales* (*aurum coronarium*) and senators (*aurum oblativum*) on the occasions of imperial celebration or anniversaries. Silver and gold (later only gold) were also produced by the tax on shopkeepers, craftsmen and merchants (*collatio lustralis*) which caused great hardship among those liable when the tax was collected at five-yearly intervals. The *sacra largitio* also received some gold revenue from the land-tax, although its share was much smaller than the prefect's revenue in kind. In addition the *largitio* seems to have obtained gold by buying-in *solidi* with debased *denarii*. The fact that a large part of the income of the *sacra largitio* arrived in five-yearly intervals suggests that the government's need for gold was cyclical also, i.e. that its main use was to pay the five *solidi* per soldier at the accession of an emperor, and subsequently at the quinquennial anniversaries of the accession.

The administrative system has been described as if it had sprung up fully grown, and remained more or less unchanged thereafter. In fact like all human institutions it was subject to evolution. The separation of military and civil administration was a gradual process completed under Constantine. The assimilation of the great offices of the court into the same career structure as the provincial governorships and other traditional honours, and the consequent integration of the two privileged groups, the senatorial and equestrian orders, into a single hierarchically graded imperial aristocracy of office, was completed under the sons of Constantine (Vogler, 1979). Under Diocletian and Constantine there had probably been as many praetorian prefects as emperors, and each had accompanied his emperor on his travels. By the second half of the fourth century they had become heads of permanent administrative subdivisions of the Empire. This in a sense preserved the tripartite division of the Empire after the death of Constantine, the prefecture of the east corresponding to the Empire of Constantius, the prefecture of Italy, Illyricum and Africa to that of Constans and the prefecture of the Gauls, which included Britain and Spain, to the short-lived Empire of Constantine II. When the Empire was divided into eastern and western halves after the death of Jovian and again after the death of Theodosius I the prefecture of the east (*Oriens*) in effect became the Eastern Empire for which it provided the administrative substructure. After 395 the Eastern Empire included most of the Balkans which were organized as a second eastern prefecture of Illyricum. But the prefecture of *Oriens* remained the core of the administration. The fact that it was essentially based on a single prefecture, was one of the factors which gave the Eastern Empire a cohesion not possessed by the west. In the course of the fourth century there developed a tendency, natural in view of the language situation, to appoint easterners to posts in the east, and this was reinforced by the creation in the reign of Constantius of a senate at Constantinople on the model of the Roman senate. The complete hellenization of the eastern administration was delayed when Theodosius I became emperor and brought many westerners into the government of the east. After his death the development resumed, and the new aristocracy of Constantinople was determined that they would not again be subject to the west. When Stilicho the powerful western *magister peditum praesentalis* tried to become the guardian and principal adviser of the eastern emperor also, the ensuing conflict was most damaging to the empire as a whole, and particularly to its western half in its struggles with the Visigoths under Alaric.

The west was itself suffering from regional separatism. For some ten years after 368 Trier had been the residence of the praetorian prefect of the Gauls and of a western emperor almost continuously. This period saw the consolidation of a Gallic aristocracy.

GOVERNMENT AND ADMINISTRATION IN THE LATE EMPIRE (TO AD 476)

The senatorial aristocracy of Gaul did not cease to think of themselves as Romans, but they did come to feel, justifiably, that the defence of Gaul was being neglected by the government in Italy, and on several occasions supported usurpers who could be expected to do more for the protection of their home country. At the same time posts in the imperial administration of Gaul came to be held almost exclusively by Gallic senators, while the administration of Italy was nearly monopolized by Italians.

The administration of the Late Empire was established in the face of terrible difficulties. It was set up rapidly in response to crisis in a society which lacked bureaucratic traditions. All action was extremely slow. An ordinary law suit might take several years. A law issued at Milan might reach Rome in twelve days but delays of three weeks are known, and six weeks are also recorded. Navigation stopped in winter and laws issued in autumn normally only reached Africa in the following spring. A law issued at Constantinople might reach any place in the east within a fortnight but the journey might take much longer, quite apart from likely bureaucratic delay. It might be many months before a communication from a province to the capital was answered. Long delay came to be expected. A court official might absent himself from his duties for six months before penalties began to be applied. A year's absence was punished with the loss of ten places of seniority, and only after he had stayed away for more than four years could the official be dismissed from the service. Soldiers were struck off the role when they had been absent for three years.

The administration, or rather the classes from which it was recruited, lacked an adequate code of public conduct. It is true that the government took an idealistic view of its duty to provide for the needs of the community, to ensure the safety and well-being of the governed, to provide justice for those who appeared in its courts. But members of the administration treated their appointments as a means to social and economic gain for themselves, and above all their friends and dependents. The city-state code of the duties which a public figure owed to his friends and dependants had not been superseded by one which proclaimed that impartiality and disinterestedness are required of a public servant. It is not therefore surprising that for men making appointments to administrative posts the problem was not to find candidates who had the right qualifications for particular responsibilities, but to find enough posts for numerous would-be officials who were socially qualified and well connected, or willing to pay for the post. The semi-legal gratuities paid to officials, shading into outright extortion, were a heavy burden on the ordinary citizen. The fact that the wealthy and influential could often obtain constitutions or other documents bearing the emperor's signature which exempted them from the scope of existing legislation amounted to a serious limitation of the rule of law. The large number of regulations by which emperors made office staff and heads of department mutually responsible for each other's conduct, and the frequency with which emperors tried to forestall anticipated legalization of illegalities, show how serious these abuses were, and how ineffective the authorities' attempts to check them. If the history of the Late Empire shows an increasing alienation of the population from the government, the conduct of an administration that appeared to exist mainly for the sake of its self-perpetuation is likely to have been a principal cause.

As it was the system could only be maintained by far-reaching regimentation to prevent individuals leaving the more unpleasant and exposed occupations to enter the more prestigious, more profitable and safer ones. Thus a large part of the population were frozen into hereditary occupations. Tenants registered on their land-lord's tax returns were forbidden to leave his farms. The duties for the feeding of Rome performed by corn-shippers (*navicularii*), bakers and butchers were attached in perpetuity to these men's land so that they would pass automatically to any purchaser. Sons of soldiers were forced to follow their fathers into the army, and of workers in government factories into the factories. Service in the offices of provincial governors was made hereditary and so was the decurions' membership of city-councils (*curiae*). The effects of this legislation are best known in the case of the decurions. It is quite clear that social mobility on their part was hampered but by no means prevented.

The inevitable movement of decurions into the civil service was one of several ways in which the growing imperial administration weakened the local government which it was supposed to supervise and direct. Since a governor now only had to supervise two or three cities in his reduced province, his intervention could become continuous. The councils ceased to be debating and policy-making assemblies, and probably no longer met for any other purpose than to elect men to perform compulsory public service. Decisions of policy were made by the governor on the advice of whomever he chose to consult. At the same time the council ceased to be composed of the natural leaders of the city. From the beginning of the fourth century the wealthiest and most enterprising decurions were drawn into imperial service. This was less serious when most of the posts involved were of equestrian rank which did not confer hereditary immunity from curial duties. But in the course of the century more and more posts were raised in status so that they came to confer senatorial rank, which was hereditary, and would deprive the councils of the service of men and property for ever. To make things worse councillors who failed to obtain imperial office might manage to get honorary rank. The government legislated again and again to keep councillors and property at the disposal of their council, evidently to little avail. One reason for the failure was the fact that information, on which enforcement of the legislation could be based, had to come from the councillors themselves, and that they, whether as a favour to friends or because they might themselves one day hope to seek imperial honours, or even because they saw opportunities of profit as leaders of a reduced council, did not provide the information. Thus a large number of decurions did succeed in getting away. Such men eventually settled either as senators at Rome or Constantinople, or in some provincial city as *honorati*, fortified with privilege of ex-officials, and with exemption from the compulsory duties of the local city-council. They would become leaders of provincial society and their patronage and opinions would be valued more highly than those of the more dutiful men who had remained councillors. Inevitably it was to them rather than to the councillors that the humbler inhabitants looked for protection. In strongly Christian areas the prestige of the councillors would be further undermined by the appearance of effective patrons of the country population in the shape of hermits or heads of monasteries.

How this development affected the administration of cities and their territories is difficult to observe as evidence for the fifth century is less than that for the fourth. Decurions continued to exist and to perform executive roles in the cities to the reign of Justinian at least, and in many places much longer. Councils became smaller and poorer, although they continued to include some men of wealth and influence (*principales*) whose status was not very different from that of members of the senatorial order of less than illustrious rank who were no longer required to live in the capital. It is likely that the administration of the city, as far as it was not in the hands of the governor and his *officium*, passed from the council to a more informal body of notables which included both *principales* and *honorati* and – a new development – the bishop and leading clergy (Jones, 1964, 758ff.; cf. also Liebeschuetz, 1973, and 1974, and Hohlweg, 1971). As early as 407 a western law transferred the election of the *defensor* to the notables. In the east it was left to Anastasius to assign to the notables the election of the *defensor, curator* (or *pater*) and corn-buyer. Anastasius' legislation, perhaps only confirming what had already been the practice for many years, may well have marked the formal end of curial administration of the cities. At any rate John Lydus in the 550s could write of curial administration as belonging to the past. Compared with decurions notables enjoyed the advantage that they would negotiate with governors and their senior officials on more or less equal terms since most notables could claim at least some privileges of official rank. There is no evidence that the authorities ever attempted to subject the notables to the hereditary compulsion to which decurions continued to be subject.

It should be noted that the decline of curial government was a consequence of the strengthening of the central administration, not of the physical decline of the cities and their population. There is evidence that cities continued to flourish in the east up to at least the first quarter of the sixth century (Foss, 1976 and 1977). In much of the west, in the Balkans, in Britain and in large parts of Gaul and Spain there was of course, in addition, a withdrawal from city-life from the third or at least the second half of the fourth century (see King and Henig, 1981: essays by Reece, Blagg, Walker, Sheldon, Keay), but where cities survived councils continued to meet, and magistrates to be elected – even if the activities for which we have evidence are notarial rather than administrative. It may even be that from the fifth century decurions were relatively more important in the shrinking cities of the west than their colleagues in the flourishing cities of the east. Documents testify to the survival of councils in Italy and Spain to the seventh and even eighth centuries (Jones, 1964, 760–1; Thompson, 1969, 118–21). In the east city councils were formally abolished by Leo the Wise (886–912) (see Ostrogorsky, 1968, 217–18; Jones, 1940, 209–10).

The history of the city councils illustrates how the strengthening of the administrative machinery for enforcing the demands of the central government set in motion other trends which would eventually make the new machinery less effective. A similar reaction happened in the area of patronages. The same officials, officers, soldiers, *honorati* who used their influence to enable decurions to escape from councils, also helped humble peasants to reduce their tax payments. The patron might physically assist his clients to resist the tax collectors. Alternatively he might use his influence when the case of the recalcitrant tax payers came to court. In the east the patron's reward seems normally to have consisted – at first at any rate – of regular payments by the client. In the west it seems to have been more usual for the peasant to hand his land over to the patron who would then resist the tax-claim as if it had been made against himself. Patrons were also used to protect tenants against their landlords. Not all patronage was voluntary. There is no doubt that powerful men often imposed their protection on unwilling peasants. The eastern government – not that of the west – legislated against patronage, but not perhaps with great success. The long-term consequence of patronage seems to have been the concentration of property in the hands of those able to offer or enforce patronage, and a reduction in the administration's ability to raise taxes.

It might therefore be said that the reforms of Diocletian and Constantine proved to some extent self-defeating. They nevertheless achieved extremely important positive results. The Empire was given a new lease of life. The frontiers were defended successfully. Usurpation became very much more difficult. In the east no usurper at all succeeded within our period, and even attempts were few and ineffective. After the death of Theodosius I stable government survived the reigns of the feeble Arcadius and the not much more effective Theodosius II. The west was less stable. Not all the provinces enjoyed continuous peace and a number of usurpations were at least temporarily successful. In spite of this the fourth century was on the whole an age of recovery.

It was only possible because the administration was able to collect the taxes required to maintain the Empire's armies or alternatively to buy off invaders. In some ways the administration was too efficient. The authorities found it easier to force money out of the tax-payer than to ensure that it was spent for the purposes for which it was collected. The level of taxation tended to rise and may well have reached crushing levels. But Jones was probably mistaken to conclude that taxation helped to bring about a reduction in the population, as rents and taxes together had not left peasants with enough income to bring up children (Jones, 1964, 1040–5). In fact the population of the east seems to have been growing through most of the fourth and fifth centuries (Patlagean, 1972, 231–5, 302–13). In the west there was a reduction in some areas which made possible the settlement of very large numbers of barbarians (de Ste Croix, 1981, 509–18). But the legislation on abandoned land is much less good evidence of depopulation than has been thought, and there seems to be evidence of actual growth of population in some areas. There is a suspicion that barbarian invasions contributed at least as much as taxation to any reduction in the rural population and abandonment of land in the west. Nevertheless taxes were resented, and when the western government eventually failed to protect the provincials in spite of the heavy taxes that they had paid to it disillusion with the Empire must have been all the more complete.

The achievement of the Late Empire was to maintain control of a civilian central administration over the provinces, and especially, because this was hardest, over the great land-owners and the army. In both crucial areas the administration of the east was more successful than that of the west. In the east it remained in clear control of its great land-owners well beyond the end of this period. In the west the senatorial aristocracy came to neutralize the provincial administration by filling a high proportion of its principal posts with its own members. In the relationship between the civilian government and the army important differences between east and west became evident when the Empire was divided between the sons of Theodosius I in 395. In the east the five commanders of field armies, the *magistri militum praesentales* and the *magistri militum* of Thrace, Illyricum and the East were all independent of each other, and each the superior of the dukes commanding frontier forts in his area. In the west the *magister peditum praesentalis* was the commander-in-chief of all armies in that half of the Empire. He was so powerful that he could only be deposed by assassination or battle. Under a weak emperor like Honorius or Valentinian III the Empire was governed by its commander-in-chief. Potentially strong emperors like Majorian and Anthemius were frustrated, and eventually destroyed, by their generals. The Western Empire came to an end when Odoacer, the *magister peditum*, deposed Romulus Augustulus, the last emperor in 476 (Croke, 1983). In the east the situation was quite different. The civilians remained in control. Under the weak Arcadius the Empire was guided by its praetorian prefects, notably Rufinus and Anthemius and for a time, Eutropius, *praepositus sacri cubiculi* and a eunuch. During the reign of Theodosius II the Empire seems to have been directed for many years by the emperor's sister Pulcheria. It was a measure of civilian supremacy in the east that the *magister officiorum* was given important duties in the supervision of the army. During all this time the Eastern Empire followed consistent, if unheroic policies when expedient, diverting threatening barbarians with large payments, so that they attacked the west instead. Thus the east weathered the storm in which the west foundered.

BIBLIOGRAPHY

Alföldi, A. (1934), 'Die Ausgestaltung des monarchischen Zeremoniells am römischen Kaiserhofe', *Mitteilungen des Deutschen Archäologischen Instituts*, Römische Abteilung, 49, 3–118.

Alföldi, A. (1935), 'Insignien und Tracht der römischen Kaiser', *Mitteilungen des Deutschen Archäologischen Instituts*, Römische Abteilung, 50, 3–158.

Alföldi, A. (1970), *Die monarchische Repräsentation im römischen Kaiserreiche*, Darmstadt.

Alföldy, G. (1974), 'The crisis of the third century as seen by contemporaries', *Greek, Roman and Byzantine Studies* 15, 89–111.

Alföldy, G. (1979), *Römische Sozialgeschichte*, Wiesbaden.

Arnheim, M. T. W. (1972), *The Senatorial Aristocracy in the Later Roman Empire*, Oxford.

Avery, W. T. (1940), 'The *adoratio purpurae* and the importance of the imperial purple in the 4th century of the Christian Era', *Memoirs of the American Academy in Rome*, 17, 66–80.

Barnes, T. D. (1981), *Constantine and Eusebius*, Cambridge, Mass.

Barnes, T. D. (1982), *The New Empire of Diocletian and Constantine*, Cambridge, Mass.

Berchem, D. van (1952), *L'Armée de Dioclétien et la réforme Constantinienne*, Paris.

Blagg, T. F. C. (1981), 'Architectural patronage in the western provinces of the Roman Empire in the third century', in A. King and M. Henig (eds), *The Roman West in the Third Century. Contributions from Archaeology and History*, British Archaeological Report, S109, Oxford.

Boak, A. E. R. (1924), *The Master of the Offices in the Later Roman and Byzantine Administration*, University of Michigan Studies, Humanities Series 14, New York.

Brown, P. (1971), 'The rise and function of the holy man in late antiquity', *Journal of Roman Studies* LXI, 80–101.

Brown, P. (1978), *The Making of Late Antiquity*, Cambridge, Mass.

Burton, G. P. (1979), 'The curator rei publicae: towards a reappraisal', *Chiron*, 9, 465ff.

Cameron, Alan (1970), *Poetry and Propaganda at the Court of Honorius*, Oxford.

Carney, T. F. (1971), *Bureaucracy in Traditional Society: Romano-Byzantine bureaucracies viewed from within*, Lawrence.

Cerati, A. (1975), *Caractère annonaire et assiette de l'impôt foncier au Bas-Empire*, Paris.

Chastagnol, A. (1953), 'Le ravitaillement de Rome en viande au Vᵉ siècle', *Revue Historique*, 77, 13.

BIBLIOGRAPHY

Chastagnol, A. (1960), *La Préfecture urbaine à Rome sous le Bas-Empire*, Paris.

Chastagnol, A. (1966), 'Le sénat romaine sous le règne d'Odoacre', *Antiquitas*, Reihe 3, volume 3, Bonn.

Chastagnol, A. (1970), 'Les modes du recruitement du sénat au IVième siècle', in C. Nicolet (ed.), *Recherches sur les structures sociales dans l'Antiquité classique*, 187–211, Paris.

Chastagnol, A. (1976), *La Fin du monde antique de Stilicon à Justinien*, Paris.

Chastagnol, A. (1978), 'L'album municipal de Timgad', *Antiquitas*, Reihe 3, volume 22.

Chastagnol, A. (1979), 'Problèmes fiscaux du Bas-Empire', in *Points de vue sur la fiscalité antique*, 127, 40, Paris.

Chastagnol, A. (1982), *L'évolution politique sociale et économique du monde romain*, 248–363, Paris.

Clauss, M. (1980), *Der magister officiorum in der Spätantike (4–6 Jahrhundert)*, Munich.

Collot, C. (1965), 'La pratique de l'institution du *suffragium* au Bas-Empire', *Revue historique de droit Français et étranger*, 43, 185–22.

Cook, S. A, Adcock, F. E, Charlesworth, M. P, Baynes, N. H. (eds) (1939), *Cambridge Ancient History*, volume 12, Cambridge.

Croke, B. (1983), 'AD 476: the manufacture of a turning point', *Chiron*, 13, 81–119.

Dagron, G. (1974), *Naissance d'une capitale: Constantinople et ses institutions de 330 à 451*, Paris.

Déléage, A. (1945), *La Capitation du Bas-Empire*, Annales de l'Est, Mémoires, No. 14.

Demandt, A. (1980), 'Der spätrömische Militäradel', *Chiron*, 10, 609–36.

Demougeot, E. (1951), *De l'unité à la division de l'empire romain, 395–410*, Paris.

Dunlap, J. E. (1924), 'The office of the Grand Chamberlain in the Later Roman and Byzantine Empires', in *Two Studies in Later Roman and Byzantine Administration*, University of Michigan Studies, Humanities Series 14, New York, 161–322.

Eck, W. (1974), 'Beförderungskriterien innerhalb der senatorischen Laufbahn' in H. Temporini (ed.), *Aufstieg und Niedergang der römischen Welt*, 2:1, 158ff, Berlin/New York.

Eibach, D. (1977), *Untersuchungen zum spätantiken Kolonat in der kaiserlichen Gesetzgebung unter Berücksichtigung der Terminologie*, Bonn.

Fitz, J. (1983), 'L'administration des provinces pannoniennes sous le bas-empire romain', *Collection Latomus*, 181, Brussels.

Foss, C. (1976), *Byzantine and Turkish Sardis*, Cambridge, Mass.

Foss, C. (1977), 'Archaeology and the Twenty Cities of Byzantine Asia', *American Journal of Archaeology*, 81, 469–86.

Garnsey, P. D. (1970), *Social Status and Legal Privilege in the Roman Empire*, Oxford.

Garnsey, P. D. (1974), 'Aspects of the decline of the urban aristocracy in the empire', in H. Temporini (ed.), *Aufstieg und Niedergang der römischen Welt*, I, 2.1, 229ff, Berlin.

Giardina, A. (1977), *Aspetti della Burocrazia nel Basso Impero*, Rome.

Goffart, W. (1974), *Caput and Colonate: Toward a History of Late Roman Taxation*, Toronto.

Goffart, W. (1980), *Barbarians and Romans*, Princeton.

Goffart, W. (1981), 'Rome Constantinople and the Barbarians', *American Historical Review*, 86, 275–306.

Gualandi, G. (1963), *Legislazione imperiale e giurisprudenza*, Milan.

Haehling, R. von (1978), *Die Religionszugehörigkeit der hohen Amsträger des römischen Reiches seit Constantins I Alleinherrschaft bis zum Ende der Theodosianischen Dynastie*, Antiquitas, 3 (23), Bonn.

Hahn, I. (1962), 'Theodoretus und die frühbyzantinische Besteuerung', *Acta Antiqua* X, 123–30.

Hahn, I. (1981), 'Das bäuerliche Patrocinium in Ost und West', *Klio* 50 (1968) 261–76, reprinted with bibliographical supplement in H. Schneider (ed.), *Social und Wirtschaftsgeschichte der römischen Kaiserzeit*, Darmstadt, 234–52.

Hohlweg, A. (1971), 'Bischof und Stadtherr im frühen Byzanz', *Jahrbuch für österreichische Byzantinistik*, 20, 51–62.

Holum, K. G. (1982), *Theodosian Empresses, Women and Imperial Dominion in Late Antiquity*, Berkeley.

Honoré, A. M. (1981), *Emperors and Lawyers*, London.

Hopkins, K. (1980), 'Taxes and trade in the Roman Empire (200 BC–AD 400)', *Journal of Roman Studies*, LXX, 101–25.

Hopkins, M. K. (1963), 'Eunuchs in politics in the later Roman Empire', *Proceedings of Cambridge Philosophical Society* 9, 62–80.

Hopkins, K. and Burton, G. P. (1983), 'Ambition and withdrawal: the senatorial aristocracy under the emperors', in K. Hopkins, *Death and Renewal*, Cambridge.

Jacques, F. (1983), 'Les curateurs des cités africaines au III siècle', in H. Temporini (ed.), *Aufstieg und Niedergang der römischen Welt*, II, 2.10, 62ff, Berlin/New York.

Johnson, A. C. and West, L. C. (1967), *Byzantine Egypt: Economic Studies*, Amsterdam.

Jones, A. H. M. (1940), *The Greek City*, Oxford.

Jones, A. H. M. (1949), 'The Roman civil service (clerical and sub-clerical grades)', *Journal of Roman Studies*, XXXIX, 38–55.

Jones, A. H. M. (1949), *The Greek City from Alexander to Justinian*, Oxford.

Jones, A. H. M. (1953), 'Census records of the Later Empire', *Journal of Roman Studies*, XLIII, 49–64.

Jones, A. H. M. (1954), 'The date and value of the Verona List', *Journal of Roman Studies*, XLIV, 21–9.

Jones, A. H. M. (1957), 'Capitatio and Jugatio', *Journal of Roman Studies*, XLVII, 88–94.

Jones, A. H. M. (1958), 'The Roman colonate', *Past and present*, 13.

Jones, A. H. M. (1959), 'Over taxation and the decline of the Roman Empire', *Antiquity*, 33, 39–43.

Jones, A. H. M. (1960), *Studies in Roman Government and Law*, Oxford.

Jones, A. H. M. (1964), *The Later Roman Empire, 284–602*, Oxford.

Jones, A. H. M. (1964), 'Collegiate prefectures', *Journal of Roman Studies*, LIV, 78–89.

Jones, A. H. M. (1968), 'The Dediticii and the *Constitutio Antoniana*', *Studies in Roman Government and Law*, 127–40, Oxford.

Jones, A. H. M. (1970), 'The caste system of the Later Roman Empire', *Eirene* 8, 79–97.

Jones, A. H. M. (1972), *The Criminal Courts of the Roman Republic and Principate*, Cambridge.

Jones, A. H. M. (1974), *The Roman Economy*, Oxford.

Jones, A. H. M., Martindale, R. and Morris, J. (1971), *The Prosopography of the Later Roman Empire (260–395)*, volume 1, Cambridge.

Jones, M. E. (1979), 'Climate, nutrition and disease, a hypothesis of Roman-British Population' in P. J. Casey (ed.), *The End of Roman Britain*, British Archaeological Reports 71, 231–5, Oxford.

Keay, S. J. (1981), 'The Conventus Tarraconsensis in the third century A.D. Crisis and change', in A. King and M. Henig (eds), *The Roman West in the Third Century: Contributions from Archaeology and History*, British Archaeological Reports, S1099, 451–86, Oxford.

Keenan, J. K. (1975), 'Soziale Mobilität im spätrömischen Ägypten', *Zeitschrift fur Papyrologie und Epigraphie*, 17, 257ff.

Kent, J. P. C. (1961), 'The comes Sacrarum Largitionum', in E. C. Dodd, *Byzantine Silver Stamps*, 31–45, Washington.

King, A. and Henig, M. (eds) (1981), *The Roman West in the Third Century: Contributions from Archaeology and History*, British Archaeological Reports, S109, 1–2, Oxford.

Knepper, A. (1979), *Untersuchungen zur städtischen Plebs des 4 Jahrhunderts nr.Chr*, Bonn.

Koch, P. (1903), *Die byzantinischen Beamtentitel von 400 bis 700*, Jena.

Kunkel, W. (1966), *An Introduction to Roman Legal and Constitutional History*, Oxford.

Lallemand, J. (1964), *L'administration civile de l'Égypte de l'avènement de Dioclétian à la creation du diocèse (284–382)*, Académie Royale de Belgique, Classe des Lettres, Mémoires LVII, 2.

Langhamer, W. (1973), *Die rechtliche und sociale Stellung der magistratus municipales und der decuriones*, Wiesbaden.

Lepelley, C. (1979), 'Les cîtés de l'afrique romaine au bas-empire', *La Permanence d'une civilisation municipale*, volume 1, Paris.

Lepelley, W. (1981), 'Notice d'histoire municipale', *La Permanence d'une civilisation municipale*, volume 2, Paris.

Liebenam, W. (1897), 'Curator rei publicae', *Philologus*, 56, 290ff.

Liebenam, W. (1900), *Städtverwaltung im römischen Kaiserreiche*, Leipzig.

Liebeschuetz, W. (1961), 'Money economy and taxation in kind in Syria in the fourth century A.D.', *Rheinisches Museum*, 104, 242–56.

Liebeschuetz, J. H. W. G. (1972), *Antioch, City and Imperial Administration in the Later Roman Empire*, Oxford.

Liebeschuetz, J. H. W. G. (1973), 'The origin of the office of the pagarch', *Byzantinische Zeitschrift*, 66, 38–46.

Liebeschuetz, J. H. W. G. (1974), 'The pagarch: city and imperial administration in Byzantine Egypt', *Journal of Juristic Papyrology*, 18, 163–68.

MacCormack, S. G. (1981), *Art and Ceremony in Late Antiquity*, Berkeley.

MacMullen, R. (1962), 'The emperor's largesse', *Collections Latomus*, 21, 159–66.

MacMullen, R. (1963), *Soldier and Civilian in the Later Roman Empire*, Cambridge, Mass.

MacMullen, R. (1964a), 'Social mobility and the Theodosian code', *Journal of Roman Studies*, LIV, 49–53.

MacMullen, R. (1964b), 'Some pictures in Ammianus Mariellinus', *Art Bulletin*, 46, 435–55.

MacMullen, R. (1969), *Constantine*, London.

MacMullen, R. (1976), *The Roman Government's Response to Crisis, AD 235–337*, New Haven and London.

Mann, J. C. (1976), 'What was the Notitia Dignitatum for?', in R. Goodburn and P. Bartholomew (eds), *Aspects of the Notitia Dignitatum*, British Archaeological Reports, S15, Oxford.

Marquadt, J. (1957), *Römische Staatsverwaltung*, Bände I–III, Darmstadt.

Martindale, J. R. (1980), *The Prosopography of the Later Roman Empire AD 395–527*, volume 2, Cambridge.

Matthews, J. F. (1971), 'Gallic supporters of Theodosius', *Collections Latomus*, 30, 1073–99.

Matthews, J. F. (1975), *Western Aristocracies and the Imperial Court, AD 364–425*, Oxford.

Mazzarino, S. (1951), *Aspetti Sociali del Quarto Secolo*, Rome.

Millar, F. (1977), *The Emperor in the Roman World*, London.

Millar, F. (1980), 'The Res Privata from Diocletian to Theodosius', in C. E. King (ed.), *Imperial Revenue and Expenditure and Monetary Policy in the 4th Century AD*, British Archaeological Reports, S76, Oxford.

Mommsen, Th. (1899), *Römisches Strafrecht*, Leipzig.

Monks, G. R. (1951), 'The administration of the privy purse: an inquiry into official corruption and the fall of the Roman Empire', *Speculum*, 32, 748–79.

Mrozek, S. (1978), 'Munificentia Privata in den Städten Italiens während der späten Kaiserzeit', *Historia*, 27, 355–68.

Neesen, L. (1981), 'Die Entwicklung der Leistungen und Aemter (munera et honores) im römischen Kaiserreich des zweiten bis vierten Jahrhunderts', *Historia*, 30, 203–35.

Nellen, D. (1977), *Viri litterati, gebildetes Beamtentum und spätrömisches Reich im Westen zwischen 234 und 395 nach Christus*, Bochum.

Noetlichs, K. L. (1971), *Die gesetzgeberischen Massnahmen der christlichen Kaiser des vierten*

Jahrhunderts gegen Häretiker, Heiden und Juden, Cologne.

Noetlichs, K. L. (1973), 'Materialien zum Bischofsbild aus den spätantiken Rechtsquellen', *Jahrbuch für Antike und Christentum*, 16, 28–39.

Noetlichs, K. L. (1981), *Beamtentum und Dienstvergehen zur Staatsverwaltung in der Spätantike*, Wiesbaden.

Noetlichs, K. L. (1982), 'Zur Entstehung der Diözesen als Mittelinstanz des spätrömischen Vervaltungssystems', *Historia*, XXXI, 70–81.

Nörr, D. (1969), *Imperium und Polis in der hohen Prinzipatszeit*, Munich.

Ostrogorsky, G. (1968), *History of the Byzantine State* (translated J. M. Hussey), second edition, Oxford.

Palanque, J.-R. (1933), *Essai sur la préfecture du prétoire du Bas-Empire*, Paris.

Patlagean, E. (1972), *Pauvreté économique et pauvreté sociale à Byzance 4e–7e siècles*, Paris.

Pedersen, F. S. (1976), *Late Roman Public Professionalism*, Odense Classical Studies, Volume 9, Odense.

Pekáry, T. (1968), *Untersuchungen zu den römischen Reichsstrassen*, Bonn.

Petit, P. (1955), *Libanius et la vie municipale à Antioche au IVe siècle après J-C.*, Paris.

Petrikovits, H. von (1978), *Altertum*, Düsseldorf (F. Petri and G. Droeg (eds), *Rheinische Geschichte*, Volume I).

Pflaum, H. G. (1976), 'Zur Reform des Kaisers Gallienus', *Historia*, 25, 109–117.

Piganiol, A. (1947), *L'Empire chrétien (325–395)*, Paris.

Reece, R. (1981), 'The third century, crisis or change?' in A. King and M. Henig (eds), *The Roman West in the Third Century*, British Archaeological Reports, S109, 27–38, Oxford.

Rémondon, R. (1965), 'P. Hamb. 56 et P. London. 419: notes sur les finances d'Aphrodito du VIe siècle au VIIIe', *Chronique d'Égypte*, XL, 401–30.

Rostovtzeff, M. I. (1957), *Social and Economic History of the Roman Empire*, second edition, Oxford.

Rouillard, G. (1928), *L'Administration civile de l'Égypte byzantine*, Paris.

Ruprecht, G. (1975), *Untersuchungen zum Dekurionenstand in den westlichen Provinzen des römischen Reiches*, Frankfurter althistorische Studien VIII, Kallmünz.

Ste Croix, G. E. M. de (1954), 'Suffragium, from vote to patronage', *British Journal of Sociology*, 5, 33–48.

Ste Croix, G. E. M. de (1981), *The Class Struggle in the Ancient World*, London.

Salmon, P. (1974), 'Population et dépopulation dans l'empire romain', *Collections Latomus*, 137, Brussels.

Schaller, W. (1975), 'Grenzen des spätrömischen Staates, Staatspolizei und Korruption', *Zeitschrift für Papyrologie und Epigraphie*, 16, 1–17.

Seeck, O. (1876), *Notitia Dignitatum*, Frankfurt (reprinted 1962).

Seeck, O. (1919), *Regesten der Kaiser und Päpste für die Jahre 311–476 n.Chr.* Stuttgart (reprinted 1964).

Selb, W. (1967), 'Episcopalis audientia von der Zeit Konstantins bis zu Nov. XXXV Valentinians III', Zeitschrift der Savigny Stiftung, 84, 167–217.

Seston, W. (1946), Dioclétien et la Tétrarchie, Paris.

Sheldon, H. (1981), 'London and south-east Britain 236–72', in A. King and M. Henig (eds), The Roman West in the Third Century : Contributions from Archaeology and History, British Archaeological Reports, S109, Oxford.

Sinnigen, W. C. (1957), The Officium of the Urban Prefecture during the Later Roman Empire, Rome.

Sinnigen, W. C. (1961), 'The Roman secret service', Classical Journal, 57, 65–72.

Stahl, M. (1978), Imperiale Herrschaft und provinziale Stadt, Göttingen.

Stein, E. (1959), Histoire du Bas-Empire (édition française par J. R. Palanque), Paris.

Stroheker, K. F. (1943), Der senatorische Adel im spätantiken Gallien, Tübingen.

Tengstrom, E. (1974), Bread for the People : Studies in the corn-supply of Rome during the Late Empire, Stockholm.

Thompson, E. A. (1969), The Goths in Spain, Oxford.

Treitinger, O. (1969), Die oströmischen Kaiser und die Reichsidee nach ihrer Gestaltung im höfischen Zeremoniell, Hamburg.

Vercauteren, F. (1969), 'Die spätantike Civitas im frühen Mittelalter', in J. C. Haase (ed.), Die Stadt des Mittelalters, I, 122–38, Darmstadt.

Veyne, P. (1981), 'Clientèle et corruption au service de l'état', Annales économies, sociétés et civilisations, 339–60.

Vogler, A. (1979), Constance II et l'administration impériale, Strasbourg.

Waldstein, W. (1976), 'Zur Stellung der Episcopalis Audientia im spätrömischen Process', in D. Medicus and H. M. Seiter, (eds), Festschrift für Max Kaser, 533, Munich.

Walker, S. (1981), 'The Third Century in the Lyon Region', in A. King and M. Henig (eds), The Roman West in the Third Century : Contributions from Archaeology and History, British Archaeological Reports, S109, Oxford.

Walser, G. and Pekáry, Th. (1962), Die Krise des römischen Reiches. Bericht über die Forschungen zur Geschichte des 3 Jahrhunderts, Berlin.

Watson, Alan (1974), Law-making in the Later Roman Republic, Oxford.

Weiss, P. B. (1975), Consistorium und comites consistoriani Untersuchungen zur Hofbeamtenschaft des 4 Jahrhunderts n.Chr. auf prosopographischer Grundlage, Würzburg.

Wes, M. A. (1967), 'Das Ende des Kaiseriums im Westen des römischen Reiches', Arch. Stud. van het Nederlands Hist. Inst. te Rome, II, s'Gravenhage.

Whittaker, C. R. (1976), 'Agri Deserti', in M. I. Finley (ed.), Studies in Roman Property, 137–65, Cambridge.

Williams, W. (1976), 'Individuality in the imperial constitutions, Hadrian and the Antonines', Journal of Roman Studies, LXVI, p. 69.

Wlassak, M. (1919), Zum römischen Provinzialprozess, Vienna.

THE SYRIARCH IN THE FOURTH CENTURY

The story of the Olympic Games at Antioch is well known. It continues through the Fourth Century A.D., a period when most festivals of this kind had already been abandoned. The evidence on the Games at Antioch has been studied by O. Seeck, A. Schenk von Stauffenberg, G. Downey and P. Petit and the resultant account, as contained in Petit's recent excellent book, is likely to remain unchallenged in most particulars[1]. The present article will touch on only one aspect of this topic, the relationship to the Games of the Syriarch.

There exists no statement in ancient sources which explicitly associates the Syriarch with the Olympic Games. A well known passage of Malalas describes the organisation of the Olympic Games by the Emperor Commodus[2]. In this passage it is implied that the Alytarch was the chief dignitary of the Olympic Games[3]. The Syriarch is mentioned a little later[4]; but since this section of Malalas' Chronicle deals with the reorganisation of a number of quite separate entertainments, including the notorious Majumas[5], the mention of the Syriarch in this context does not make him a participator in the Olympic Games.

In spite of the absence of explicit evidence, previous writers have come to the conclusion that the Syriarch did participate in the organisation of the Olympic Games[6]. This conclusion appears to be based on an argument in three parts. The Syriarch is first argued to be one of the officials responsible for the

---

[1] O. Seeck: 'Die Briefe des Libanius zeitlich geordnet', Leipzig 1906. (Cited as Seeck). A. Schenk von Stauffenberg: 'Die Römische Kaisergeschichte bei Malalas', Stuttgart 1931. G. Downey: 'Malalas on the History of Antioch under Severus and Caracalla', T.A.P.A. 68, 1937, pp. 141–156. Same author: 'The Olympic Games of Antioch in the 4th Century A.D.' T.A.P.A. 70, 1939, pp. 428–38. P. Petit: 'Libanius et la vie municipale à Antioche au 4 ème siècle ap. J.C.' Paris 1956. (Cited Petit.)

[2] Malalas, 'The Chronicle' books 9–12, edited by Stauffenberg in the work cited in note 1. The remaining books in the edition of L. Dindorf volume 15 of Corpus Scriptorum Historiae Byzantinae, Bonn 1831. The present reference is to Malalas 284,1 ff. (Both editions use the same divisions for reference).

[3] Malalas 286,12–14, ibid. 289,14, where the manuscript reading ἀλυτάρχης found in the apparatus criticus is to be preferred to Stauffenberg's emendation Συριάρχης. The difficulty produced by the fact that the two passages give the first Alytarch different names are plausibly resolved by Downey in the article in T.A.P.A. 68 cited in note 1. Malalas 417,5 shows that Olympic Games were numbered by their Alytarchs. Malalas 286,12 ff. mentions Scribe and Amphithales but *not* the Syriarch as officials of the Olympic Games.

[4] Syriarch; Malalas 285, l. 17. Beast Chases ibid. ls. 12–16.

[5] Malalas 284,18–285,11; ibid. 285,20.

[6] Stauffenberg, Kaisergeschichte p. 422 ff. supplemented by Downey's article in T.A.P.A. 1937 cited in note 1 and Petit pp. 128–136 especially p. 131.

show of the assembly of Syria. The Olympic Games are then identified with the games of the province of Syria. Lastly, the conclusion that the Syriarch played a part in the organisation of the Olympic Games is confirmed by the evidence of two laws which mention him together with the Alytarch[7], and of some letters of Libanius in which the Syriarch is reported to be preparing animal hunts for a festival, which is taken to be the Olympic Games[8].

The three stages of this argument are not equally cogent. The problem of the relationship of the Syriarch to the provincial assembly of Syria is linked with that of the status of the Asiarchs and of dignitaries in other provinces bearing titles of the same type. It has been argued that the Asiarch was associated with the activities of the assembly of Asia. If this conclusion regarding the status of the Asiarch were beyond dispute, we could reasonably apply it to that of the Syriarch. Unfortunately, in spite of a great deal of research, the precise significance of the Asiarch title has not been established, and the question whether the title was bestowed by a provincial assembly, or by a city, or even by the temple of a city remains to be answered[9]. It is, however, possible that the inconclusive outcome of the debate over the nature of the Asiarchate is due to the fact that much of the relevant evidence dates from the first two centuries A.D., during which time the institution of the Asiarchate might well have been still evolving. The later evidence, on the other hand, seems far more definitely to associate the Asiarchs and similar dignitaries with the provincial assemblies[10].

[7] C.T. 15,9,2 (409), C.J. 1,36,1 (465). On them Stauffenberg, Kaisergeschichte p. 423 ff. See also Bruns, 'Fontes Juris Romani Antiqui' ed. 7, no. 97b (375 A.D.).

[8] Letters of Libanius mentioning Syriarch; ep. 1400, 1459 (363). The evidence of Libanius is discussed by Downey in the article in T.A.P.A., 1939 cited in note 1. See also Petit, work cited in note 1.

[9] This is the conclusion of D. Magie in 'Roman Rule in Asia Minor,' Princeton, 1950, t. I, p. 450. Ibid. t. II, p. 1298–1301 has references to numerous earlier writers on the subject and provides a survey of the evidence. Of earlier writers particularly relevant are Kornemann's article 'κοινόν' in P. W. Suppl. IV, 1, col. 936 ff. and Brandis's article 'Asiarches' P. W. t. II, col. 1564 ff. Also Stauffenberg as cited in note 7.

[10] 1. Digest (Modestinus) 27,1,6,14. This exempts from guardianships during their term of office those who held an ἔθνους ἱεραρχία, οἷον ᾿Ασιαρχία, Βιθυναρχία, Καππαδοκαρχία. ἱεραρχία is a restoration of Mommsen but is confirmed by the repetition of this measure in the Basilika ed. Heimbach 3,681. The scholia to this passage in the Basilica explain οἱ ἱερεῖς τῶν ἐπαρχιῶν τοῦτ᾿ ἔστιν ἀσιάρχαι καὶ οἱ λοιποί as meaning Alytarchs, Syriarchs and Phoenicarchs.

2. C.J. 5,27,1 (336) quos in civitatibus duumviralitas vel sacerdotii, id est Phoenicarchiae vel Syriarchiae ornamenta condecorant ... Of this the version in C.T. 4,6,3 does not mention Phoenicarch or Syriarch. It has instead ... quos in civitatibus duumviralitas ... vel sacerdotii provinciae ornamenta condecorant. Nov. Marc. 4,1,16 is similar to the version in the Theodosian Code. The reference to the Syriarch and the Phoenicarch in the Code of Justinian may therefore be an interpretative insertion, as Brandis suggests, in the P.W. article cited in note 9. But there is no reason to believe that the interpretation was a false one.

3. C.T. 15,9,2 (409) limits amounts producers of shows might spend ... exceptis alyt-

I would therefore conclude that during the Later Empire, at any rate, the Asiarch and the Syriarch were provincial dignitaries and responsible for the production of spectacles for the assembly of their province.

The second stage in the argument, the identification of the Olympic Games with the Games of the Province of Syria, is plausible but not conclusive. Olympic Games were produced in association with a meeting of the assembly of Asia at Ephesus[11]. We also know that in the reign of Domitian an athletic festival accompanied the joint meeting of the assembly of Syria, Phoenicia and Cilicia. On the other hand, the Olympic Games at Antioch were held every four years, while provincial assemblies as a rule met annually[12]. It would thus have been possible to arrange for the Olympic Games to be held at the same time and in conjunction with a meeting of the assembly of Syria every four years. But it still remains a possibility that there existed at Antioch, apart from the Olympic Games, a second, annual festival with the specific function of marking the occasion of the provincial assembly and of celebrating the Emperor, in whose honour the assembly had come together.

The third stage in the argument associating the Syriarch with the Olympic Games is the least satisfactory. The fact that two laws and one inscription mention Syriarch or Asiarch together with the Alytarch[13] can be explained on the ground that the dignitaries bearing these titles produced shows of the same status. It need not mean that they shared the production of the same show. The evidence of Libanius, in the opinion of the author of the present article, provides no support for the association of the Syriarch with the Olympic Games. In the following pages an attempt will be made to prove this and to show that in the Fourth Century the animal hunts produced by the Syriarch took place annually at the meetings of the provincial assembly in honour of the Emperor, while the Olympic Games were held every four years in honour of Zeus.

archis, Syriarchis, agonothetis itemque Asiarchis et ceteris quorum nomen votiva festivitatis sollemnitas dedicavit. Of these three passages 1 and 2 show the Asiarch type dignitaries to have been priests associated with provinces. Passage 3 shows them to have been show-producing priests. Another reference to Asiarch (and Alytarch) in connection with a show of the province of Asia is found in C. G. Bruns, 'Fontes Juris Romani Antiqui', ed. 7, p. 272–4, no. 97b– Abbott and Johnson, Municipal Administration of the Roman Empire, p. 503 no. 158. On this inscripti compare note 71.

[11] The Games at Ephesus, B. V. Head, Historia Nummorum, ed. 2, p. 577. The Games of Syria, Phoenicia and Cilicia I.G.R. t. 1, no. 445.

[12] Olympic Games at Antioch every four years; Stauffenberg as in note 1, p. 438; Petit p. 130. Provincial assemblies meet annually; P.W. suppl. 4 article 'κοινόν' col. 937 (Asia) Kornemann. P.W. 4,1, article 'Concilium,' Huelsen, col. 814, ibid. 824/5. Festival of Asia annual D. Magie, as cited in note 9, t. 2, p. 1295–7.

[13] References in note 7. The inscription of course refers to Alytarchs in Asia not at Antioch. Alytarch and Syriarch are also mentioned together in the scholia to the Basilica (cf. note 10). But this is late and probably not independant evidence.

Libanius tells us much about the Olympic Games but not the official titles of the men who produced them. He mentions the Syriarch title twice. Libanius gives this title to Celsus, who in the year 364 performed a liturgy, of which the most important part was the production of an animal hunt for the seventeen cities of Syria[14]. 364 was indeed a year in which the Olympic Games were held, but this coincidence proves no more than that the Syriarch might also perform his liturgy in an Olympic Games year. It does not prove that he produced them as part of the Olympic Games, or even that he only produced them in Olympic Games years.

Libanius does not mention the Syriarch title again. There are, however, in his letters two groups of passages dealing with animal hunts produced under conditions recalling Celsus' liturgy. Both belong to years in which the Olympic Games were celebrated, respectively 356 and 360. Accordingly, Seeck and Petit, but not Downey, assume that these shows were associated with the Olympic Games[15]. This is most unlikely in the case of the spectacle of the earlier of the two years. The decisive passage reads: τῷ μὲν Ὀλυμπίῳ Διὶ πάλαι τὸν ἀγῶνα τέθεικεν οὑμὸς ἀνεψιός, νῦν δὲ εἰς λειτουργίαν εἰσῆλθεν ἧς οὐκ ὀλίγα μὲν ᾔδει, τὸ δὲ ἐν πλείστῃ σπουδῇ τὰ τῶν ἀνθρώπων ἀγωνίσματα πρὸς τὰ θηρία. This passage is from a letter of autumn 356[16]. It is therefore improbable that the πάλαι refers to a time as recent as the summer of that year. The passage surely implies that the man's Olympic Games lay some years back and that he was now entering a new and formidable liturgy. It must also be remembered that the preparation of a *venatio* took time[17]. Since Libanius' cousin started his preparations late in 356[18], he would certainly not have been ready to produce a show in time for the Olympic Games of that year.

---

[14] Libanius cited in the edition of R. Foerster, Teubner Texts, Leipzig, 1903–26. *All references which do not name an author are to Libanius.* Syriarch title; ep. 1400, 1459. About the same liturgy; ep. 1399 (early summer 363), 1231–2 (later in the summer of the same year.) ep. 1147–8 (spring 364). Dates according to Seeck cited in note 1, p. 410,416,420. The seventeen cities ep. 1399. 17 cities of Syria are named by A. H. M. Jones, 'Cities of the Eastern Roman Provinces', Oxford 1937 p. 531 as follows; Antioch, Seleucia, Laodicea, Gabala, Paltus, Beroea, Chalcis, Anasartha, Gabbula, Apamea, Epiphaneia, Arethusa, Larissa, Mariamne, Balanea, Raphanea, Seleucia ad Belum.

[15] Ep. 544–5 (356–7), Seeck as cited in note 1, p. 333. Ep. 217,218,219 (360), Seeck ibid. p. 372. Ep. 113 (Winter 359–60), Seeck ibid. p. 372. See also Petit, p. 128; Downey in T.A.P.A. 1939, p. 433.

[16] Ep. 544: t. 10, p. 509, l. 9; Seeck p. 333. On same liturgy: ep. 545.

[17] Wild animals and their hunters were obtained from distant provinces and cannot have been obtained quickly. Negotiations for beasts in Bithynia ep. 586–8, 598–9 (357). An unfortunate quest for hunters in Pamphylia ep. 1509 (365), cf. Downey's article in T.A.P.A. 1939, cited note 1, p. 432. Celsus started preparations in summer 363. (See note 14.) Yet in March or April 364 he was still looking for wild beasts and seeking his subsidy (ep. 1147–8; Seeck p. 106).

[18] Seeck p. 333.

The arguments against associating the beast chase of 360[19] with the Olympic Games of that year are again strong, even if not quite conclusive. First, the show could be postponed indefinitely[20]. Had it been part of the Olympic Games we would have expected its date to have been linked with that of the rest of the Games, which were held in July and August[21]. Then, Libanius states that invitations were extended to the cities specifically for this show[22]. There is no suggestion that the invitation was to the Olympic Games as a whole and that the animal hunts would be only one of many spectacles the visitors would see. Finally, Libanius' explanation of his cousin's actions would not make good sense if the cousin's liturgy was the production of the Olympic Games. For Libanius tells us that his cousin had issued the invitations and was preparing an exceptionally splendid show, because he was resigning his liturgy and the present show would be the last to be given by him[23]. Had the spectacle been part of the Olympic Games there would have been no occasion to proclaim the end of a liturgy which would have ended automatically with the conclusion of the Olympic Festival.

Another man is described as preparing an animal hunt late in 359 or early in 360[24]. This was Obodianus, who was providing the *venatio* in the name of his schoolboy son, Argyrius. It is possible that Obodianus was preparing the show for the Olympic Games of summer 360, though there is no hint to that effect in Libanius' letter. The letter does, however, show that preparations were only just beginning and it is doubtful whether Obodianus would have completed his preparations by July or August, in time for the Games.

The writings of Libanius thus provide little support for the thesis that the shows of the Syriarch formed part of the Olympic Games. It must also be noted that Libanius never reminded the men, whose support for an animal hunt he was trying to obtain, that they would be honouring Zeus if they did him the favour[25]. Only few letters written explicitly for the purpose of requesting help

[19] Ep. 217–219 (360) liturgy of Libanius' cousin. Ep. 113 (winter 369–60) liturgy of Obodianus and Argyrius.

[20] Ep. 218, t. 10, p. 200, l. 19 ff.

[21] Malalas 284,16.

[22] i.e. for the last production of the animal hunt liturgy. Ep. 218, t. 10, p. 200, l. 18; Cf. Ep. 219, p. 202, l. 1.

[23] Ep. 217, t. 10, p. 198, l. 12 ἐπ' ἐξόδῳ τῆς λειτουργίας ὁ ἀνεψιός ἐστί μου. νόμος δὲ τὰ τελευταῖα καὶ μέγιστα εἶναι τῆς γε τοιαύτης λειτουργίας.

[24] Ep. 113 (winter 359–60) I see in him the successor to the liturgy of Libanius' cousin. I agree with Petit, p. 129, that this show was never held and that this was the reason why Celsus in 364 could restore a spectacle which had been long omitted. (ep. 1399 (363) t. 11, p. 441, l. 22).

[25] Ep. 843, 1181, 1183, 1182, 1180, 1179, 1167, 440, i.e. 8 letters in all, explicitly refer to Olympic Games and at the same time mention that the Games belong to Zeus or that they are sacred. The following 9 letters mention Olympic Games but have no reference to the sacred character of Games; ep. 1243, 1278, 1279, 1189, 1038, 36, 552, 1017. 439. Of this

for the Olympic Games are without some reference to the Games' divine patron. The explanation might be that the ardent Hellene, Libanius, refused to recognise that the Syriarch's show with its Roman associations had become part of the Olympic Games. This is suggested by Petit[26]. Another explanation is that it had not in fact done so.

In order to establish the real nature of the Syriarch's office it will be necessary to survey the passages of Libanius which deal with wild beast chases more closely. It has already been mentioned that in 363 Celsus, a senator and ex-governor of Cilicia, and as such personally immune from civic liturgies, was preparing a liturgy to be performed in the name of his son[9] and that Libanius expressly gives him the title of Syriarch[27]. We are also told that the provider of this liturgy wore a special robe and crown[28]. He received a subsidy out of the Imperial treasury which was paid out rather tardily[29]. The entertainments provided by him included chariot races, theatrical shows and, most popular of all, wild beast chases, δεῖ δὲ αὐτὸν τὰ αὐτοῦ νῦν μὲν ἡνιόχων ποιεῖν, νῦν δὲ τῶν εἰς τὸ θέατρον εἰσιόντων κυνηγέτας τε ἀγείρειν κούφους καὶ θηρία κρείττω τέχνης ἁπάσης[30]. He provided these spectacles not for Antioch only but for the seventeen cities of Syria[14].

It is probable that the liturgy prepared by Celsus in 363 was actually performed in 364[17]. Yet, in the following year, 365, we are again informed about a man called Celsus who was producing a wild beast chase in the name of his son (Cynegius) to be given to the province of Syria in this year[31]. He was not very lucky. First, an agent who was trying to bring hunters from the province of Asia for the show at Antioch was arrested for some illegality and condemned[32]. Then, when Celsus had already invited the province to the show, a letter from Constantinople forbade the killing of the more impressive of the wild beasts, which were to be reserved for the Emperor[33]. We do not know whether Libanius' letter obtained the reversal of this command.

It would be reasonable to assume that the Celsus who was performing a liturgy in 365 was the same individual as the Syriarch of 364. Neither Seeck nor Petit approves of this conclusion. Seeck identifies the Celsus of 365 with another man of the same name[34]. Petit prefers to date the two letters in 364, in spite of the fact that they stand in a sequence of letters of 365[35]. Neither suggestion is very convincing. But then the date and identification provide a

group only two letters, eps. 1189, 439, request help for the Games and are thus strictly comparable with the letters seeking assistance for animal hunts. Concerning animal hunts we have 18 letters. Not one of them has a reference to Zeus or any other divinity interested in the success of the spectacle.

[26] Cf. Petit, p. 129.   [27] Ep. 1400, 1459.   [28] Ep. 1399, t. 11, p. 442, l. 2.
[29] Ep. 1459, 1147–48.   [30] Ep. 1400, t. 11, p. 443, l. 10–11.
[31] Ep. 1509, 1520 (365). 'To Syria': t. 11, p. 543, l. 10–11. 'The show of the province,' ibid. l. 13. Described as πανήγυρις ibid. l. 23.   [32] Ep. 1509.
[33] Ep. 1520.   [34] Seeck, p. 106–7.   [35] Petit, p. 131, note 12.

difficulty only if you assume that the liturgy of the Syriarch was performed with the Olympic Games only every four years. Once it is granted that the Syriarchy had to be produced annually and that it could be held by the same liturgant for several years the difficulty disappears.

It must be added that the liturgy of the Syriarch was surely the provision of spectacles to the assembly of the province of Syria. As we have seen the title Syriarch recalls the titles of the officials who are known to have produced shows at assemblies of other provinces[36]. Again, the statements that the show is "the show of the province", is given "to Syria"[37], is watched by "the seventeen cities"[14], must mean that the other cities of the province were officially represented at the spectacles; in other words, that they accompanied a meeting of the provincial assembly.

Since we have now obtained some sort of idea of the functions of the Syriarch we can inquire whether some of the other beast chase liturgies mentioned by Libanius can be identified with that of the Syriarch. The liturgy prepared by Libanius' cousin late in 356 has already been mentioned[16]. About this liturgy Libanius wrote a letter to his kinsman Spectatus who was a notary at court. In this letter he reminds Spectatus that the cousin's liturgy has not yet been confirmed by the Emperor's "nod" and that Spectatus ought to help obtain this[38]. We cannot be certain what was meant by the Emperor's nod. Does Libanius mean that this particular liturgy had to be sanctioned by the Emperor, or is he asking for a financial subsidy?[39] Perhaps Spectatus' mission was concerned with both these topics. At any rate, the Emperor was directly interested in this show and such interest would be most easily explained if this show was the show of the assembly of the province and thus directly in honour of the Emperor.

In the course of the year 357 there are several references in the letters to certain negotiations undertaken by Libanius in order to arrange an exchange of wild beasts between the cities of Bithynia and Antioch[40]. Libanius' uncle Phasganius also took an interest in this deal. The interest of the two members of the family in beast chases would be explained if Libanius' cousin was still preparing his show.

Libanius' cousin is mentioned again in letters of the year 360[41]. We are told that he is now ἐπ' ἐξόδῳ τῆς λειτουργίας and intends to follow the custom, which is to make the last show the greatest of all[23]. We are told this in a letter of the year 360, in which Libanius asked the governor of Phoenicia to send some of the

---

[36] See above p. 114; also note 10. See also G. Downey's article in T.A.P.A., 1939, cited in note 1, on page 434 note 33.   [37] See note 31.

[38] τῷ μὲν γὰρ ἀνεψιῷ τὴν λειτουργίαν ἐφ' ἣν κέκληται δεῖ βασιλέως βεβαιωθῆναι νεύματι. [ep. 545].

[39] A subsidy mentioned eps. 970–1 (390) also eps. 1459 (363), 1147–8 (364).

[40] Eps. 586–8, 598–9. Phasganius interested: ep. 586, t. 10, p. 550, l. 20.   [41] Eps. 217–19.

hunters for which the province was famous to take part in the show. Immediately after, an Imperial edict from Constantinople forbade the killing of the beasts. The Emperor intended to come to Antioch and the animals were to be preserved to be hunted by him[42]. Two alternatives now faced the cousin. He could either not invite the σύνοδος and postpone his show through the winter, which would be ruinously expensive. Or he might invite the cities and produce a rudimentary show, regardless of the ridicule and unpopularity this would bring him[43]. The σύνοδος referred to by Libanius in his passage was surely the assembly of Syria, composed of the representatives of the seventeen cities. The spectacle prepared by Libanius' cousin was therefore in all probability the Syriarchy. The probability is strengthened by a reference to a crown and robes which the producer of the show would wear[44], since we know from the account of Celsus' show that a crown and robes were worn by the Syriarch[28].

The show which Libanius cousin was due to hold late in 360 was only the last of an extremely expensive series. When did he hold the others? He could have produced them earlier in the same year but it is just as likely that they had taken place in previous years. Since the cousin had entered on a very similar liturgy late in 356 and since he is never praised for performing this most expensive beast liturgy twice, but rather chidden that a reasonable man would not have drawn out expenses over such a long time[45], I prefer the view that he assumed in 356/7 the liturgy from which he resigned in 360. This may seem too long and expensive for a single liturgy. Yet he will not have performed his first show until autumn 357 or even later, and the shows were not necessarily equally expensive every year[46].

Little detail is known of the beast show which, as reported earlier[24], Obodianus was preparing in the name of his son late in 359 or early in 360. Obodianus' immediate action was to go on embassy to the Emperor[47]. It is not said that he went to make requests in the interest of his liturgy but that is quite likely. We are also told that Argyrius, as the nominal provider of the spectacle, would wear a special robe at the performance. The embassy and the robe recall features

[42] Ep. 218, t. 10, p. 200, ls. 3–5, ibid. p. 201, ls. 7–8. Ep. 219, t. 10, p. 202, ls. 5–9, and 11–13.

[43] Ep. 218, t. 10, p. 200, l. 19ff. Cf. ep. 219, t. 10, p. 202, ls. 5–9.

[44] The σύνοδος mentioned ep. 218, t. 10, p. 200, l. 19 is surely the assembly of Syria that will be assembled as a result of the invitation to the cities, ibid. l. 18 and ep. 219, t. 10, p. 202, ls. 6–7. On 17 cities see note 9. The crown: ep. 218, t. 10, p. 201, l. 2 and ep. 219, t. 10, p. 202, l. 1.

[45] Ep. 218, t. 10, p. 200, ls. 15–17. καὶ ἦν μὲν σωφρονοῦντος μὴ πρὸς τοσοῦτον χρόνου τὴν δαπάνην ἐκτεῖναι καὶ πολλάκις τοῦτο παρηνέσαμεν. Cf. ibid. ls. 12–15 and ep. 217, t. 10, p. 198, ls. 15–18 which shows that earlier shows also involved beast fights. Cf. also ep. 219, t. 10, p. 201, ls. 19–22.

[46] The last show was the most expensive (note 23). Also, the Imperial subsidy may at times have borne a high proportion of the cost of the shows. Cf. also note 65.

[47] Ep. 113.

of the liturgies of Celsus[28] and of Libanius' cousin[44]. If the resemblance is significant we may consider that Obodianus was producing for his son the liturgy of the Syriarch but this cannot be proved. If he was producing the Syriarchy it would be necessary to suppose that he was preparing to be the successor of Libanius' cousin, and his show would only have been due to come on in 361. This would be the probable year of his performance in any case, for it is very doubtful whether Obodianus would have had sufficient time to bring to a successful end his embassy and to complete the preparations for his show before the end of 360.

Wild beast chases became the subject of controversy at Antioch in 386. The Consular of Syria, Tissamenes, ordered the Council of Antioch to produce a beast fight. The Council refused[48]. Tissamenes got a councillor of Beroea, the modern Aleppo, to produce the show[49]. He did this by bringing wild beasts and hunters from his native Beroea, and staging the chase at Antioch. In this Libanius saw a deliberate public insult to Antioch. Tissamenes' insistence on having a beast chase was particularly reprehensible because a law had been issued by the Emperor in the previous year but one, προπέρυσιν ... τὴν μὲν ἀνάγκην τῆς τοιαύτης δαπάνης ἀναιρῶν, γνώμης δὲ τὸ πρᾶγμα ποιῶν.

This law Pack and Foerster[50] have taken to be C.T. 15,9,1, issued in 384, – the year before last, reckoned from the date of the speech in which the incident is reported. But this law does not mention beast chases. Its effect is to limit the amount that might be spent on donations, *sportulae* etc., at shows, but nothing is laid down about conditions under which an entertainment liturgy should be assigned to councillors. Yet Libanius was evidently thinking of a law that explicitly permitted a Councillor to refuse to undertake such a liturgy, perhaps even of one that referred precisely to beast chase liturgies[51]. Then, C.T. 15,9,1 is addressed to the Senate of Constantinople and may apply only to shows held in that city. It is therefore unlikely that this is the law to which Libanius appealed.

More relevant to Libanius' purpose in the speech against Tissamenes is the law C.T. 12,1,103 published in 383: "Each and every person who undertakes the Syriarchia must do so of his own free will and not by imposition of compulsion." We have learnt that the production of beast chases was the most spectacular and most popular performance by the Syriarch. It is therefore quite possible that in the public mind the Syriarch was so much identified with wild beast chases that Libanius could refer to a measure making the function

---

[48] Or. 33, cs. 14–15.   [49] Or. 33, c. 21.

[50] Or. 33, t. 3, p. 173 note on line 11. R. Pack, Studies in Libanius and Antiochene Society, Ann Arbor 1935.

[51] Cf. Or. 33, t. 3, p. 173, ls. 11–12 τῆς τοιαύτης δαπάνης. i.e. a specific kind of expense. Cf. ibid. ls. 19–20. .... θηρία δὲ οὐκ ἐβούλοντο τρέφειν .... κατ' ἐξουσίαν ἔφευγον ἂν τὸ ἀνάλωμα.

of the Syriarch voluntary as the law which removed compulsion from the provision of beast chases.

If Libanius did in fact appeal to C.T. 12,1,103 it would necessarily follow that the dispute between the governor and the council in 386 arose over the performance of the wild beast show of the Syriarch. In favour of this is the emphasis with which Libanius denounces the disgrace suffered by Antioch when the show was eventually produced by a citizen of Beroea[52]. The disgrace would indeed have been blatant if the liturgy was one which it had hitherto been the privilege of Antioch, as metropolis, to provide for the humbler cities of the province[53].

Whatever the law at issue in the dispute between Tissamenes and the council of Antioch, the existence of the law of 383 and the fact that there was a dispute prove that it was at that time getting difficult to find Councillors who would undertake these extremely expensive liturgies. A few years later the Praetorian Praefect Tatianus tried to relieve the Councillors of part of the weight of this burden. He ordered the senators who had property in Syria to contribute to the expenses of the Syriarchy[54]. A very sound scheme, but as was not uncommon at the time, the senators disliked the imposition and shortly after succeeded in throwing it off.

The last reference to a beast fight in the writings of Libanius dates from the year 390. Argyrius, probably the same as the youth in whose name Obodianus had prepared a chase in 359, following in the tradition of his family, is preparing a wild beast chase. To lighten this task he requires from the Praetorian Praefect Tatian the grant of the subsidy which his father had once received from the man who was then Praetorian Praefect. This liturgy with its traditional imperial subsidy might well be the Syriarchy[55].

I have suggested that all beast chases mentioned in the writings of Libanius represented the liturgy of the Syriarch. It would follow from this conclusion that there was only one recurring beast chase liturgy at Antioch. There is evidence in favour of this view. When the Syriarch Celsus produced his show he gave the city a spectacle it had not seen for a long time[56]. This suggests that when the Syriarch did not produce a show nobody else did. But there is further reason for supposing that beast chases were rare.

[52] Or. 33, c. 22.

[53] Against the identification is that 383 was not 'the year before last' in 386. But Libanius is not always exact in indications of time. Thus, πρῴην in Or. 49, c. 31 of after 388 refers to an incident already mentioned in a speech of 381 (Or. 2, c. 34).

[54] C.T. 6, 3, 1 (393), Praef. Urb. abolishes the contribution to the Syriarchy. Cf. C.T. 12, 1, 131, Praef. Urb. which abolishes a contribution towards the heating of the baths imposed by Tatian.

[55] Eps. 970–1.

[56] Ep. 1399 (363) t. 11, p. 441, l. 22. τοῦτο δὴ τὸ θέαμα does not refer to the Syriarchy in general but to beast chases in particular.

We learn from inscriptions of the early Empire that wild beast chases and gladiator fights usually formed part of the same programme[57]. Such programmes were rarely given by a private citizen. It was normally provided only by priests of the Imperial cult, whether priests of cities or priests of provinces[58]. The combats were under central control. Sometimes imperial authorisation was required. Robert cites as an example the inscription of an ἀρχιερεύς of the assembly of Crete, who by special grants had been allowed to produce an exceptionally bloody programme[59]. The Imperial Indulgence laid down the number of days that might be devoted to this spectacle. It established how many gladiators might fight, how many pairs would be permitted to fight to death. The Imperial decree apportioned the time that might be given to beasts fighting each other or to fights between animals and men, and gave the priest authority to have as many animals killed as he wished. It therefore appears that the right to produce beast and gladiator shows was a boon and a privilege, which the Emperor only granted sparingly and on condition that it was performed by a priest of the Imperial cult in his honour[60]. It is therefore reasonable to assume that the liturgy of the Syriarch was the only civic duty at Antioch entailing the production of beast chases.

We may now summarise what has been learnt about the Syriarch. He was normally a Councillor of Antioch, elected to produce certain spectacles. These were enormously expensive, even though the liturgy received an Imperial subsidy, which was granted anew to each holder of the office[61]. While the Syriarch may have produced chariot races and theatrical entertainments at various times throughout the year[62], his greatest effort was the organisation of

[57] L. Robert 'Les Gladiateurs dans l'Orient Grec', Paris 1940, p. 309.

[58] Ibid. p. 271. But this is denied by Magie in the work cited in note 9, t. 1, p. 656 and t. 2 p. 1526.   [59] Ibid. p. 118, no. 63.

[60] Certain features of the beast chases at Antioch are likely to be the result of the Imperial ownership and control of beast chases. Such features are the prohibitions of killings so that beasts might be kept for the Emperor (notes 33 and 42), and the suggestion that it was illegal to entice hunters out of one province into another (ep. 1509). Perhaps also there were restrictions on the traffic in beasts, for when Libanius tried to arrange an exchange of beasts with friends who were producing a beast chase in Bithynia (eps. 586–8 and 598–9) it seems that the friends had to obtain permission to send beasts from the Council of their city. (Or is the κοινόν of ep. 587, t. 10, p. 551, l. 14 the assembly of Bithynia?) Possibly governor's permission was also needed for export, eps. 588 and 599. It seems that lions were preserved for the Emperor's amusement since C.T. 15, 11,1 (415) implies that up to then it had been an offence to kill a lion, even if he was a public danger. Finally, the Emperor's 'nod' (ep. 545, see note 38) may refer to the permission that was required from the Emperor for a beast show.

[61] That definite resources were set aside for it follows from C.J. 1, 36, 1. That subsidy had to be granted again each time, references in note 39.

[62] I conclude this from the use of νῦν ... νῦν in ep. 1400 t. 11, p. 443, l. 10. This suggests that the different kinds of expense mentioned were not made at the same time. See also note 65.

a show for the seventeen cities of Syria. Of this show wild beast chases formed the most important and characteristic part. There is no evidence that gladiators took part and there is reason to believe that this cruel spectacle was no longer seen at Antioch in the second half of the 4th Century[63]. The principal show of the Syriarch was probably held in summer or autumn[64]. Preparations, including the search for beasts in provinces as distant as Bithynia and Pamphylia, might start a year earlier[17]. The Syriarch might perform his liturgy for several years in succession[65].

The title of Syriarch, the reference to the seventeen cities and the connection with beast chases all suggest that the Syriarch performed his liturgy for the provincial assembly of Syria and that his office was a vestige of the provincial imperial cult, which was too popular, or too important for the maintenance of loyal feelings among the provincials, to be abandoned when the Emperor became a Christian[66]. The office of the Syriarch in Syria was in no way unique. Quite similar roles were played by the *sacerdotes provinciarum* and *coronati* who appear in numerous laws and on a few inscriptions of this period[67].

[63] Only reference to gladiators in Libanius's writings Or 1, c. 3. This was in c. 330 A.D. Since Libanius tells us so much of beast chases, which had formerly been linked with gladiator fights, we may conclude from his silence that gladiator shows were abandoned later in his life. This conclusion is also reached by J. C. Baur from the study of writings of St. John Chrysostomus. 'Johannes Chrysostomus und seine Zeit', Munich 1929, t. 1, p. 129.

[64] Seeck dates ep. 218 in summer or autumn 360. Seeck p. 372.

[65] According to Malalas 285, ls. 12–16, the Emperor Commodus arranged that beast chases were to be held for 32 (a transmission error for 42 ?) months of a four year cycle. The remaining 6 months were to be filled with the collection of beasts for hunting at the festival of Ares and Artemis. If these lines refer to the liturgy of the Syriarch the full-term of office would have been four years, which we have seen may have been the time the liturgy was performed by the cousin of Libanius. But Libanius emphasises that his cousin was not obliged to perform as long as he did. Other details are not confirmed by Libanius. He does not suggest that beast chases were produced over a 32 (or 42) months period but that they were produced at one festival once a year. It is however possible that the small shows of the Syriarch, composed of races or theatricals, might in more prosperous times have been beast shows also. Libanius mentions a festival of Artemis held in spring (Or. 5, c. 43) which was celebrated with boxing competitions. He says nothing of beast shows.

[66] On reduction of Imperial cult until only the production of shows was left see P.W. IV, 1 'Concilium' (Huelsen) col. 824. Also Th. Mommsen 'Das Fest-Verzeichnis aus Capua' (C.I.L. 10, 3792), Gesammelte Schriften vol. VIII, pp. 14–24. There is room for considerable amount of research on the history of various aspects of the Imperial cult under the Christian Emperors.

[67] For the evidence on the later assemblies and their officials see P. Guiraud 'Les assemblées provinciales dans l'Empire Romain', Paris 1887, pp. 219–85. The duties of the priests of the Flavian cult recorded on the Hispellum inscription Dessau, I.L.S. 705; Th. Mommsen 'Gesammelte Schriften,' vol. VIII, p. 25–45 correspond closely to those of the Syriarch; so do those of the officials variously described as Coronati, holders of the 'honor Asiae', or Asiarchae in the edict sent to the proconsul of Asia in 375, Bruns, 'Fontes Juris Romani Antiqui' ed. 7, no. 97b.

The Syriarch had nothing to do with the Antiochene Olympic Games, which took place every four years[68] and was the responsibility of a number of officials, but principally of the Alytarch[69]. The Olympic Games, too, may have been held in association with the provincial assembly of Syria[70], but the fact that its main attraction consisted of athletic contests, and the dedication to Zeus, show that the Olympic Games was basically a Hellenic cultural and religious festival, not a political Roman one, even though this distinction would tend to disappear with the progress of Christianity[71].

The Emperors of the 4th Century made great efforts to keep the provincial assemblies alive and even to use them for new purposes[72]. There is, for instance, evidence in a few laws of the Theodosian Code that the high priests of provinces were gaining the function of legally representing private individuals before the local governor, before governors of other provinces, or even the Emperor himself[73]. Unfortunately, Libanius does not tell us anything about this development. He does not mention a single example of political or legal activity on the part of the assembly of Syria. How comprehensive the suggestions of a provincial assembly could be is shown by the topics debated at one session of the assembly of the province of Cyrene. These included the large number of barbarian mercenaries stationed in the province and the question whether the province should continue as a separate military command or be united with

[68] Petit p. 130. Stauffenberg p. 438.

[69] On Alytarch see note 3. It follows that of the men listed by Petit on p. 131 of his work, as Syriarchs responsible for the production of Olympic Games, only Celsus and Libanius' cousin should receive that title, though they should have it on account of the 'venationes' they had produced not for any part they had in the production of Olympic Games. The other men listed by Petit are likely to have been Alytarchs. Incidentally, Letoius, who produced the Olympic Games at a time when both Libanius and Themistius were at Constantinople, (ep. 551, t. 10, p. 514, 1, 14 – 15 and ep. 552, t. 10, p. 517, 1, 16–17) certainly did not produce them in 356, as Petit suggests, but in 352.

[70] See above p. 115.

[71] One effect may have been that the Imperial Government began to treat all the major spectacle-producing priesthoods on the same level, whether they originally had been associated with the Imperial Cult or not. This would account for the laws cited in note 7 which mention Syriarch and Alytarch together. It might also explain why the inscription, Bruns, 97b, treats Asiarchs and Alytarchs in the province of Asia as equivalent dignitaries in the same regulation. Their respective shows may well have stood in the same relationship as the Olympic Games and the shows of the Syriarch at Antioch.

[72] J. A. O. Larsen, 'The Position of the Provincial Assemblies in the Government and Society of the Late Roman Empire', Classical Philology 1934, p. 209–20. By the same author, 'Representative Government in Greek and Roman History', University of California Press, 1955, p. 145–157.

[73] Priests of Provinces as 'patrons' of individuals or corporations, C.T. 12, 1, 46 (358) Vicar of Africa. C.T. 16, 2, 38 (407) Proconsul of Africa and Coll. Concil. ed. Mansi t. III, p. 802 = t. 4, p. 501 cited by Th. Mommsen 'Gesammelte Schriften' t. VIII, p. 487.

Egypt[74]. Clearly, the final resolution taken by Synesius to Constantinople contained requests on these matters, as well as the customary plea for relief from taxation. But we do not know whether the assembly of Syria sent such embassies or not.

The last topic of interest raised by the liturgy of the Syriarch is the manner of its abolition. In 465 a law abolished the liturgy and transferred its funds and functions to the Consular of Syria. The same regulation transferred responsibility for the Olympic Games to the Comes Orientis[75]. Henceforth Councillors were expressly prohibited from performing either liturgy. Thus the Council of Antioch was relieved of the burden of its two most expensive duties[76]. But why? Since Councillors had to be prevented from volunteering for these performances, there evidently remained in the Council men able to afford the financial responsibility for the Games. The evidence of Libanius, too, would have led us to expect that some very wealthy families would remain in the Council of Antioch, in spite of conditions unfavourable to the Council as a whole. A few powerful members were benefiting from the hardships of their colleagues[77]. The reasons, then, which led the government to reverse its normal policy of compelling Councillors to undertake duties are still obscure. Perhaps they are also behind the disappearance from new legislation in the second half of the 5th. Century of references to priests of provinces[78]. More research is required on this, as on other problems of 5th. Century municipal government.

---

[74] C. Lacombrade, 'Synesius, discours sur la royauté,' Paris 1951, p. 11–20.

On the varied activities of assemblies of other provinces in the 4th Century see P. Guiraud's work cited in note 67, p. 272 ff.

[75] C.J. 1, 36, 1.

[76] Nullique penitus curialium nec si voluerint idem munus, vel honorem subeundi licentia permittatur.

[77] Or. 49, c. 8; Or. 48, c. 4. On the wealth of the Councillors of Antioch see Petit, p. 330 ff.

[78] On this see P.W. IV, 1, col. 829 'Concilium' (Hülsen), according to whom C.J. 10, 65, 5 = C.T. 12, 12, 12 (392) is the only law concerning provincial assemblies taken over into the Code of Justinian. See also on the end of the Imperial Cult O. Hirschfeld, 'Zur Geschichte des römischen Kaiserkultus,' S.B. der Berliner Akademie, 35, 1888, p. 833–62 in O. Hirschfeld, 'Kleine Schriften,' Berlin, 1913, on p. 503; and E. Kornemann, 'Zur Geschichte der antiken Herrscherkulte', in Klio, 1, 1901, on p. 140–2. The last reference to a provincial priest in a new law is in Nov. Marc. 4 of 454.

XII

THE FINANCES OF ANTIOCH IN THE FOURTH CENTURY A. D.

The single city state, governed by its Council, formed the basic unit of government in the Roman Empire. The fourth Century saw a weakening of City government everywhere. It was catastrophic in the West, serious in the East. The degree of the decline is most easily estimated from the condition of the city of Antioch. For, thanks to the Sophist Libanius, we are much better informed about this city than about any other in the East.

The present essay will approach the problem of the survival of civic constitutions from the aspect of finance. The traditional method of financing civic services was by means of a combination of liturgies (the munificence of decurions), endowments, revenues from civic estates, and taxes.[1] In the fourth Century these means of paying for civic servives were breaking down. The councillors were becoming too few and too poor to be able to perform the necessary liturgies.[2] The civic estates and civic taxes were confiscated by the Imperial treasury.

The act of confiscation probably took place during the reign of Constantius. Its exact date is not known but the evidence is strong that during the second half of the fourth Century, the brief reign of Julian excepted, estates of the cities were in Imperial ownership and the cities allowed the use of only a fraction of their old income from land and taxes.[3] Clearly, these unfavourable developments must have brought about far-reaching changes in the financial organisation of the cities and the civic services financed by them. The present study will attempt to assess the nature and extent of the changes at Antioch.

Any study of the finances of Antioch must start from the problem of the city's estates. For, in apparent contradiction to the evidence suggesting

---

[1] W. Liebenam: ,,Städteverwaltung im Römischen Kaiserreiche". Leipzig, 1900, pp. 2–68.

[2] See for instance A. H. M. Jones, "The Greek City from Alexander to Justinian". Oxford, 1940, p. 193 ff. on depletion of Councils.

At Antioch, as Petit has well shown, the impoverishment of the Council was caused as much by the wealthiest Councillors rising above it as by the poorer members succumbing to their burdens. P. Petit: "Libanius et la vie municipale à Antioche au 4ième siècle après J.-C." Paris 1955 (henceforth cited as "Petit".) p. 335.

[3] See A. H. M. Jones: "Greek City", pp. 149, 251, 331 and note 98. – A. Piganiol: "L'Empire Chrétien", Paris, 1947, p. 281. – E. Stein: "Geschichte des Spätrömischen Reiches", t. i. Wien 1928, p. 279. – J. Declareuil: "Quelques problèmes d'histoire des institutions municipales au temps de l'Empire romain" in Nouvelle Revue historique de droit Français et étranger, vol. 32 of 1908. The view summarised is that of Jones who also believes that the third of the land whose revenues went to the cities was later placed in the charge of the civic authorities.

that the civic estates had been confiscated everywhere, the evidence of Libanius on conditions at Antioch leaves no doubt that that city was closely concerned with the administration of its estates for much of the second half of the fourth Century. In his „De Rhetoribus" of c. 360[4] Libanius mentions civic estates at the disposal of the Council.[5] The Council had let the larger estates to members[6] but was entitled to let estates to outsiders as well,[7] to Zenobius the Sophist, Libanius' predecessor at Antioch, for instance,[8] or if it were so minded to Libanius' underteachers.[9] This was in the last part of the reign of the Emperor Constantius, at a time when the civic estates were in all likelihood already confiscated.

Leaving aside for the moment the reign of Julian, the remaining evidence belongs to the last decade of Libanius' life, the eighties of the fourth Century. Libanius leaves us in no doubt that at this period also the city of Antioch administrated and drew rents from estates. The estates were farmed for the city and their produce was, or should have been, the property of the city.[10] Thus argued Libanius, who wished animals to be requisitioned from these estates to carry building rubble out of Antioch. Next, after the riot of the statues, Libanius suggests that his city first lost and then received back from a forgiving Emperor what he calls τὴν αὐτῆς γῆν[11] or τὰς οὐσίας,[12] which is most easily explained as the civic estates. Lastly, we are informed about a doctor, who farmed the land of the Council, always paying his rents and sometimes exceeding them.[13] These estates were not recently acquired but had been left to the city by men of old.[14] They do not therefore represent resources which the city had acquired after the loss of its ancient properties and endowments.

How can the fact that the city of Antioch did administer ancient estates be reconciled with the evidence strongly suggesting Imperial confiscation? Petit proposes the solution that there existed at Antioch and elsewhere two distinct categories of civic estates from which revenues flowed

---

[4] Or. 31 in R. Foerster's edition of Libanius in the Bibliotheca Teubneriana. All references to Libanius are to this edition and all references which do not mention an author are to Libanius. – The date of Or. 31 – P. Wolf: "Vom Schulwesen der Spätantike", Baden-Baden, 1952, p. 91.

[5] Or. 31, c. 16 ff. Γεωργεῖτε τοὺς ἀγροὺς τῆς πόλεως σχεδὸν ἅπαντας οἱ βουλεύοντες ὑμεῖς, ὃ τῇ μὲν παρασκευάζει Φοιτᾶν ἐντελῆ τὴν πρόσοδον . . .

[6] Or. 31, c. 16, t. 3, p. 132, ls. 12–15.

[7] Ibid. p. 132, l. 19 ff. The Council also had the right to withdraw all tenancies Ibid. p. 133, l. 1.

[8] Or. 31, c. 20.

[9] Or. 31, c. 17.

[10] Or. 50, c. 5 ἐστι τῇ πόλει Χωρία παρὰ παλαιῶν ἀνδρῶν ἐν διαθήκαις δεδομένα τῇ πόλει. ταῦτα γεωργεῖται τῇ πόλει καὶ τούτων ἐστὶν ἡ πρόσοδος τῆς κεκτημένης.

[11] Or. 20, c. 7, t. 2, p. 424, l. 19 recording the restoration of the land.

[12] Or. 20, c. 38.

[13] Or. 52, c. 33. ἣν γὰρ ἡ βουλὴ γῆν ταύτην ἐγεώργησε τιμὰς μέν τὰς προσηκούσας τιθεὶς καί που καὶ μείζονας . . .

[14] Or. 50, c. 5., t. 3, p. 473, ls. 7–8.

into two quite separate treasuries and that the Emperors confiscated only estates belonging to one class.[15] This is in itself a perfectly reasonable solution. The financial resources of Greek cities were often not administrated in as unified a manner as efficiency might be thought to require.[16] Nevertheless, the particular arguments upon which Petit bases his case are quite unconvincing. His main support is a statement in the Emperor Julian's "Misopogon", according to which the citizens of Antioch at that time possessed 10,000 (or just very many?) κλῆροι of land.[17] The term κλῆρος he considers to date back to the time of the foundation of Antioch, when King Seleucos Nicator granted the Greek and Macedonian settlers land from his own royal domain, which was appropriately divided into "lots".[18] Accordingly, Petit contrasts these civic estates derived from the Seleucid royal domain with those mentioned by Libanius as derived from legacies. Only the lands which had originally been royal possessions were taken over by the Imperial Government, which might in a sense be described as having resumed a long-lapsed ownership.

This argument is unacceptable. First, it is not very likely that the Seleucid "lots" still formed a significant proportion of the civic estates of the cities of the East after so long an interval of time. Then, I cannot find a hint at this particular definition of the nature of the civic estates under Imperial ownerships in the laws dealing with the matter in the Codes. Lastly, Julian's use of the word κλῆρος is surely only determined by his Atticising sensibility. Like Libanius himself, Julian disdained to disfigure his literary prose with contemporary jargon. This is shown most relevantly by a passage, also from "The Misopogon", in which the word κλῆρος is used in a context where, as Déléage has seen, the Latin "jugum" would have been appropriate.[19] We cannot therefore make the use of the word κλῆρος by Julian the basis of a classification of civic estates and we cannot use any classification derived from it to establish the existence of two separate treasuries at Antioch. The apparent contradiction between the evidence of Libanius and that of the Laws over the confiscation of the civic estates by the Government must be resolved in some other way.

Libanius' information on the civic estates really resolves itself into four statements. The estates continued to be in real sense the estates of the city. The rents were paid entirely to the city. The estates were largely leased to decurions. The leasing was in the hands of the Council. The task of re-

---

[15] Work cited in note 2, p. 99.

[16] Jones: "Greek City", p. 241.

[17] Julian: "Misopogon", 362, C. μυρίους κλήρους γῆς ἰδίας κεκτημένη [ἡ πόλις]. — A. H. M. Jones suggests that "very many" should be the translation of μυρίους.

[18] Petit suggests that a special tax on this category of land preserved the memory of the original 10,000 "lots". He cites Digest 50, 15, 8 in support but there is no reason to suppose that the "tribute" there mentioned was a tax on civic estates.

[19] "Misopogon", 370, D; 371, A. Déléage: "La capitation du bas empire", Maçon, 1945, p. 160. Petit himself cites Julian and Déléage's comment but rejects their implication, Petit., p. 97.

conciling these statements with the laws is complicated by the fact that evidence is not plentiful. Moreover, in the period after Julian, divergencies began to appear in the administration of the two halves of the Empire which make it unsafe to make deductions about conditions in one half from evidence relating to the other.[20] This is particularly troublesome because the bulk of the evidence comes from the West, while we are concerned with the East.[21] The scheme of estate administration which we can build up from the Laws, such as it is, is not inconsistent with the evidence of Libanius.

The estates had probably been confiscated by Constantius;[22] they were restored by Julian.[23] But very shortly after Julian's death, the Emperors, in great need of money to make good the losses suffered by the army on Julian's Persian Campaign, took the civic estates over once more.[24] The earliest evidence for this is an inscription recording instructions sent by the Emperor Valens to the Proconsul of Asia in 370 or 371.[25] The inscription suggests that by the original edict of confiscation the Emperor had taken over both the ownership and the whole revenue of the estates. The estates were joined to the Res Privata, and "actores" of the Res Privata collected rents and arranged leases. The cities received no income at all.

---

[20] On the differences in the sphere of financial administration see J. P. C. Kent's unpublished thesis: "The office of the Comes Sacrae Largitionis". Thus for example in the later 4th Century in the West the revenue of the "nationalised" civic estates went to the sacra largitio, together with the revenue of all other state lands in perpetual or short lease, while in the East they went to the Res Privata. – Of course, the practice of administration was not necessarily uniform within one half of the Empire.

[21] This is true of the laws contained in the Theodosian Code as a whole. Cf. O. Seeck, "Geschichte des Untergangs der antiken Welt", t. 6, p. 173 ff.

[22] This must be deduced from the fact that Julian restored them. Nothing is known of the time and circumstances of the confiscation. Petit p. 102 follows S. Mazzarino, "Aspetti sociali del quarto secolo", pp. 323–6, in supposing that C. T. 4, 13, 5 of 358 refers to the confiscated corporate revenue of the cities. I see no evidence for this view. The term "vectigalia" is explained in the "interpretatio" of C. T. 4, 13, 1. They were a kind of toll collected by the Imperial authorities.

[23] Julian's restoration of the estates: C. T. 10, 3, 1; C. T. 15, 1, 10; C. T. 15, 1, 8 = C. J. 8, 11, 4; C. T. 15, 1, 9; C. J. 8, 11, 3; C. J. 10, 70, 2. Ammianus 25, 4, 15. Libanius Or. 13, c. 45; ep. 828.

[24] The probable motive for confiscations: Ammianus 30, 8, 8. I have seen no evidence that any class of estates escaped confiscation. As far as I have seen, the evidence suggests that confiscation was complete. The inscription, Bruns, "Fontes Juris Romani Antiqui" ed. 7 no. 97 A, written some years after the confiscation, grants to Ephesus 100 juga of land, which that city might hold together with a certain estate, called Leuke, which was already in the city's administration by special grant of the Emperor "nostra iam liberalitate". The suggestion is that apart from the Emperor's generosity the city had no estate left at all.

[25] Bruns: "Fontes Juris Romani Antiqui", ed. 7, no. 97. A, S. Riccobono: "Fontes Juris Romani Antejustiniani", Florence 1940, t. 1., p. 511, no. 108. Commentaries by Schulten and Heberdey in Jahreshefte des Österreichischen Archäologischen Instituts, no. 9, 1906, p. 43 ff. and p. 182 ff. On the whole I follow the interpretation of Heberdey.

348

Some time later the cities of Asia were granted the use of varying pro-
portions of the revenue of their former estates to help them rebuild their
fortifications and possibly other structures, but certainly only for definite
and approved purposes.

Next, an embassy of the city of Ephesus asked the Emperor to restore
to the city the management of its estates. Valens refused at first, but then
returned to the city 100 juga of land. This land, together with an estate
granted on an earlier occasion, Ephesus might administer, and if Ephesus
made good use of this favour in the interest of wall-building, other cities
would be granted similar benefits.

At about the same time or earlier, a report from the proconsul of Asia
had reached the Emperor Valens, in which that official advocated the restoration of the civic estates to the cities. At present the "actores" were
refusing the cities the share of the revenues which the Emperor had allowed
them. They were also putting into their own pockets "id quod amplius
ex isdem fundis super statutum canonem colligitur", that is, the excess
of the actual rents of the estates over the "canon", fixed once and for all,
which the Res Privata drew from the lands. The restoration of the estates
to the administration of the cities would end both these abuses. Moreover,
it would give the cities a chance to increase their share of the income of the
estates beyond the quota allotted them by the Emperor, through efficient
management.[26]

On consideration Valens appears to have accepted these arguments. In
his reply, he suggested to the proconsul that he might divide all the civic
estates in his province between the various cities. He would have to
arrange for the collection of the "canon" and its transmission to the Res
Privata through his officium, leaving to the cities that proportion which
Valens had previously allowed them,[27] together with any surplus by
which the revenue from the estates exceeded the canon fixed by the Res
Privata.[28]

Valens' edict is phrased in the form of advice, not command. Nevertheless, we may assume that the Emperor's advice was taken and that
the estates were distributed among the cities. What administrative changes
would follow on this act of distribution? The aim of the reform was to enable
the cities to benefit by the higher revenue that they might get from the
estates through better management. The only way of increasing the
revenue would be through new leases. The only guarantee that the new
rents would go to the cities would be to allow the cities, by means of their

---

[26] ... possitque a curialibus vel excultione majore vel propensiore diligentia non-
nullus praestitionis cumulus ad gratiam concessionis accedere.

[27] ... ut arbitrio tuo per curias singulas omni jugatione dispersa retracto eo redi-
tuum modo quem unicuique civitatum propria largitate concessimus reliquam summam
per officium tuum rei privatae nostrae inferre festines.

[28] ... et si quid extrinsi(cus luc)ri est cedat rationibus civitatum. This is earlier
stated to amount to 3000 solidi.

Councils, to collect the rents themselves.[29] It is therefore likely that as a result of Valens' edict the cities of Asia received back the right to arrange leases and collect rents on their estates. Its effect might be summarised as the restoration of the estates to the cities, together with a heavy fixed tax on their revenues. I suggest that this situation would be perfectly compatible with the evidence of Libanius.

I would further suggest that Valens' settlement lasted. It gave advantages to both parties. The cities did not get back all they had had under Julian. They did not get back ownership. There was probably some redistribution of land between cities. Some lands had probably already been disposed of by the Emperor for the benefit of powerful or influential people.[30] These would never again pass under full civic control. The revenue left to the cities will have been only a fraction of the figure they had drawn in Julian's day. On the other hand, the cities were now sure of getting their share of the canon and any surplus as well. Besides, since the leasing of the estates was now in the Councillors' hands, they could lease them to colleagues and thus lighten each other's burden of liturgies. As for the Emperor, he was now assured of a fixed yearly income. He could no longer be cheated, since he knew the amount in advance and was no longer dependent on agents of direct administration, a system which Emperors had often tried out in various branches of state finance, never with lasting success.[31] Thus there were advantages in the arrangements for both parties and neither would be overeager to change them. It is my contention that they were not changed but adopted in essentials, at first in the East only, but later all over the Empire.

---

[29] I refer the clause, si . . . suscipere propria praestatione non abnuis, to the collection of the rents from the cities, not directly from the estates. The proconsul is asked to accept responsibility for the payment of the dues to the Res Privata, a responsibility which had been that of the actores. It does not exclude the possibility that the Council collected the rents from the estates.

[30] The last part of the inscription requires the proconsul to furnish the Emperor with full details of the estates, their rents and tenants ". . . qui in praesentem diem ha(bita licitati)one possideant, et quantum per juga singula dependant, qui etiam opimi adque utiles fundi (fisc)o gr(ati si)ngulis quibusque potentissimis elocati fuerint." Heberdey suggests that this information would provide the Emperor with a basis for the final settlement of the administration of the estates, pending which the proconsul's provisional arrangements would remain in force. Perhaps so. Certainly, the information would enable the Emperor and his officials to keep a very close watch on any departure the Councils might make from the status quo of tenants and rents. Another interpretation is possible. Riccobono reads "ha(bita donati)one" for "ha(bita licitati-)one". He cites references to donations in C. J. 11, 61, 6 and Nov. Theod. 5, 1. If Riccobono is right, the return requested of the proconsul might be of such lands as could not be returned to full civic management, because the Res Privata had either given them away, or leased them to powerful men, probably senators, or had not found tenants for them. The last group would require special action of the kind represented by C. J. 11, 59, 5 and C. T. 10, 3, 4.

[31] For the almost contemporary attempt to take tax collecting from the Councils begun in 364, C. T. 12, 6, 5; partly abandoned in 383, C. T. 11, 7, 12; over in 386, C. T. 12, 6, 20.

The earliest evidence for the West excludes curial management of civic lands. "Curialibus omnibus conducendorum rei publicae praediorum ac saltuum inhibeatur facultas."[32] This would be an impossible order, if its enforcement would depend on the very decurions against whom it was directed. The date of the law is 372. We can be sure that at that date the cities in the West did not administer their lands. But four or five years later the law had been dropped.[33]

A Western law of 374 contains the earliest reference to the rule that one-third of a city's income (canon) might be used for the benefit of the city while two-thirds must be sent to the Imperial treasury.[34] This rule was still in force in the time of Justinian.[35] In itself it was equally compatible with administration of the estates by the cities or by the Res Privata. The law of 374 does however show that in that year the accounts of the estates of the various cities were kept separate. It also shows that administration was not any longer in the hands of "actores" of the central finance department, for the revenue now passed to the treasury through the department of the provincial governor.

Next, a law of either 376 or 377 proves that decurions were at that time admitted as tenants of civic lands. Indeed, they were now the normal tenants. "They who hold fertile land belonging to a municipality . . . must also take up waste land . . . if they object to the addition of these lands . . . let them give way to *other decurions* . . . who . . . will hold the good with the bad . . ."[36] But the participation of decurions and Council, as revealed by this law, went further. If any land went out of cultivation and there was no tenant who might pay its rent, the Imperial government would nevertheless still require to receive its share and the burden of the government's demand would have to be met by the decurions as a body, the "municipes".[37] The law from which we gain this information was addressed to a Western

---

[32] C. T. 10, 3, 2 (372) Probus Pr. Prefect. Valens' inscription shows that the actores leased the land to "potentissimi" cf. note 30.

[33] C. J. 11, 59, 5 to Antonius Pr. Prefect Gaul 376–7.

[34] C. T. 15, 1, 18 (374) Probus Pr. Prefect Illyr. – Si civitatis eius res publica tantum in tertia pensionis parte non habeat quantum coeptae fabricae poscat impendium ex aliarum civitatum rei publicae *canone* praesumant, tertiae videlicet portionis.

[35] C. T. 4, 13, 7 (374) Proc. Afr. ibid. 15, 1, 26 (390) Pr. Prefect It. & Ill. ibid. 15, 1, 32 (395) C. S. L. Occ. = C. J. 8, 11, 11. – C. T. 15, 1, 33 (395) Pr. Prefect Gaul. – C. T. 5, 14, 35 = C. J. 11, 70, 3 excludes revenue of local taxes from the gross sum out of which a third is allowed the cities. It is paid to government completely. But C. J. 11, 61, 33, 3 (431) restores one-third of taxation revenue to cities.

[36] C. J. 11, 59, 5. – Qui utilia rei publicae loca possident, permixtione facta etiam deserta suscipiant, ut si earum partium graventur accessu, quas antea per fastidium reliquerunt, cedant *aliis curialibus*, qui utraque hac condicione retineant ut praestatione salva cum desertis et culta possideant sublata a paucis quos iniquum est electa retinere, cum municipes gravatura sit pars relicta.

[37] Municipes in sense of curiales C. T. 12, 1, 4; ibid. 12, 1, 89. In C. T. 15, 1, 41 municipes stands in the place in which curiales stands in C. T. 10, 3, 5. In C. T. 12, 1, 62 decurion. described as municipalis.

official. In 384, however, a law expressing a similar policy was published in the East.[38]

This law shows that in the East too the civic estates were at this time normally let to decurions. It does not state that the Councils were held responsible for the payment to the government of the whole of its share of the fixed "canon", but the analogy of the earlier Western law makes it likely that the Councils were held responsible.

Active participation by the Councils in the administration of the civic estates in the West is expressly assumed in a law of 395 . . . "Singuli igitur ordines civitatum ad reparationem moenium publicorum nihil sibi amplius noverint praesumendum praeter tertiam portionem eius canonis . . ."[39] The implication is that the Councils collected the whole canon of the estates before passing two-thirds to the governor.

A law of 400 provides further information on the status of civic estates in the West. "Edifices, gardens . . . and such lands of municipalities which are enclosed within the walls of the municipality or adjoin its boundary . . . shall remain in the hands of the decurions . . . and members of guilds and corporations of that city. The lease shall be perpetual on the understanding that the fixed rent which is proved on full examination to have been imposed on the land continues to be paid."[40] So at this time the civic properties were exclusively let to decurions and members of guilds and the tenancies were unending, provided the rent fixed once and for all was paid. The law does not create a new situation. Its purpose was to protect existing tenants from dispossession as the result of the intrigues of influential men at Constantinople. But in this purpose it was not successful. The powerful continued to intrigue and the Emperor or his officials continued to abuse the rights of Imperial ownership by granting them land.[41]

---

[38] C. T. 10, 3, 4 (384) C. R. P. Or. – In this law "antiquos possessores" is not to be understood as ancient owners, as Petit takes it. (Petit p. 99.) In laws dealing with state lands, as this one does, the „possessor" is not the proprietor but the tenant. Thus, the first line of this very law, "Ut quisque *conductor* fuerit inventus *possessor* fundi . . ." – Cf. use of "possessio" in C. T. 10, 5, 1: "conductas possessiones" in C. T. 10, 3, 3; C. J. 11, 71, 4: "veteros possessores fundorum publicorum . . ." C. T. 5, 15, 15 "Enfyteutica praedia . . . a priscis possessoribus . . . retinenda. . ." ibid. 5, 15, 20 "fundorum patrimonialium possessores . . ." etc. – Comparison with C. J. 11, 59, 5 shows that the "antiquos possessores id est decuriones" of C. T. 10, 3, 4 are the tenants who have been dismissed because they refused to take on waste land.

[39] C. T. 15, 1, 33 (395).

[40] C. T. 10, 3, 5 (400) Pr. Prefect Afr.

[41] C. T. 15, 1, 41 (401) Pr. Prefect Occ. – C. T. 15, 1, 42 (404) Pr. Prefect Or.; C. T. 15, 1, 43 (405) Pr. Prefect Occ. Nov. Theo. 17, 2, c. 5 (444) Nov. Theod. 23 (443) making significant exception for lands that have been sold ". . . vel a procuratore divinae domus vel a viro illustri comite rerum privatarum jussu nostrae clementiae vel communi consensu civitatum cum scripturae interpositione . . ." – Lastly, Nov. Marc. 3 = C. J. 11, 70, 5 deals with men who have by gift or purchase obtained possession of civic land without the liability to pay the "canon civilis" to the cities. Some of them pay a smaller sum to the Res Privata instead.

352

Our survey of the evidence on the administration of the civic estates in the fourth Century has revealed a system which is compatible with three of the four features of management suggested by the evidence of Libanius. The estates continued in real sense to be the estates of a particular city.[42] The estates were to a large extent let to Councillors. The Council collected the rent. Only the Council's control over leasing has not been proved. But this too is likely under the circumstances. The logic of Valens' settlement for Asia, as we have seen, required the arranging of leases by the Councils, and the arguments for this procedure, as argued to Valens, always remained valid. Moreover, if the Councillors as a body were obliged to make up any deficit in the share of the canon paid to the government,[36] it is likely that they had a controlling say in the assignment of tenancies. After all, they would foot the bill if a tenant proved unable to pay his rents, and their liability was sufficient guarantee against abuse of their function.[43]

To conclude, Libanius and the laws do not give contradictory evidence and there is no need to postulate different categories of civic estates in order to reconcile them.

So far, I have only discussed one form of civic property, estates of farm land. Apart from the rents of landed estate, Libanius informs us of two kinds of civic revenue: rents from shops, first exacted by the Comes Orientis Proculus in 384, and a tax reintroduced after a long interval by the consular Tissamenes, to pay for the construction of cages for wild beasts.[44] These passages suggest that new sources of income could only be created by the governor. We hear nothing of older taxes or of their confiscation.

As far as we can judge from very meagre evidence, all the revenue went into the same treasury, which was also the one to receive the product of the Imperial tax in kind. This arrangement will have simplified the task of supervision by the governors and their officials. This was evidently very close, for we are informed that the teachers who received a civic salary were paid very irregularly and only after prolonged pleading with the governor, his officials, and the ἀποδέκται,[45] the curial officials in charge of

---

[42] See Passage cited in note 34. Cf. also Nov. Th. 23 "... praedia tam urbana quam rustica nec non etiam taberna ... universis civitatibus adsignentur ..." – Nov. Marc. 3 "possessiones juris civilis cuiuslibet civitatis".

[43] But very soon after the death of Libanius (393) the application of perpetual tenancies to civic estates will have greatly reduced the councils' opportunities for reletting. – C. J. 11, 71, 3 (400–5) Hadrian Pr. Prefect. – "loca omnia fundive reipublicae propositis prius licenter edictis dehinc, ubi in eum canonis modum contendentium augmenta succreverint, ut extendi ultra aut superari alterius oblatione non possint, perpetuariis conductoribus locentur." – But cf. C. J. 11, 71, 4 which gives present tenants the right to keep their land, provided they agree to pay increased rent offered by others. If this law is later than the previous one it suggests that perpetual tenancies were not yet universal.

[44] Or. 26, c. 20. – 6 rents destined for actors. – Or. 33, c. 13 tax.

[45] Or. 31, c. 19.

the public granary.[46] It further appears that the Council of Antioch could not easily increase the salaries which were paid out of civic funds.[47] This would be quite in accordance with the spirit of a law of 349, which states that salaries may only be paid out of civic resources with permission of the Emperor.[48]

We now come to the expenditure of civic resources. Civic resources are known to have been used for the payment of certain, but not all, building work.[49] This is what we would expect, after observing in the Codes that when the government released a proportion of the revenues of civic estates, it generally did so for the benefit of public works. Civic money was also used for the payment of the civic police,[50] and of a number of teachers.[51] The rents of certain shops were assigned to the actors.[43] The income of an otherwise unknown levy contributed to the heating of the baths.[52]

The writings of Libanius suggest that the bulk of the current expenses of the civic services was still met out of liturgies. These included the production of the Olympic Games[53] and of the show of the Syriarch,[54] the maintenance of horses and the organisation of chariot races,[55] the heating of the baths,[56] certain building tasks,[57] the import of food at times of famine,[58] the provision of theatrical entertainment.[59] The Council used its control of the leasing of civic estates to let them to members with a view to helping them to support their burdens.[60] In fact, the estates were

---

[46] ἀποδέκται also mentioned Or. 57, c. 51. Or. 28, c. 16. cf. Petit pp. 53–5.

[47] Or. 31, c. 15 Libanius does not suggest a straight increase in salary. The alternative to a grant of land is private munificence.

[48] C. T. 12, 2 (349) Comes Orientis = C. J. 10, 37, 1.

[49] Or. 27, c. 3 bridge repair profitable. Also Or. 50, t. 3, p. 472, ls. 1–14.

[50] Or. 48, c. 9.

[51] Or. 31, cs. 19–20.

[52] C. T. 12, 1, 131 (393).

[53] Petit p. 125 ff.

[54] Treated by Petit together with Olympic Games, wrongly in my opinion; cf. Historia 8 (1959) 113–126.

[55] Petit p. 124. There is no reference to factions or other contractors in connection with chariot races. Or. 35, c. 14 shows that the Councillors bought the horses when they assumed a chariot racing liturgy and sold them when they had completed it. The herdsmen who looked after the horses on the meadows may have been employees of the city. How else could the Comes Orientis forbid them to pay a tribute to the robbers? Or. 27, c. 4.

[56] Bath Heating: Or. 26, cs. 5–6 and Or. 27, c. 13, Or. 28, c. 6; Or. 1, c. 272; ep. 381; Or. 49, c. 10; Or. 49, c. 31 and Or. 2, c. 34 mention some of the tasks that had to be performed in baths; Libanius does not tell us how the humble ones were normally performed at Antioch.

[57] Building liturgies. ep. 196 (358–59), ep. 617 (361), ep. 242 (358–59) ep. 620 t. X, p. 571, l. 18.

[58] Or. 11, c. 134. Or. 27, c. 6 shows that the Imperial representatives were also called upon to help.

[59] Ep. 1400 (364).

[60] Or. 31, cs. 16–17.

let out to the most powerful rather than to the most needy members.[61] Julian had presented 3000 juga of land to the city for the specific purpose of assisting the men feeding horses for the chariot races;[62] we do not know what happened to them after Julians' death. Probably they suffered the same fate as the remaining civic estates.

Liturgies were not all financial. We hear that beside the six hundred Councillors who performed the financial liturgies there were six hundred others, who only performed services for the city with their bodies, on the instructions of the former group.[63] Nothing else is known about these second six hundred. Petit's explanation of the passage is not conclusive, but he is probably right to consider that the institution was dead at the time of Libanius' writings.[64] Certain forced labour in connection with repair of public buildings was also required of the shopkeepers, who were however entitled to hire substitutes to do the work for them. Shopkeepers were also required to maintain the rest house belonging to the Cursus Publicus, to make a certain contribution to charity, and to maintain lights outside their shops at night.[65]

The city also benefited from the generosity of the powerful men, other than Councillors, who resided in the city. Some Honorati provided new public buildings voluntarily, even if they could not be compelled to do so.[66] Governors tried to make their period of office memorable through building, sometimes at their own expense, sometimes at the Emperor's.[67] There is no evidence that these great men contributed to other aspects of the civic services. The Theodosian Code does, however, tell us of a Praetorian Prefect who gave 600 solidi to the Council of Antioch for the benefit of public spectacles.[68] Two fragments of a law of 393 show that an attempt had been made to compel senators to contribute to the heating of the baths and to the production of the games of the Syriarch.[69] Both show that the attempt had to be abandoned.

---

[61] The estates were probably the most important of the profits of the decurionate which, according to Libanius, the most powerful of the Councillors kept to themselves. Or. 48, c. 4. Or. 49, c. 4.

[62] Julian "Misopogon" 370 D and 371 A.   [63] Or. 48, c. 3, t. 3, p. 429.

[64] Petit, pp. 53–54. I am not convinced that C. J. 10, 42, 8 (Diocletian) is relevant.

[65] Shopkeepers' building duties; Or. 46, c. 21. Furnishing of hostel Or. 46, c. 19. Support for beggars, Or. 46, c. 21. Street lighting, Or. 33, cs. 35–36.

[66] Datian, favourite of Constantius, built a stoa and two baths (ep. 441 [355]) and a house with a fine garden (ep. 114 [359–60]). Hellebichus, the general, built a house and a bath (ep. 898 [388]). Some of the buildings of the Comes Orientis Proculus may also have been at his own expense. So the enlargement of the "Plethron". (Or. 10.) Libanius opposes this scheme but does not say it would cost the Council money. Other buildings of Proculus (ep. 852 [388]), a stoa and work on roads, baths and markets. Proculus' governorship ended in 384 but he was in Antioch again in early summer 388, conceivably to supervise the completion of his buildings, ep. 840. Also on building by honorati Or. 11, t. 1, p. 503 l. 19.

[67] Reference in Petit, p. 314 ff.   [68] C. T. 12, 1. 169 (409).

[69] C. T. 12, 1, 139 (393) (Baths) C. T. 6, 3, 1 (393) (Syriarchy) Both to Praef. Urbis Cpl.

In the fourth Century finances of Antioch were assisted by certain subsidies from the Imperial treasury. The Great Imperial building schemes have already been mentioned. In addition, the heaviest liturgies, the spectacles of the Syriarch and the Olympic Games, were regularly subsidised, even if the subsidies had to be requested anew by each holder of the liturgies.[70] Libanius himself, and probably several other leading teachers in the city, received their salary from the Emperor.[71] There is some reason to suppose that Antioch, like the other great centres of the Empire, Rome, Constantinople, Alexandria, Carthage, received distributions of cheap corn or bread.[72] It is likely that, as in the other cities, the distributions were financed out of Imperial taxation. Lastly, the not very effective civic police was reinforced by an Imperial force, probably attached to the officia of the governors, but commanded by a „Night Prefect" appointed by a diploma from the Imperial court.[73] The importance of the Imperial contribution to the finances of Antioch must not be underestimated.

Does the evidence on the income and expenditure of Antioch reveal any significant trends? First, there are certain signs of reduced expenditure. In this strongly Christian city we hear little of expenditure on pagan cults. Julian had already remarked on the fact.[74] Then, there is no reference to the maintenance of a gymnasium. This institution would appear to have ceased to function, as had ephebic training. This was a change of very great cultural significance. „Das Gymnasium war der Herd und die Hochburg der griechischen Kultur, das Wahrzeichen des Griechentums, das die Griechen von den Eingeborenen unterschied."[75] The Museion too was decrepit, for at one time it was made the headquarters of the Comes Orientis.[76] Considering that we are observing Antioch through the eyes of

---

[70] Subsidy of Syriarch eps. 1459 (363), 1147–8 (364), eps. 970–1. Subsidy of Olympic Games ep. 439. C. J. 1, 36 shows that certain sums were definitely set aside for these subsidies.

[71] Libanius eps. 28, 740, 258, 800. His rival Euboulos, Or. 1, c. 110. Even a sophist in the small city of Elusa, ep. 132.

[72] A private foundation, Malalas 289 l. 16–290, l. 1. An Imperial foundation (3rd Century) Malalas 302 ls. 10–12 of text as emended by A. Schenck von Stauffenberg in his "Römische Kaisergeschichte bei Malalas", p. 392. Lines suggesting that food distributions existed in Libanius' time, Or. 20, c. 7. – Or 22, c. 37, where the πινάκια might correspond to the καλαμίων συντόμια of the first passage of Malalas. cf. J. J. Reiske's note t. 2, p. 24 of his edition of Libanius.

[73] The "soldiers" who appear frequently in the role of policemen in Libanius. eg. Or. 54, c. 42; Or. 45, c. 5; Or. 46, c. 18; Or. 26, c. 30; etc. The archers who broke the riot of the statues, Or. 19, c. 35–36, were also probably part of this Imperial force. – The Night Prefect: Palladius "Dialogus de vita S. Joannis Chrysostomi" ed. Coleman-Norton, p. 97, ls. 8–10.

[74] Julian "Misopogon", 362.

[75] M. P. Nilsson, "Die Hellenistische Schule", p. 84. A reference to end of Ephebic training? Or. XI, c 157.

[76] Malalas in P. G. t. 97, col. 477. Or. 1, c. 102 refers to the "Museion" as occupied by teachers but P. Wolf in his "Schulwesen der Spätantike", pp. 43–5 argues plausibly that the word is used figuratively and that the school in the town hall is meant.

a Sophist, it is surprising how little we hear of competitions in rhetorics or poetry organised by the city.[77] Patronage of great men rather than festive competition provided the rewards of artists. We might note in passing that while there was thus a reduction in many of the activities characteristic of Hellenic life, literary schooling for children was probably more widespread and systematic than ever before.[78]

Reductions in other than cultural branches of the civic services are difficult to establish. Libanius makes statements implying that the standards of the civic services were being reduced.[79] But while his writings provide examples of strain and tension in the maintenance of certain liturgies,[80] he does not mention any liturgy that had definitely been abandoned. Of course, this may be due to the fragmentary nature of the evidence.

Other signs of the time are the cessation of voluntary public building by the Councillors, the building activities of the honorati, and the importance of funds from the Imperial treasury in the maintenance of certain services. It may be that these signs indicate the direction in which civic finances were moving – to face an age in which the degeneration of the Councils would bring about the end of the liturgical system.[81]

---

[77] Reduction in number of literary festivals and competitions, Or. 48, c. 32.

[78] Cf. H. I. Marrou "Histoire de l'éducation dans l'antiquité", p. 406 ff.

[79] A general lowering of standards: Or. 49, cs. 8–9.
Cf. also C. T. 12, 1, 169 (409). – Very striking in comparison with situation under the Early Empire, as revealed in the 10th book of Pliny's letters or some orations of Dio of Prusa, is the almost complete end of voluntary public building by the Councillors.

[80] Strain and tension: bath heating Or. 26, cs. 5–6 and other references in note 56. Syriarchy: ep. 1399, t. 11, p. 441, 1. 22; C. T. 12, 1, 103 (383) and Or. 33, cs. 14–18. Olympic Games: Or. 38, c. 5; Or. 53, c. 16.

[81] That, by the time of Justinian, liturgies were suppressed almost completely is the opinion of Jones in "Greek City", p. 258. Cf. A. C. Johnson and L. C. West, "Byzantine Egypt: Economic Studies", Princeton, 1945, pp. 104–5. – Justinian's 13th edict gives some information on the finances of Alexandria in this late period.

XIII

MONEY ECONOMY AND TAXATION IN KIND IN SYRIA IN THE FOURTH CENTURY A. D.

It is well known that for the greater part of the fourth century the government of the eastern half of the Roman Empire carried out most of its financial transactions in kind, while private individuals continued to use money [1]). The present essay is a discussion of evidence, taken from the writings of the Antiochene Sophist Libanius, which shows this dual system in operation, and may help to explain why the government found it advantageous [2]).

A number of passages dealing with compulsory transport services — sometimes described as σιτηγίαι — required by the government, provide a starting point for this study.

1. In 358 one Julianus, a former governor of Bithynia, travelled to Egypt in order to supervise the transport of corn from Alexandria. It had once been possible to make much money out of this duty, but when Julianus accepted it, this opportunity was no longer open [3]). On the other hand, Libanius says nothing of financial losses, which Julianus, a "poor man" [4]), might suffer in the course of his duty. So he will not have had to pay for the transport out of his own purse. Libanius hopes that Julianus will be rewarded for his services with a governorship of several provinces [5]).

---

1) G. Mickwitz, „Geld und Wirtschaft im römischen Reich des vierten Jahrhunderts", Helsingfors, 1932, especially cs. V and VI. S. Mazzarino, „Aspetti Sociali Del Quarto Secolo", Rome 1951.

2) Libanius cited in edition of R. Foerster, in the Bibliotheca Teubneriana. References not naming an author are to Libanius.

Dates of the letters of Libanius were established by O. Seeck in „Die Briefe des Libanius zeitlich geordnet" (cited Seeck) in Gebhardt-Harnack, Texte und Untersuchungen, Neue Folge, 15, Leipzig, 1906.

3) Julianus' journey eps 349—50 (358?); no longer profitable ep. 350: ἐπεὶ δὲ τὰ κέρδη ἑτέρωσε τέτραπται ...

4) ibid., l. 12 γενοῦ δὴ πάντα ἀνδρὶ ... πένητι.

5) ep. 349, t. 10, p. 331, l. 13. κυβερνήτης ἐθνῶν. cf. Petit, „Libanius et la vie municipale à Antioche au 4ᵉ siècle après J. C.", Paris 1955 (cited as Petit) p. 255.

2. A little later in 358 Libanius appears to have made some request connected with σῖτος to the Praetorian Prefect, Strategius Musonianus, which the Prefect had turned down [6]. While Petit [7] refers this passage to a σιτηγία, I prefer to see in it the refusal to someone of an Annona [8]).

3. In 360 we hear of one Antoninus, who has been required to transport corn for the second time. He had been unable to perform the duty when first commanded and had handed over his property to his nominators. Thereupon, he fled from his home town and Libanius sent him to an official in the financial administration for help [9]. This Antoninus may be identical with an Armenian of that name, whose brother belonged by marriage to a curial family at Antioch [10]. If so, he was neither a Councillor nor a resident of Antioch [11]).

4. In 362 we hear of the case of Megistus [12]. Petit has acutely explained this man's obscure career as that of a small decurion of an Egyptian city, who had escaped from his curial obligations by going into the service of the powerful family of the Praetorian Prefect Thalassius [13]. Now he has been called back to Egypt and his duties, and Libanius asks an official, probably a governor, either to release him for the service of his powerful patrons, or if this was not possible, to let him be included among those who export corn out of Egypt [14]).

---

6) ep. 356 (358) t. 10, p. 338, l. 4.

7) Petit, p. 159, n. 9 and p. 163.

8) σῖτος as Annona. eps. 55, 258, 545, 1397. Perhaps ep. 356 (358), like ep. 545 (356/7), concerns a request made by Libanius for himself.

9) ep. 210, date: 358, according to Foerster, following Silomon, "De Libanii epistularum libris I—VI", p. 42 Dissert. Göttingen 1909. 360, according to position of letter, and Seeck p. 78: Antoninus II, and p. 372, Ἀντωνῖνος ἐκεῖνος ὁ τῶν πατρῴων τοῖς ὡς εὐπορεῖ λέγουσιν ἀποστάς .... αὖθις ἠνάγκασται σιτηγεῖν.

10) ep. 1495 (365). see Petit, p. 397, "Acontius"; Seeck pp. 77—8: Antoninus I—III.

11) "Petit" p. 160 follows Silomon p. 42 in identifying this man as the Antoninus whose desertion to the Persians is related by Ammianus 18, 3, 1. But that two men of the same name were both unable to meet demands of the government is not proof that they were identical, and Seeck's objection, that the place of ep. 210 in the collection is not among the letters of 358, has force.

12) ep. 705 (362), on same man ep. 626 (361).

13) Petit, pp. 340 and 402.

14) ep. 705, t. 10, p. 639, l. 5. ἐν τοῖς κομίζουσιν ἀπ᾽ Αἰγύπτου σῖτον τετάχθω.

5. In 363 Alexander, the formidable consular of Syria, appointed by Julian, threatened Eusebius (XXI), a Councillor of Antioch, with a περὶ τὴν ναῦν λειτουργία. Libanius opposed this with the argument that Eusebius was too poor [15]).

6. In 365 a man contrived to obtain his brother's property by the following device. He volunteered for a σιτηγία and then asked that his brother should be required to share the liturgy. The brother Meilichius was at the time studying at Antioch. If he refused to participate in the liturgy, his brother would be entitled to take over his property [16]). We have already met a similar case of exchange of property in the case of Antoninus. A remarkable aspect of this affair is that the governor concerned was the governor of Galatia, an inland province, while the corn transport was definitely by sea [17]).

7. In 388 the governor of Syria, Eustathius, tried to compel one Romulus to undertake a σιτηγία [18]). Romulus was a member of an impoverished, probably curial, family of Antioch [19]). The governor's object, in making this second attempt to compel Romulus to undertake a liturgy that was far too expensive for him, was to force him to launch an accusation against Libanius.

8. About the same time, the same governor refused Libanius' request to exempt the ship of his friend and assistant, Thalassius, from the duty of corn transport [20]). There were plenty of ships available at the time and this governor had already given many such exemptions [21]). The transport would have been destined to feed "the Emperor, the soldiers and the two capital cities", Rome and Constantinople [22]). It is not certain that Thalassius was at the time already a decurion of Antioch. Attempts were certainly being made to enrol him. He

---

15) ep. 1414, t. 11, p. 455, 1. 24.
16) ep. 1496 (365).
17) The letter written to governor of Galatia, Seeck, p. 438. transport by sea, ep. 1496, t. 11, p. 524, 1. 1.
18) Or. 54, c. 40. Ῥωμύλος πάλιν σῖτον πέμπειν ἐπὶ νεῶν ἀναγκαζόμενος.
19) Petit, p. 400.
20) Or. 54, c. 47. ἠξίουν μὲν αὐτὸν ἐλευθερῶσαι τῆς σιτηγίας τοῦ θεοῖς ἐοικότος .... τοῦ φιλοσόφου τὴν ναῦν.
21) ibid. τουτὶ δὲ αὐτῷ πρὸς πολλοὺς ἐπέπρακτο δι' ἀφθονίαν πλοίων.
22) ibid. ἀλλ' ἡ ναῦς αὕτη τὴν σωτηρίαν ἔφερε καὶ βασιλεῖ καὶ στρατιώταις καὶ πόλεσι ταῖς ὑπὲρ ἄλλας.

resisted strenuously and tried to enter the senate at Constantinople as a refuge [23]).

9. A letter of 390 describes the corn transport liturgy as a most dangerous hazard, which would threaten Libanius' son, Cimon, if he were to become a member of the Council of Antioch [24]).

These passages have been discussed by P. Petit, in his recent book. Petit argues that the σιτηγία was a liturgy which entailed the supervision of the loading of corn into ships in Egypt and the transport of the corn to its destination, normally Constantinople. This liturgy had originally been purely supervisory, involving no expenditure, as in the case of Julianus. Later, the performer of the liturgy was also obliged to make a heavy financial contribution to the cost of transport. The liturgy had become a "munus mixtum", but the governors could at their discretion lighten the burden by providing a government-owned ship. The duty normally fell on decurions, but in times of special need it could be imposed on landowners outside the Councils [25]).

In this article an attempt will be made to show that Petit's interpretation is too simple. I will try to show that the scrappy passages of Libanius used in evidence show too much variation in detail to fit convincingly into the reconstructed evolution of a single liturgy. I will also argue that the compulsory duty which Libanius calls σιτηγία was not necessarily, or even most frequently, connected with the transport of corn exacted in Egypt, but furnishes an example of a practice of much wider scope: the use of compulsory transport services to make the system of taxation in kind more flexible, and to convey the produce of taxation to wherever the exigencies of the moment created a demand for it.

The view that our passages illustrate the evolution of a single liturgy, connected with the transport of government corn from Egypt, largely depends on the cases of Julianus and Megistus, for these alone involved duties that were relatively

---

23) Attempts to enter Senate: Or. 54 cs. 5—6, threatened with Council Or. 42 c. 6 ff. and Or. 54, c. 66. Perhaps the σιτηγία would have been Thalassius' first liturgy.

24) ep. 959 (390) definitely links σιτηγία with service in Council, to avoid the latter would be to escape the former.

25) Petit pp. 159 and 162.

attractive and explicitly connected with the transport of corn from Egypt. Yet, the social positions of the two men and the circumstances in which they came to Egypt and obtained their duties were quite different. Julianus was "honoratus", a former governor of Bithynia [26]). For the performance of his duty in Egypt he might hope to be rewarded with the office of Vicar [27]). There is no suggestion that Julianus was performing a civic liturgy. Megistus was man of much humbler rank and prospects. He may have belonged to a curial family. He certainly lived in a position of dependence on a great Antiochene family, the senatorial house of Bassianus, for whom he came to Egypt as agent [28]). He was prevented from leaving Egypt by a local official and he asked "to be assigned to the men carrying corn out of Egypt" in order to avoid the more unpleasant obligations — possibly curial service — which the official was forcing him to undertake [29]). Also Libanius' words suggest that the tasks which faced the two men in Egypt were different. Julianus was sent to supervise the loading of ships with corn [30]). Although this task was no longer profitable and involved for Julianus a lengthy separation from his family, it was of some dignity and might become a stepping stone in an official career [31]). Megistus

---

26) Ep. 349, Seeck, p. 190/1: Julianus V.

27) The Vicarate: see above Note 5. It is not stated what authority sent him to Egypt. In Egypt he is commended to the "dux" Sebastianus, who can be of assistance to him but is not necessarily his chief. See Seeck, p. 271, Sebastianus II.

28) Curial background suggested by Petit pp. 340 and 402. Agent of house of Bassianus: ep. 625 (361) and 705 (362), addressed to Apolinaris, an official, perhaps provincial governor in Egypt. Seeck p. 384.

29) See note 14 above.

30) ep. 349 τὴν περὶ τὰ πλοῖα φροντίδα
ep. 350 ἀνδρὸς ὁ σῖτος ἄμισθον εἰσοίσοντος ....
ibid. ... ὑπέστη τὰς ὁλκάδας ἐμπιμπλάναι.

31) In spite of the reward which Libanius expects for Julianus, his language makes clear that the task was troublesome — a burden rather than an honour.
ep. 349 μοχθήσων οὐκ ἐπὶ κέρδει
ep. 350 μὴ δόξαι τοῖς ἀπείροις αὐτοῦ φεύγειν τὸν πόνον διὰ τὸ μὴ λαβεῖν ἐνεῖναι ....

These suggest a munus rather than an official post. I would suggest an unpaid or badly paid post concerned with the handling and loading of the corn tax destined for Constantinople at Alexandria. Possible duties are suggested in Justinian's 13th edict cs. 4 and 6. See also P. W. t. 44, i, col. 1276 art. "Praefectus Annonae Alexandriae". Perhaps the lost pay was a perquisite which had recently been stopped. Cf. Justinian ed. 13, praef. and c. 7.

asked to be assigned to a group of men engaged in the actual
transport of the corn from Egypt. This might well have been
the guild of "navicularii" of Alexandria, membership of which
would have given him immunity from curial duties [32]).

It therefore appears that Megistus and Julianus were not
involved in the same compulsory service and that their cases
cannot be used to illustrate the development of a single liturgy.
Furthermore, there are considerable differences between the
cases of Megistus and Julianus and those of the other men
engaged in a compulsory corn transport duty for the government, sometimes described as σιτηγία. First, these σιτηγίαι were
frighteningly expensive. Then, there is no reference to any
of the men threatened with a σιτηγία anticipating a voyage to
Egypt. Lastly, while Megistus was subject to an Egyptian
official, and Julianus worked in co-operation with an official
in Egypt, the others were subject to the governors of their home
provinces [33]). Moreover, the remaining cases fall into two
groups. Four of the men concerned — Eusebius XXI in 363 [34]),
Romulus and Thalassius in 388 [35]), and Cimon in 390 [36]), were
citizens of Antioch and either decurions or at least liable to be
enrolled in the Council of Antioch. All four were ordered by
the consular of Syria to transport corn by sea. It therefore
appears likely that among the services required by the government from the city of Antioch was an extremely expensive
sea transport liturgy, to which decurions were liable. The
second group consists of two cases, involving men who were
not citizens of Antioch — Antoninus, who may have been an

---

32) See note 44 below.

33) Officials i/c of corn transport duties:
(i) Antoninus, subject to Euphemius I, whose authority extended over
several provinces. A high ranking subordinate of the Comes Sacrae
Largitionis? (Seeck p. 136).
(ii) Eusebius XXI, subject to Alexander, consular of Syria.
(iii) Galatian brothers, subject to Leontinus IV, consular of Galatia (Seeck
pp. 438 and 195).
(iv) Romulus — subject to Eustathius V, consular of Syria (Seeck pp. 147/8).
(v) Thalassius IV, to Eustathius V, consular of Syria.
On the other hand, Julianus V and Megistus dealt with Egyptian
Officials. Megistus with Apolinaris, a praeses? (note 28), Julianus co-operated with Sebastianus, the „dux" (note 27).

34) See note 15. Seeck, p. 143. Petit, p. 398.
35) See notes 18, 23. Petit, p. 400.
36) See note 24. Seeck, p. 81. Petit, p. 398.

Armenian [37]), and the Galatian brothers — all inhabitants of inland provinces. The fact that the Galatian brothers [38]) were called upon to transport corn by sea, although they lived inland, need not occasion surprise. A law survives directed against officials who exacted sea transport from inland cities [39]), and the liturgy of the Galatians may be an example of the abuse against which this law was directed. In any case, it is clear that Antioch was not the only city to be burdened with sea transport duties and it is quite likely that most cities around the Mediterranean had to bear them from time to time, not necessarily always on identical terms.

There remains the question of the origin and destination of the corn which the citizens of the eastern cities were obliged to transport.

As we have seen, Julianus and Megistus were probably associated in different capacities with the transport of corn from Egypt. Their cases have special features, and since Egypt is not mentioned in connection with any of the other cases, it is not necessary to assume that these too involved transport of corn from Egypt. With the possible exception of Megistus, none of the men mentioned by Libanius as obliged to transport corn by sea belonged to one of the two [40]) guilds organised by the Emperors to transport corn from Egypt to Constantinople [41]), the "Navicularii Alexandriae" and the "Navicularii Orientis". For, while we hear that Syrians were enrolled into the second of these guilds [42]), the conditions of service of a "Navicularius" were quite different from those suggested by the passages of Libanius. "Navicularii" performed a lifelong hereditary duty [43]). The men mentioned by Libanius performed their duty once or twice only, on the command of their provincial governor. The "Navicularii" were exempt from membership and

---

37) See notes 9—11.
38) See notes 16—17.
39) C. T. 11, 1, 22 P. P. O. (386). cf. Cicero 2 in Verrem III, c. 81 ff.
40) C. T. 13, 5, 7 (334) ⎫
    C. T. 13, 5, 14 (371) ⎬ mention both fleets.
    C. T. 13, 5, 32 (409)
41) C. T. 13, 5, 32 shows that both fleets transported corn from Alexandria.
42) C. T. 8, 4, 11 (365?) exempts officials of consular of Syria from conscription among navicularii.
43) C. T. 13, 5, 1 (314) Pr. Urb.
    C. T. 13, 5, 19 (390) P. P. O.

compulsory services of the city councils [44]). The σιτηγία, at Antioch at least, was particulary incumbent on decurions.

But if these men were not "Navicularii", there is no reason why they should have transported corn only or mainly from Egypt. It is just as likely that they were required to transport the product of taxation of their own home provinces. In fact, if the corn which the decurions of Antioch had to transport by sea came from Syria, the σιτηγία at Antioch would be absolutely parallel to certain compulsory land transport duties which the Councillors of Antioch were obliged to perform. A letter of the year 358 suggests that the garrison of the fortress of Callinicum on the Euphrates was supplied from Syria [45]). A sentence from a much later speech tells us that at the time of Constantius' wars against the Persians, councillors of Antioch were sent to the River Tigris and suffered severe financial losses there [46]). Combining the two passages, we may draw the conclusion that at the time of the Persian wars the councillors of Antioch were obliged to transport supplies to the army in Mesopotamia at their own expense. Libanius does not use the term σιτηγία in connection with this duty, but otherwise this land transport duty seems not to have differed very much from the sea-transport liturgies discussed earlier. If this land transport liturgy furnishes a true parallel to the sea transport duties, the σιτηγία of Antioch is another example of the practice, already known from the codes [47]), of making the transport of the produce of taxation itself into a tax.

---

44) C. T. 13, 5, 5 (326) P. P. O.   ⎫ exemption from compulsory
C. T. 13, 5, 7 (354) Nav. Or.   ⎬ services, and civic functions.
C. T. 13, 5, 17 (386) P. P. Occident.
C. T. 13, 5, 16 (380) Corp. Nav. Navicularius may not be enrolled into Council.
C. T. 12, 1, 149 (395) Procos. Af. Councillors try to escape from Council by enrolling as Navicularii.

45) ep. 21 (358) cf. "Petit", p. 256, n. 2. τοῦτο δὴ τὸ χωρίον ἔχει στρατιὰν ἱδρυμένην, ἣν δεῖ τρέφεσθαι παρ' ἡμῶν οὐκ ἐκεῖσε κομιζόντων ἀλλ' ἑτέρωσε τὴν τροφήν, ἐκεῖθεν δὲ εἰς Καλλίνικον ἄγειν νόμος τὸν ἄρχοντα τῶν περὶ τὸν Εὐφράτην.

46) Or. 49 c. 2. The circumstances of the Persian War proved disastrous for the Councils: τὰ περὶ τὸν πόλεμον .. πράγματα .. καθ' ἕκαστον αὐτὰς ἔτος ἐπὶ τὸ χεῖρον ἄγοντα τῶν ἐπὶ τὸν Τίγρητα πεμπομένων βουλευτῶν ταῖς ἐκεῖ βλάβαις τὰ πατρῷα πωλούντων. cf. Petit, p. 110.

47) e. g. "translatio annonae" as a tax:
C. T. 7, 5, 2 (404) P. P. Occident = C. J. 12, 38, 2.

The destination of the corn sent by the decurions of Antioch presumably varied according to circumstances. Only once, in the late 380s, are we told the destination of a σιτηγία. Rome, Constantinople, the court and the army are possible recipients of the corn Thalassius had been asked to transport over-seas [48]). The location of the army changed according to the military situation. At the time of this reference it was fighting the usurper Maximus in Italy. That corn from the taxation of Syria helped to feed the growing citizen body of Constantinople is confirmed by the evidence of Eunapius, a contemporary of Libanius [49]). The σιτηγία with which Eusebius XXI was threatened in 363 is likely to have been rather exceptional. At that time there was a famine in Antioch [50]), and it thus is very unlikely that corn was then exported from Syria. It is more likely that Eusebius was required to transport corn to Syria, probably from Egypt [51]).

We have only the vaguest information about the manner in which the decurions of Antioch actually performed their σιτηγία. Thalassius was probably required to transport the corn in his own ship [52]). Since the Orontes was navigable from An-

---

C. T. 1, 5, 14 (405) P. P. O. = C. J. 1, 26, 5.
C. T. 16, 2, 15 (359?) P. P. Occident = C. J. 1, 3, 3.
C. T. 16, 2, 40 (412) P. P. Occident = C. J. 1, 2, 5.
or the supply of frontier troops in Africa:
C. J. XI, 60, 1 (385) C. T. XI, 1, 11 Vic. Afr. (365) = C. J. 10, 16. 6.
C. T. XI, 1, 21 P. P. O. (385), transport to Eastern frontier = C. J. 10, 16, 8.
See also C. T. VII, 4, 15, P. P. O. (369) = C. J. 12, 37, 4.
cf. also the difficult and fragmentary African taxation regulations discussed by Ch. Saumagne, „Un tarif fiscal du 4e siècle de notre ère", Karthago I, 1950, which lists a tax, "limitis nomine", together with one, "naviculariorum nomine", as well as others.

48) See note 22.
49) Eunapius 'Lives of the Philosophers', life of Aedesius 462: οὐδὲ τὸ ἀπ' Αἰγύπτου πλῆθος τῶν ὁλκάδων οὐδὲ τὸ ἐξ 'Ασίας ἁπάσης, Συρίας τε καὶ Φοινίκης καὶ τῶν ἄλλων ἐθνῶν συμφερόμενον πλῆθος σίτου, κατὰ ἐπαγωγὴν φόρου ἐμπλῆσαι καὶ κορέσαι τὸν μεθύοντα δύναται δῆμον.
50) On Eusebius see above note 15.
On the famine at Antioch see Petit, pp. 109—118, also G. Downey in "Essays in honor of A. C. Johnson", edited by Coleman-Norton, Princeton 1951, p. 312, "An economic crisis at Antioch under Julian the apostate".
51) Julian, Misopogon, 369 B.
52) Or. 54, c. 47, τοῦ φιλοσόφου τὴν ναῦν.

tioch to the sea[53]), it is possible that there were other ship-
owners among the decurions of Antioch, and that the liturgy
was most frequently imposed on them[54]). It is likely that
Libanius himself at one time owned a ship[55]). This could be
the reason why he worried so much that his son might be forced
into the shipping liturgy, if he became a member of the Council[56]). On the other hand, the pressure exercised on Romulus in
connection with a σιτηγία seems to have been designed to force
him to contribute money[57]). In this case the government will
have provided the ship, perhaps by requisition[58]), compensated

---

53) P. W. article "Orontes", t. 18, i, col. 1163. Pausanias VIII, 29, 3.

54) Or. 54 c. 47. τουτὶ δὲ αὐτῷ πρὸς πολλοὺς ἐπέπρακτο δι' ἀφθονίαν
πλοίων shows that there was no shortage of ships. Petit takes these ships
to have formed a fleet of publicly-owned vessels, which, at his discretion,
the governor could place at the disposal of the men performing a σιτηγία
— or withhold. He bases his view on C. T. 13, 5, 14 of 371, but this law
deals with the building of ships out of taxation for men who were newly
enrolled into the navicularii orientis. These were owned by individuals,
clearly not ship owners to start with, who would henceforth have to
transport corn for life. The case of our men performing a single liturgy
was quite different and it does not follow from the law that the government built up a fleet of ships which might be supplied to performers of the
liturgy. It is more likely that the σιτηγία was in the first place imposed
on ship owners, and that if others were required to pay for the transport
of corn, a ship was found for them by requisition, with or without com-
pensation. Requisition of ships: C. T. 13, 7, 1—2. The ships would presumably be requisitioned from ship owners of Antioch or Seleucia at the
mouth of the Orontes.

55) Eps. 177—8. Two slaves sent to Constantinople and Sinope by
ship. On these Petit, p. 305, note 5, ibid. p. 408, note 1. H. Bouchery:
"Themistius in Libanius' Brieven", Antwerp, 1936. p. 182 explains that the
servants were to sell the house which Libanius had inhabited during his
stay at Constantinople. They did, however, go on to Sinope κατ' ἐμπορίαν,
and the ship as well as the slaves had been sent by Libanius. So the ship
may have been Libanius' own.
Cf. also the other small scale domestic trading venture noted by
Petit, p. 305 n. 5, ep. 709, wine sent to Cilicia; ep. 568 buys wood in Cilicia, also eps. 649 and 1191. It is important to realise that these activities
arose from Libanius' domestic needs as a landowner. He was in no sense
a trader. There is similarly no evidence at all that any of the many well-
to-do citizens of Antioch whom we meet in Libanius' writings engaged in
commerce for its own sake or owed his wealth to commerce. cf. Petit p. 305.

56) ep. 959 (390).

57) Or. 54, c. 41. στήσας βίᾳ τὴν εἰσπραξιν suggests an exaction of
money. Cf. tax raised in Egypt to pay for transport of corn by sea to
Constantinople, A. C. Johnson and L. C. West, "Byzantine Egypt: Economic Studies", p. 160 ff.

58) On the source of the ship, cf. note 54 above.

the owner and paid for the voyage out of the money supplied by Romulus. Perhaps Romulus would also have had to supervise the transport for which he had paid. It seems that personal supervision was required from the Galatian brothers[59], whose liturgy will have resembled Romulus' since as inhabitants of an inland province they had surely not been required to supply a ship.

Did these long distance transport duties form a normal part of the annual demands made on the cities by the government, or were they required only at times of special emergency? The fact that all the cases mentioned by Libanius belong to periods of crisis — the Persian Wars[60] and the revolt of Maximus[61] — suggests that they were extraordinary impositions. But it must be remembered that by chance the greater part of Libanius' surviving writings dates from these two periods.

In connection with the compulsory land transport it may however be significant that transport of supplies to the armies in Mesopotamia, which had such a disastrous effect on the finances of the Council of Antioch during the Persian War, is not mentioned in the writings of the later period, when there was peace on the Persian frontier. On the contrary, we are told that a consular of Syria was sent to Mesopotamia to buy corn[62]. We also learn that a certain Councillor of Antioch was obliged, in the course of some compulsory service, to deliver gold at the depot of taxation in kind at Barbalissos, the military headquarters on the Euphrates[63]. The explanation of this

---

59) ep. 1496 t. 11, p. 524, l. 1 συμπλεῖν suggests that liturgy required personal supervision. Otherwise, if it was nothing but a tax, it would not have interfered with the young man's studies.

60) The Persian War lasted with varying intensity from 337—351. There was another Persian invasion in 359. In 363 there was Julian's campaign and lasting peaceful conditions were only re-established by the terms accepted by Jovian later in 363. On the details of the war, see P. W. article "Constantius" in P. W. t. 4, i, cols. 1047—8, 1053—4, 1055, 1061—2, 1063—4, 1091—3.

61) On Theodosius' campaign against Maximus see A. Piganiol, L'Empire Chrétien, pp. 253—5.

62) Or. 33, cs. 6—7, also c. 27. Ibid. t. 3, p. 168, l. 10 shows that corn purchase in Euphratensis was normal, but not normally supervised by the governor of Syria himself.

63) Or. 28, c. 16. ἡ γὰρ δὴ Βαρβαλισσὸς καὶ ὁ σῖτος καὶ πάντα τὰ τοιαῦτα τὸν ἀποδέκτην εἰς τιμωρίαν ἦγε ... ἀλλ' οὐ τὸν Λάμαχον, ᾧ τὸ ἔργον ἦν δοῦναι χρυσίον καὶ ἐδεδώκει.

might be that in peace time it was no longer necessary to transport supplies from Syria to Mesopotamia, and that the taxes were now changed into money, with which supplies could be bought on the frontier[64]). If this was indeed the case, this land-transport duty had been an extraordinary one.

The account of the corn transport duties puts us in a position to understand why the government continued to collect taxes in kind, in a province where, as Petit has conclusively shown[65]), money was used by all classes in all private transactions[66]). To feed its armies and capital cities the government needed large quantities of corn. Frequently war or famine created additional needs in different localities. Through its practice of raising taxes in kind the government could obtain the corn to meet these needs, and a system of compulsory transport duties made it possible to transport the corn wherever it was needed.

Means had, moreover, been found to reduce the inconvenience inherent in this system of state finance. Thus, there is evidence to suggest that occasionally a tax in kind was converted into a money levy. We have already noted some evidence which suggested that the tax which had gone to feed the army in Mesopotamia had been converted into money, with which corn could be bought on the frontier[67]). A letter of 357 records that a man owning an estate near Boroea (Aleppo) was forced to sell grain to men in an official position[68]). Mazzarino sees in this a case of compulsory purchase at a price fixed by the government, such as was used to obtain supplies for the troops when the tax had been raised in money. There is, further, a

---

Barbalissos was the H. Q. of the Dux Syriae et Euphratensis, "Martyrium Sergii et Bacchi", Anal. Bolland. XIV, 1895, p. 384. Libanius uses the term ἀποδέκτης to describe the men in charge of the stored taxation in kind. Petit p. 154 and below note 72. The situation described is very obscure. I suggest that the decurion Lamachus had been accused because of some deficit in the matter of σῖτος in the public corn store at Barbalissos, and that his defence is that he had been ordered to deliver gold, and that the amount of corn in the store was not his concern but that of the storekeeper.

64) For an example of a tax raised in gold followed by corn purchase at fixed price in Egypt see A. Segré "Annona Militaris in Egypt", Byzantion 16, 1942—3, p. 441 ff.
65) Petit pp. 299—303.
66) See above note 1.
67) See above p. 249 and notes 62—64.
68) Ep. 276 (361) Mazzarino p. 161.

suggestion that the Councillor in charge of that department of tax collecting which dealt with garments for the soldiers, collected money from the taxpayer, and with that purchased garments, either from the government directly, or at least at prices over which the provincial governor had control [69]. But these possible cases of "adaeratio" do not alter the impression that the bulk of the φόρος of Syria was raised in kind [70].

More widespread were arrangements for converting salaries in produce into money wages. There is no doubt that the salaries to be paid to officials out of the product of taxation were assigned in kind. This is indicated among other things by the terms Libanius uses to describe state salaries, whether he is talking of the salary of the Comes Orientis, or of a humble sophist of the little city of Elusa in Palestine. The words used are βασιλικὴ τροφή, τροφή or σῖτος [71]. But the fact the salaries were assigned at a rate calculated in kind did not necessarily mean that they were always drawn in kind. Thus, in his speech against the former governor Severus, Libanius charged him with bullying the ἀποδέκται in connection with the wages due to him in agricultural produce. He forced the storekeepers to buy his rations from him, and further cheated them by using measures not in accordance with the law. No doubt, he managed in this way to get more for his rations than they were worth [72]. Severus used force and deceit when turning his rations into money, but the same matter could also be arranged in a more friendly way, by men of less power than the consular of Syria. Thus in 359/60 Libanius wrote to a leading Councillor of Elusa

---

69) ep. 602 (357). On the exaction of a gold tax followed by compulsory purchase of garments at fixed price in Egypt see A. Segré "Annona Civica and Annona Militaris" Byzantion XVI, 1942—3, p. 418 ff. esp. 420 on P. Oxy. 1905.

70) As in Or. 33, c. 19; Or. 47, c. 8; Or. 30, c. 42; Or. 25, c. 43. Petit, p. 153, note 2 and p. 298.

71) e. g. ep. 132 (359—60) sophist of Elusa; ep. 207 (360) Imperial pension; ep. 258 (361) sophist tries to get σῖτος; ep. 348 τροφή salary of official; ep. 356 (358) Libanius himself seeks σῖτος; ep. 345 (356—7) same matter; ep. 55 (359) Libanius asks for increase of σῖτος for Comes Orientis from P. P. O.; ep. 1397 σῖτος as kind of pension promised by governor. Libanius' own salary ep. 28 (359/60) τροφή also ep. 207 (360) ep. 740 (362).

72) Or. 57, c. 51. ὃς καὶ τοὺς ἀποδέκτας ἐπλεονέκτησεν ἐν ταῖς τιμαῖς ὧν βασιλεὺς [ἐν] ταῖς ἀρχαῖς ἐκ τῶν παρὰ τῆς γῆς αὐτῷ προσιόντων δίδωσιν, ὠνεῖσθαί τε ἀναγκάζων ὧν οὐδὲν ἐδέοντο καὶ προσέτι μέτροις ἀδικῶν οὐ συμβαίνουσι τῷ νόμῳ.

that the local sophist wished his βασιλικὴ τροφή to be changed
into money. The point seems to be that Libanius wished the
decurion to use his influence with the local ἀποδέκται to get them
to buy the sophist's rations at a reasonable price[73]). Both parties might benefit by a bargain of this kind. The sophist would
be saved the embarrassment of disposing of a quantity of corn
larger than he required for food. The storekeeper could obtain
for himself a stock of corn which he might sell when prices
were favourable.

Further light is thrown on the case of the sophist of Elusa
by a chapter of a speech written by Themistius, the great sophist
of Constantinople, in 377/8. Themistius argues that he might
have had a very large salary in wheat, oil, pork and wine, but
accepted only the rations which the Emperor granted to every
citizen of Constantinople. Large payments, far above a man's
needs, must be turned into money and this involved quarrelling
with ταμίαι, behaviour unworthy of a philosopher[74]). I imagine
that the ταμίαι were the people Libanius calls ἀποδέκται, store
keepers in charge of the produce of taxation. Thus, Themistius
considered this practice of bargaining with storekeepers about
"adaeratio" an inevitable consequence of being assigned a salary
out of public funds.

Libanius himself received a salary in wheat and barley,
part of which he drew in gold at a price fixed by the governor
of Phoenicia[75]). That this portion of Libanius' salary came
from Phoenicia and not from the immediate environment of
Antioch reveals a disadvantage of the policy of collecting taxes
in kind. It made it troublesome, but not impossible, to organize
expenditure at a distance from collection. On the other hand,
the disadvantage was modified from the salary earner's point of
view by the possibility of selling the salary in kind on the spot,
and transferring the proceeds.

---

73) Ep. 132 (359—60).
74) Themistius ed. Dindorf, p. 353 D. Or. 23 (Winter 377—8).
ὅστις .... ἱστᾷ τε ὕεια ταρίχη καὶ ζυγομαχεῖ τοῖς ταμίαις, τὸν οἶνον καὶ τὰ
ὄψα ἀπαργυρίζων.
75) Ep. 800 (362—3).
On the various sources of Libanius' income and the difficulties in
which he became involved as a result, see Petit p. 409.
Petit also points out an occasion when the government required
Libanius to repay in gold a salary he had received in kind: Petit p. 409,
on ep. 454 (355—6), mentioning reclaiming in gold of farm produce,
granted Or. I, c. 80.

I imagine that such agreements for the adaeratio of salaries in kind were extremely common, if not universal. It is difficult to suppose that they were even strictly speaking illegal. They were far too convenient for that. What was wrong with them was that they lent themselves to grave abuse by powerful officials, to the ruin of the storekeepers and of the territories whose taxation was in the stores. Mazzarino gives many examples of the abuses of this system, which frequently must have given rise to most ruinous situations for the tax payers[76]). In turn, this produced much legislation, prohibiting, restricting, and regulating adaeratio under various circumstances[77]).

It is hard to believe that the prohibitions, at any rate, were generally observed, and they should be taken to indicate the prevalence of abuse and the despair of the government, rather than the rarity of turning wages in kind into money.

The examples given in this essay illustrate how the apparently clumsy system of taxation in kind could be made to work to distribute the resources of the Empire wherever the government needed them, provided that this did not involve too distant transport by land[78]). It has also been shown that the practice of adaeratio, prevalent in Syria, mainly in connection with the paying out of government salaries, greatly modified the inconveniences involved in any system of payment of salaries in kind.

---

76) Mazzarino pp. 136—168.

77) The numerous laws issued by the government in its attempts to control the abuses of "adaeratio" are summarized by Mickwitz, pp. 170—173.

78) Of course, land transport of bulky loads over all but the shortest distance was enormously expensive. See F. W. Walbank in "Cambridge Economic History of Europe", t. c. 2 pp. 76—7. Also A. Segré in article cited in note 69, p. 395 ff. Also the disastrous effect of the transport duties on the financial strength of the Council of Antioch, recalled in Or. 49, c. 2.

XIV

SYNESIUS AND MUNICIPAL POLITICS
OF CYRENAICA IN THE 5TH CENTURY AD

In a well known article C. H. Coster remarked that 'the central fact in the life of Synesius was that he was a *curialis*', and proceeded to use his writings to shed light on the position and opinions of the *curiales* of his time. He also tried to explain 'how it is possible that in the time of Arcadius we come across a figure that we might almost have expected to find in the age of the Antonines'. It is the purpose of the present paper to supplement this picture by pointing out ways in which the position and opinions of Synesius, the civic politician, were quite different from those of *curiales* of earlier periods, and that the fact that Synesius was a *curialis*, and thus a member of the *curia* of Cyrene, was comparatively unimportant as far as his local power and influence were concerned. I will argue that his writings shed light on the development of a form municipal government which was to succeed government of each city by its *curia* [1].

EP 95 (94) AND AN EMBASSY OF PENTAPOLIS

The 95th Letter of Synesius is important in two ways. Firstly it throws light on the life of Synesius at the time at which he wrote the letter, and so fills a gap in his biography. Secondly it contains information about the discussions that preceded the sending of an embassy from the province of Pentapolis to the emperor at

---

(1) C. H. COSTER, 'Synesius, a *Curialis* of the Time of the Emperor Arcadius', *Byzantion*, XV (1940-1), pp. 10-38, also in C. H. COSTER, *Late Roman Studies* (Cambridge, Mass., 1968), pp. 145-82. The letters of Synesius have been cited in the numeration of R. HERCHER, *Epistolographi Graeci* (Paris, 1873), pp. 638-739, which was followed by A. FITZGERALD in his translation, '*The Letters of Synesius of Cyrene*' (Oxford, 1926). The numbering of J. P. MIGNE, *Patrologia Graeca*, LXVI (Paris, 1864), where different, is given in brackets. Column references are to Migne. Where the numbering of A. GARZYA, *Synesii Cyrenensis Epistolae* (Rome, 1979), differs from Hercher it is given last.

Constantinople. It is one of the principal sources for the pre-liminaries of such an embassy. More specifically it has been understood to refer to the preparations of the embassy which Synesius himself undertook in 399. It has therefore been used to provide a background for the *De Regno*, Synesius' important address to the emperor Arcadius (²). The present paper presents an argument that the letter has no bearing on the events of 399, but is concerned with events of 410. I will argue that the letter throws a good deal of light on the position of Synesius in the months between his election as bishop by the people of Ptolemais and his consecration. It also illumines the character of politics in Cyrenaica in the early 5th century.

The letter was written at a time when Synesius could claim that he had no influence with the provincial governor, as he was a wanderer, fleeing his own city without hope of return, while barbarians were in occupation of his property, and using it as a base against Cyrene (³). When could this have been ? We know of two invasions by the nomadic Ausurians that were more than raids, and resulted in a kind of occupation of the Cyrenaican countryside : First the invasion which was ultimately thrown back by Anysius and then, a year later, the 'great invasion' (⁴). Now the events of the 'great invasion' happened entirely within the period of Synesius' episcopacy at Ptolemais (⁵). As bishop, active in the defence of that city (⁶) Synesius could not have described himself as 'wandering', nor could he have attributed his lack of influence with the governor to misfortune. So the letter must belong to the time of the first invasion. When Anysius defeated this invasion Synesius was already bishop, and in a position to support the general with the prayers (⁷). The letter must therefore be earlier than that. Now we have no precise date for Synesius' consecration. The nearest to a

---

(2) C. LACOMBRADE, *Synésios de Cyrène, hellène et chrétien* (Paris, 1951), 73 ; IDEM, *Le discours sur la royauté de Synésios de Cyrène* (Paris, 1951), pp. 13-15. T. BARNES, *op. cit.*, note 8 below, argues that Synesius arrived at Constantinople in winter 397/8.

(3) *Ep.*, 95 (94, 1461C).

(4) *Catastasis*, 1568A.

(5) C. LACOMBRADE, *op. cit.*, p. 234.

(6) *Catastasis*, 1572-3.

(7) *Ep.*, 14, cf. 6, *Constitutio*, 1575a.

dating document is *Ep.*, 13. This letter accompanied the first letter announcing the date of Easter to have been sent out by Synesius as bishop. Lacombrade has pointed out that the announced date, namely the 19th of the Egyptian month of Pharmuthi, which corresponds to the 14th April, was the date of Easter 412. Since the date of Easter was announced by the bishop of Alexandria around the festival of Epiphany, Lacombrade concluded that the letter was written in January 412, and that since it evidently was Synesius' first Easter letter, Synesius cannot have been consecrated in time to write the Easter letter of 411 [8]. On the other hand we cannot have been consecrated later than summer 411 [9]. Lacombrade therefore concluded that Synesius was consecrated sometime in the first quarter of 411 [10]. If we accept that, it follows that *Ep.*, 95 (94), was written either very early in 411 or late in 410.

Why should Synesius have spent the time before consecration wandering (or 'in exile') fleeing his city, rather than encouraging its defenders or otherwise assisting the struggle against the invader ? Lacombrade has suggested that Synesius has suffered a major political set-back in Cyrene, that he had gone into voluntary exile to Ptolemais, and thus given the citizens of that city a chance to elect him their bishop [11]. It is however unlikely that Synesius had suffered a major political set-back. Apart from the fact this would contradict Synesius' assertion that everything had gone well for him until he became a bishop [12], it is unlikely that the people of

---

(8) C. LACOMBRADE, *Synésios de Cyrène*, pp. 211-2. Easter also fell on the 19th Pharmuthi in 407, but C. Lacombrade rejected the earlier date for the consecration thus made possible, against O. SEECK, 'Studien zu Synesius', *Philologus LII* (1893), pp. 461-2. J. R. MARTINDALE, *P.L.R.E.*, *II*, s.v. Synesius I, followed Lacombrade. More recently T. Barnes has strengthened Seeck's argument by arguing that Synesius returned from Constantinople not in 402 but in 400, see his forthcoming article in *J.R.S.* The evidence is not conclusive. In my opinion the later date remains more likely, as I hope to show in another article.

(9) Andronicus was deposed after Synesius had been bishop for almost a year (*Ep.*, 72, 1436B) and this was some time before the death of Theophilus of Alexandria on 15th October 412. That Synesius survived Theophilus is argued convincingly, if not absolutely conclusively, on the basis of *Ep.*, 12 by C. LACOMBRADE, *Synésios de Cyrène*, 251-2.

(10) *Ibid.*, 212.

(11) *Ibid.*, 205-7.

(12) *Ep.*, 57, 1388C ; 1389C = 41. p. 57, GARZYA.

Ptolemais and the bishop of Alexandria would have elected a man who was a political failure. They knew as well as the villagers of Palaebisca that an effective bishop must be able to injure his enemies, or at the very least be useful to his friends [13]. Indeed this was precisely what was expected of Synesius when he was bishop [14]. I would therefore suggest that the reason for Synesius' departure from Cyrene was precisely the fact that he knew that he was to be chosen bishop of Ptolemais, and was evading consecration. He knew that the pressure on a man to accept a bishopric or a priesthood could become irresistible [15]. Archaeologists excavating the burnt remains of temples and the shattered fragments of cult-statues have found evidence of the violence of which Christians of Cyrene were capable [16]. A letter written then, or earlier, suggests that Synesius felt that departure to Athens was the only way in which he could avoid something unpleasant, quite possibly consecration, which certain priests and laymen were eager to inflict on him [17]. He certainly thought that if he rejected the bishopric he would not be able to stay in his home-town [18]. So he left Cyrene to make up his mind free from pressure. He relates that before accepting the office he had come to God in many places and as a suppliant prayed for death rather than the priesthood [19]. He was several times on the point of evading consecration by flight. He discussed his problem with monks without being satisfied with their arguments [20]. He spent at least six months [21] away from his home city, moving from place to place in uncertainty until at last he

---

(13) *Ep.*, 67, 1413C = 66. p. 108, GARZYA.

(14) See below pp. 162-163.

(15) C. LACOMBRADE, *op. cit.*, 219 n. 19 ; MARC LE DIACRE, *Vie de Porphyre*, ed. H. Grégoire and M. Kugener (Paris, 1930), 16 ; 93. P. BROWN, *Augustin of Hippo* (London, 1967), pp. 138-9 ; 294.

(16) See R. G. GOODCHILD, *Kyrene und Apollonia* (Zürich, 1971) for evidence of destruction of temples.

(17) *Ep.*, 54. Consecration had worried Synesius long before it materialised ; *Ep.*, 105, 1481C = p. 184, GARZYA.

(18) *Ep.*, 96 (95).

(19) *Ep.*, 57, 1389A = 41. p. 57, GARZYA, cf. *Ep.*, 11.

(20) *Ep.*, 57, 1389A-B = 41. p. 59 GARZYA.

(21) *Ep.*, 96 (95).

allowed himself to be consecrated by Theophilus at Alexandria [22]. I would suggest that he wrote *Ep.*, 95 (94) during these six months.

It follows that the lack of influence on which Synesius insists so much in *Ep.*, 95 (94) was self-inflicted. In fact this weakness was something of a pose. After all the letter is a response to an attempt by Synesius' brother Euoptius [23] to reconcile Synesius with one Julius, and the attempt seems to have been made at Julius' request [24]. Now Julius was a powerful citizen of Cyrene, whose position was so strong that not many months later he would be in a position to criticise the ruthless governor Andronicus with impunity [25]. Such a man would not have sought reconciliation if Synesius had been a powerless exile. In fact Euoptius was trying to heal a rift between two leading citizens of Cyrene, a city in which contention between notables seems to have been common.

In this case we are informed about the origin of the quarrel. It began when Synesius saw that the army and the decurions were being reduced to a condition of menials and attempted to resist the process [26]. It developed in the course of a debate over sending of an embassy to Constantinople, in which the abuse attacked by Synesius was one of the topics discussed [27]. The question now arises what kind of embassy was being prepared. It has usually been assumed that the embassy concerned is the only one about which we happen to be well informed, that is the embassy which brought Synesius himself to Constantinople in 399 [28]. But of course there were many others. Imperial anniversaries regularly provided occasions for cities to send embassies with gold-wreaths to the emperor [29]. The death of Arcadius and the succession of Theodesius II in Spring 408 will certainly have called for ambassadors, congratulations and gold. The embassy mentioned in *Ep.*, 95 (94) could have been the embassy sent to honour the accession of Theodosius II, but if so it would

---

(22) *Ep.*, 11 written by new bishop before entering his city.
(23) *P.L.R.E.*, II, p. 422.
(24) *Ep.*, 95 (94, 1459C).
(25) *Ep.*, 79.
(26) *Ep.*, 95 (94, 1461D-1464A).
(27) See below p. 152.
(28) SO C. Lacombrade, *Discours sur la royauté* (Paris, 1951), pp. 13-15.
(29) A. H. M. Jones, *The Later Roman Empire* (Oxford, 1964), p. 430.

have arrived rather long after the event. For *Ep.*, 95 (94) suggest that the embassy had been discussed not very long before the writing of the letter. The quarrel which that discussion helped to provoke was recent. 'Only yesterday' Synesius had done Julius the very considerable fvaour of freeing him from the threat of an imminent treason trial, by forcefully removing the accuser [30]. This is incidentally only one of several known cases of the use of private coercive power by a local magnate of Pentapolis [31]. However the point of immediate relevance is that Julius and Synesius had been on good terms not long before the writing of the letter, and that the present violent antagonism, and therefore also the embassy which had helped to cause it, were recent. This is confirmed by the end of *Ep.*, 95 (94). Synesius agrees that in the debate Julius gained his point, but he warns that the disastrous consequences of Julius' victory are yet to come [32].

The detail of the letter thus suggests that this particular embassy had been sent not very long before the writing of *Ep.*, 95 (94), most probably in 410, but certainly at least six months before Synesius was consecrated as bishop, since he clearly did not take part in secular policies during his period of retirement. On the other hand the interval between the debate about the embassy and Synesius' consecration cannot have been very long since two, unfortunately obscure, matters related to this embassy were still 'live' in the governorship of Andronicus which followed soon after Synesius' taking up his duties as bishop of Ptolemais [33]. One of the items of business discussed in the debate preceding the embassy was the affair of Dioscurides. The problem must have been to decide what attitude the embassy was to take in this matter [34]. Tw other letters briefly mention Dioscurides to correspondents at Constantinople [35]. It is not certain, but likely, that all three letters refer to the

---

(30) *Ep.*, 95 (94, 1460D).
(31) *Ep.*, 6 and 14 ; *Ep.*, 57, 1393A (41. p. 62, GARZYA) ; *Ep.*, 91 illustrate direct action carried out or expected on the part of Synesius as bishop.
(32) *Ep.*, 95 (94, 1464C).
(33) *Ep.*, 57, 1389C = 41. p. 59, GARZYA.
(34) *Ep.*, 95 (94, 1464C).
(35) *Ep.*, 47 = 49, GARZYA and 79.

same man (³⁶). If so, the two letters are later than *Ep.*, 95 (94), for Synesius seems to assume that his addressees already know about Dioscurides. This they would have done if the embassy had taken his case to Constantinople. Now one of the letters was written when Andronicus had refused to be influenced by Synesius on Dioscurides' behalf (³⁷). The affair of Dioscurides, whatever it was, had not therefore been settled by the embassy and was causing problems in the governship of Andronicus.

That an embassy and – as I would argue – *the* embassy went not long before the governorship of Andronicus is confirmed by another detail of *Ep.*, 79. One Anastasius was being threatened by henchmen of Andronicus with charges arising from his behavior as ambassador, presumably not long before (³⁸). Now an Anastasius, who seems to be an ambassador (³⁹), was recommended to Pylaemenes at Constantinople in *Ep.*, 100 (99). At the time Synesius was worried that he might be compelled to perform curial duties (⁴⁰). This must have been before he was elected bishop, and before he went into 6 months of voluntary exile to make up his mind whether he would allow himself to be consecrated bishop – in other words the letter confirms that an embassy did go to Constantinople around the time which I have argued for the debate described in *Ep.*, 95 (94).

One reason why it has often been assumed that *Ep.*, 95 (94) must refer to the embassy of 399 is that the principal business of the embassy mentioned in that letter seemed to be the same as that explained by Synesius in his speech *De Regno* in 399. But this, I would argue, is a mistake. The discussion must centre on the sentence in which Synesius defined his disagreement with Julius. Τὸ στρατιωτικόν τε καὶ τὸ βουλευτικὸν εὑρων εἰς θητικὸν ... (⁴¹). In the translation of Fitzgerald this reads : 'I saw the army and senate falling under the yoke of mercenaries and I endeavoured to

---

(36) In all passages Dioscurides is in trouble. In *Ep.*, 95 (94) and 47 he is in the wrong. In 79 Synesius has been unable to help him.

(37) *Ep.*, 79, 1449A.

(38) *Ibid.*, 1445C.

(39) *Ep.*, 100 (99, 1468-9).

(40) *Ibid.*

(41) *Ep.*, 95 (94, 1461D).

resist' (⁴²). This version fits the preoccupation of 399 with the danger threatening the Roman Empire from its German mercenaries – but is it right ? A more literal translation would be 'I saw the soldiers and the decurions reduced to a 'thetic' condition', i.e. to a condition of menials ... By itself this is very obscure. By what process were soldiers and decurions being humbled ?

Fortunately Synesius tells us of a measure which was presumably intended to put a stop to this abuse. He proposed that foreigners (ξένοι) should no longer be enrolled in the army, because foreigners retrain (μεταδιδάσκουσι) even the most soldierly governors (ἄρχοντες) into merchants (⁴³). The problem is clearly connected with recruiting. In this way, but in this way only, it recalls the situation in 399. But in 399 Synesius was concerned with a danger to the security of the Empire caused by the recruitment of foreigners. In 410 he was worried by the consequences of corruption and illicit gains. He believed that Julius and the otherwise unknown Helladius and Theodorus were continuing the present system because it profited them (⁴⁴).

To my mind the most probable interpretation of this allusion to illicit profits at the expense of soldiers and councillors is that it refers to a well-known abuse of the Later Roman Empire : the commutation of conscription. The furnishing of recruits was a tax like the supply of corn, and like other taxes in kind it could be commuted into a money payment (⁴⁵). Governors could make huge profits by demanding enormous sums of gold instead of men, and using a small part of it to purchase worthless recruits (⁴⁶). I would suggest that the allusions of *Ep.*, 95 (94) fit into this situation. In Pentapolis, as in the provinces of the West, the readiest source of recruits may well have been among the barbarians across the frontier (⁴⁷). Provincials would be asked to provide the money with which foreigners could be hired. Councillors would be reduced to menials by the size of the tax demanded from them, the army would

---

(42) A. FITZGERALD, *The Letters of Synesius of Cyrene* (Oxford, 1926), p. 183.
(43) *Ep.*, 95 (94, 1464B).
(44) *Ibid.*
(45) A. H. M. JONES, *L.R.E.*, pp. 615-16.
(46) *C.T.*, VII, 13, 7 (375), cf. also *ibid.*, 8 (380), 9 (380).
(47) Cf. *C.T.*, VII, 13, 7 preface.

be reduced to the same condition because its recruits were derived from have-nots across the frontier rather than Roman peasants. Defenders of this kind of recruitment could indeed argue that it was advantageous for the wretched (ταπεινοί) to become soldiers [48], and it would be the governors not the generals who could become merchants since the commutation of the levy was the responsibility of the civilian governor [49]. It is not clear how this situation could have been improved by Synesius' proposal that the separate military command (στρατηγία) in Pentapolis should be ended, and the cities returned to the traditional system of government (εἰς ἀρχαίαν ἡγεμονίαν), i.e. that the cities of Libya should be subject to the governor of the cities of Egypt [50]. It does however seem that some kind of supervision from Egypt was restored − with results not to Synesius' liking [51].

Synesius and other Magnates of Pentapolis

Synesius has not told us where the debate of *Ep.*, 95 (94) was held. It has been concluded that it must have been in the curia of Cyrene [52], but since the occasion was the sending of a delegation to Constantinople, and the matter under debate problems of military administration without any reference to the sending of crown-gold, it is more likely that the meeting described by Synesius was an extraordinary meeting of the provincial assembly of Pentapolis [53].

(48) *Ep.*, 95 (94, 1464B).
(49) *Ep.*, 79, 1445B.
(50) *Ep.*, 95 (94, 1464B).
(51) *Catastasis*, 1569B.
(52) C. H. Coster, *Late Roman Studies*, pp. 234 and 236, cf. Lacombrade, *Synésios*, p. 73.
(53) Regulations for such a meeting : *C.T.* XII.2.12-3 (P. P. III., AD.392). It may have been held at Cyrene but more likely at Ptolemais, the residence of the governor. The embassy of 399 had also been sent to carry requests 'of the cities', i.e. of the provincial assembly (*De Regno*, 1108C). But this sentence also shows that *De Regno* was a festival speech. The speech which would outline the requests of the cities, was yet to come. That is why in *De Regno* Synesius could say that Cyrene (his native town) had sent him.

If this was so it was a meeting not only of decurions but of *honorati* as well, in fact of everybody in the province who counted ([54]).

There is another reason for believing that the debate did not take place in the council of Cyrene : the writings of Synesius provide no explicit evidence that matters of this kind were still being debated in city-councils. It would not be surprising if city councils, had ceased to be concerned with basic questions of policy, since at this time many of the most powerful citizens were likely to be outside the council ([55]). The local councils of course continued to exist and the *curiales* continued to be threatened with impoverishment ([56]), as they continued to perform their compulsory public services ([57]). Not unnaturally they continued to seek ways of escaping their curial obligations ([58]). But the *curiae* appear to have ceased to provide the actual and symbolic leadership which had been theirs in earlier centuries.

When we compare the role of the council (whether of Cyrene or of Ptolemais) as revealed in the writings of Synesius with that of the council of Antioch in the writings of c. 40 year older Libanius a considerable change is apparent. Traditionally possession of a council (*curia* or βουλή) was a symbol of civic identity, and indeed of a community's status as a city ([59]). Libanius, who like Synesius was descended from a long line of decurions ([60]), compared the council of a city to the root of a tree ([61]), to the keel of a ship ([62]), to the soul

---

(54) *C.T.*, XII.12.12-13 ; Honorius' decree of 418AD on assembly of Gaul : *M.G.H.*, *Epistolae*, III, 13 ; cf. J. A. O. LARSEN, *Representative Government in Greek and Roman History* (Berkeley, 1966), pp. 150-3.

(55) A. H. M. JONES, *L.R.E.*, pp. 758 and 760, W. LIEBESCHUETZ, *Antioch* (Oxford, 1972), pp. 186-92.

(56) See above p. 153.

(57) E.g. Magnus (*Ep.*, 72), and Leucippus (*Ep.*, 79 (78) also probably 57. 1392C-93A = 41 p. 62, GARZYA and *Ep.*, 58 = 42, GARZYA. Leucippus probably incurred the debt in tax-collecting.

(58) See below notes 65-7.

(59) A. H. M. JONES, *The Greek City from Alexander to Justinian*, Oxford, 1940, pp. 93 and 272.

(60) P. PETIT, *Libanius et la vie municipale à Antioch* (Paris, 1955), p. 283, W. LIEBESCHUETZ, *Antioch*, pp. 101-5.

(61) LIBANIUS, *Or.*, XI. 133.

(62) *Or.*, XXVIII. 4.

of the body [63] ; he considered it the source of everything that is worthwhile in a city [64].

Synesius did not ascribe anything like as lofty a role to the council of Cyrene. It is not significant that he tried to free himself [65], his brother [66] and at least one other [67] from curial service, such behaviour had been normal among *curiales* for a long time [68]. But Synesius was openly contemptuous of curial status [69]. He did not consider it part of the ancient traditions but as a disagreable chore to be performed, significantly, not on behalf of his fellow citizens but of the Roman Empire [70]. When he made his speech to the emperor Arcadius he spoke as a man sent by Cyrene but said nothing about the city council [71]. Similarly he very rarely identifies individuals as decurions, so that unless they happened to be involved in liturgies [72] or were trying to escape from curial status [73], it usually is impossible to tell whether significant personalities mentioned by him were decurions or not. Was Julius a decurion [74], or Joannes the magnate accused of murder [75], or Anastasius the ambassador [76], or Andronicus even, the tyrannous governor [77] ? It may well be that some or all of these men were *curiales*, but Synesius does not say it of any one of them.

---

(63) *Or.*, XVIII. 147.

(64) *Or.*, XLIX. 32.

(65) *De Providentia*, 18. 1253C immunity gained, *ibid.*, 1256C lost again, *Ep.*, 100 (99) regained but not securely.

(66) *Ep.*, 93 (92).

(67) *Ep.*, 79.

(68) Cf. W. LIEBESCHUETZ, *Antioch*, pp. 178 ff.

(69) *Ep.*, 93 (92) 'the unlucky book', 100 (99) 'The accursed liturgy' – thought a service to the Roman empire not to his city.

(70) *Ep.*, 100 (99).

(71) *De Regno*, 2. 1056C.

(72) See note 57 above.

(73) See above notes 65-7.

(74) See above p. 153.

(75) See below p. 162.

(76) See above p. 152, notes 38-9.

(77) *Ep.*, 73 (1440A). δεσπότης ὁ πρῴην ἀντιπολιτευόμενος καὶ τὴν ἐν πολιτείᾳ διαφορὰν ἀπὸ τοῦ βήματος ἀγωνίζεται. This may suggest that he was a decurion, but need only mean that he had engaged in local politics. Synesius never accused him of having deserted his council.

I would suggest that these men's curial status was not mentioned because in most contexts it was no longer important. When local opinion on some political matter was required, or an embassy had to be sent to Constantinople, I would suggest that there was a gathering of leading men, whether of honorary imperial rank or decurions or clergy, and these would meet in the governor's court [78], or under the chairmanship of the bishop [79], or as a provincial assembly, and reach the necessary decisions. This development was eventually formalised by imperial legislation. In the reign of Anastasius, the election of corn buyer [80] and defensor [81] and perhaps curator ($ἔφορος$) [82] was assigned legally to a gathering of notables. In the West the election of the defensor had been assigned to notables as early as 409 [83]. Cyrene and the province of Pentapolis were of course in the East, but perhaps the actual transfer of political power from the *curia* to the notables was earlier than its legal recognition. A reason could be that the magnates of Pentapolis became increasingly involved in the defence of the country-side against nomads whom the regular troops were unable to keep out [84]. This military capacity must have given men like Synesius [85] a much more powerful position vis-à-vis mere decurions and even the provincial governor than great landowners would have had elsewhere.

It must be admitted that my argument depends to a considerable extent on negative evidence : the fact that a debate preceding an

(78) *Ep.*, 62 implies that the governor's court (not the council) was where the citizens of Ptolemais would formally thank a retiring general.

(79) *Constitutio* seem to have been spoken by Synesius as bishop and spokesman of a joint meeting (of the notables ?) of the cities of Cyrene and Ptolemais (*P.G.*, LXVI. 1576).

(80) *C.T.*, I. 4.7.

(81) *Ibid.*, 19 (505AD).

(82) *M.A.M.A.*, III. 197A.

(83) *C.T.*, I. 55.8.

(84) C. LACOMBRADE, *Synésios de Cyrène*, pp. 199 ff. ; see *Ep.*, 130 (129), 133 (132), 132 (131), 107, 108, 122.

(85) Joannes too had a military following : *Ep.*, 44. 1363B. (43 p. 76.5, GARZYA). He is probably the long-haired Joannes with long-haired followers who rode away from barbarian invaders as related in *Ep.*, 104. *Ep.*, 2 is probably the same man. On Joannes see also below pp. 163-164.

158

embassy is described, and the council is not mentioned, that we are never told that the council passed a motion in praise – or criticism – of an official [86], that the council – as opposed to individual councillors and the bishop – played no part in the conflict between leading citizens and the governor Andronicus [87], that the council is not mentioned in connection with the organisation of defence against raiders [88], that we never hear that the imperial authorities held the council responsible for the conduct of its city [89]. Singly these negatives mean little, cumulatively, they become significant. We do after all have quite a lot of information about Cyrene and Ptolemais in the writings of Synesius. If we never hear about one of the city councils acting collectively, the reason is quite likely to be that they no longer did so, and that what mattered in these cities were the governor, the general and a number of powerful individuals, of whom by far the best known – and probably also one of the most powerful – was Synesius himself. If there was a formally established representative of the city it was its bishop, but the bishop's secular role in order to be effective required the support of at least either the local magnates or of the governor [90].

The character of the magnates of Pentapolis is of course best illustrated by Synesius' own life. Unlike the decurions of Antioch, but like the magnates of the West, he was not by preference a city dweller. He preferred the life of a country-gentleman, with leisure for the pursuit of philosophy [91], varied from time to time by a little hunting. He resented, or at least professed to resent, life in the city with the demands that it made on him as a local politician or as a patron [92]. In fact his life was far from leisurely. He painted an idealised picture of the idyllic life that he and his peasants might live on his inland country estate. In practice he had to use his wealth and influence to raise a militia and to defend the countryside against

---

(86) See above p. 157, note 79.
(87) C. LACOMBRADE, *Synésios de Cyrène*, pp. 237-48.
(88) *Ibid.*, pp. 230-36.
(89) Contrast situation at Antioch. See W. LIEBESCHUETZ, *Antioch*, pp. 101-5.
(90) Synesius eventually seems to have lost the support of both.
(91) *Ep.*, 105. 1484.
(92) *Ep.*, 148 (147), the reality e.g. *ep.*, 132 (131).

nomads [93]. Synesius belonged to a family which for many centuries had been one of the leading families, if not the leading family of Cyrene. He claimed descent from the original colonists, the predigree going back to Heracles [94]. What may have been the city house of the family has been excavated in the public centre of Cyrene [95]. If it was, Synesius had probably been brought up in a Christian family. This will explain why he was to express qualms about becoming a bishop, but none whatsoever about becoming a Christian.

Synesius' family had clearly been wealthy for a long time, and even in the early 5th century when so many pressures were bearing down on decurions, he was evidently a rich man still. He could boast of his indifference to property as only a wealthy man can [96]. He could afford to give away a horse [97], and to hire a ship [98]. His country-estate had a fortified house behind whose walls he could endure a siege [99]. Synesius' brother also seems to have owned a fortified country-house [100]. It was situated near salt-marshes, not far from the port of Phicus [101], and within walking distance of

(93) See R. S. O. TOMLIN, 'Meanwhile in North Italy and Cyrenaica ...' in P. J. CASEY, ed. The End of Roman Britain, B.A.R. British series 71 (Oxford, 1979), pp. 253-70.

(94) Catastasis. 1572, Ep., 113, 57. 1393B = 41 p. 63, GARZYA.

(95) R. G. GOODCHILD, Kyrene und Apollonia (Zürich, 1971), pp. 89-90. An inscription shows that the house belonged to Hesychius, and another that he was Libyarch, probably president of the provincial assembly of Libya. (See J. M. REYNOLDS, J.R.S., LIX (1969), pp. 100-1. Hesychius was the name of Synesius' father, and of his son (P.L.R.E.; II Stemma 34), and Synesius' family was clearly one of the presumably small number wealthy enough to provide the Libyarch. So it is reasonably likely that this was their family house. It was not rebuilt after the earthquake of 365. So Synesius did not live there as an adult. The inhabitants were Christians.

(96) Dio, 1157C, Ep., 134 (133).

(97) Ep., 40 = 37, GARZYA ; horses were scarce because of the difficulty of feeding them Ep., 109. His brother had two, Ep., 132 (131).

(98) Ep., 41 = 38, GAZYA.

(99) On the location near Balagrae (El Beid) 15 KM S.W. of Cyrene in the hills see R. C. GOODCHILD, Libyan Studies (London, 1976), p. 241. The siege : Ep., 132 (131).

(100) Ep., 132 (131).

(101) Ep., 118. Phycus was the nearest port, through which Synesius received his letters. See Ep., 51 = 53, GARZYA, 101 (100), 129. On Phycus see G. D. B. JONES

Synesius own property ([102]). One has the impression that both brothers spent most of their lives on their estates ([103]).

We have seen that Synesius and his brother were *curiales* but that for them the city-council was anything by a focus of local patriotism ([104]). Synesius repeatedly struggled to free himself from curial burdens ([105]), and his brother did the same ([106]). Since each ended his life as bishop of Ptolemais ([107]), their efforts were eventually successful though perhaps not in the way they had hoped. We cannot be sure that either brother had been absolutely secure before he became a bishop. Synesius describes members of his family as 'eager for office'. A number of relatives are known to have obtained imperial posts, though none is known to have achieved great distinction ([108]). We have also seen that lack of loyalty to the council did not in the case of Synesius imply absence of love for his city, or of a sense of duty towards his fellow citizens ([109]).

We know of only one liturgy performed by Synesius, the embassy to Constantinople ([110]). Presumably there were others. Strangely enough the surviving letters do not mention that Synesius feared tax-collecting, the most notorious hazard in the life of

---

and J. H. LITTLE, 'Coastal Settlements in Cyrenaica', J.R.S., LXI (1971), pp. 64-79, esp. 73-4 and Pl. IV.

(102) *Ep.*, 109.

(103) *Ep.*, 114, 105. 1484C suggest that Synesius visited Cyrene rather than lived there. Was the fact that leading decurions had become countrymen linked with the decline of Cyrene, which was no longer provincial capital, and had not been fully rebuilt after the earthquake of 365 ? See R. G. GOODCHILD, *Kyrene und Apollonia*, pp. 46-7, 66, 68, 74, 97, 114, 119 for archaeological evidence, cf. also SYNESIUS, *De Regno*, 2, the city a 'vast ruin'.

(104) See above p. 156, note 69.

(105) See above p. 156, note 65.

(106) See above p. 156, note 66.

(107) See *P.L.R.E.*, II, s.v. Euoptius.

(108) Maximianus father of Synesius' cousin Diogenes spent much time at court (*Ep.*, 118). Diogenes held a military command in Cyrenaica (*Ep.*, 118-9, 131 (130)), and eventually lived in Syria (*Ep.*, 23). Herodes a senator by birth and a member of senatorial order by office (*Ep.*, 38). *P.L.R.E.*, II, s.v. Herodes, argues that he was a decurion by birth.

(109) See above p. 155.

(110) *De Regno, passim, De Insomniis*, 1309 ; *Hymn*, III, 460 ff.

decurions of the Later Empire [111]. This may indicate that at Cyrene, as at Antioch [112], that unpleasant burden fell more heavily on humbler *curiales* [113]. On the other hand Synesius did take a leading part in political debate and he was frequently involved in the legal infighting of leading citizens of Cyrene [114]. His patronage was sought by many [115], and his intercession was often effective without much effort on his part [116]. He did not however always win his point, he was only one of a group of magnates.

It is significant that the basis of Synesius' influence was local. It derived from the antiquity, status and wealth of his family, and no doubt the strength of his own personality. His standing was not based on active or honorary rank in the imperial administration or army, as was the effectiveness of patrons encountered in the writings of Libanius or the chapter *De patrociniis* in the Theodosian Code [117]. Synesius' patronage was mainly exercised in his native province, though his family evidently had close links with Alexandria [118]. Synesius' connections at Constantinople were, with one important exception, comparatively minor figures whose acquaintance he happened to have made when he was studying at Alexandria, or later during his stay as ambassador at Constantinople [119]. He was not born to be a member of an empire-wide net-

(111) Magnus beaten to death (*Ep.*, 72, 1436C), torture of tax-payers (*Ep.*, 79, 1445A).

(112) LIBANIUS, *Or.*, 49, 8 ; *C.T.*, XI, 24, 1-6 ; my *Antioch*, p. 176.

(113) Was Zenas who 'last year collected double-tax', and threatened to persecute Anastasius (*Ep.*, 79, 1445C) a leading decurion who made his liturgy a source of power and wealth ?

(114) See below p. 162.

(115) *Ep.*, 50. 1380 = 52, GARZYA.

(116) *Ep.*, 57. 1388C = 41. p. 57, GARZYA.

(117) A. H. M. JONES, *Later Roman Empire*, pp. 775-8, my *Antioch*, pp. 201 ff.

(118) Euoptius was frequently at Alexandria, sometimes with family (*Ep.*, 4. 1341B = 5 p. 25, GARZYA ; *Ep.*, 105. 1486. Synesius studied at Alexandria (C. LACOMBRADE, *Synésios de Cyrène*, pp. 38-71), and his children were born there (*Ep.*, 18). Theodorus of Alexandria had been host to Synesius' parents (*Ep.*, 20). Synesius may have had land in Egypt at Leontopolis (The puzzling fragment *Homilia*, II. 1564B).

(119) Aurelian, the praetorian prefect, became a 'dear friend' (*Ep.*, 61), but there is no reason to suppose that Synesius knew him before the embassy (*De Providentia*, 18. 1253).

work of influential individuals. What had brought him and his acquaintances together was a common interest in philosophy or literature ([120]). He was essentially a provincial aristocrat.

Surveying his life before becoming a bishop, Synesius claims that he was successful in all that he had undertaken. Overlooking minor set-backs that may well have been right ([121]). Not long before he became bishop he wrote a very depressed letter. Synesius was not only living away from Cyrene, but was completely disillusioned with the city of the Joannes and the Julii. He complained that his way of life separated him from his fellow citizens even more than distance ([122]). It is a pity that we do not hear more about the way of life of these other magnates. Compared with Synesius they remain shadows. One of their characteristics does however emerge clearly enough : their habit of ruthlessly attacking each other, and each other's property. In their intensive feuding they made use of the local legal machinery — one, Andronicus of Berenice, even managed to do so from the position of judge, since he had illegally managed to get himself appointed governor of Pentapolis. But they also exploited to the full the possibilities offered by the courts of the capital. *Ep.*, 95 (94) reveals that not long before the debate about the embassy, somebody had accused Julius of treason. Since the governor was afraid to reject the case Synesius used force to compel the accuser to drop proceedings ([123]). The embassy itself carried a resolution against one Dioscurides ([124]). We don't know who he was, but he was well known to Synesius and his correspondents. The alleged offence of Dioscurides is not described, but it was evidently not unlike that of one Peter, who is described as 'even more shameless than Dioscurides'. Peter had been seizing other people's property by force. When the decision of the provincial court went aganist him, he refused to give in and even threatened the police. Synesius rallied leading men of the province to uphold

---

(120) Apart from Aurelian the most influential connections at Constantinople in the later years were Troilus, a sophist (*P.L.R.E.*, II, 1128), and Anastasius 2, probably the tutor of the imperial children (*P.L.R.E.*, II, 77).

(121) See above p. 148, note 12.

(122) *Ep.*, 50 = 52, GARZYA.

(123) Andronicus : see above note 77. On Julius : *Ep.*, 95 (94. 1460D).

(124) See above p. 151, notes 34-5.

the court-decision. Thereupon Peter appealed to the praetorian prefect Anthemius at Constantinople. Synesius sent Martyrius, a friend, to oppose the appeal ([125]).

Litigation was not the only way in which the rivalry of the local magnates was carried on. About the same time as the affair of Peter there occurred a sensational murder. Joannes, who has been mentioned earlier was thought to have employed one of his followers to kill his brother Aemilius – at least so it was alleged by Joannes' enemies among the decurions (or just 'local politicians' πολιτευομένους ἐχθρούς) ([126]). The truth was uncertain. Synesius was as opposed to the accusers as to Joannes. He grieves that famous Cyrene should have become the home of the likes of the Julii and the Joannes. Evidently it was Julius and his friends who had originated the accusation against Joannes. Synesius was resolved to remain neutral.

But Synesius did not stick to that resolve. Some time later he wrote a letter in which he addressed Joannes sternly, but as friend whose interest he had at heart. Joannes is to hand himself over to the authorities and to submit to punishment. Alternatively he is to demand a rigorous examination of the man alleged to have carried out the actual killing, and in this way to prove his own innocence ([127]).

One migth ask what produced the change from the scornful neutrality of the first letter to the almost paternal concern of the second. The most probable explanation is that the second letter was written by Synesius when he had become a bishop and saw in Joannes not simply a murderous magnate but also a soul for whom he was responsible. It is true that the letter does not contain a word that is explicitly Christian, and that the vaguely Christian ideas of Synesius' letter can be parallelled in Plato ([128]). Nevertheless the

(125) Ep., 47 (49, GARZYA), considerably later and written by Synesius as bishop Ep., 91 (90) ; Ep., 42 (GARZYA, 39) may deal with same case. For a similar case, the harrassing of Synesius' cousin Diogenes see Ep., 118-9, 131 (130), 134 (133), cf. P.L.R.E., II, p. 360, s.v. Diogenes, 2.

(126) Ep., 50 (52, GARZYA), see note 85 above for his armed followers. Joannes marriage was in some way scandalous : Ep., 44. 1372D (43, GARZYA).

(127) Ep., 44 (43, GARZYA).

(128) For references see C. LACOMBRADE, Synésios de Cyrène, p. 209, and Edition of GARZYA, pp. 78-80.

balance of the argument with its stress on punishment after death, and on its mitigation through repentance and voluntarily accepted punishment in this life is thoroughly Christian, and the expression of Christian ideas in terminology that is altogether derived from Greek classical authors is characteristic of Synesius, and his brand of Hellenic Christianity ([129]).

Quite apart from literary taste there was very good reason why on this occasion Synesius avoided the language of the priest. He was dealing with a criminal offence, which was the business of a secular court, which might use torture to assist its inquiries ([130]), and which was empowered to inflict capital punishment ([131]). Synesius was still too much a man of the world to reject torture and judicial killing, but he was aware that as representative of the Church, he could not have anything to do with them ([132]). If he was going to advise a man to submit himself to the secular court he could not do so with the authority of a priest. The incident is an example of the mixture of secular and religious duties that faced Synesius as bishop. When taking it up he had hoped against all the evidence that the priesthood would mean not a stepping down from philosophy but an ascent towards it ([133]). In fact his worst fears were realised, as bishop he assumed a heavy new responsibility for the souls of his charges, while becoming ever more deeply involved in the secular and political affairs which had already been taking up too much of his time as a secular magnate ([134]).

---

(129) Cf. *De Providentia*, 1256C.

(130) *Ep.*, 44. 1373A calls for use of torture.

(131) *Ep.*, 121.

(132) J. GAUDEMET, *L'église dans l'empire romain* (Paris, 1958), pp. 265 and 278-9. A. H. M. JONES, *L. R. E.*, p. 984.

(133) *Ep.*, 11.

(134) I hope to make this subject of a separate paper.

XV

WHY DID SYNESIUS BECOME
BISHOP OF PTOLEMAIS ?

In a lecture to the Roman Society ([1]) T. Barnes has thrown the accepted chronology ([2]) of the life of Synesius into confusion by arguing that Synesius returned from his embassy to Constantinople not in 402, but in 400. This provides two extra years for the events of the later part of Synesius' life and has made 407, Seeck's date for Synesius' consecration more attractive ([3]). It is therefore worthwhile to examine the evidence for the date of Synesius' consecration once more.

Ep. 13 is the only source giving an explicit date. The letter accompanies what seems to have been the first Paschal letters to be sent by Synesius as bishop. The Easter date announced is 19 Parmuthi, that is 14th April ([4]). This date would fit either 407 or 412 ([5]).

The choice between the two dates could be decided by *Ep.* 12 — if only the interpretation of that letter was certain. It is addressed to 'brother Cyril', who ought to be a fellow bishop, and concerns the death of our 'common father', who ought to be an ecclesiastical

---

(1) Letters of Synesius have been cited in the numeration of R. HERCHER, *Epistolographi Graeci* (Paris, 1873), pp. 638-739, which was followed by A. Fitzgerald in his translation, *The Letters of Synesius of Cyrene* (Oxford, 1926). The numbering of J. P. MIGNE, *Patrologia Graeca, LXVI* (Paris, 1864), where different, is given in brackets. Column references are to MIGNE. The numbering of A. GARZYA, *Synesii Cyrenensis Epistolae* (Rome, 1979) is given where it differs from Hercher. Where helpful, page and line references to Garzya are given in brackets. Where my dating of letters differs from Garzya's this is deliberate. The lecture of T. Barnes will appear in a fortcoming volume of J.R.S. The ref. to Aurelian as consul in *Ep.* 61 is the key evidence.

(2) C. LACOMBRADE, *Synésios de Cyrène Hellène et Chrétien* (Paris, 1951) see table at end.

(3) O. SEECK, 'Studien zu Synesius', *Philologus*, LII (1983), pp. 442-83, esp. 461-2.

(4) A. CAPELLI, *Chronologia, Cronografia e Calendario Perpetuo* (Milan, 1930), p. 82.

(5) E. BICKERMAN, *Chronology of the Ancient World* (London, 1968), p. 48.

superior of both Cyril and Synesius. If this deduction is right it is not easy to think of anyone who this could be if not Theophilus the patriarch of Alexandria ([6]). This is confirmed by the fact that Synesius describes the deceased as τὸν ἱερὸν ἐκεῖνον καὶ θεοφιλῆ πρεσβύτην which would be a pun on Theophilus' name (as in *ep.* 105 near end). Theophilus died on 15th October 412. So on the face of it, it is likely that Synesius was bishop in 412 ([7]).

It would still be possible to concede that Synesius was consecrated in 407 if there is evidence showing him in office before 411 ([8]). *Ep.* 66 (67 Garzya) was written in the first year of Synesius' episcopacy ([9]). In it Synesius asks Theophilus how he should behave towards one Alexander, a bishop who had been driven from his see in Bithynia as a follower of John Chrysostomus, and had not returned even though there has been an amnesty and a reconciliation ([10]). Three years have passed since this possibily of return had been offered to Alexander. What was the year of the 'amnesty'? Synesius writes that the reconciliation was initiated by a pamphlet which Theophilus sent to 'the blessed Atticus', although he seems not to have been absolutely sure of this ([11]). Now if 'the blessed Atticus' was Atticus, patriarch of Constantinople, the amnesty must have been later than Atticus' consecration in March 406. In that case the earliest possible date of *Ep.* 66 would be March 409, and there could be no question of Synesius having been consecrated in time to send out the Paschal letter of 407.

But Seeck, on the basis of Synesius' uncertainty as to the addressee of the pamphlet and his use of the epithet 'μακάριος', argued that Theophilus' pamphlet had been sent to a deceased bishop, and proposed that in the letter Synesius had written Atticus in mistake for Atticus' deceased predecessor at Constantinople, Arsacius ([12]). If Arsacius was in fact the bishop concerned, *ep.* 66 could have been

(6) So C. Lacombrade, *Synésios*, p. 269.

(7) Since we have no figure for the length of Synesius' episcopate it would still have been possible for him to have been consecrated in 406/7.

(8) Cf. C. Lacombrade, *op. cit.*, pp. 210-11.

(9) Garzya, p. 127, 3.

(10) *Ibid.*, p. 122, 12.

(11) *Ibid.*, p. 122, 8.

(12) O. Seeck, *op. cit.*, 461-2.

written as early as say September 407 ([13]), and would be reconcilable with 406 as the date of Synesius' consecration. But Seeck', argument is weak. The epithet μακάριος was sometimes given to living bishops ([14]), so Synesius could have applied it to the current bishop of Constantinople. Even if Synesius' memory deceived him, and Theophilus pamphlet had not been addressed to Atticus, it is quite arbitrary to conclude that it must have been addressed to Arsacius. It could have been addressed to any bishop. We have no other evidence that certainly refers to the amnesty and reconciliation mentioned in *ep.* 66. The fact that persecution of the followers of Chrysostom seems to have intensified in the course of 404 ([15]) makes it rather unlikely that the attempted reconciliation was as early as this ([16]). There is, moreover, evidence that precisely Atticus did attempt a reconciliation. He succeeded in making peace with some Thracian bishops ([17]). 'Martyrius' *Life of John Chrysostom* seems to be a warning to Chrysostom's followers not to accept Communion with Atticus ([18]). The author had heard reports of Chrysostom's death but was still uncertain of their truth. Chrysostom died on 14th September 407. The months after Chrysostom's death would seem a suitable time for an initiative to bring the dispute to an end ([19]). If so Alexander may well have been offered a return to his see in 408 which would put *ep.* 66, written three years later in 411.

(13) Arsacius died on 11.11.405 (SOCRATES, VI, 20, 1), and thus could have initiated a reconciliation between autumn 404 and autumn 405. In which case *ep.* 66 could have been written in autumn 407, and Chrysostom might have been bishop just early enough to have sent a Paschal letter for Easter 407.

(14) BASIL, *ep.* 225 (*P.G.*, XXXII, 841) refs. to Gregory of Nyssa, 'blessed' applied to living Athanasius of Alexandria : *P.G.*, XXV, 364 C, 372 A, 372 B ; to bishops in general *ibid.*, 301 A, 407 C.

(15) See my 'The Deposition of John Chrysostom', *Nottingham Medieval Studies*, XXIX (1985), pp. 1-31, esp. 23-6.

(16) There was pressure on all followers of Chrysostom to recognise Arsacius, and later Atticus, and some individuals yielded, *e.g.* the bishops of Tarsus and Aegae (JOHN CHRYS., *Ep.* 204, the Goths on estate of Promotus refused, *ibid.*, 206-7). But individual acts of submission could not be described as 'reconciliation' or 'amnesty'.

(17) PALLADIUS, *Dial.* 71 (p. 127, 17-19).

(18) See fragment of 'Martyrius' printed *P.G.*, XLVII, xlvi-liv.

(19) On 13th June 407, even before death of Chrysostom a synod of African bishops petitioned Pope Innocent I to resume communion with Theophilus of Alexandria — unsuccessfully (MANSI, IV, 502 nr. lxviii = *P.L.*, XX, 618, nr. xxi).

A final approach to the dating of Synesius' consecration makes use of references to nomadic invasions of Cyrenaica. Sometime after Synesius had become a bishop the dux Anysius had inflicted a decisive defeat on the invaders, and put an end to seven years of exhausting war. Anysius won the province one year's respite ([20]). Then there came another and devastating invasion. Can the beginning of the 'seven years war' be dated ? In *ep.* 130 Synesius complains that the corrupt general Cerealis had demoralised the army, and that knowledge of this had attracted the invaders. In *ep.* 132 and 133 we realize that Synesius is organising the defence of his locality against the nomads. *Ep.* 132 was written in 405, after Cerealis had taken over the command, *ep.* 133, earlier in 405 ([21]). If these letters describe the start of the war which was temporarily ended by Anysius, this would give a date for Anysius of late 411 or early 412 ([22]). The fact that the nomads, had come north to invade the coastal area suggests that the time of year was spring or early summer. This is confirmed by reference to a record plague of locusts ([23]). To sum up, the evidence if not absolutely conclusive, nevertheless, strongly suggests that Lacombrade was right and that Synesius began his episcopate in 411, probably in spring of that year.

SYNESIUS' OBJECTIONS TO CONSECRATION

When Synesius was elected bishop he was not in orders or even baptised. This was not, however, the reason why he was so reluctant to accept consecration. The causes of his hesitation were more complex. Even when he was close to giving in he made his acceptance depend on the fulfilment of certain conditions. First he must be allowed to go on living with his wife. Then he stated in advance that

(20) SYNESIUS, *Catastasis, P.G.*, LXVI, 1568A.

(21) *Ep.* 130, 132 and 133 are numbered one less in *P.G.*, 133 was written after the consulate of Aristaenetus, *i.e.* 404 AD.

(22) This was not the first invasion. There was war when Synesius returned home from Constantinople in 400 (or 402) (*Ep.* 61 end). Was that the invasion of PHILOSTORGIUS, XI, 8, — which struck Egypt as well as Libya ?

(23) On nomadic migrations : W. B. FISCHER, *The Middle East* (7th Ed., London, 1978), p. 554. Locusts : *Ep.* 57 = GARZYA, 41 (p. 55, l. 15), 58 = GAR-ZYA, 42 (p. 71, l. 2). On their season : L. CARLSON, *Africa : Land and Nations* (New York, 1967), p. 90.

he would not preach dogma in which he did not believe. In fact he would not teach doctrine at all. He would let his congregation believe what they believed already. He felt that he as a philosopher was closer to the truth than ordinary members of his congregation could ever be. 'Now you know that philosophy rejects many of those convictions which are cherised by the common people. For my own part, I can never persuade myself that the soul is of more recent origin than the body. Nor would I admit that the world and the parts which make it up must perish. This resurrection which is an object of common belief, is for me nothing but a sacred and mysterious allegory' ([24]). Synesius did believe that popular religion was a separate and inferior entity ([25]). The reason for this was that ordinary people lacked education and a trained faculty of reasoning ([26]). The attitude was common place among educated members of the upper class. From a Christian point of view the attitude was arrogant and sinful. Nevertheless, even Christians found it difficult to shake off. Augustine abandonned it only gradually, as he designed a new Christian scheme of education based on the bible and research into its many layers of meaning ([27]). John Chrysostom through his close contact with Syrian ascetics saw quite clearly that Christian wisdom was independent of education and social status. He proclaimed it often enough — but even for him it remained a paradox ([28]). Synesius, although as I would insist, a practising Christian ([29]), was much less emancipated from traditional attitu-

---

(24) Synesius' doubts : *Ep.* 105, 57 = GARZYA, 41, 11. Translation of *Ep.* 105 from A. FITZGERALD, *The Letters of Synesius of Cyrene* (London, OUP, 1926), p. 200. On Synesius' philosophical outlook see A. BREGMAN, *Synesius of Cyrene, Philosopher and Bishop* (Berkeley, 1982).

(25) Differing from P. BROWN, *The Cult of the Saints* (London, 1981), pp. 12-21.

(26) Synesius believed that ordinary people could not understand philosophy and that it should not be presented to them. They should be taught through myth and allegory as recommended by PLATO, *Rep.*, III, 21. See SYNESIUS, *Ep.* 143 (142), 137 (136). In contrast, for Augustine research into the many levels of meaning of the Bible, accessible through allegorical interpretation, was open to all whether educated or not. See AUG., *Ep.* 137, 18 cited by E. AUERBACH, *Literary Language and its Public* (London, 1958), pp. 48-51, cf. P. BROWN, *Augustine of Hippo* (London, 1967), pp. 252-5, 259-63.

(27) P. BROWN, *op. cit.*, chaps. 12-16 traces Augustine's development.

(28) *E.g. Panégyriques de S. Paul*, ed. A. Piédagnel (Paris, 1982), iv, 10.

(29) Cf. my review of A. BREGMAN, *op. cit.*, n. 222-3, p. 24 above in *J.H.S.*, CIV (1984), pp. 222-3.

des (^{30}). Indeed there is no indication that he felt any need for emancipation.

Synesius' unwillingness to become a bishop derived from more than reluctance to separate from his wife and to have to teach theological dogma. Beneath the formulated objections we can recognise a deep unwillingness to take on the full-time, life-consuming professionalism of the bishop's office. Men of the highest social rank were not accustomed to full-time, life-long careers. The empire was governed by a large professional civil-service, but the heads of department had not normally been promoted from the career grades, and held office for only a comparatively short time (^{31}). A bishop was consecrated for life. The fabric of Synesius' life was woven out of study and recreation, the latter provided by sociability and hunting. Study of philosophy to raise his soul from defilement to purity through knowledge and understanding was the real centre of his life (^{32}). Visits to the city for whatever business forced him back to earth, covered with more stains than anyone could imagine (^{33}). In contrast the role of a priest, above all that of a bishop, required on one hand 'a man above human weaknesses, a stranger to every kind of diversion, even as God himself' (^{34}), and on the other one who was prepared to undertake an enormous amount of business of a kind that Synesius could only endure within strict limits, administration, patronage and involvement in law suits and disputes of every kind. 'How shall I who have devoted my youth to philosophic leisure and to the idle contemplation of abstract being, and have only mingled as much in the cares of the world as to be able to acquit myself of duties to the life of the body and to show myself a citizen — how, I say, shall I ever be equal to a life of daily routine ? Again if I deliver myself over to a nest of practical matters shall I ever be able to apply myself to the fair things of the mind which may be

---

(30) Cf. P. BROWN, *op. cit.*, 113 on Augustine at Cassiciacum.

(31) Traditional senatorial and equestrian offices were held for relatively short periods and not consecutively. The career posts of the civil service of the Later Empire were originally of much lower social standing, thought the status of some of them rose rapidly from the later 4th century. See A. H. M. JONES, *LRE*, pp. 521-601.

(32) *Ep.* 105 (1484 A).

(33) *Ibid.* (1485 C).

(34) *Ibid.* (1484 B). Translations here and in following notes are Fitzgerald's.

gathered in happy leisure alone ? Without all this would life be worth living to me, and to all those who resemble me' ([35]) ?

Thus Synesius could write that he should have preferred many deaths to the bishopric ([36]). But it would be a mistake to conclude that he did not respect the office or bishop or recognise its validity. Quite the opposite : he was deeply concerned that it should be held by a man as unsuitable as he felt himself to be. 'The city ought to be understand the imprudence it commited towards me in appointing one to the priesthood who had not sufficient confidence in his mission to enable him to go to God and pray on behalf of the whole people, but one who has need of the prayer of the people for his own salvation' ([37]). In other words he feared that his lack of qualifications would make any prayer he might offer on behalf of the community unacceptable to God. Worse, he feared punishment and when his consecration was immediately followed by a long series of disasters : the governorship of Andronicus, the great Asurian invasion, and finally the deaths of his own children Synesius saw his worst forebodings confirmed. These calamities came upon him and his community because he was un-worthy to handle the 'mysteries of God', *i.e.* the eucharist, — that surely is the implication of the way the sequence of events is repre-sented in *Ep.* 57 ([38]).

SYNESIUS AS BISHOP

Synesius' reluctance was overcome and he was duly consecrated by Theophilus as metropolitan of Ptolemais ([39]). No sooner had he taken over his duties than his worst fears were realised ([40]). Apart from holding service he had to combat heresy ([41]), to deal with delicate matters of diocesan diplomacy, to consecrate one bishop, to confirm the position of another inspite of a technical defect in his consecration,

(35) *Ep.* 11.
(36) *Ep.* 96 (95).
(37) *Ep.* 13.
(38) *Ep.* 57 (1389 B) = GARZYA, 41 (p. 59, 1.13). See also *Ep.* 67 (1432 C) = GARZYA, 66 (p. 122).
(39) *Ep.* 57 (1392 C) = GARZYA, 41 (p. 62, 1.11), Ptolemais described as πατρίς.
(40) C. LACOMBRADE, *Synésios*, pp. 209-11.
(41) *Ep.* 5.

to decide to what diocese a particular church belonged ([42]). But besides his ecclesiastical functions he continued to perform the whole range of political duties which he had performed as a layman, — only they had become more numerous, difficult and invidious. He had prayed that the priesthood might not seem a descent from philosophy but rather a step up to it ([43]). He soon discovered that his consecration as metropolitan was a long stride into the world of politics.

That a bishop was expected above all to be an effective protector and patron of his community is vividly illustrated by Synesius account of his visit to the village of Palaebisca in western Cyrenaica. This village was part of the diocese of Erythrum, but as the bishop was old and weak and incapable of protecting them, the villagers seceeded, and managed to get a separate bishop consecrated for their village, choosing Siderius, a retired officer, a man who had the reputation of being able to injure his enemies and aid his friends. At the time the consecration seems to have been recognised by Theophilus of Alexandria. One sees how ecclesiastical administration could bring about the break-up of large civic territories. Theophilus wished to continue the arrangement after Siderius' death and nominated a successor to be bishop of Palaebisca only. But the villagers had put themselves back into the diocese of Erythrum which was now governed by the popular bishop Paul. Synesius was given the invidious task of persuading the villagers to foresake Paul and to accept the nominee of Theophilus. He failed ([44]).

While Synesius was inclined to think that dogma should be interpreted allegorically, he was quite certain that the Churches rulings on heresy and heretics must be enforced, irrespective of what his own feelings might be. Thus Synesius publicly boycotted Alexander, the follower of John Chrysostom who was refusing to return to his see. He clearly did not like doing this and continued to entertain Alexander in the privacy of his house. But he was evidently ready to stop this too if Theophilus ordered him to do so ([45]).

Synesius, philosopher that he was, fully joined in the war of words against 'the godless heresy' of Eunomius whose followers are said to

---

(42) *Ep.* 67 (1425 ff.) = GARZYA, 66 (p. 105 ff.) ; cf. also *Ep.* 76.
(43) *Ep.*, 96.
(44) *Ep.* 67, 1412 ff. = GARZYA, 66 (p. 105 ff.).
(45) *Ep.* 66 = GARZYA, 67 ; also *Ep.* 67 (1432) = GARZYA, 66 (p. 120).

be using influence at court to 'sully' the Church. Their 'false teachers' were 'spreading their net' to catch weaker brethren. Their elder were an 'adulterous generation, modern apostles of the devil'. It was well known which estates haboured these bandits ([46]). Synesius was evidently in no doubt that Church discipline, what he calls the law of the Church, must be maintained, and that after he had argued his view of the matter, the last and decisive word must be that of Theophilus of Alexandria, his ecclesiastical superior ([47]).

Quite soon after entering Ptolemais as bishop, that is as I have argued in spring 411, Synesius faced conflict with a new governor, Andronicus. Andronicus is represented as a monster but we have only Synesius' version of the dispute and the issues are not really made clear. Andronicus was a citizen of Cyrene, and a man of low birth — or so Synesius claims, but presummably a decurion, and evidently one who had been a political opponent. Synesius seems to have opposed him from the first. He protested against the appointment, arguing that it was illegal since no man was allowed to govern his home province ([48]). Andronicus cannot have been governor very long when Synesius held a synod of bishops to excommunicate him. We have the letter which was to proclaim the excommunication ([49]), and a sermon, the *Contra Andronicum*, which Synesius delivered, or at least intended to deliver, before the public reading of the letter ([50]). At this point Synesius was unable to put the excommunication into effect. He was persuaded to put Andronicus as it were on probation. Eventually the excommunication was reimposed and Andronicus deposed from

(46) *Ep.* 5 = Garzya, 4.

(47) *Ep.* 66 (end) = Garzya, 67.

(48) Adronicus appointed soon after Synesius' consecration : *Ep.* 57 = Garzya, 41 (p. 59, l. 15). Protest at appointment of fellow citizen and political opponent : *Ep* 73. Andronicus had been in office for some time but was only now on way to Ptolemais by sea. CJ I, 41 is a later restatement of law that no one may govern his home province.

(49) *Ep.* 58 = Garzya, 42.

(50) *Ep.* 57 = Garzya, 41. In favour of view that letter was not written a very long time after Andronicus had taken office : 1. Anysius had not yet won his victory 1385 C = Garzya, p. 56, l. 2 (assuming the general refered to is Anysius). 2. Synesius still hopes that the people might elect another bishop in his place 1397 B = Garzya, p. 69, l. 14. 3. Synesius has lost only one son 1392 B = Garzya, p. 61, l. 15. 4. We are still in the year in which Synesius had taken over the bishopric *Ep.* 72 (1436 B) = Garzya, p. 128, l. 6.

office. We can't date this precisely, but the interval of 'probation' was long enough for many rich to be exiled or reduced to beggars ([51]).

The original, and ecclesiastical, justification for excommunication had been that Andronicus had refused to recognise the Church's right of asylum. The bulk of Synesius' charges against Andronicus were however secular, and of the kind that had always been made against corrupt governors whether by prominent provincials or prosecutors in the capital. Andronicus had obtained his office by bribery. He had exercised it cruelly and greedily, beating and torturing his victims. Some men, forced to sell property in order to pay debts to the state had been compelled to sell to nominees of Andronics. The context, as so often, was collection of taxes. Andronicus introduced unprecedented forms of torture to extort, among other levies, the tironicum ([52]). Needless to say Synesius' account is completely one-sided. Andronicus imprisoned a man in order to induce him to prosecute Gennadius, the previous governor. The implication is that he was simply jealous of Gennadius ([53]). Another is said to have suffered imprisonment and torture because he was preventing a marriage which Andronicus ([54]), and perhaps the woman concerned ([55]), wanted. He had the decurion Magnus beaten to death ([56]). He refused to release the presbyter Evagrius from curial service ([57]). In most of these cases the bishop's role appears to have been no different from that of a traditional secular patron, and his basic grievance was that the intercession on behalf of so many victims of the administration had been unsuccessful.

In order to have his way as bishop, Synesius continued to exploit the traditional instruments of a powerful patron. He tried to use influence in the capital to get Andronicus removed from office. Unfortunately his connections were not men of first rate impor-

---

(51) *Ep.* 72 (1436 C) = GARZYA, p. 129, l. 2 ff. Garzya's *paulo post epp.*, 41 et 42 is too brief.

(52) Debts incurred in paying for office : 73 (1140 A). Forced sales to nominees : *Ep.* 72 (Magnus) ; *Ep.* 79 (1448 B) ; 57 (1392 C-1393 A) = GARZYA, 41 (p. 62, l. 14) on Leucippus. Taxes : *Ep.* PL 78 (1448 B).

(53) *Ep.* 73 (1440 B).

(54) *Ep.* 58 (1401 A) = GARZYA, 42 (p. 73, l. 2).

(55) *Ep.* 73 (1440 B).

(56) *Ep.* 72.

(57) *Ep.* 79.

tance ([58]), and one of them, Anastasius ([59]), the tutor of the imperial children, seems actually to have favoured Andronicus ([60]). Andronicus, for his part, seems to have striven for the support of the all-powerful praetorian prefect Anthemius, who was not one of Synesius' correspondents ([61]).

Synesius influence was much more formidable at home. As a mere magnate he had once compelled a would-be prosecutor to drop a treason charge against Julius ([62]). As bishop Synesius was able to compel soldiers to surrender a prisoner, admittedly one whom they had arrested on Synesius' own complaint ([63]). More significantly Andronicus decided to keep the accused Leucippus in a fortress so that Synesius should not be able to rescue him ([64]). Synesius did not rescue Leucippus, but some time later when Andronicus himself had been deprived of his post, and faced prosecution, Synesius removed the ex-governor from the tribual which was to try him ([65]).

As bishop, Synesius could give fugitives from the governor refuge in his church. We have seen that it was Andronicus' provocative refusal to allow church-asylum that induced Synesius to make his first attempt to excommunicate the governor ([66]). Then Andronicus had promised repentance, and Synesius yielding to the advice of other bishops of the province had suspended the sentence ([67]). An unknown number of months later, Andronicus caused the death of the decurion Magnus and the excommunication was put into effect. It carried with it not only exclusion from church, but complete social ostracism. 'I exhort every private individual and ruler not to be under the same roof as them (Andronicus and his agents), not to be seated at the same

---

(58) They included none of the great officials. The most influential was probably Troilus, a literary man close to Anthemius (PLRE II s.v. Troilus 1). On Aurelian see below p. 5.

(59) PLRE II s.v. Anastasius 2.

(60) *Ep.* 79, cf. 46 = Garzya, 48.

(61) Andronicus claimed to be suppressing a conspiracy against Anthemius : *Ep.* 79 (1448 B).

(62) *Ep.* 95 (94).

(63) *Ep.* 6, 14.

(64) *Ep.* 57 (1393 A) = GARZYA, 41 (p. 62).

(65) *Ep.* 90.

(66) *Ep.* 58.

(67) *Ep.* 72.

table ; particularly priests, for these shall neither speak to them while living nor join in their funeral procession when dead' ([68]). Andronicus was dismissed from his governorship after perhaps a year in office ([69]), and it was only thanks to the physical intervention of Synesius that he avoided prosecution ([70]).

As a layman Synesius had organised a militia to defend the country-side from Ausurian raiders. As bishop he continued to be involved with defence. As we had seen the raids had become very serious. Soon after their resumption in 404, they had begun to interfer with communications, and the loading of ships at Phycus ([71]). Indeed they seem to have grown into something like a permanent occupation ([72]). After seven years Anysius, *dux Libyae,* managed to expel the invaders through the skillful use of a striking force of only 40 horsemen, the Unnigardae, operating in advance of the solid defensive phalanx of the more orthodox forces of the province ([73]). The enemy was compelled to return to raiding tactics ([74]), evidently a great improvement. But then the news that Anysius would be replaced caused great concern in the province and the spokesman of this concern was Synesius, the bishop of Ptolemais.

The two cities of Cyrene and Ptolemais decided to honour the retiring general. They held a joint meeting at which speeches were made. One of the speakers was Synesius whose speech was only very marginally theological. Essentially he provided a tactical analysis of Anysius' victory. He proposed that the Unnigardae, which had already been reinforced from 40 to 200, should be increased by another 200 men, and that the command of Anysius should be prolonged. An

---

(68) *Ep.* 58.

(69) *Ep.* 72 : at the time of the final excommunication Synesius had been bishop for less than a year and Andronicus therefore governor for a shorter period still.

(70) *Ep.* 90.

(71) *Ep.* 134 of 405 written soon after the start of the war of above, p. 1.

(72) *Ep.* 13 of 411/12 cf. above.

(73) *Constitutio,* 1575 B-C, *Catastasis,* 1568 C. *Ep.* 77 shows that Anysius' generalship overlapped with Andronicus' governorship. In note 50 above I argue that the victory was won after Andronicus had been governor for some time. That Anysius' command at least overlapped with Synesius' episcopacy is shown by *Ep.* 6, 14 and 94 (93).

(74) *Catastasis,* 1568 H.

embassy was to take the proposals to Constantinople ([75]). We don't know whether an embassy was sent. At any rate Anysius was not kept in command and the Unnigardae did not receive further reinforcements.

When Anysius had left the province for Constantinople the new commander attempted to merge the Unnigardae with the regular garrison. This would have meant that they lost donatives, extra pay, special equipment and relays of horses. The troops turned to the bishop to petition the emperor. Synesius presented their case in a letter to Anysius who was presumably in a position to influence decisions on policy in the capital ([76]). It looks as if the initiative was successful. For a year later ([77]), when the military situation had deteriorated again, the Unnigardae survived — even though they could not repeat their success under Anysius ([78]).

The unprecedentedly severe invasion cannot be dated precisely. Almost certainly it happened after the deposition of Andronicus, that it perhaps in late summer of Autumn of 412 ([79]). Pentapolis was completely over-run by nomadic horsemen. The enemy wore captured Roman equipment, shields of the Marcomanni, breastplates of the

---

(75) *Constitutio*, 1573-6 is the speech. *Ep.* 78 : 40 Unnigardae. At the time of *Constitutio* there were 200.

(76) *Ep.* 78.

(77) *Catastasis*, 1568 A.

(78) *Ibid.*, 1568 B.

(79) The date of the 'great' invasion :

1. One year after the victory of Anysius, and therefore more than one year after the coming into office of Synesius and Andronicus, *Catastasis*, 1568 A.

2. During the siege Synesius lost his 2nd son *Ep.* 89 (88) it was therefore later than the *Contra Andronicum* = *Ep.* 57 = GRZYA, 41 which mentions loss of only one son. It is unlikely that the bishop would have excommunicated the governor during so dangerous a foreign threat. Therefore the invasion was probably later than *Ep.* 72, which proclaims the excommunication — and says nothing of war.

3. According to its M.S. heading *Catastasis* was spoken when Gennadius was governor and Innocentius general, *P.G.*, LXVI, 1565. This is impossible since Gennadius was Andronicus' predecessor (*Ep.* 173), and the great invasion described in *Catastasis*, happened a year after Anysius' victory (1568 B), which happened while Andronicus was governor. The notice can only be true if Gennadius was governor twice.

4. Since Synesius could ask Theophilus to pray for the province (*Ep.* 69) the invasion happened before 15.10.412 when Theophilus died.

Thracian cavalry. Evidently the invasion had begun with a severe defeat of the regular forces. The remaining regular units were besieged in the fortified cities, and too dispersed to take the offensive. The enemy carried-off countryfolk, animals and plunder, bringing 5,000 camels into the province to help with the booty ([80]). For a time even Egypt seemed to be in danger ([81]). Meanwhile the bishop of Ptolemais shared guard duties on the walls at night and posted pickets ([82]). When the crisis had eventually been ended by the leadership of Marcellinus a new general, who in a single battle brought back peace to the province, it fell to Synesius to thank the general formally on behalf of the people of Pentapolis ([83]). The outcome proved that Synesius' *Catastasis* had been far too pessimistic. Pentapolis survived the great invasion. Its countryside recovered. But the fact that the frontier had become penetrable meant that numerous villages of the province has to build fortification ([84]).

SYNESIUS IN ECLIPSE

Synesius' progress from curialis to bishop so far can be read as a success-story. This was not however the way Synesius himself saw it. His latest letters were written by a deeply depressed man. Synesius' sadness was natural enough in view of the fact that he had lost all three of his sons ([85]), and that his occupation as bishop was profoundly incongenial. But there was a political reason too. Synesius felt abandoned by his friends, and deprived of all his former influence ([86]). What had gone wrong ? Perhaps the starting point was that he has over-reached himself when he excommunicated the governor Andronicus.

(80) Captured Roman equipment : *Catastasis*, 1568 B. Camels : 1569 A.

(81) *Catastasis*, 1569 D.

(82) *Ibid.*, 1572 C.

(83) *Ep.* 62. Marcellinus has freed cities from siege. Synesius is bishop. This fits only the 'great' invasion

(84) R. GOODCHILD, *Libyan Studies*, ed; J. Reynolds (London, 1976), pp. 203-4.

(85) The first son died during Andronicus' governorship *Ep.* 57 (1392 B) = GARZYA, 41 (p. 61). The second during the siege *Ep.* 98 (88). The third in winter 412-23 *Ep.* 70 ; 126.

(86) *Ep.* 16, 17 (all children dead) ; *Ep.* 10 ; 81 (80) without children, friends or influence.

At any rate about this time he lost the friendship of one of his most influential contacts at Constantinople, Anastasius, tutor of the imperial children ([87]). Loss of influence in Pentapolis is suggested by the fact that his brother Euoptius had gone into voluntary exile at Alexandria. It seems that he fled to avoid membership of the curia. Synesius interceded for him with the governor Hesychius, but in vain ([88]).

Then in October 412 came the death of Theophilus bishop of Alexandria who had been a powerful patron of Synesius for many years ([89]). Our sources only give us isolated glimpses of the process by which Synesius became politically isolated. It is clear that his combination of the power of a landed magnate with the prestige of a bishop was not enough to ensure the continued enjoyment of the degree of influence to which he was accustomed. He also needed the support of his peers and that, in some way or other, he had lost. In this period he lost the third of his sons, but in the letters grief at the bereavement is regularly combined with complaints that he has lost friends and influence. Four desperately sad letters were addressed to his friend and teacher the pagan philosopher Hypatia ([90]). The letters show little or no traces of Christianity ([91]). It would however be a mistake to conclude that he lost his faith. At the same time he was building a monastery not far from his estate ([92]).

The letters of Synesius contains no information that is certainly later than 413. Neither the fact that Cyril succeeded Theophilus late in 412, nor the murder of Hypatia in 415, are mentioned. Lacombrade concluded that *Ep.* 16 was Synesius' last letter and that he died soon after of the illness mentioned in it ([93]).

---

(87) *Ep.* 46 = GARZYA, 48 ; cf. 79 (78) : Anastasis and Anthemius favoured Andronicus.

(88) *Ep.* 93 (92). *Ep.* 8 shows that Euoptius was at Alexandria. If *Ep.* 8 and 9, both mentioning the Paschal letters, are contemporary the date was early January 412.

(89) *Ep.* 12, cf. above p. 1.

(90) *Ep.,* 10, 15, 16, 81 (80).

(91) *E.g.* opening of *Ep.* 126, but cf. A.-M. Malingrey on Chrysostom's Christian Stoicism in her introduction to *Jean Chrysostome, Letters à Olympias,* Sources Chrétiennes, 13 bis (Paris, 1968), pp. 53-64.

(92) *Ep.* 126.

(93) C. LACOMBRADE, *Synésios,* p. 272.

The conclusion may be mistaken. I have argued elsewhere that Synesius did live to experience Aurelian's second prefecture of the East ([94]). Synesius' *De Providentia* asserts quite unambiguiosity that Osiris (*i.e.* Aurelian) would eventually regain the throne of Egypt (*i.e.* the praetorian prefecture of the East) ([95]). Now this prophecy might simply be a polite fiction. But vague as the forecast is, it does nevertheless mention two concrete facts. First, several men must hold the supreme post before Osiris will be able to resume it. They will have to perform a purifying role in preparation for his government ([96]). Secondly, the interval between Osiris return from exile and his resumption of office would be a very long one ([97]). The circumstantial detail makes it likely that the prophecy was written with *post-eventum* knowledge of Aurelian's second prefecture. I have suggested that Synesius rewrote the *De Providentia* in order to make it a fitting compliment to Aurelian on the occasion of his return to the prefecture in December 414 ([98]).

The *De Providentia* contains no factual information about the prefecture. Synesius may well have died soon after completing the *De Providentia.* One of three surviving letters addressed to Aurelian was adressed to him in office, and the circumstances make it quite likely that the office was the second prefecture ([99]). If this is right, the last glimpse we get of Synesius is that of a man who after set-backs and bereavements had reestablished a relationship with an old acquaintance who had become the most powerful man in the Empire, and was just beginning to use it in the interest of a relative.

(94) 'The date of Synesius' *De Providentia*', Actes du VIIe congrès de la F.I.E.C., Vol. II (Budapest, 1983), 39-46.

(95) *De Providentia*, 215.

(96) 1273 B.

(97) 1272 C. If Synesius had simply wished to compliment Aurelian he could have prophecied a return to office, without adding that he would only achieve it in old age, and, that first he would have 'to see and hear many things' (1273 B).

(98) See *PLRE*, I, s.v. *Aurelianus*, 3. The second prefecture began in December 414. K. G. HOLUM, *Theodosian Empresses* (London, 1982), p. 96 argues that Aurelian's appointment was instigated by Pulcheria then almost 16 years old, cf. *PLRE*, II, s.v. *Aelia Pulcheria.*

(99) *Ep.* 38 = GARZYA, 35.

XVI

Antioch and the Villages of Northern Syria in the Fifth and Sixth Centuries A.D.: Trends and Problems

In collaboration with Hugh Kennedy

Study of Antioch in the fifth and sixth centuries, as for earlier periods, must start from G. Downey's *A History of Antioch in Syria*.[1] The central theme of this great book is the history of the buildings and topography (naturally so, since the author was a member of the team from Princeton that excavated Antioch in the nineteen thirties) and the central problems of the book are those posed by the requirements of excavation. Nevertheless the student of political history and its social and religious ramifications finds plenty of information.

Paradoxically the excavations themselves contributed comparatively little to Downey's *History*—even on the topographical level.[2] The principal reason is the depth at which the excavators had to work. Virgin soil is no less than 11 metres below today's ground level and the buildings of imperial Rome 8 metres. The difficulties have been outlined by J. Lassus in his report of the excavation of the colonnaded main street.[3] Lassus sought to modify Downey's assessment of the long-term effect of the destruction of Antioch in 541 by the Persians: 'The real greatness of the city must have come to an end by AD 540'.[4] He points out that the great portico and road were rebuilt in careful work on the same scale (40 metres wide) as the structures destroyed by the Persians. Only the actual carriage-way was narrowed by a raised footpath.[5] But Lassus also noted clear evidence that the rebuilt monumental street was invaded subsequently by small buildings of poor workmanship which blocked the road and diverted traffic. He assigned these encroachments on the Justinianic lay-out to the Arab period.[6] In fact the new

---

[1] G. Downey, *A History of Antioch in Syria from Seleucus to the Arab Conquest* (Princeton, 1961). This is a bibliographical treasure house.

[2] *Antioch on the Orontes* (Princeton, 1934–72, 5 vols): i, *The Excavations of 1932*, ed. G.W. Elderkin (1934); ii, *The Excavations, 1933–36*, ed. R. Stillwell (1938); iii, *The Excavations, 1937–1939*, ed. R. Stillwell (1941); iv, pt. 1. *Ceramics and Islamic Coins*, ed. F.O. Waagé (1948); iv, pt. 2. *Greek, Roman, Byzantine and Crusaders' Coins*, ed. D.B. Waagé (1952); v, *Les Portiques d'Antioche*, ed. J. Lassus (1972).

[3] Lassus, *Les Portiques d'Antioche*.

[4] Downey, *op.cit.*, p. 559; cf. pp. 575–6.

[5] Correcting Downey, *op.cit.*, p. 548.

[6] For transformation of colonnaded streets elsewhere, see J. Sauvaget, *Mémorial Jean Sauvaget*, (Damascus, 1954), pp. 101–20 (Laodicea); *Syria*, xxvi (1949), 314–18 (Damascus); *Rév. biblique*, lxiv (1957), 22 (Petra). D. Claude, *Die byzantinische Stadt* (Munich, 1969), pp. 58–9, suggests that this development generally belongs to the post-Byzantine period.

structures seem to have been built directly upon the Justinianic pavement. As silt accumulates very rapidly upon the site of Antioch, this suggests that the process of disintegration of classical urban monumentality began not long after the Justinianic rebuilding.[7] It is likely that the process by which the classically planned city was transformed into an Arab town with an irregular street pattern like that of the large villages in its territory was well on the way by the end of the sixth century. But dense urban occupation continued on the site. The narrowing of the road-way by irregular building was followed by a further reconstruction after destruction. This cannot be dated precisely, but probably falls into the Arab period. But even then the new buildings were massive and appear to have covered a large area. Even though there seems to be no archaeological evidence for habitation outside the present built-up area after c. 540, it was probably only after its destruction by the Mamluks in 1258 that Antioch became the small country town it is today.

Our understanding of urban development in Syria in Late Antiquity can be supplemented by the excavations at Apamea begun 1930–8 by the Musées Royaux d'Art et Histoire of Brussels,[8] and resumed in 1965.[9] As at Antioch prosperity is reflected in ambitious building operations during the fifth and early sixth centuries. When in 526–8 the city was largely destroyed by earthquakes, a real attempt was made to rebuild it in its old splendour, though the rebuilding took several decades to complete.[10] Half a century later Apamea suffered a terrible disaster as a result of its capture by the Persians in 573. The city was plundered and set on fire, and a vast number of inhabitants deported to Persia. Once again Apamea had to be rebuilt, but this time on the basis of much weakened resources. This shows clearly both in the use of cheaper materials, and in the incompleteness of the rebuilding. By now the great colonnaded street was closed to through traffic, like the one at Antioch. At Apamea it was blocked by a church.[11] But in one important respect continuity with the tradition of classical Apamea was maintained. A striking feature of the city had always been a series of great town houses with state-rooms

---

[7] H. Kennedy, 'The last century of Byzantine Syria: a reinterpretation', *Byzantinische Forschungen*, x (1985), 141–83, esp. 153.

[8] F. Mayence, 'Fouilles à Apamée, *L'Antiquité Classique*, i (1932), 233–42, pl. I–III; iv (1935), 199–204, pl. XII–XXVI; v (1936), 409–20, pl. XLI–LII; viii (1939), 201–11, pl. III–XI. H. Lacoste, *L'Antiquité Classique*, x (1941), 115–21, pl. I–XI; 'Restitution du plan antique d'Apamée de Syrie', *Académie Royale Belgique, Bulletin de la Classe des Beaux-Arts*, xliii (1961), 53–62.

[9] Janine Balty, Jean Chr. Balty, *Actes du Colloque Apamée de Syrie. Bilan des recherches archéologiques* (Brussels, 1969–80, 3 vols), i (1969), ii (1972), iii (1980).

[10] *Ibid.*, iii. 495–7.

[11] *Ibid.*, i. 17, 41–3, 77.

situated around a pillared courtyard, invariably including a great reception hall. A number of these mansions were restored after the disaster and it seems that the urban magnates continued to inhabit them, less lavishly perhaps, but otherwise in the same manner as before.[12] It seems that this style of urban gracious living continued into the seventh century, up to the Persian occupation (613–20) and the Arab conquest (636). After this the peristyle and surrounding apartments of former mansions came to be used for agricultural purposes, while other parts of the building fell into ruin. There clearly had been a fundamental transformation in the character of the town.[13] But the site continued to be densely inhabited for several centuries under Arab rule. New building was unambitious and the use of old buildings more chaotic, but the site was only abandoned after a series of destructive earthquakes between 1157–70.

Syria is remarkable for its very large number of sites of ruined villages and small towns. This is a consequence of the fact that there has been a great reduction in the permanently inhabited areas as compared with Late Antiquity. Archaeology has begun to benefit, but very much remains to do. Many of the ruins have been published in a series of surveys, which supplement each other.[14] Among the most striking are the remains of villages on the limestone hills to the east of Antioch which once were part of the territories of Apamea and Antioch. The solidly built ruins include buildings of many kinds—farms, social buildings, hostels for pilgrims, churches. The architecture and indeed the whole civilisation of the northern part of this area has been described and brought to life in a remarkable book by G. Tchalenko.[15] The remains of the churches have provided a great deal of material for Lassus' study of the churches of Syria, their furnishings and their accompanying buildings.[16] The architecture of the villages seems to have

---

[12] *Ibid.*, iii. 19–38, 471–97.

[13] *Ibid.*, iii. 497–503, but it is also significant that the town remained inhabited and coin finds are at least as common after 638 as before. *Ibid.*, iii. 239–48.

[14] M. de Vogüé, *Syria centrale. Architecture civile et religieuse du Ier au VIIe siècle* (Paris, 1864–77, 2 vols). *Publications of the American Archaeological Expeditions to Syria* (1903–1930); *Publications of the Princeton University Archaeological Expedition to Syria* (1934–72); A. Poidebard, *La trace de Rome dans le désert de Syrie: Le limes de Trajan à la conquête Arabe, Recherches aériennes 1925–34* (Paris, 1934, 2 vols). J. Lassus, *Inventaire archéologique de la région au nord-est de Hama* (Paris, 1935); R. Mouterde and A. Poidebard, *Le limes de Chalcis: organisation de la steppe en haute Syrie romaine* (Paris, 1945, 2 vols).

[15] G. Tchalenko, *Villages antiques de la Syrie du nord. Le massif du Bélus à l'époque romaine* (Paris, 1953–58, 3 vols).

[16] J. Lassus, *Sanctuaires chrétiens de Syrie* (Paris, 1947); 'Syrie', *Dictionaire d'archéologie chrétien et de liturgie*, xv (1951) cols. 1855–1942. See also G. Tchalenko, *Églises de village de la Syrie du Nord* (Paris, 1979–80, 2 vols).

developed independently of urban architecture. But the highest level of urban art entered the countryside with the building of the great monastery around the pillar of Symeon Stylites at Qual'at Sem'an c. 476–90.[17] After this a new monumentality and greater use of ornament also appears in village churches.

A feature of the architectural remains of Syria is the abundance of work dating from the fifth and sixth centuries. It looks at least in all areas that have visible remains—the coastal region is the exception[18] —as if building continued right up to the Arab conquest. It follows that in some areas the population was expanding, that new areas were being brought under cultivation and that in the steppe new irrigation work was being carried out.[19]

But recently attention has been drawn to an important distinction. Tchalenko already noticed that in many areas civil building seems to fade out around the middle of the sixth century, while the building of churches and monasteries continues until the early seventh.[20] The evidence is compatible with the view that the area saw a steady rise in population up to around 542 when the great plague described by Procopius passed over the Near East, followed by a series of further visitations. There is a considerable amount of evidence that this resulted in long-term population decline,[21] comparable to that which followed the Black Death in England in 1348–9. In England the fact that there were fewer people meant that the survivors were better off, earned higher wages and paid lower prices.[22] Numerous perpendicular churches witness to the prosperity of their

---

[17] M. Écochard, 'Le sanctuaire de Qual'at Sem' an', *Bulletin des Études Orient.*, vi (1936), 61–90; S. Guyer, 'Kunstgeschichtlichen Stellung der Wallfahrts Kirche von Kal'at Sim'ân', *Archaeologisches Jahrbuch*, xlix (1934), 90–6; G. Tchalenko, *op.cit.*; J.-L. Biscop and J.-P. Sodini, 'Qal'at Sem'an et les chevets à colonnes de Syrie du Nord', *Syria*, lxi (1984), 287–330; J.-L. Biscop and J.-P. Sodini, 'Travaux récents au sanctuaire Syrien de Saint-Syméon le Stylite', *Comptes Rendus des Séances de l'Académie des Inscriptions et Belles-Lettres* (Paris, 1983), 335–72.

[18] J.H.W.G. Liebeschuetz, *Antioch. City and Imperial Administration in the Later Roman Empire* (Oxford, 1972), pp. 90–100.

[19] A. Poidebard, *La trace de Rome*, pp. 170–91; Mouterde and Poidebard, *Le limes de Chalcis*, pp. 13, 110 *et seqq*, 112 *et seqq*, 117 *et seqq*, 150 *et seqq*; M. Evenari, L. Shanan, N. Tadmor, *The Negev* (Harvard, 1971). Presumably the possibility of exploiting land that had not been exploited before was an important factor in the prosperity of Syria in the Later Empire.

[20] H. Kennedy, 'The last century of Byzantine Syria', *Byzantinische Forschungen*, x (1985), esp. 160–2; *idem*, 'Recent French archaeological work in Syria and Jordan', a review article, *Byzantine and Modern Greek Studies*, xi (1987), 245–352.

[21] E. Patlagean, *Pauvreté économique et pauvreté sociale à Byzance 4e–7e siècles* (Paris, 1977), pp. 84–92.

[22] J. Hatcher, *Plague, Population and the English Economy 1348–1530* (London, 1977), pp.

patrons. It may be that the churches and monasteries built in Syria in the later sixth century owed their existence to the same phenomenon. The transfer of economic activities from towns to monasteries and their estates seems to have occurred in Russia after the disaster of the Mongol invasions.[23] Did something of the kind happen in Syria?

Late Roman Syria has produced many inscriptions. These are being assembled in the *Inscriptions Grecques et Latines de la Syrie*.[24] They include few inscriptions recording legislation, munificence or careers of the kind put up so freely in Asia under the Early Empire. Most items merely commemorate the building, the date of the building and perhaps seek divine protection. They are useful all the same. Tchalenko has used inscriptions to trace the progress of Christianity in the countryside, more specifically to show that the conversion of the villages of the limestone massif took place in the second half of the fourth century. It also seems that the conversion of the countryside of Syria proceeded from north to south. It was significantly later in the territory of Apamea than of Antioch and later still around the cities further south along the Orontes. It seems that in the countryside around the upper Orontes conversion to Christianity became widespread—or at least traceable on inscriptions—only in the late fifth century, and in many localities later still.[25]

Inscriptions also throw light on the composition of the population of the frontier areas of Syria which certainly experienced Arab settlement long before the Arab conquest, including penetration of nomad tribes right up to the walls of Chalcis and Aleppo.[26] It would probably be possible to analyse the names found on inscriptions to trace the origins and movements of the population and to supplement Dussaud's work on the penetration of the Arabs into the Hauran and

---

49–50.

[23] G. Vernadsky, *A History of Russia* (New Haven and London, 1943–69, 5 vols), iii, *The Mongols and Russia* (1953), pp. 378–9.

[24] *Inscriptions Grecques et Latines de la Syrie* [*IGLS*], edited by L. Jalabert, R. Mouterde and others (Paris, 1929–). The latest volume: xiii.1 *Bostra*, ed. M. Sartre (Paris, 1982).

[25] J.H.W.G. Liebeschuetz, 'Epigraphic evidence on the Christianisation of Syria', *Akten des XI. Internationalen Limes Kongresses* (Budapest, 1978), pp. 485–508.

[26] H. Kennedy, 'The last century of Byzantine Syria, *Byzantinische Forschungen*, x (1985), 167–8.

the area of Palmyra.[27] It might also be worthwhile to compare the distribution of inscriptions in Greek and inscriptions in Aramaic at different times.[28]

The abundant archaeological remains of Syria provide opportunities for the economic historian of which the exploitation has only begun. Tchalenko has sketched a social and economic history of the region surveyed by him.[29] He concluded that its ever-increasing population depended largely on the cultivation of olive trees. In the course of the development estates, some owned by veterans of the Roman army, who seem to have settled in this area in the second century, were divided into a large number of small holdings.[30] The area seems to have reached its peak of population and prosperity in the early sixth century, but the trend had been set in the fourth.[31] Tchalenko's work is based on the mapping of visible remains. The urgent task of checking his results by excavation has been begun by G. Tate and P. Sodini. Their findings suggest that village economy was less exclusively based on the cultivation of olives than Tchalenko had thought. They have found evidence for animal rearing. More sensationally lion bones turned up in the excavation.[32] The evidence of the hill villages contradicts the widely held gloomy estimate of the condition of the peasantry in the Later Roman Empire which has been presented with fullest documentation by A.H.M. Jones[33] and G.E.M. de Ste Croix (1981).[34] Yet the prosperity of the limestone hills is parallelled by at least some other areas of eastern Syria[35] and the Negev region of

---

[27] G. Tchalenko, *Villages*, p. 145 n.2; R. Dussaud, *La pénétration des Arabes en Syrie avant l'Islam* (Paris, 1955); M. Sartre, *Trois études sur l'Arabie romaine et byzantine* (*Col. Latomus* clxxviii, Brussels, 1982), ch. 3: 'Les nomades et l'empire en Arabie', pp. 121–203; I. Shahid, *Rome and the Arabs: a prolegomenon to Byzantium and the Arabs* (Washington, 1984); *idem*, *Byzantium and the Arabs in the fourth century* (Washington, 1984).

[28] E. Littmann, ed.: *Publ.Am.Arch.Exp.Syr.* vol.iv, and *Publ.Princeton.Exp.Syr.* vol.iv. G. Ryckmans, ed., *Corpus inscriptionum semiticarum*, vol.v (Paris, 1900). E. Littmann, *Publ.Princeton.Arch.Exp.Syr.* vol. iv, p. 24, notes great predominance of Greek inscriptions over Syriac. He also remarks on the increase in Syriac inscriptions in fifth and sixth centuries. But even so the great majority of inscriptions from the little towns and stone-built villages of N. Syria are Greek, even though this was a Monophysite area.

[29] Tchalenko, *Villages*, pp. 377–438.

[30] *Ibid.*, pp. 406–9.

[31] *Ibid.*, p. 417–31, but Tchalenko's view that prosperity of hill villages was unaffected by successive calamities after 540 is extremely doubtful.

[32] G. Tate and J.-P. Sodini, 'Déhès, recherches sur l'habitat rural', *Syria*, lxvii (1980), 1–303.

[33] A.H.M. Jones, *The Later Roman Empire* (Oxford, 1964, 3 vols).

[34] G.E.M. de Ste Croix, *The Class Struggle in the Ancient World* (London, 1981), esp. pp. 226–51.

[35] J. Lassus, *Inventaire archéologique de la région au nord-est de Hama* (Damascus, 1935); Mouterde and Poidebard, *Le limes de Chalcis*, cited n. 14 above; M. Sartre, *Bostra: des origines à l'Islam* (Paris, 1985).

Palestine.[36] The question arises whether coastal areas were prosperous too. It could be supposed that exploitation by the cities and the limited amount of land available for cultivation might over a long period of time reduce the peasantry to destitution. There is less evidence for Late Empire building activity from this area. This could be due to the fact that since this land has never been abandoned successive occupiers have destroyed the work of their predecessors.[37] On the other hand it does seem as if Seleucia, the harbour city of Antioch, was becoming depopulated even before the Arab conquest.[38]

Tchalenko has opened the discussion of the economy of Syria in Late Antiquity. We are still far from a full understanding of the causes of the economic expansion along the Eastern frontier from the fourth century. It is still an open question to what extent, if at all, the village economy was related to the rise and fall of Mediterranean trade. More recently attention has turned to trade with Mesopotamia and south Arabia.[39] Among negative factors affecting social life and the economy of Syria plague has come to loom very large.[40] It seems plausible, but yet remains to be proved, that the plague of 541 marked the beginning of the decline.[41] Archaeology has only just begun to provide answers to these questions.[42] Meanwhile more evidence could probably still be gained from Lives of saints.[43] It

---

[36] Evenari, Shanan, Tadmor, *The Negev*; see also Patlagean, *Pauvreté*, pp. 309 *et seqq.*

[37] Liebeschuetz, *Antioch*, pp. 99–100.

[38] But earlier in the sixth century Seleucia was still an active port: G. Dagron, 'Un tarif des portules à payer aux *curiosi* du port de Séleucie de Piérie (VIe siècle)', *Travaux et Mémoires*, ix (1985), 435–55.

[39] M. Gawlikowski, 'Palmyre et l'Euphrate', *Syria*, lx (1983), 53–68; M. Sartre, *Bostra des origines à l'Islam* (Paris, 1985); *idem, Trois études*, pp. 121–203.

[40] H. Kennedy, *Byzantinische Forschungen*, x (1985), 154–5; see also n. 135 below.

[41] Patlagean, *Pauvreté*, pp. 88–92. It may be more than a coincidence that the latest dated inscription of Bostra is from 541 (*IGLS*, xiii.1.9131).

[42] J. Mécérian, *Expedition archéologique dans l'Antiochène occidentale* (Beirut, 1969); W. Djobadze, 'Second preliminary report on excavations in the vicinity of Antioch-on-the-Orontes', *Türk Arkeologi Dergisi*, xiii.2 (1964), 32–5; *idem*, 'Vorläufiger Bericht über Grabungen und Untersuchungen in der Gegend von Antioch am Orontes', *Istanbuler Mitteilungen*, xv (1965), 218–42. J. Lafontaine-Dosaque, *Itinéraire archéologique dans la région d'Antioche* (*Bibliothèque de Byzantion*, iv, Brussels, 1967).

[43] Barlaam: H. Delehaye, 'S. Barlaam, martyr à Antioche', *Analecta Bollandiana*, xxii (1903), 28 *et seqq.*; P. Peeters, 'S. Barlaam du Mont Casius', *Mélanges de la faculté orientale de Beyrouth*, iv (1909), 805–15. Dometius: 'Acta S. Dometii', *Analecta Bollandiana*, xix (1900), 285–317; cf. P. Peeters, *Analecta Bollandiana*, lvii (1939), 72–104. Symeon Salus: *PG* xciii, 669–1748. Theodosius: John Moschus, *prat.spirit.*, *PG* lxxxvii, 2937 *et seqq.* Symeon Stylites the Younger: P. van den Ven, *La vie ancienne de S. Symeon Stylite le Jeune* (521–92) Brussels, 1962, 2 vols), and its review by R. Riedinger, *Byz.Zt.*, lxv (1972), 90–2.

is likely that the study of emigration from Syria could throw light on the economic condition of the region and its links with other parts of the Roman world. Tombstones of Syrians have been found in many parts of the Empire, including Western provinces. What makes these monuments particularly useful for the historian is the fact that they often record not only the date of the death of the deceased but also his village of origin.[44]

Meanwhile it is important that the gloomy analysis of the condition of the Late Roman peasantry in A.H.M. Jones' *Later Roman Empire* does not seem to apply to Syria, or at least to inland Syria. This area in all likelihood still had a large number of free peasants.[45] In fact it is not yet established that huge estates like those of the West ever became prevalent in the East.[46] When the 'dark ages' came to Asia Minor c. 600–750 the old nobility of the Later Empire simply disappeared, and recovery of the Empire was accompanied by the rise of a new nobility. This would be surprising if the old nobility had been as heavily landed as that of the West.[47] Moreover the fact that a peasant is a tenant does not necessarily mean that he is exploited to the limit. The peasant who grows nothing but corn in this arid land, is in an extremely weak position *vis à vis* his landlord. The tenant who employs more sophisticated cultivation, involving irrigation and the planting

---

[44] L. Ruggini, 'Ebrei e orientali nell' Italia settentrionale fra il IV e il VI secolo d.Cr.', *Studia et documenta historiae et juris*, xxv (1959), 186–308; D. Hoffman, *Das spätrömische Bewegungsheer und die Notitia Dignitatum* (Düsseldorf, 1971, 2 vols), pp. 63–5; *Monumentae Asiae Minoris Antiquae* (Manchester, 1928–62, 8 vols), iii, J. Keil and A. Wilhelm, *Denkmäler aus dem Rauhen Kilikien* (1931), p.138 n.248; R. Florescu, 'Relations éntre la Syrie-Palestine et la Scythie Mineure à l'époque du bas empire', *Roman Frontier Studies* (Tel Aviv, 1971), pp. 166–70; Keune, *Paulys Realencyclopaedie der classischen Altertumswissenschaft*, x, col. 1918, s.v. Kaprazabadon. Villages of Apamea especially provided emigrants.

[45] P. Petit, *Libanius et la vie municipale à Antioche au IVe siècle après J.-C.* (Paris, 1955), p. 307; Liebeschuetz, *Antioch*, pp. 67–9.

[46] Jones, *Later Roman Empire*, pp. 778–80.

[47] G. Ostrogorsky, 'Observations on the aristocracy in Byzantium', *Dumbarton Oaks Papers*, xxv (1971), 1–32, esp. 2–5. Much less is known about great estates in the East. Numerous senators, officials and even curiales owned a great deal of land (e.g. see Liebeschuetz, *Antioch*, pp. 41–8), but it may be that landholding on the scale of the Egyptian Apions (E.R. Hardy, *The Large Estates of Byzantine Egypt* (New York, 1931)) was untypical in the East; see A.K. Bowman, 'Landholding in the Hermopolite Nome in the Fourth Century', *JRS*, lxxv (1985), 137–63.

and maintenance of trees, is in a much stronger position.[48] Such cultivation was much commoner in Byzantine Syria than it is today.[49]

It is also a traditional view that patronage was the means by which the peasant was first subjected and then exploited by men of wealth and position. This could and did happen,[50] and is still happening today.[51] But it has been observed in contemporary peasant societies that patrons also confer essential benefits. He provides protection, arbitration and finance which but for him would simply not be available.[52] It has been suggested that ancient patrons, whether notables, soldiers or monks, conferred similar services;[53] indeed, that it was precisely the existence of patrons that enabled peasants of such areas as the limestone massif to prosper as much as they did.[54]

The beginnings of a new and ultimately extremely important form of rural patronage are the subject of Peter Brown's study of holy men.[55] The Lives of prominent hermits,[56] especially that of St Symeon Stylites the Elder[57] show that, in

[48] D. Warriner, *Land and Poverty in the Middle East* (London, 1948), pp. 84–91: income of irrigated land two to three times that of dry. J. Weulersse, 'Essai de géographie urbaine', *Bulletin d'études orientales*, iv (1934), 27–79, esp. 33: replacement of corn-growing by fruit or vegetables favours tenants. *Idem, Paysans de Syrie et du Proche Orient* (Paris, 1946), pp. 36, 97, 129, tenants of plantations (fruit trees, olives or vines) given better terms.

[49] Weulersse, *Paysans de Syrie*, pp. 34; 160 *et seqq.*, lack of irrigation in contemporary Syria.

[50] Libanius, *Or.*, xxxix, 10–11; Jones, *Later Roman Empire*, pp. 775–7.

[51] Weulersse, *Antioche*, pp. 30–31.

[52] R. Redfield, *The little community: Peasant society and culture* (U. Chicago P., 1960), pp. 23–39. 'It will not do to describe these relations only as relations of ruler and ruled or exploiter and exploited... The student will also want to describe the feelings of prestige or contempt, of excellence to be emulated, of baseness to be avoided... present in the relationship between peasant and élite'.

[53] P.R.L. Brown, 'The rise and function of the Holy Man in Late Antiquity', *JRS*, lxi (1971), 80–101, esp. 85–7.

[54] R.M. Price, *The role of the military in Syria and Egypt from Constantine to Theodosius* (D Phil thesis, Oxford University, 1974). This unpublished thesis includes the best analysis of Libanius' *De patrociniis* (*Or.*, xlvii), especially the lawsuit between Libanius and his Jewish tenants.

[55] P.R.L. Brown, *JRS*, lxi (1971), 80–101.

[56] Surveyed by Theodoret, *Historia Religiosa*, to be read in *Théodoret de Cyr, Histoire des moines de Syrie—histoire philothée* ed. and trans. P. Canivet, A. Leroy-Molinghen, *Sources chrétienes*, 234 and 257 (Paris, 1977–79, 2 vols); John of Ephesus, *Ecclesiastical History*, ed. and trans., E.W. Brooks, C.S.C.O. 106, Scr.Syri 55 (Louvain, 1952).

[57] H. Lietzmann, *Das Leben des heiligen Symeon Stylites = Texte und Untersuchungen*, xxxii no.4 (Leipzig, 1908) has translations of the Greek Lives by Theodoret (*PG*, lxxxii, 1464–84) and Antony, as well as of the Syriac Life. A.J. Festugière, *Antioche païenne et chrétienne* (Paris, 1959), pp. 347–401, 493–506, has French translations of the Lives of Antony and Theodoret and a full précis of the Syriac Life. See also *Life of Symeon Stylites the Younger,*

at least some cases,[58] they engaged in a good deal of arbitration, debt regulation mediation, 'trouble-shooting' such as one might expect a good system of local government to perform. It may be that the social work of ordinary holy men covered a narrower field and was exercised chiefly through prayer and healing.[59] The fact remains that a village with a holy man by virtue of the saint's influence with God had access to a recognised source of power such as had not resided in the countryside—apart from exceptional sanctuaries—since the beginnings of Graeco-Roman civilisation. Eventually the power was institutionalised and the hermit was replaced or supplemented by the abbot of a monastery. The development, nevertheless, brought about a shift in the balance of power from city to country, the importance of which can hardly be exaggerated.

In the East the monastic movement was remarkable for the way in which it ignored social barriers which were rarely crossed in the Graeco-Roman world. The ascetic ideal appealed to city dwellers and country folk, to the educated and illiterate, to Greek speakers and speakers of Aramaic, to inhabitants of Persian Mesopotamia no less than to citizens of the Roman Empire. Ascetism took a great variety of forms.[60] Hermits might roam along the desert fringe or they might remain through life fixed in a single spot. They might live singly, or in groups with, or without, common organisation. Monasteries might be self-governing, or united with others under a common rule. Some hermits remained completely outside institutional Christianity, ignorant of the priesthood and never taking the eucharist.[61] Some hermits worked for a living but the majority of the Syrian hermits got what little they needed through charity. The whole movement existed outside the organisation of the church with its bishops and their itinerant inspectors, even though some bishops chose to act in close cooperation with monks—to combat heresy[62] or to suppress paganism.[63] In fact the establishment of

---

ed., P. van den Ven, cited n. 43 above.

[58] Peter Brown's picture is modified by M. Whitby, 'Maro the dendrite, an anti-social Holy Man', in *Homo Viator*, ed. M. Whitby, P. Hardie, Mary Whitby (Bristol, 1987), pp. 309–17.

[59] R.M. Price, *The Role of the Military*; J. Seiber, *The Urban Saint in Early Byzantine Social History*, British Archaeological Reports, Supp. Ser., 37 (Oxford, 1977).

[60] The vast material is surveyed by A. Vööbus, *A History of Ascetism in the Syrian Orient*, vol. 1: *The Origin of Ascetism, Early Monasticism in Persia* (Louvain, 1958); vol. 2: *Early Monasticism in Mesopotamia and Syria* (Louvain, 1960) = *Corpus Scriptorum Christianorum Orientalium*, 184 (Subsidia 14) and 197 (Subsidia 17); see also P. Canivet, *Le monachisme syrien selon Théodoret de Cyr* (Paris, 1977).

[61] Theodoret, *Historia Religiosa*, 13 (1401–3) Macedonius does not understand ordination; 15 (1416C) Acepsimas only accepts ordination when dying; 19 (1428D) Salamanes ordained by force.

[62] *Ibid.*, 2 (1317–19); cf. *Eccl.History*, IV, 24 (*PG*, lxxxii, 1187) Julianus Sabas used against Arians. So too *Historia Religiosa*, 8 (1372–76), Aphraates.

monks on the fringe of the Syrian countryside was followed by rapid progress of Christianity among country folk.[64] It is easy to over-emphasise the role of the great organisers like Pachomius and St Basil. In the fourth century the practice of ascetism arose spontaneously in many widely separated places and individuals. The full story of the movement and its gradual institutionalisation and integration into the church organisation,[65] not to mention its influence on the church when a high proportion of bishops came to be chosen from monasteries, has still to be written.

A feature of the early monastic movement is the wide social range of the monks. A large proportion evidently were countrymen and only Syriac speaking.[66] Some of them came from a propertied village aristocracy.[67] But these were outstanding men, perhaps ordinary peasants predominated among the mass of the hermits.[68] Certainly the ideology of monasticism was independent of Hellenism in a way that institutional Christianity with its city-born and city-educated bishops was not. But the ascetic movement also had enormous appeal among city folk including the young, well-born and highly educated.[69] The selling or giving away of property was part of ascetic idealism.[70] How the classically educated might

---

[63] *Historia Religiosa*, 13 (1404 B-C), Macedonius pleads for city after Riot of Statues. Monks co-operate with bishops in destroying temples: Libanius, *Pro Templis* (*Or.*, XXX) 15; cf. J.F. Matthews, 'A pious supporter of Theodosius I, Maternus Cynegius and his family', *J.Theol.St.*, ns. xviii (1967), 438–446. Also on destruction of temples see G. Tchalenko, *Villages*, p. 145 n.2; W. Liebeschuetz, *Antioch*, p. 237; C. Mondesert, 'Inscriptions et objets chrétiens de Syrie et Palestine', *Syria*, xxxvii (1960) 116–30; M.-T. and P. Canivet, 'Sites chrétiens d'Apaméne', *Syria*, xlviii (1971) 295–321, esp. 305–6 (church on site of temple).

[64] G. Tchalenko, *Villages*, pp. 145–6.

[65] G. Dagron, 'Le monachisme à Constantinople jusqu'au Concile de Chalcédoine', *Travaux et Mémoires*, iv (1970), 229–76 describes the introduction, conflicts and eventual control of monasticism at Constantinople. Excavation might help to answer the question: how far did monasteries dominate the countryside economically?

[66] Theodoret, *Historia Religiosa*, 28 (1488): that Thalalaeus speaks Greek is explained by his Cilician origin. Evidently most Syrian hermits spoke no Greek. Further references in Liebeschuetz, *Antioch*, p. 235 n.1.

[67] Monks from propertied village families: Symeon Stylites (Syriac Life 11); Sabas son of a soldier from Cappadocia (*V. Sabae* 1; 25). So too the Egyptians: Antony (Athan. *Vita Ant.* 1–2); Pachomius (*V. Pach.* 29) and Theodore (*ibid.* 33).

[68] Sabas and Pachomius paid for monastic buildings. We are not given information about the economic background of the majority of the early monks.

[69] From Theodoret's *Historia Religiosa*: Asterius, 2 (1312C); Marcianus, 3 (1324D); Publius, 5 (1352B); Theodosius, 10 (1389A); Zeno, 12 (1396B); Marana and Cyra, 29 (1489C); Domina, 30 (1493C) at least of wealthy family. Aphraates, 8 (1368A) was a Persian aristocrat (*Magus*) who had emigrated to the Roman Empire.

[70] Theodoret, *Historia Religiosa*, 12 (1204D) Zeno; 5 (1161C) Publius, *Syriac Life of Symeon Stylites*, 11;

interpret the monastic ideal in terms of literary traditions concerning the moral advantages of philosophical, simple or rural life is shown in the ascetic writings of John Chrysostomus, as has been pointed out by A.J. Festugière.[71]

An influential by-product of the monastic movement was a new genre of literature, the biography of the holy man.[72] It is characteristic of saints' Lives that they are full of miracles, the evidence that the subject of the biography was genuinely close to God. The great majority are miracles of healing, but in addition from time to time the saint brings about the discomfiture of a man who had rejected his moral advice or mediation by an effective curse. This literature gives a very unclassical picture of the world. It provides contemporary confirmation of the biblical teaching that there is constant divine intervention and that illness and other misfortunes, individual or social, are sent by God as punishment for identifiable offences. Henceforth Christianity exercised an ever wider and a deeper influence. The limited toleration of paganism which had prevailed more or less since Constantine came to an end.[73] There were an increasing number of attacks on Jews.

Doctrinal controversies became a matter of concern for whole populations rather than clergy. More positively Christianity could now become a national religion and help to maintain the morale of Mesopotamian cities under attack by Persians.[74] Monks provided leadership in all these spheres.[75] But monks also provided leadership and mass support for the highly divisive Monophysite movement.

---

[71] A. J. Festugière, *Antioche païenne et chrétienne*, pp. 329–46. John Chrysostomus: *In Matth. hom.*, 55 *PG*, lviii, 545–6; *hom. 68 (646); hom.* 69 (652–3). In *ep. I ad Tim. hom.* 14 *PG* LXII, 574–5.

[72] A.J. Festugière, *Les moines d'orient* (Paris, 1961–65, 4 vols). A. Momigliano, 'Pagan and Christian historiography in the fourth century', in *Paganism and Christianity in the Fourth Century*, ed. A. Momigliano (Oxford, 1963), pp. 78–99, esp. 92–3 with references to earlier work especially by K. Holl and R. Reizenstein. Patricia Cox, *Biography in Late Antiquity, a Quest for the Holy Man*, Transformation of Classical Heritage, 5 (Berkeley, 1983).

[73] Matthews, cited n. 63 above. Cynegius was a type of the new generation of officials, influenced by the monstic ideal, who carried out the suppression of paganism. See also J.F. Matthews, *Western Aristocracies and Imperial Court AD 364–425* (Oxford, 1975), pp. 127–45.

[74] N.H. Baynes, *Byzantine Studies and Other Essays* (London, 1955), pp. 248–60. Averil Cameron, 'The virgin's robe', *Byzantion*, xlix (1979), 42–56, also *The Sceptic and the Shroud*, inaugural lecture King's College (London, 1980), esp. pp. 5 *et seqq*.

[75] Monks lead opinion against Eunomianism and Appolinarianism: Sozomen, *HE*, VI, 27; destroy synagogue of Callinicum: Ambrose, *ep.* XLI, 27.

The late fourth and early fifth century saw the triumph of monasticism and of the growing up of a monastically influenced generation of court officials. It may or may not be a coincidence that for the subsequent century there is a great reduction in surviving secular literature so that the nature of the history it is possible to write of Antioch changes. With the exception of the chronicle of Malalas,[76] the abundant evidence for society and administration comes to an end. This means that we hear very little about internal developments apart from sensational occurrences like riots and earthquakes.[77] But it is certain that fundamental changes in the institutions of Antioch, as of other cities in the East, were taking place. Traditionally the well-to-do provided entertainment and other civic services as well as public building for their city at their own expense. In this way they both promoted their personal reputations and conciliated the less well-off. The Later Empire for a number of reasons saw a decline in private secular munificence. Civic services declined or were paid for out of imperial taxation, and giving became religious, with the church rather than the city as its chief beneficiary. We witness a stage in this development when we learn that the two greatest of the Antiochene entertainment liturgies, the Syriarchy and the Olympic Games, came to an end in 465.[78] Another stage is represented by the introduction, sometime in the fifth century, of a comprehensive organisation of public entertainment based on the factions. The date of this reform is not known. In the last years of Zeno's reign (after 484) the factions were involved in heavy rioting on at least three occasions, and there was more factional rioting in the first decade of Anastasius. There is no indication in the sources of the causes of this rioting. This was an age of religious divisions, but the sources never mention religion in connection with factional riots or the factions in religious ones. Perhaps it was the creation of the permanent organisations of the factions and the consequent division of the spectators in the hippodrome into mutually opposed groups of supporters that was responsible for the strife.[79]

We have a single glimpse at the way public decisions were made at Antioch in the sixth century. When the city faced attack by the Persians in 540 the Antiochenes 'took counsel' and decided to offer ransoms to the Persian king.[80] We

---

[76] *The Chronicle of John Malalas, a Translation*, ed. E. Jeffreys, M. Jeffreys, R. Scott and others, *Byzantina Australiensia*, iv (Melbourne, 1986).

[77] For the facts see Downey, *Antioch in Syria*, pp. 476–507.

[78] *Codex Justinianus*, 1, 36,1 of 465.

[79] For a discussion of the rioting late in the reign of Zeno and under Anastasius see Alan Cameron, *Porphyrius, the Charioteer* (Oxford, 1973), pp. 232–44. For the history of factional organisation see *idem, The Circus Factions* (Oxford, 1976).

[80] Procopius, II, 6, 16. The old office of *comes orientis* had been abolished. His title and salary were assigned to the consular of Syria I (Justinian, *Nov.* VIII, 5).

78

are not told what kind of body decided: most likely it was a council of lay and clerical notables which is mentioned in laws of Anastasius and Justinian and can be seen to have taken over some of the functions of the old *curia* and *curiales*.[81] Surprisingly, in view of his importance in the fourth century, the governor of Syria I is not mentioned in the account of the discussion. The imperial government was represented by a special envoy of the emperor, his nephew Germanus, and later by certain ambassadors travelling to negotiate with the Persian king. The bishop Ephraemius favoured ransom.[82] Eventually payment was stopped on orders of the ambassadors. In the defence of the city citizens played a considerable part.[83]

We lack the evidence to decide how far the decision-making at Antioch in 540 was typical of the last period of Byzantine rule and how far a result of an exceptional military situation, the almost complete breakdown of military cover for Syria. The development of the civic authority at Antioch in the fifth–seventh centuries remains obscure. The continuous history of the years is largely the story of the conflict between Chalcedonians and their opponents and indeed of divisions within the main conflicting groups. But these conflicts nevertheless had political and administrative implications as far as the city was concerned since their effect was to reduce the authority of the bishop of Antioch over a great part of the patriarchate. But by this time the administrative importance of Antioch was to a considerable extent involved with that of its bishop.

This is not the place for a full narrative of the religious controversies of the fifth and sixth centuries as they affected Antioch. It must suffice to point out that while Asia Minor came to stand solidly behind Constantinople, and Egypt behind Alexandria, the huge patriarchate of Antioch began to crumble. Between 413 and 417 the province of Syria Secunda was taken out of the province of Coile Syria and was given Apamea as civil provincial capital. Subsequently the bishop of Apamea became the metropolitan of the churches of the new province. A new cathedral

---

[81] Municipal government in the sixth century was certainly very unlike municipal government in the fourth. But the functioning of 'post-curial' institutions remains to be worked out. The fullest treatment to date is D. Claude, *Die byzantinische Stadt im 6. Jahrhundert*. Byzantinisches Archiv, Heft 13 (Munich, 1969), pp. 107–61. See also a note on the pagarch, Liebeschuetz, 'The origin of the office of the pagarch', *Byz. Zt.*, lxvi (1973), 38–46 and J. Gascou, 'La détention collégiale de l'autorité pagarchique dans l'Égypte byzantine', *Byzantion*, xlii (1972), 60–72.

[82] Procop., II, 6, 16; II, 7, 6. On Ephraemius, the *comes orientis* who became patriarch and persecuted Monophysites in both offices, see G. Downey, 'Ephraemius, Patriarch of Antioch', *Church History*, vii (1938), 364–70.

[83] Resistance by 'young men' who in peace engaged in factional strife: Procop., II, 8, 8; 11; 17; 28. Most were unarmed, cf. Cameron, *Circus Factions*, ch.5.

was built at Apamea and it is likely that the visible prosperity of Apamea in the fifth century owed something to the city's heightened status.[84] No doubt Apamea's gain was Antioch's loss.

This was only the first of a series of setbacks for the patriarchate of Antioch. Cyprus became independent.[85] The bishop of Jerusalem became a patriarch.[86] Even in the field of liturgy the predominant influence of Antioch in the oriental provinces was increasingly replaced by that of Jerusalem.[87] But the most far-reaching setback was in the condemnation of Antiochene theology.

Lucian of Antioch (martyred in 312) founded a school of theology which was particularly devoted to biblical scholarship. Lucian's recension of the Bible came into general use. In their attitude to the Bible the Antiochene theologians differed from those of Alexandria in favouring literal rather than allegorical exegesis.[88] This literalness still characterised Antiochene theologians, Diodorus, bishop of Tarsus (who died c. 395) and Theodore, bishop of Mopsuestia (350–428), towards the end of the fourth century. Theodore even rejected the traditional interpretation of Old Testament passages as prophecies of Christ and denied that the Song of Songs referred to Christ and his Church.[89] Two younger theologians of the same school were Theodoret, bishop of Cyrrhus (423–57),[90] and Nestorius, patriarch of Constantinople.[91]

[84] Janine Balty, 'La maison aux consoles', Colloque Apamée de Syrie, bilan de recherches archéologique 1973–79 (Brussels, Musées Royaux d'Art et d'Histoire, 1980), pp. 19–47, 59–78.
[85] G. Downey, 'The claim of Antioch to ecclesiastical jurisdiction over Cyprus', Proceedings Am. Philosoph. Soc., cii (1958), 224–8.
[86] E. Honigmann, 'Juvenal of Jerusalem', Dumbarton Oaks Papers, v (1950), 211–79. The weaknesses of the patriarchate of Antioch as compared with Alexandria are well analysed by W.H.C. Frend, The Rise of the Monophysite Movement (Cambridge, 1972), pp. 83–8.
[87] On increasing liturgical influence of Jerusalem see J.A. Jungmann, Missarum Sollemnia (Vienna, 1952, 2 vols), i.53.
[88] On Lucian of Antioch and the school of Antioch see D.S. Wallace-Hadrill, Christian Antioch (Cambridge, 1982).
[89] On Eustathius, bishop 324 to 326 or 330, see R.V. Sellers, Eustathius of Antioch (Cambridge, 1928); on Diodorus, R.A. Greer, 'The Antiochean Christology of Diodore of Tarsus', J.Theol.St., n.s., xvii (1966), 327–41; on Theodore of Mopsuestia, R.A. Greer, Theodore of Mopsuestia, Exegete and Theologian (London, 1961); F.H. Sullivan, 'The Christology of Theodore of Mopsuestia', Analecta Gregoriana, lxxxii (Rome, 1956); R. Devréesse, Essai sur Théodore de Mopsuestie = Studi e Testi, cxli (Vatican, 1948).
[90] Theodoret, Thérapeutique des maladies hellénique, ed. and trans. P. Canivet, Sources Chrétiennes, 57 (Paris, 1958, 2 vols). Canivet discusses Theodoret's work in Histoire d'une entreprise apologétique au Ve siècle (Paris, 1959), an analysis of Theodoret's polemic against pagans and Jews.
[91] F. Loofs, Nestorius and his place in the history of Christian doctrine (Cambridge, 1914).

The views of the four men came to be at the centre of the christological controversies of the fifth century. The Antiochene theologians insisted on the independent existence of the human element in the personality of Jesus. Their position can be seen to follow from their distrust of allegory, and their insistence that the gospel narrative must be accepted in its literal meaning. They saw salvation as essentially a moral problem, the filling of the gulf between God and man caused by man's immorality, rather than the divinification of human nature. Only if Jesus had full humanity could his overcoming of temptation and his resurrection set an example and offer hope to man.[92] It may not be too fanciful to see in the Antiochene theology a reflection of the intellectual atmosphere of the city. Theodore of Mopsuestia was a pupil of Libanius.[93] Theodoret, as seen through his letters, clearly belongs to the same atticising rhetorical civilisation. Libanius had shown comparable moral concern, respect for classical texts and reluctance to draw practical conclusions from metaphysical concepts. Antioch in contrast to Alexandria had no tradition of philosophy.

Here is not the place to tell the full story of Cyril of Alexandria's attack on the Antiochene theology. It suffices to record the result. At the First Council of Ephesus (413) Cyril of Alexandria achieved the deposition of the Antiochene theologian Nestorius from his see at Constantinople and the condemnation of his doctrines. After Ephesus a new theological party at Constantinople sought to wipe out all traces of Nestorianism in Syria. It gained the emperor's support and an imperial edict condemning the works of Nestorius was sent to Antioch. At this time the attack on the local theology could still provoke popular demonstrations.[94] At the Second Council of Ephesus (449) Dioscorus of Alexandria obtained the deposition of Theodoret of Cyrrhus, Ibas of Edessa and even of Domnus of Antioch itself. Theodoret and Ibas were later reinstated but Nestorianism remained condemned and the Antiochene theology was driven out of the Empire.

---

[92] Frend, *Monophysite Movement*, pp. 126–30.

[93] P. Petit, *Les étudiants de Libanius* (Paris, 1957), pp. 40–1. Theodoret's letters are printed in *Theodoret: Correspondences*, ed. Y. Azéma, *Sources Chrétiennes*, 40, 98, 111 (Paris, 1955–65, 3 vols). They deserve a full historical commentary. R.V. Sellars, *The Council of Chalcedon* (London, 1952), pp. 152 *et seqq.* suggests that the strong Jewish community influenced the theology of Antioch. On possible Jewish influence at an earlier stage, see F. Millar, 'Paul of Samosata, Zenobia and Aurelian. The church in local culture and political allegiance in third-century Syria', *JRS*, lxi (1971), 1–17, esp. 17.

[94] G. Hoffmann and J. Flemming, *Akten der ephesinischen Synode vom Jahre 449, syrisch mit Georg Hoffmanns deutscher Übersetzung, Abh.K.Ges.Wiss.Göttingen, phil.hist.Kl.*, n.f. 15, 1 (1917), pp. 58–9, 61.

The original rivalry was between Constantinople and Alexandria but Antioch was squeezed between them.[95]

The defeat of Antioch was not only due to external pressure. A decisive factor was that the monks of the territory of Antioch turned against the theology of Antioch so that a split developed between the bishop and the territory immediately surrounding his see. This involved a reversal of the attitude of the monks. Under Constantius and Valens the 'orthodox' party (i.e. the upholders of the view that was to prevail under Theodosius I), among whom the Antiochene theologian Diodorus of Tarsus was prominent, had used the prestige of hermits to oppose the imperially supported Arians.[96] In the 370s the monks of Syria led public opinion against Apollinarianism which was a predecessor of Monophysitism.[97] But in the fifth century the predominating tendency among the monks began to change. Theodoret of Cyrrhus had cultivated his relations with monks carefully over a long period.[98] But after the First Council of Ephesus Syrian monks including St Symeon Stylites tried to bring him closer to the position of Cyril of Alexandria,[99] and in 448 monks accused him of Nestorianism.[100] The centre of the pro-Cyrilian anti-Antiochene radicals was the monastery of Barsaumas situated on a rocky hill now known as Der Bar Sam between Melitene and Samosata.[101] The Syriac-speaking archimandrite Barsaumas is to us a shadowy figure, although in his day he was obviously a figure of enormous influence, whom the Emperor Theodosius II invited to represent all the archimandrites of the East at the Second Council of Ephesus. Needless to say he followed the Alexandrian line. Seven years later at

[95] Frend, *Monophysite Movement* p. 188 n.2. M.V. Anastos, 'Nestorius was orthodox', *Dumbarton Oaks Papers*, xvi (1962), 117–40 argues that the conflict between Cyril and Nestorius was largely personal, ecclesiastical, political and terminological.

[96] See n.62 above.

[97] Soc. *HE*, VI, 27. Frend, *Monophysite Movement*, pp. 115–16.

[98] *Historia Religiosa, passim.* M. Richard, 'Theodoret, Jean d'Antioche et les moines d'Orient', *Mél.Sc.Rel.*, iii (1946), 147–56; Festugière, *Antioche païenne et chrétienne*, pp. 418–23, especially the exchange of letters between Theodoret and Alexander of Hierapolis; *Synodicon* 234–5 = E. Schwartz, *Acta Conciliorum Oecumenicorum*, iv. 170. 23 *et seqq.*.; 171. 7 *et seqq.*

[99] H. Bacht, 'Die Rolle des orientalischen Mönchtums in den Kirchenpolitischen Auseinandersetzungen um Chalcedon 431–519', in A. Grillmeyer and H. Bacht, *Das Konzil von Chalcedon* (Würzburg, 1953–62, 2 vols), ii,199–200, points out that monks around Antioch supported Cyril and put pressure on their bishop before the Formula of Reunion.

[100] Hoffmann and Flemming, *Akten der ephesinischen Synode*, p. 87. Bacht in Grillmeyer and Bacht, *Konzil von Chalcedon*, ii.229–31.

[101] E. Honigmann, *Le Couvent de Barsauma et le patriarcat Jacobite d'Antioche et de Syrie, Corpus Scriptorum Christianorum Orientalium*, 146, subsid. 7 (Louvain, 1954).

Chalcedon when the decision of the Second Council of Ephesus was reversed, Barsaumas resisted to the end. His opponents charged him with corrupting the whole of Syria and even with being responsible for the murder of a deposed bishop of Constantinople.[102]

Christological controversy continued after the condemnation of the Antiochene theologians. The church of Antioch had now dissociated itself from the condemned theology but the definition of the relationship between the divine and human elements in Christ continued to be a matter of extreme importance. The attempt to end the controversy by a comprehensive series of definitions at the Council of Chalcedon only made matters worse since a large number of people, particularly among the monks of Egypt, felt that the definitions of Chalcedon struck at the heart of their religion. Opposition to Chalcedon soon began to make progress among the monks of Syria as well. Symeon Stylites, the greatest of the hermits, seems to have supported Chalcedon,[103] though retrospectively he was represented as an anti-Chalcedonian.[104] Certainly the monastery established at the site of the pillar at Tell Neshim soon became anti-Chalcedonian[105] and in due course all the monasteries in the Antiochene area of the limestone massif took the same anti-Chalcedonian line.[106]

In Antioch itself progress of the anti-Chalcedonians was much slower. Indeed they may never have become the majority party in the city. Their greatest advance occurred after 470 when Peter the Fuller, a Monophysite priest, came to Antioch in the following of Zeno, the *magister militum per orientem* and later emperor. He brought Monophysite monks into the city to preach their doctrine,[107] and he rallied his followers round the Monophysite version of the trisagion.[108] Henceforth every service became a demonstration for or against Chalcedon and a Chalcedonian patriarch could expect strong and violent opposition in the city. Martyrius eventually resigned (471). Stephen was murdered (479). His successor

---

[102] *Op.cit.*, 8 in G.D. Mansi, *Sacrorum Conciliorum Collectio Nova*, vii, col. 68 = *Acta Chalc.* 77–8.

[103] Evagrius, *HE*, II, 10.

[104] Frend, *Monophysite Movement*, p. 148 n.5 on Michael the Syrian, *Chron.*, VIII, 12 (p. 92).

[105] Frend, *op.cit.*, p. 166, n.5.

[106] A. Caquot, 'Les couvents du massif calcaire dans quatre lettres monophysites du VIe siècle', in Tchalenko, *Villages*, ii. 63–85.

[107] Theodore Lector, *HE*, 1, 20 = *PG*, lxxxvi.176.

[108] 'Holy God, holy and strong, holy and immortal, *who was crucified for us*, have mercy on us'. Neither Peter the Fuller nor Philoxenus of Mabbog (Hierapolis) originated the underlined insertion: A. de Halleux, *Philoxène de Mabbog, sa vie, ses écrits, sa théologie* (Louvain, 1963), pp. 34–5.

Calandio had to wait a year before he could enter the city.[109] Peter the Fuller himself was bishop intermittently (469–70, 470–1, 475–6, 484–94).[110] The Monophysites achieved their greatest triumph in 512 when the orthodox patriarch Flavian was deposed and the Monophysite Severus appointed.[111] But even this was not necessarily a result of their party having become the majority at Antioch. The factor that decided who was to be bishop of Antioch was always the policy of the emperor—or intermittently under Zeno the policy of usurpers.[112] Ultimately it was the emperor Anastasius who made possible the deposition of Flavian and the election of Severus.[113] At Antioch itself the anti-Chalcedonians could exert physical pressure with the help of the monks of the province of Syria I, but among the citizens there was a strong Chalcedonian party which, aided by monks of Syria II, could answer force with force and actually rose on behalf of their patriarch Flavian against the Monophysites.[114] While Severus was patriarch, Antioch was the centre of the Monophysite world. Severus was a great figure. Highly educated in classical literature and Roman law in his youth and an admirer of Libanius, he was also thoroughly versed in christian writings, particularly those of the Cappadocian fathers. While studying at Berytus he was converted to the monastic ideal and as bishop of Antioch became the intellectual as well as hierarchical leader of the anti-Chalcedonians. He wrote in Greek. A considerable number of his writings survive, but only in Syriac translation. Most of his works are theological. The letters do however throw light on the problems of administration that would face

---

[109] E.Schwartz, 'Publizistische Sammlungen zum acacianischen Schisma', *Abh. bayer. Akad. Wiss.*, *Phil.-hist. Abt.*, n.f. x (1934), 193.

[110] A full account and references: Downey, *Antioch in Syria*, pp. 484–97. Also important, Schwartz, *Publizistische Sammlungen*, esp. pp. 182 *et seqq.*; E. Honigmann, *Évêques et évêchés monophysites d'Asie antérieure au VIe siècle*, CSCO 127, subsid. 2 (Louvain, 1951) pp. 1–6; E. Schwartz, 'Codex Vaticanus gr. 143, eine anti-chalkedonische Sammlung aus der Zeit Kaiser Zenos', *Abh. bayer. Akad. Wiss.*, *Phil.-hist.* Abt. xxxii, 6 (1927), 96. Peter the Fuller was forced by monks to curse Chalcedon.

[111] On the deposition of Flavian through Philoxenus and Severus, see Frend, *Monophysite Movement*, pp. 215–20. A. de Halleux, *Philoxène*, pp. 55–79.

[112] E.g. in 475–6, Peter the Fuller's return was made possible by the usurper Basiliscus. In 476 the victorious Zeno deposed and exiled Peter. In 484 the orthodox Calandio favoured the usurper Leontius. After crushing the rebellion, Zeno restored Peter the Fuller. Nine other senior bishops were replaced at the same time: Theophanes, *Chron.* A.M. 5982; Evagrius, *Ecclesiastical History*, III, 16.

[113] Evagrius, *HE*, III, 32.

[114] Evagrius, *loc.cit.* After the death of Anastasius, a letter accusing Severus was sent by 25 monks and clerics of Antioch to Constantinople. viii, col. 1039E, 1042 A-C = *Acta Conciliorum Oecumenicorum*, vol. 3, p. 61,2–62,17.

any bishop of Antioch as well as those specific to the propagation of the anti-Chalcedonian cause. A monograph is needed.[115]

After the death of Anastasius (518) imperial protection was withdrawn from the Monophysites and replaced by intermittent persecution of varying intensity. Monophysite bishops were deposed and monks expelled. Antioch was under orthodox bishops. But the strength of Monophysitism among the monks in the territory and further east was not reduced—quite the contrary.[116] When the Monophysites eventually organised a church of their own they also appointed a patriarch of Antioch. But the Monophysite patriarch rarely visited the city, residing rather at monasteries on the Euphrates or later at what had been the monastery of Barsaumas,[117] and they continued to do this after the Arab conquest when the fear of persecution by the imperial government had disappeared.[118] As has been mentioned, Monophysitism was not city-centred. In as much as the importance of Antioch in the Later Empire was based on its being a religious centre, the rise of Monophysitism reduced the importance of Antioch.

The Monophysite movement in Syria and Egypt has been seen as an expression of local nationalism. 'Nationalism in Syria as in Egypt then found its strongest expression in a religious cause'.[119] It is one of many merits of W.H.C. Frend's *Monophysite Movement* that it enables us to see much more cleary how far the modern concept of nationalism is applicable to Monophysitism. The closest parallel lies in the fact that Monophysitism was linked with language. The Monophysites were strongest in areas where Aramaic and Coptic were the predominant languages. In the case of Syria this meant the countryside and cities around and across the Euphrates. The facts are beyond doubt whether one looks at the distribution of Monophysite bishoprics in 512–18[120] or 793–1199.[121] The

---

[115] *A collection of letters of Severus of Antioch from numerous Syriac manuscripts*, ed. and trans. E.W. Brooks, *Patrologia Orientalia*, XII, 2 and XIV (Paris, 1916 and 1920); *The Sixth Book of the Select Letters of Severus Patriarch of Antioch in the Syriac version of Athanasius of Nisibis*, ed. and trans. E.W. Brooks (London, 1902–4, 4 vols).

[116] Frend, *Monophysite Movement*, p. 333 citing Michael the Syrian, *Chron.*, X, 22 (ed. Chabot, ii.336); *ibid.*, X, 21, 5 (Chabot, ii.380) on strength in villages.

[117] Honigmann, *Évêques et évêches monophysites*, p. 20.

[118] Honigmann, *Le couvent de Barsauma*, pp. 52–3.

[119] E.g. Downey, *Antioch in Syria*, pp. 474–5. On general problem E.L. Woodward, *Christianity and Nationalism in the Later Roman Empire* (London, 1916); A.H.M. Jones, 'Were ancient heresies national or social movements in disguise?', *J.Theol.St.*, n.s. x (1959), 280–98, repr. in A.H.M. Jones, *The Roman Economy*, ed., P.A. Brunt (Oxford, 1974), 308–29).

[120] Honigmann, *Évêques et évêches*, map 1 also in Frend, *Monophysite Movement*, fig. 1, pp. 250–1.

[121] Honigmann, *Le couvent de Barsauma*, map 3.

complex of attitudes known as Monophysitism certainly had a particularly strong appeal to Aramaic speaking inhabitants of the fertile crescent—even beyond the boundaries of the empire. It is also true that some Monophysite writers took a special interest in developing the Aramaic language in order to make it a suitable vehicle for theological discussion.[122] It is not chance that the bulk of Syrian Monophysite writing, whether originally written in Greek or Aramaic, has survived in Aramaic.

But if Monophysitism was strong among speakers of Aramaic it in no way saw itself as a religion for Aramaic speakers, nor did it assign them a privileged position. For Monophysites their religion was simply the true form of Christianity which ought to prevail everywhere. Moreover numerous Greek speakers shared this belief. After all Severus of Antioch was as much a Greek as Libanius had been, and Monophysite bishops were consecrated in not a few Greek cities of Asia Minor. No doubt their strength in these areas was greatest in the reign of the sympathetic Anastasius,[123] but Monophysite communities survived in the hostile atmosphere of Justinian and successors.[124]

Again, like the nationalism of Europe, Monophysitism had a mass[125] following and appealed to both educated and uneducated. It united all its adherents in passionate loyalty and equally passionate opposition to Chalcedon and its followers.[126] It aroused a readiness to riot and a readiness to persecute as well as to suffer persecution.[127] But unlike modern nationalism or city-state patriotism, Monophysitism created no sense of political community. It produced no call for political action whether on a linguistic or any other basis. Frend shows that Monophysites were long loyal to the emperor: that they only reluctantly established a separate hierarchy and that it was persecution that induced them to

---

[122] A. de Halleux, *Philoxène*, p. 21. Eventually, as shown by the terminology of Michael the Syrian, 'Syrian' was equated with Monophysite, 'Chalcedonian' with Greek, just as in Egypt 'Copt' was the Monophysite and 'Chalcedonian' was Greek. So Frend, *Monophysite Movement*, p. 334.

[123] Honigmann, *Évêques et évêches*, map 2.

[124] *Ibid.*, map 3.

[125] Cf. the Egyptian bishops at Chalcedon: 'We shall be killed if we subscribe to Leo's epistle. Every district in Egypt will rise against us' (*Mansi* VII, 58–60). But the actual rioting and violence were usually carried out by monks.

[126] E. Schwartz, 'Johannes Rufus, ein monophysitischer Schriftsteller', *S.B. heid. Akad. Wiss.*, *Phil.-hist.*, K1. III, 16 (1912), esp. 12 *et seqq.*

[127] The staple form of persecution on either side was the expulsion of monks from monasteries and clergy from churches. Imprisonment and torture of monks or clergy only happened ocasionally. Executions were rare. Battles of monks might be bloody. Naturally the literature makes the most of atrocities or martyrdom.

support or at least to accept foreign rule—so that Persians and Arabs favoured them.[128] There is a great contrast with Mohammedanism which was an Arab national as well as a universal religious movement. If Monophysitism had had a political component, the Arab conquest might never have happened or—to adapt Horace—the conquered Syrians might have led the victorious Arabs captive.[129]

The division between Chalcedonians and anti-Chalcedonians was an aspect of a phenomenon which had much further to go under Arab rule: the disintegration of the citizen-body of the Graeco-Roman city state into religious and racial groups. This may well have become an important factor obstructing the imperial government's efforts to enrol soldiers and collect taxes. It certainly showed itself in the relations between Christians and Jews. The Jews had a long history as an organised community at Antioch and the relationship between them and the other inhabitants had varied a great deal. But the fourth century saw the beginning of a steady intensification of antagonism. Intellectually Jews and Christians were closer at Antioch than in some other cities.[130] But the very closeness produced problems. John Chrysostomus was worried by the prestige of Jewish rites and Jewish doctors among Christians and preached a succession of virulent sermons against them.

Anti-Jewish feeling also found expression in the taking over of the synagogue of the Seven Maccabee Brothers and in the conversion of a synagogue into a church at Apamea. A century later the letters of Severus show strong antagonism to Jews.[131] Nevertheless in the sixth century the Jews of Antioch still possessed a

---

[128] Persians expelled Chalcedonians, left Monophysites in peace: Frend, *Monophysite Movement*, pp. 336–7; similarly the Moslems, *ibid.*, 356–7.

[129] Horace, *Ep.* II, 1, 156. G. Downey, *Antioch in Syria*, pp. 521–59 relates the history of Antioch 526–641. The reduced scale of the narrative reflects the reduced volume of information, and perhaps of the importance of Antioch. See also R. Devréesse, *Le patriarcat d'Antioche* (Paris, 1945), pp. 192–205. Honigmann, *Évêques et évêches*, gives biographies of the monophysite patriarchs Sergius and Paul the Black. On the latter also E.W. Brooks, 'The patriarch Paul of Antioch and the Alexandrian schism of 575', *Byz.Zt.*, xxx (1929–30), 468–76.

[130] M. Simon, 'La polémique anti-juive de S. Jean Chrysostome et le mouvement judaisant d'Antioche', *U.libre Bruxelles, Ann. inst. phil. et hist. orient. et slav.*, iv (1936), 403–21; *idem*, *Verus Israel* (Paris, 1948). R.L. Wilken, *John Chrysostom and the Jews, Rhetoric and Reality in the Late Fourth Century* (Berkeley, London, 1983). The religious challenge of Judaism is also evident in the Christian apologetic of Theodoret; see n. 90 above.

[131] Severus, *Select Letters*, ed. Brooks, nos. 15–16; Liebeschuetz, *Antioch*, pp. 232–4; Downey, *Antioch in Syria*, pp. 447–9. While Christian doctrinal disputes are not mentioned in connection with factional riots, anti-semitism is. Jews were attacked by the Greeks as associates of the Blues, e.g. Malalas, 389, 15–390, 3. *Ibid.*, 396, 3–4 on events of 507. A church was established on the site of a synagogue at Daphne: Downey, *op.cit.*, p. 506.

social centre, a *triklinion*.[132] In 592–3 Jews were compelled to have their heads partly shorn and were expelled from the city.[133] But the explusion was either only temporary or partial, for we hear that between 708 and 710 Jews were involved in serious rioting at Antioch. In the course of the disturbances the patriarch Anastasius was murdered. The sources of these events, as for much else in the disturbed reign of Phocas, are confusing.[134] Internal conflict was consuming the resources which the Empire would need first against Persians, then against Arabs.

The sixth and early seventh century were a bad period for Antioch. It was a period of destructive earthquakes and recurrent plague no less than hostile invasion.[135] Earthquakes, plague and deportation must have carried off a high proportion of the city's population. At the same time we have observed long-term trends which impeded the city's recovery. The ecclesiastical disputes weakened the authority of the patriarch. The city's role in the secular administration of the empire was reduced. Monasticism brought a new source of power to the countryside. It may be that the flourishing condition of the countryside until at least the middle of the sixth century was ultimately at the expense of the city. It is possible that there had been a movement of craftsmen and manufacture from the city to the country and that the economic organisation which had previously been controlled by urban magnates had partly passed into the hands of men living in villages, and especially to monasteries. Unfortunately the available evidence makes it very difficult to trace structural changes in the economy. It is of course even more difficult to assess the relative importance of changes in the balance of social and economic power from city to countryside and other factors such as the plague or the decline of sea trade in wine and oil.

---

[132] *Inscriptions Grecques et Latines de la Syrie*, 770 and 1344.

[133] Agapius of Menbidj, *Patrologia Orientalia* VIII, 439–40; J. Starr, 'Byzantine Jewry on the eve of the Arab conquest', *J.Palest.Orient.Soc.*, xv (1935), 283.

[134] G. Downey, *Antioch in Syria*, pp. 572–4; A.N. Stratos, *Byzantium in the seventh century*, vol. 1 (1968), 76 and note IV, 357 distinguishes between a rising at Antioch in 608 which was suppressed by Bonosus and a subsequent revolt by Jews under their patriarch. A. Sharf, 'Byzantine Jewry in the 7th century', *Byz.Zt.*, xlviii (1955), 106–7 argues that the Jews were blamed for riots in which they had participated with many others; idem, *Byzantine Jewry from Justinian to the Fourth Crusade* (London, 1971), pp. 47–8.

[135] Malalas, XVIII.27 (442–3) for 528 AD = *The Chronicles of John Malalas, a translation*, ed. E. Jeffreys, M. Jeffreys, R. Scott and others, pp. 256–7. See Evagrius, *HE*, IV.29 on recurring nature of plague, with commentary by Pauline Allen in *Evagrius Scholasticus, The Church Historian* (Louvain, 1981), pp. 190–94; also by same author, 'The Justinianic Plague', *Byzantion*, xlix (1979), 5–20. The most thorough study: L. Conrad, 'The plague in Bilad al-Sham in pre-islamic times', in *Proceedings of the Symposium on Bilad al-Sham*, ed., Muhammad Ad-nad Bakhit and Muhammad Asfour Amman (Amman: U. of Jordan, 1986), ii.143–63.

What is clear is that the society which succumbed to the Muslim invasion was very different from that described by Libanius and regulated by the laws of the Theodosian Code. The immediate cause of defeat was of course military failure but the system that failed bore little resemblance to that of the fourth century.[136] The army no longer held—or so it seems—a continuous line of forts at the frontier along the *Strata Diocletiana*. For instance, a dispute as to whether the area known as *Strata* was or was not part of the Roman empire could not have arisen if the frontier was continuously held and patrolled.[137] Instead of holding a line of forts, the Romans seem to have left defence of the steppe and semi-desert of the frontier area to the Arab nomads who roamed there. The tribesmen of each frontier province were under a phylarch appointed or at least recognised by the Roman government and all or most were under the supreme command of a prince of the Ghassanid family.[138] In fact, as far as the government of the nomad population was concerned, the Ghassanid Arethas (al Harith) and his son, al Mundhir, were practically client kings.[139]

[136] W. Liebeschuetz, 'The defences of Syria in the sixth century', *Akten des X. Internationalen Limes Kongresses* (Cologne-Bonn, 1977), 487–99; T.S. Parker, *Romans and Saracens*, a History of the Arabian Frontier, American School of Oriental Research Dissertation Series, 6 (Winona Lake, Eisenbrauns, 1986); *idem*, 'Retrospective on the Arabian frontier after a decade of research', in *The Defence of the Roman and Byzantine East*, ed. P. Freeman and D. Kennedy, BAR Int. Ser. 297(i) (Oxford, 1986), pp. 633–60.

[137] Procopius, II, 1–15 on events 539. *Strata Diocletiana* had been the name of the road linking the frontier forts south-west of Palmyra in the system of Diocletian, cf. D. van Berchem, *L'armée de Dioclétien et la réforme Constantinienne* (Paris, 1952), pp. 10, 13 n.4, 14; also E. Honigmann, 'Syria', *RE*, 2 ser. viii (1932), cols 1549–1729. On the line of forts 10–20 miles apart between Euphrates and Palmyra, see the classic Poidebard, *La trace de Rome*; they are still garrisoned in *V. Alex. Acoem.* 32–5 (*PO* VI, 683).

[138] Th. Nöldeke, 'Die Ghassanidischen Fürsten aus dem Hause Gafnas', *Abh. Preusz. Akad. Wiss. phil.-hist. Kl.* (1887), II no. 11; I. Kawar, 'Procopius and Arethas', *Byz.Zt.*, 1 (1957), 39–67, 362–82; *idem*, 'Procopius on the Ghassanids', *J.Am.Or.Soc.*, lxxvii (1957), 79–87; *idem*, 'The patriciate of Arethas', *Byz.Zt.*, lii (1959), 322–43; P. Goubert, 'Le problème ghassanide à la veille de l'Islam', *Actes du VIe congrès internationale d'études byzantines, Paris 1948* (Paris, 1950, 2 vols), i.103–18. See also Sartre, *Trois Études*, cited n. 27 above.

[139] This is the theory expounded by J. Sauvaget, 'Les Ghassanides et Sergiopolis', *Byzantion*, xiv (1939), 115–30. It has been criticised especially by A. Alt, 'Der Limes Palaestinae im sechsten und siebten Jahrhundert', *Ztschft. Dt. Palaest. Ver.*, lxiii (1940), 129–42, on the grounds that it overlooks evidence for the continued existence of *limitanei* on the eastern frontier and particularly across southern Palestine. For northern Syria there is astonishingly little evidence for the presence of frontier soldiers. We would agree that there probably were some forts with soldiers. We would however argue that soldiers had been moved from the desert to the edge of settled land. This was where Romans preferred to station their troops, cf. P. Trousset, *Recherches sur le limes tripolitanus* (Paris, 1974). See also T.S. Parker, *Romans and Saracens*, and in *The Defence of the Roman and Byzantine East*, ed. Freeman and

The defensive organisation of Syria broke down with calamitous consequences on a number of well-known occasions in the sixth and early seventh centuries. But this should not be allowed to obscure its success. Until 610 there was no permanent occupation by the enemy of Syrian territory. After that came the collapse. But the breakdown under the emperor Phocas happened at a time when the empire was torn by strife, and after the organisation of the tribesmen under the supreme command of the Ghassanids had been broken up.[140] The subsequent Arab invasion struck an empire that was exhausted by a long and desperate struggle with Persia. Moreover, the Roman defensive organisation was not designed to meet a massive invasion from another direction then Mesopotamia. Nevertheless, when the Arabs invaded southern Palestine, Roman defences came into action in due order.[141] Only at each stage the Arabs won the resulting battle.[142]

In 638 the Arabs entered Antioch. There was very little resistance, and the Arab historians do not make much of the capture of what had been the metropolis of the Roman Orient.[143] This in itself, together with the fact that the only Syrian city to offer prolonged resistance to the Arabs was Damascus, suggests that some fundamental transformation had already taken place in the structure of Syrian society. Since its foundation Antioch had been a centre of Hellenism and a centre of administration from which first Greeks and then Romans governed a large part of the Near East. More recently it had also been a centre of Christian thought and

---

Kennedy, cited n. 136 above.

[140] P. Goubert, *Byzance avant l'Islam* (Paris, 1951–65, 3 vols), i, *Byzance et l'orient sous les successeurs de Justinien: l'empereur Maurice*, 251–60. While the supreme phylarchate was ended the empire was at least superficially reconciled with the princely family and an Arab force under the Ghassanid chief Jabala was in the Byzantine army at the battle of the Yarmouk.

[141] There was no resistance in the steppe *limes* area. Aila had surrendered to Mohammed in 630, P. Mayerson, 'The first Muslim attacks on Southern Palestine (AD 633–634)', *Transactions of the American Philological Association*, xcv (1964), 155–99, esp. 169–73. In 634 the Arabs were challenged first in Araba valley in front of the line of forts on the edge of cultivated land, then by a striking force at Dathin: A. Alt, *Zt. Dt. Palaest. Ver.*, lxiii (1940), 140–2. Finally, the fate of Palestine was decided by the defeat of the field army at Ajnadayn, south of Jerusalem.

[142] Considering its enormous importance—and interest—the Arab conquest has been made the subject of surprisingly little modern research. The main work is now F. Donner, *The Early Islamic Conquest* (Princeton, 1981) which effectively replaces S. Caetani, *Annali dell' Islam* (Milan, 1905–26, 10 vols), for the conquest of Syria especially vols. iii–iv; also S. Caetani, *Studi di storia orientale* (Milan, 1911–14, 3 vols), and M.J. de Goeje, *Mémoire sur la conquête de la Syrie* (Leiden, 1900).

[143] H. Kennedy, *Byzantinische Forschungen*, x (1985), 151.

ecclesiastical administration. The city's importance had been declining in all these roles but after the Arab conquest they all rapidly came to an end. What remained was Antioch's skilled population—or some of it[144]—and the strategic and economic advantages of its geographical position. These assets enabled Antioch to continue as a centre of more than local importance for another six centuries.[145]

University of St Andrews   HUGH KENNEDY

University of Nottingham   J.H.W.G. LIEBESCHUETZ

---

[144] Plague which devastated settled Syria, but not the nomads of the desert, had presumably helped the Arab victory. Subsequently it must have made it difficult for the farmers of Syria to resist the advance of nomads and their herds with the result that villages and rural towns were abandoned over a wide area. See L. Conrad, *op.cit.*, n. 135 above, pp. 156–7. There was also emigration. Syrians were replaced by Arabs from Arabia and Arabs of the border areas of Syria who had been quickly converted to Islam. See M.A. Shaban, *Islamic History AD 600–750. A new interpretation* (Cambridge, 1971), pp. 41–44; E. Ashtor, 'Nouvelles réflexions sur la thèse de Pirenne', *Schweizer Zeitschrift für Geschichte*, xv (1970), 601–7.

[145] See also C.I. Cahen, *La Syrie du Nord à l'époque des croisades*, Institut français de Damas, Bibliothèque Orientale, tome 1er (Paris, 1940), pp. 27–33 on Antioch in the time of the crusades.

XVII

THE ORIGIN OF THE OFFICE OF THE PAGARCH

From papyri of the 6th and 7th centuries it appears that an increasingly important part in the civil administration of Egypt was played by the official known as the pagarch.[1] Unfortunately there is no evidence about this official from the 5th century[2] and the origin of the office and its significance in the evolution of municipal institutions remains obscure. In the present paper an attempt is made to compensate for the lack of Egyptian evidence by examining what is known about the pagarch against the background of developments in civic institutions elsewhere in the Eastern Empire.

The title of the pagarch was not a creation of the 5th or later centuries. It was already applied to the *praepositi pagorum*,[3] the curial officials who controlled village government and tax collection in the municipal organisation introduced to Egypt by Diocletian.[4] But the pagarchs of the 6th and 7th centuries were not simply successors of the *praepositi pagorum*. Not one of the later pagarchs is known to have been a *curialis*.[5] Unlike the *praepositi pagorum* pagarchs – as far as the evidence goes – never received orders from a civic superior.[6] It also appears that a pagarch wielded greater coercive power than any earlier civic official. He could back his demands not only with civil police but also with units of the army. He might inflict imprisonment and confiscate property.[7] Finally there was, as a rule, only one pagarchy per city[8] even though this might be headed,

---

[1] H. I. Bell, the Aphrodito Papyri, J. H. S., XXVIII (1908), 97–119; idem, Pap. Lond. IV, general introduction; idem, An Egyptian village in the age of Justinian, J. H. S. LXIV (1944), 21–36.
G. Rouillard, Administration civile de l'Égypte byzantine, (Paris 1938), 52–62.
A comprehensive study is needed.
[2] The lack of evidence is related to social changes by R. Rémondon, L'Égypte au 5e siècle de notre ère, Atti dell'XI Congresso Internazionale di Papirologia, (Milan 1966), 135–48.
[3] C. T. VII, 4, 1 (325); P. Oxy. VXII, 2110 (370).
[4] J. Lallemand, L'administration civile de l'Égypte, (Brussels 1964), 97–107.
[5] Praepositi pagorum had been decurions: P. Oxy. 2110 (310); P. Goodsp. 13 (341).
[6] Praepositi pagorum had been subject to exactor: P. Amh. II, 142 = Chr. 65 (after 341).
[7] Troops and police: P. Cair, Masp. 67002, II, 23; 67021, V, 8 ff, (after 567 acc. to Bell P. Lond, V, p. 31 n. 1); police (παγανοί): P. Lond. 1674, 79. (c. 570); violence: P. Cair. Masp. 67024, 35 (551), cf. 67283; confiscation of property and arrest: P. Lond. 1677, 10–20; 26 ff.
[8] Pagarchies named after cities or city territories: see Bell's list: J. H. S. (XXVIII), 1908, 101–2; F. Preisigke, Wörterbuch der Griechischen Papyrusurkunden, (Berlin

collegially, by several pagarchs. The old *pagi* and their *praepositi* had been numerous. The territory of Oxyrhynchus was divided into 24 *pagi*.[9] The 6th century pagarchy of Antaeopolis certainly was a comparatively recent institution for the pagarch Menas, in office in 567,[10] appears to have been only the 9th holder of the office.[11]

In the 6th century the pagarch's main function was financial.[12] He was responsible for the collection of imperial taxes from villages and estates of the city territory that were not specifically exempted from his authority[13] and so allowed to pay their taxes to the officials of the governor directly.[14] But even the privileged taxpayers paid local taxes to the pagarch.[15] Collection was still, at least partly, in the hands of decurions.[16] But the pagarch's department, which at Antaeopolis drew the considerable sum of 301 solidi, 22^1/$_2$ carats in wages from imperial taxation,[17] signed receipt[18] and the pagarch exercised severe pressure on reluctant tax payers.[19]

The essential role of the pagarch could be described as that of director of taxation. As such he appears to have carried out functions which had

1925–31), III 139. Antaeopolis spent 124 solidi 6^1/$_2$ carats out of taxation on staff of the pagarchy: P. Cair. Masp. 67057, II, 25.

Collegiality: At Aphrodito c. 553: Julian, Patricia, Menas (P. Lond. 1660); Julian and Menas (ibid 1661); P. Cair Masp. 67002 (after 567) has Menas only, but ibid 6700 of same year shows that Colluthus has recently been pagarch and may be still; ibid. 6732 (after 585) receipts by pagarchs Severus and John; ibid. 67045 and 67047 receipt signed for pagarchs; so also P. Lond. 1665–6.

τῶν . . . κοινῶν δεσποτῶν παγάρχων of P. Lond. 1660 (c553) suggests joint administration, but in P. Cair. Masp. 6732, III, b. John is πάγαρχος τοῦ διμοίρου μέρους and Serenus τοῦ τρίτου μέρους. That this was a territorial division is suggested by payments ὑπὲρ τοῦ μέρους τῆς παγαρχίας and ὑπὲρ τοῦ ἄλλου μέρους τῆς παγαρχίας at Oxyrhynchus in P. Oxy. 2040. There was a pagarch τοῦ βορρινοῦ σκέλους at Heracleopolis (B. G. U. 304, 3 of 7th cent.) and so presumably also τοῦ νοτινοῦ σκέλους. The latter is known from Hermopolis (P. Lond. IV 1461, 14 of c. 709); cf. νυκτοστράτηγος νοτινοῦ μέρους (Preisigke S. B. 10287 (504).

[9] P. Oxy. 2110, 16; Hermopolis had at least 14 pagi (B. G. U. 21 of 340), Heracleopolis at least 11 (P. Amh. 147).

[10] J. Maspero B. I. F. A. O. (X) 1912, 131–57; H. I. Bell, P. Lond. V, p. 22.

[11] P. Cair, Masp. 67002, II, 18 of 567 (acc. to. Bell. o. c. 31 n. 1): 8 pagarchs had accepted the autopragia, granted by the Emperor Leo (457–74) acc. to P. Cair. Masp. 67019. This need not mean that pagarchs went back to Leo.

[12] In P. Cair. Masp. 67003, 25 (c. 567) the pagarch has a wider law-enforcing duty but perhaps significantly jointly with the τοποτηρητής, the duke's deputy. P. Lond. 1677, 22–4: pagarch appoints head of village, but these were concerned with tax collection.

[13] Supervises tax collectors: P. Lond. 1660 (553); accepts pledge of property from ἀπαιτηταὶ τῶν λειτουργῶν: P. Lond. 1661 (553); decisions on rate of tax: P. Lond. 1674 (c. 570).

[14] Autopragia of Aphrodito: P. Cair. Masp. 67019, 6702,36. No other autopract village is known. On the status M. Gelzer, Arch. f. Pap. V, (1913) 188–9.

[15] P. Cair. Masp. 67045–6; 67060.

[16] P. Cair. Masp. 67134–5; Nov. CXLVII, 2 (553); CLXIII, 2 (575).

[17] P. Cair. Masp. 67057, 25.

[18] P. Lond. 1665–6; P. Cair. Masp. 67045–7.

[19] See above n. 7.

earlier been performed by the *exactor civitatis*[20] and before Diocletian introduced the municipal system by the στρατηγός of the nome.[21] It is therefore unlikely to be a coincidence that there are very few references to the *exactor* in papyrus documents of the 6th century or later.[22] It is probable that the office had been reformed and its title changed to pagarch. The very few papyrus references in the late period to *exactores* might be accounted for by linguistic conservatism. The choice of the title pagarch to describe the reformed official might be explained if the reform included the abolition of the *praepositi pagorum* and the transfer of their functions to the enlarged officium of the new officials and of their alternative title to the official himself.

For the date of the reform it is significant that the Emperor Anastasius (491–518) reformed the taxation system of the empire. As a result of this reform, we are told, the cities were placed under *vindices* who gained their position through competitive bidding and replaced the decurions in the supervision of taxation.[23] The reform marked an epoch in the history of the cities. John Lydus, the literary civil servant who lived under Justinian thought that it put an end to the traditional government of cities by decurions and even to the decurions' distinctive dress.[24] This opinion is difficult to check. Papyrological and legal evidence shows that actual collection of taxes remained with decurions.[25] But it is certainly no coincidence that it was in the reign of Anastasius, or soon after, that the election of the principal officers in the cities, the *defensor*,[26] the cornbuyer[27] and the *curator*[28] was taken from the council and given to the notables of the city, that is to a body including not just decurions but all the important landowners, the clergy and the bishop.

It would be reasonable to suppose that the reform of tax collecting which introduced the office of pagarch in Egypt was in some way linked with these radical innovations. The simplest explanation would be that pagarch

---

[20] J. D. Thomas, The office of Exactor in Egypt, Chronique d'Égypte, XXXIV (1959) 124–40. A. H. M. Jones, The Greek City (Oxford 1940) 332 n. 104.

[21] J. Lallemand o. c.

[22] Thomas o. c. 137 knows only one named exactor of 6th cent: Theognostus of P. Lond. III, 1014 (summarised only). He takes the ἐξακτορικὴ τάξις of P. Oxy. 1, 126 and XVI, 1887 to be a private bureau. Nov. CXXVIII, 5 (545) mentions exactores among tax collectors.

[23] John Lydus Mag. III, 46; 49. Euagrius H. E. III, 42; Malalas XVI, 400; A. H. M. Jones L. R. E. 457 n. 111.

[24] Lydus I, 28.

[25] P. Cair. Masp. 67134–5. Nov. Just. CXXVIII, 5; 8 (545) Ed. XIII pr. (339); C. J. I, 3, 52, 1 (531) and older regulations e. g. CJ. X, 19, 7; 20, 1; 32, 40; 72, 8; 72, 14, taken over into the Justinian Code show that decurions continued to play an important part in tax collection.

[26] C. J. I, 55, 11 = I, 4, 19 (505).

[27] C. J. I, 4, 17 (491–505).

[28] Nov. Just. CXXVIII, 16 (545). On identity of pater with curator see A. H. M. Jones, L. R. E. III, 242 n. 104.

is a local Egyptian term for *vindex*. But this does not appear to have been the case. Edict XIII of Justinian contains regulations for pagarchs. It also refers to a budget drawn up by the *vindex* of Alexandria. Thus pagarch and *vindex* were both official titles and there is no suggestion at all that they were synonymous.[29] The fact that the title *vindex* has not yet been found on papyrus documents suggests that in Egypt the office existed only at Alexandria and that pagarch and *vindex* represent alternative forms of organisation.

It is possible – Lydus' evidence notwithstanding – that the reform of Anastasius and his praetorian prefect Marinus did not result in the appointment of *vindices* in all cities of the empire. The fact that only very few cities are known to have possessed a *vindex* suggests that the office was never universal. On the other hand the disparate character of the cities concerned Alexandria, Antioch,[30] Tripolis and Anazarbus[31] makes it difficult to see on what criterion they should have been selected to share a particular financial organisation. Alternatively it could be that *vindices* were appointed universally at first and that the experiment proved a failure with the result that in most areas other forms of organisation were introduced. The Emperor Justinian admitted that *vindices* had won a very bad reputation.[32] In any case it appears that the uniformity that had been a feature of the imperial organisation of tax gathering before Anastasius was not maintained in the 6th Century. A law of 545 suggests that the assignment of financial liability for arrears of taxation differed from province to province.[33] The law also envisages as normal an organisation of local finance under a *pater civitatis* which is different from the organisation under a *vindex* found at Alexandria according to Edict XIII of 538.[34]

The existence of two titles suggests that the position of pagarch and *vindex* differed significantly but the evidence allows comparison to be made only of the procedures followed in their respective appointments. Regulations for deposition and appointment of pagarchs are found in Edict XIII.[35] If a pagarch had failed in his duties the provincial governor i. e. either the *Augustalis* or the duke of the Thebaid might arrest him and 'look out' for a successor.[36] We are not told how he did this but if we bear

---

[29] Just. Ed. XIII, 14–15 vindex and curiales at Alexandria; 12 and 25 pagarchs and curiales elsewhere.

[30] Chron. Pasch. 626 (AD 532).

[31] Sev. Ant. Ep. I, 9; 27.

[32] Nov. Just. XXXVIII pr. τοὺς ὀλεθρίους μισθωτὰς οὓς δὴ βίνδικας καλοῦσι.

[33] Nov. CXXVIII, 5; 8 (545); cf. CXXXIV, 2, 5 (556) εἰ δὲ ἐν ταῖς ἐπαρχίαις ἢ βίνδικες ἢ ἐκλήπτορές εἰσι τῶν δημοσίων.

[34] The pater: Nov. CXXVIII, 16; vindex of Alexandria Ed. XIII, 14–5. Pagarchs collected local taxes, ἀστικά or κωμητικά, G. Rouillard, L'administration civile de l'Égypte byzantine, (Paris 1928), 60 and 118, and thus may have controlled local finance, but the topic requires further study.

[35] Ed. XIII, 12; 25.

[36] ibid. 12. περισκοπήσει, ibid. 25 ἀναζητήσει.

42

in mind that at this time the chief civic officials the *defensor, curator* and corn-buyer were elected by the notables of the city it appears likely that this group was at least consulted over the selection of a pagarch. But the final decision to depose the existing pagarch and to appoint his successor was made neither by notables nor by the provincial governor. It was made by the praetorian prefect and required imperial confirmation. At the time of his appointment the pagarch took over some property forfeited by his predecessor.[37] Presumably a pagarch on entering office was obliged to pledge his property for the satisfactory performance of his tax-collecting duties.

Vindices according to Lydus were appointed by the praetorian prefect who managed to make a lot of money out of the appointments.[38] This could mean that the post was simply sold to the highest bidder. Sale of office was widespread under the predecessors of Justinian.[39] But the parallel of the pagarch points in a different direction: perhaps the post was given to the candidate who would offer security for the largest tax payment and thus guaranteed the lowest arrears of taxation.[40] There is no evidence to indicate what kind of persons became *vindices*. Lydus' tantalisingly brief description is compatible with the view that the whole process of appointment took place at the headquarters of the praetorian prefect at Constantinople. If that was the case the distinctive characteristic of a *vindex* could have been that he was an outsider sent by the central government to take charge of tax collection, and local finance,[41] in a provincial city, while a pagarch was a local man selected, even though not appointed, by provincial authorities namely the governor of the province and the notables of the city.

The pagarch received his orders from the provincial governor and the governor could be held responsible for the pagarch's actions,[42] but since the governor could not on his own dismiss him a pagarch enjoyed a certain amount of independence. The independence was increased by the fact that the tenure of governorships was short while pagarchs remained in office for many years if not for life.[43] The governor might appoint

---

[37] Ibid. 12. παραδόσει τῶν τε εἰς τὰς παγαρχίας ἀνηκόντων τῶν τε εἰς τὰς οὐσίας τὰς αὐτῶν. Ibid. 25 καὶ εἰς τὰς ἐκείνων παγαρχίας τε καὶ οὐσίας ἐμβαινόντων.

[38] Lydus III, 49 ἀπεμπολῶν τοὺς ὑπηκόους παντί, ὡς ἔτυχεν εἰ μόνον αὐτῷ τὸ πλέον ὑπόσχοιτο . . . καὶ γίνεται μὲν πολύχρυσος, εἴπερ τις ἄλλος, ὁ βασιλεὺς καὶ μετ' αὐτὸν ὁ Μαρῖνος καὶ ὅσοι Μαρινιῶντες ἁπλῶς. Nov. XXXVIII pr. μισθωτάς.

[39] Jones L. R. E. 393–5.

[40] Cf. pledging of governor's property against abuses of tax collecting: Nov. App. VIII (Const. Prag). 12 (554); Nov. CXLIX (569).

[41] See n. 34.

[42] Ed. XIII, 12 ἅπασι διακελεύεσθαι καὶ στρατίωταις καὶ παγάρχαις; ibid. 25 ὑπὲρ ὧν καὶ κινδυνεύει . . .

[43] If pagarchs were instituted under Anastasius (491–518). Aphrodito in 567 (n. 11 above) had 9 pagarchs in at least 49 years. Menas pagarch c. 553 (P. Lond. 1660) was still in office in 567.

deputies τοποτηρηταί[44] and sometimes an individual held the titles of deputy and pagarch concurrently.[45] But the very fact that there were two titles shows that the offices were distinct and that the pagarch's standing was independent of the governor.

The situation is in accordance with the policy of Anastasius and successors who pursued the policy of building up the power of civic officials, and to reverse the long continued decline of civic self determination vis-à-vis the governor. Thus Novel XV of 535 expressly forbids that a governor should depose a *defensor*. A *defensor* is to be elected by the chief inhabitants of the city who are to hold the office in turn for a period of two years. During absence of the governor the *defensor* is even given authority over locally stationed members of the provincial *officium*.[46] It is not clear how far Novel XV succeeded in strengthening the position of the *defensor*. But the evidence of papyrus documents suggests that in the pagarch Egyptian cities had a local official of a standing comparable to that which Justinian tried to give the *defensor*. In Egypt the pagarch was in fact evidently much more important than the *defensor*.[47]

Pagarchs were drawn from the ranks of the notables. All had honorific titles, not a few official ranks.[48] The rank need not have been conferred by sinecures. A law of Anastasius requires that notables and bishop should elect a corn-buyer from active or retired members of the provincial *officium*, because his experience of public business would help him to bear the burden of the σιτωνία.[49] A pagarch whose duties were more complicated than those of a corn-buyer would find experience of public business an even greater advantage.

Membership of a provincial officium did not at this period exclude great landowners. Colluthus the *cancellarius*, pagarch of Antaeopolis was a descendant of governors and evidently belonged to the landed aristo-

---

[44] C. Kunderewicz, Topoteretai, J. Jur. Pap. XIV, 1962, 33–50; the τοποτηρητής of Antaeopolis: P. Cair. Masp. 67003; ibid. 67279. Dios and Helladius τοποτηρηταί. The former was T. under the dux Athanasius when Menas and perhaps Colluthus were pagarchs. The posts were therefore distinct.

[45] P. Flor. 295.

[46] Nov. Just. XV, (335); aim: praef.; not to be deposed by governor: 1; officiales to obey: 3; election: 6.

[47] On the Egyptian defensor see B. R. Rees, The Defensor Civitatis, J. Jur. Pap. VI (1952) 73–102, esp. 94: It is this custody of the acta this responsibility for the verification of the actual facts of a dispute and for recording them which forms the source of his municipal authority. The activity of the pagarch extends into the judicial sphere of the defensor: Rouillard o. c. 153 on P. Cair. Masp. 67094; P. Lond. V, 1683 cf. 1682; P. Cair. Masp. 67005.

[48] Eg. 6th century pagarchs of Antaeopolis: Patricia: ἐνδοξοτάτη, (P. Lond. 1660) Menas: scriniarius, λαμπρότατος, (P. Cair. Masp. 6702). Julian: μεγαλοπρεπεστατος ἀπ᾿ ἀρχόντων, (P. Lond. 1660). Colluthus: cancellarius, λαμπρότατος, (P. Cair. Masp. 67005, 19). John: ἐνδοξότατος, (P. Cair. Masp. 67325). Serenus: ἰλλούστριος, ibid. Fl Alexander ἰλλούστριος (S. O. C. 283, 5). Without title Macarius (before 553?) (P Cair. Masp. 67055, II, 10). cf. Preisigke, Wörterbuch, III, 139–40.

[49] C. J. X, 27, 3 (491–505).

44

cracy.[50] It is indeed likely that great wealth was in itself a qualification for the pagarchy. The illustrious Patricia who exercised the pagarchy together with her manager Menas, the *scriniarius*, can only have owed her position to rank and wealth. Since women did not normally perform public functions it is likely that her qualification for office lay in the possession of property out of which the government might make up deficits.[51] Presumably the administrative work was carried out by Menas, by the senatorial colleague Julian, ἀπ' ἀρχόντων, and the permanent officials of the pagarchy.

At Oxyrhynchus the great house of the Apions, which owned two fifths of the combined territories of Oxyrhynchus and Cynopolis[52] appears to have obtained a permanent grip on the pagarchy. At any rate the formula describing a village situated in the pagarchy held by the head of the family[53] is so similar to that describing a village of subject peasants[54] as to suggest that the village of the pagarchy had been reduced to a state of permanent dependency.

To judge by the evidence of the village notable Dioscorus[55] the pagarchs of Antaeopolis were powerful officials able to back their demands with soldiers as well as civil police.[56] But they might also employ unofficial means of coercion. When the pagarch Menas wished to enact payments from the villagers of Aphrodito he came to an agreement with the μεγαλοπρεπεστάτῳ Σερήνῳ τῷ λογιωτάτῳ σχολαστικῷ, evidently a landed magnate, who arranged for his agent to seize a number of villagers while they were visiting an annual market and held them for a time in his private gaol.[57]

The pagarchs appear to have been less formidable to other landed magnates than they were to a wealthy villager like Dioscorus. When the headman of the village Aphrodito was away on an embassy of complaint to Constantinople the taxes of the village were collected by the magnificent Theodosius – perhaps a chosen patron of the village. Unfortunately for the villagers the great man failed to hand over the money to the imperial authorities. The pagarch thereupon extorted a second payment from

---

[50] P. Cair. Masp. 6705; 67120 cf. J. Maspero, Un dernier poète Grec d'Égypte, R. E. G. 1911 esp. 441–3.

[51] P. Lond. 1660. Exemption of women from munera: Dig. L, 17, 2; C. J. X, 32, 11; but not from financial ones C. J. X, 42, 9; Dig. L, 4, 3, 3 or some personal ones C. J. X, 52, 5. Financial liability of pagarch? Just. Ed. XIII, 25; cf. 12.

[52] Jones, L. R. E. 780.

[53] P. Oxy. 139; cf. 133 and P. Lond III, 776, 6. κώμη . . . παγαρχουμένη παρὰ τῆς ὑμετέρας ὑπερφυείας.

[54] P. Oxy. 137., ibid. 134, 19; 135, 14 cf. P. Lond. III, p. 279 and 280, ἀπὸ ἐποικίου διαφέροντος τῇ ὑμῶν ὑπερφυείᾳ.

[55] H. I. Bell, J. H. S. LXIV (1944), 21–36. J. Maspero, Un dernier poète Grec. d'Égypte, R. E. G. XXIV (1911), 426–481.

[56] Civic police and soldiers: P. Cair. Masp. 67002; 67021 ver. 8; P. Lond. 1674, 78.

[57] P. Cair. Masp. 67002, II, 2 ff.

the village.[58] It was evidently beyond his power to extract the money from the magnificent Theodosius. On a smaller scale an otherwise unknown Senuthes could ignore a pagarch who ordered him to release a woman from his private prison.[59] In a period when great landowners had private soldiers, *bucellarii*[60] and prisons[61] the scope of even a powerful official was limited.

To sum up: the origin of the office of pagarch as known from 6th and 7th Century sources was linked with the reforms of the Emperor Anastasius. These reforms sought to revive civic institutions disastrously weakened by the decline of the curial class. The decurions reduced in numbers and wealth[62] and overshadowed by a new aristocracy exempt from curial service[63] had become incapable of asserting themselves against the governor or their more powerful fellow citizens. In this situation the imperial government transferred the most important civic offices *defensor*, *curator*, corn-buyer to members of the new aristocracy and made their election the responsibility of the notables as a whole. At almost the same time supervision of tax collection passed from the curial *exactor* and the council collectively either to a *vindex* or a pagarch. Pagarchs were recruited from the new aristocracy of great landowners or ex-officials. In addition they had greater scope for independent decision, a much larger clerical department and a stronger military and police backing than their predessors had ever had. Their authority implies some decentralisation of the traditional power of a Roman governor. The disorderly condition of Egypt in the 6th Century suggests that the new system was accompanied by a weakening of the administration.[64] It was left to the Arabs to restore strong centralised authority.[65]

If the view outlined above is correct the pagarch was an official whose responsibility extended over both city and territory.[66] In a sense he represents the last of a series of attempts by the imperial government to control individual cities through an official appointed by the central au-

---

[58] P. Cair. Masp. 67024, 8 ff.; 67029; R. G. Salomon, J. E. A. XXXIV (1948), 98–108 on P. Hamb. Inv. 410.

[59] P. Cair. Masp. 67005.

[60] Duke to expel bucellarii: P. Masp. 67089, rect. 13. On private troops see also P. Oxy. 150; 156; P. Lond. III, 871; B. G. U. 836. J. Maspero, Organisation militaire de l'Égypte byzantine, 66–8.

[61] P. S. I. 953.

[62] Nov. Just. XXXVIII pr. εἰς ἄνδρας ὀλίγους περιστάντα τὰ λειτουργήματα . . . ὥστε (τὰς πόλεις) ὑπὸ τούτους εἶναι . . . οὓς δὴ βίνδικας καλοῦσιν.

[63] Jones, L. R. E. 760 n. cities Mansi IX, 277–8 for Mopsuestia in 550.

[64] H. I. Bell, Egypt from Alexander the Great to the Arab conquest (Oxford 1956), 101–34; G. Rouillard l. c. 184–95.

[65] On growing local autonomy in 6th century see D. Claude, Die byzantinische Stadt im 6. Jahrhundert, (Munich 1969) 114–36.

[66] This is the view argued by G. Rouillard, L'administration civile de l'Égypte byzantine, 67–62 against M. Gelzer, Studien zur byzantinischen Verwaltung Aegyptens, (Leipzig 1909) 90 ff.

thority: the institution of the pagarch repeats the early history of *curator*, *defensor* and *exactor*.[67] The earlier control officials were rapidly assimilated to the condition of local magistrates and became part of the curial institutions which governed cities until the reforms of Anastasius. The pagarch was not absorbed. Documents never show a pagarch acting in consultation with other civic authorites. The reason for this, I would suggest, is that 'the notables' never became the continuosly available collective city authority which the city council had been. Hence the pagarch was left to act on his own. In practice he became the officer who passed the administration's financial orders to the city and its territory and was expected to ensure that they were obeyed. It is not by chance that a number of pagarchs are known to have doubled their office with that of governor's deputy τοποτηρητής[68] or even that of garrison commander, tribunus or στρατη- λάτης.[69] Under Arab administration all these offices fused into that of pagarch who was the official through which the Arab governor enforced his commands to the subject population.[70]

---

[67] B. R. Rees, The Curator Civitatis in Egypt, J. Jur. Pap. VII–VIII (1953–4), 83–105 and o. c. n. 46 above and J. D. Thomas o. c. n. 20 above.

[68] P. Flor. 295, 11.

[69] At least at Arsinoe: S. B. 4721, 3; 4857; Stud. XX, 240, 4.

[70] R. Rémondon, Papyrus Grecs d'Apollonos Ano, (Cairo 1953), correspondence of a pagarch c. 703–14. H. I. Bell, The Aphrodito Papyri, J. H. S. XXVIII (1908), 97–19, esp. 107 ff. on correspondence of Basilius pagarch of Aphrodito c. 710.

I owe gratitude for suggestions and corrections to professor A. H. M. Jones who read a version of this paper some time before his death.

XVIII

THE PAGARCH: CITY AND IMPERIAL ADMINISTRATION
IN BYZANTINE EGYPT*

The administration of the Roman Empire, even the post-Diocletianic Empire depended on the fact that the bulk of administration was done not by imperial officials but by the authorities of self-governing cities. The cities were governed by a hereditary oligarchies, the *curiales*, who staffed the city council of every city in the Empire.[1] In the course of the 4th century the councils were gravely weakened and became incapable of performing their traditional role.[2] This development represents a crisis in the administrative history of the Roman Empire. Lack of evidence about municipal government during the 5th and 6th centuries hinders the historian seeking to find how the crisis was overcome. It is only in Egypt that we can watch the working of "post-curial" institutions in any detail.

In the last centuries of Byzantine rule in Egypt the principle of local autonomy is represented by the *pagarch*.[3] This official appears as the leading man in the city territories of Egypt. His position was kept independent of the imperial governor or duke[4] by the fact that he was not appointed by him but by the praetorian prefect of the East with confirmation by the emperor.[5] Governors must have influenced appointment.[6] But since pagarchs held their office

---

* This paper originated as a communication read to the 14th International Congress of Byzantine Studies at Bucharest in September 1971. Dr K. T r e u supplied references to prayers for the pagarch and family.

[1] A. H. M. J o n e s, *The Greek City*, (Oxford, 1940); J. L a l l e m a n d, *L'administration civile de l'Égypte* (Brussels, 1964).

[2] See my *Antioch* (Oxford, 1972), 186—92.

[3] A general survey G. R o u i l l a r d, *Administration civile de l'Égypte byzantine* (Paris, 1938), 52—62; see also R. R é m o n d o n, *Papyrus Grecs d'Apollonos Ano*, (Cairo, 1953).

[4] On changing administration of Egypt see J. K a r a y a n n o p u l o s, *Die Entstehung der byzantinischen Themenordnung* (Munich, 1959), 61ff; R. R é m o n d o n, *Le P. Vind. inv. 25838 et les commandants militaires en Égypte au IVe siècle et au Ve, Chr. É.* XL (1965), 180—97.

[5] Justinian, *Ed.* XIII, 12; 25.

[6] Appointment of *pagarch* by *praef. Augustalis*: John N i k i u (henceforth cited J. N.) 97, 3; by Emperor Phocas: J. N. 107, 4; 107, 26; by Nicetas representing Heraclius: J. N. 107, 15.

for long periods, if not for life,[7] while governors changed much more frequently,[8] the pressure a governor could exert on a pagarch in office was very limited. A pagarch was often a local man,[9] a big landowner,[10] with honorary or retired rank in the imperial service. The office might become hereditary. He was evidently not an easy man to depose. Moreover while a governor might propose the deposition of a pagarch, the actual dismissal required the decision of the praetorian prefect and emperor.[11]

We have no detailed account of the appointment of a pagarch. As a result we cannot form a clear picture of the relations between the official and the other great landowners of the city. The analogy of *defensor*,[12] *curator*,[13] and corn-buyer,[14] suggests that a man was picked by the notables of the city meeting together with the bishop and that the governor would put the name before the central authorities for the formal appointment.

The pagarch's basic function was financial. He was responsible for the collection of imperial taxes from villages and estates of the city territory that were not specifically exempted from his authority.[15] He appears to be the successor of the *exactor civitatis* in the role of director of taxation.[16] Under him individual councillors, *curiales*, continued to collect some of the taxation.[17]

---

[7] Menas, *pagarch* between 553 and 567, was the ninth *pagarch* of Antaeopolis (P. Cair. Mas. 67002, II, 18 of 567). If, as is argued by me in *B.Z.* LXVII (1974), *pagarchs* were instituted by Anastasius (491—518), this suggests an average length of office of not less than 4 years. Since some *pagarchs* held the office concurrently the real average is probably considerably greater. Papas, whose correspondence was published by R. R é m o n d o n, was *pagarch* for at least ten years. The "most illustrious Patricia" (P. Lond. 1660, 7) surely inherited the pagarchate; so did Flavius Christophorus and Theodoracius sons of *pagarch* Apa Cyrus (S.B. 9749—51; 55; 76—7 of 642—3 A.D.)

[8] L. C a n t a r e l l i, *La serie dei prefetti di Egytto pt. 3* (A.D. 395—642) in *Atti della R. Accademia dei Lincei*, Ser. 5 (1909), 385—440. H. H ü b n e r, *Der Praefectus Aegyptii* (Munich, 1952) adds little to prosopography. See also J. M a s p e r o, in: *B.I.F.A.O.* X (1912), 143 and A. H. M. J o n e s, *L.R.E.* 883.

[9] So the Apion family (R o u i l l a r d, *op. cit.*, 204, n. 1); Papas of Apollonopolis (R. R é m o n d o n, *op. cit.*, p. VII). Perhaps Julianus (cf. P. Cair. Masp. 67,060 and P. Lond, 1661, 5.

[10] E.g. Colluthus (J. M a s p e r o in R.E.G. 441—53), but not *pagarch* in home-town. See also the "prefect" Theodosius J. N. 95, 3—5. Prayers for pagarch and his family: W e s s e l y, *Stud. Pal. Pap.* XV, No. 251 b; P l e y t e - B o e s e r, p. 127—9.

[11] *Ed.* XIII, 12: 25.

[12] *CJ.* I, 55, 11 (505).

[13] *Nov. Just.* CXXVIII, 16 (545).

[14] *CJ* 1, 4, 17 (491—503).

[15] References in R o u i l l a r d, *op. cit.*, 97 whose interpretation is followed.

[16] J. D. T h o m a s, *The Office of Exactor in Egypt, Chronique d'Égypte*, XXXIV (1959), 124—40.

[17] P. Cair. Masp. 67045—7; 67060; 67326—7.

There even is evidence that they were still doing this in early Arab times.[18] But the precise role of these councillors in the financial organisation of the city is not yet clear. Certainly the pagarch was not a councillor himself, and he did not work under the supervision of the city council as the *exactor* had done.[19] The pagarch's duties must have involved much negotiation with leading tax payers,[20] but there is no evidence that a pagarch ever had, or was expected to have, dealings with any formally organised collective body. Evidently the notables who dominated the cities from the 5th century onwards were completely successful in avoiding corporate responsibility for taxes or any other aspect of civic life of the kind that had burdened the *curiales*. They had their say in emergency such as a foreign invasion.[21] Normally they remained in the background and left administration and relations with imperial officials to the pagarch.

The pagarch also had far greater coercive power than his curial predecessor. He could back his orders not only with local policy (*paganoi*), with men drawn from the provincial *officium*, or the private power of powerful men, but also with soldiers.[22] He might confiscate property or inflict imprisonment.[23] A punitive visit of the pagarch might bear resemblance to a hostile invasion. Such authority on the part of a city, as opposed to a provincial, official implies significant decentralisation of the traditional power of a Roman governor.

Such decentralisation was paralleled — if not indeed made possible — by dispersal of the units of the army as garrisons throughout the cities of Egypt. Many units — whether originally *limitanei* or *comitatenses* had remained in the same station for many generations and formed strong local ties. In some communities they are likely to have formed a considerable proportion of the population. Mamy soldiers had part-time civilian jobs.[24] Garrisons were commanded

---

[18] J o h n s o n - W e s t, *Economic Studies*, 323; R. R é m o n d o n, P. Apoll. 76; *P.E.R.F.* 566.

[19] Old system well exemplified by E. B o s w i n k e l, *Ein wiener Papyrus mit bezug auf die exactores civitatis, Actes du Xe congrès international de papyrologues* 1961 (Warsaw, 1964), 117—20.

[20] P.R.G. IV, No. 6, P. Lond. 1356 (both under Arabs); also Makrizi Hitat 1, 77, 5, 77, 5 (ed. Wiet. I, 323).

[21] J. N. 97, 11 (obscure); 107, 19; 115, 10.

[22] P. Cair Masp. 67002 (great man and "soldiers"), 67021 ("soldiers" and "pagans"); 67024, 37 (*ibid.*, 45 shows that *officiales* were involved). P. Kond. 1674, 78 ("pagans"). P. Lond. 1677, 26. P. Lond. (1435, 117, Arab rule).

[23] Confiscation: P. Cair. Masp. 67002, P. Lond. 1677. Arrest: P. Apoll. 18; 37; 39; 42 (all Arab. rule). More general authority P. Cair. Masp. 67003; 67005; perhaps 67313; 67322. Pagarch's jurisdiction: A. S t e i n w e n t e r, *Studien zu den koptischen Rechtsurkunden aus Oberägypten* = C. W e s s e l y, *Studien zur Palaeographie und Papyruskunde* XIX (Leipzig, 1920 repr. Amsterdam, 1967), 6—18.

[24] J o n e s, *L.R.E.* 660—63 based on P. Monac. and P. Lond. V, 1719—37.

by a tribune. These were appointed in theory by the emperor, in practice no doubt by the duke. We have little biographical information. Such evidence as there is suggests that like pagarchs, tribunes belonged to the landowning aristocracy.[25] It is not clear whether they were normally natives of the city in which their unit was stationed. The tribune's position was in many ways parallel to that of the pagarch.[26] He was the military as the pagarch was the civil head of each city.[27] When the two co-operated — or when the two posts were combined[28] — the arrangement comprised a degree of local power very rarely found in Roman provincial administration earlier.

There is no evidence for pagarchs outside Egypt and even at Alexandria his functions were in all likelihood performed by the *vindex*.[29] The position of the pagarch in the provincial cities of Egypt is incompatible with the enhanced powers which *defensores* appear to have been given by Justinian.[30] We also lack evidence that his regulations concerning the *pater civitatis* were observed there.[31] It looks as if the municipal arrangements of Anastasius and Justinian were of more limited application than the sources suggest.[32] It is likely that the regulations were made necessary by local developments such as the weakening of city councils, the power of citizens outside the curial class and the dispersal of the army and that these developments took different shape in accordance with varying local conditions. The imperial government merely recognised and regulated these changes. It was unwilling or unable to restore the former uniformity of provincial administration.[33]

The reforms were to some extent successful. The treasure left by Anastasius and the campaigns on which Justinian spent it witness to the restored strength of the Empire. But the history of Justinian's wars dragging on endlessly because

---

[25] J. M a s p e r o, *Organisation militaire de l'Égypte byzantine*, (Paris 1912, 95). The important paper of R. R é m o n d o n, *Soldats de byzance d'après un papyrus trouvé à Edfou, Recherches de papyrologie* I (1961), 43—93, besides much else "rehabilitates" the pagarch Menas and the tribune Florentius. Domentianus the last tribune (and pagarch) of Arsinoe was brother-in-law of the patriarch of Alexandria (J. N. 109, 10), therefore presumably a landowner.

[26] With some overlapping e.g. receipts (P. Cair. 67040; P. Gen. II, 95 — or violence P. Cair. Masp. 67009).

[27] C. K u n d e r e w i c z, *Les topotérètes, J. Jur. Pap.* XVI (1962), 33—50; *P.W.* IV A2 *s.v. tribunus civitatis.*

[28] Regularly at Arsinoe (J. M a s p e r o, *Organisation militaire*, 140—1). John N i k i u simply refers to "prefects" of individual towns but in some cases he mentions a civilian as well as a military leader.

[29] Ed. XIII, 13ff. On vindices: J o n e s, *L.R.E.* 457; *P.W.* 22, IX, A1 *s.v. vindex* (2).

[30] Ed. XV, 16.

[31] *Pater* in Egypt: *P.R.G.S.* III, No. 46; *P.R.K.F.* 67; 176; but he was important in Asia Minor: H. G r e g o i r e, *I.G.C.* 101, 219, 264, 270, 307, 309.

[32] Vindices are known only from Alexandria, Antioch, (*Chron. Pasch.* 626, A.D. 532), Tripolis and Anazarbus (Sev. Ant. *Ep.* 1.9., 27).

[33] D. C l a u d e, *Die byzantinische Stadt* (Munich, 1969), 114ff.

the Emperor could not finance large enough armies to finish them shows that the restoration was incomplete. The same impression is created by Justinian's reorganisation of Egypt by means of the famous *Edict* XIII.

The administration of Egypt was not performing its primary function:[34] the taxes were not coming in. If the revenue was collected — and it looks as if tax-payers paid a great deal — it failed to reach its destination. The various officials concerned handled matters in such a way that it was impossible to find out what had happened to the taxation.[35]

Justinian's cure was to simplify administration and to strengthen the governors by combining military and civil authority in the hands of "dukes" each responsible for two of the Egyptian provinces. The new official would have greater coercive power as a result of his being able to give orders to soldiers directly and he would not be obstructed by the patronage of a rival military commander.[36]

The reader of the edict may well doubt whether its object was achieved. A large part of the edict is taken up with threats against various officials. The Emperor evidently could not rely on the men who would have to carry out the law. He anticipates dishonesty at every level.[37] The various collecting departments will obstruct each other by granting (no doubt corruptly) exemption from taxes due to other branches of the administration.[38] He anticipates that officers and men will refuse to enforce the demands of the tax collectors.[39] Bishops, especially the bishop of Alexandria, will enable tax payers to escape their obligations.[40]

The later history of Egypt justifies the Emperor's fears. John, Bishop of Nikiu's *Chronicle* includes an account of the troubles of Egypt at the end of the 6th and the beginning of the 7th century.[41] There is no time for a full account of the "Aikelah rising", the overthrow of Phocas or the Arab invasion, but some general observations can be made. The military effectiveness of the army of Egypt was very low.[42] The same is true of the civil administration.

---

[34] R. R é m o n d o n, *P. Hamb. 56 et P. Lond. 1419*. Notes sur les finances d'Aphrodito du VIe siècle au VIIIe, *Chr. É.* XL (1965), 401—30, analyses in detail the tax registers of Aphrodito and reveals a steady rise in the level of tax demanded.

[35] *Ed.* XIII, *praef.*

[36] R o u i l l a r d, *op. cit.*, 36ff., see also n. 3 above.

[37] E.g. *Ed.* XIII, 6; 9; 14.

[38] *Ibid.*, 7; 9.

[39] *Ibid.*, 11; 20.

[40] *Ibid.*, 10; 28.

[41] Chronique de Jean, éveque de Nikiou, text and translation by M. H. Z o t e n b e r g, in: *Notices et extraits des manuscrits de la bibliothèque nationale*, Vol. 24 (Paris, 1883). English translation by R. H. C h a r l e s (London, 1916). A new commentary is needed.

[42] J. M a s p e r o, *Organisation militaire*, 114—32; R. R é m o n d o n, *Recherches de papyrologie* I (1961), 143—93; also J. J a r r y, *B.I.F.A.O.* (LXII) 1964, 174—206.

Important decisions are made by the local "prefects". Nikiu's language is ambiguous but most of the "prefects" are probably garrison commanders.[43] Some may be pagarchs. Perhaps the two offices were now frequently — not universally[44] — combined. The local element in decision-making was increased by the fact that at this time civilians did have a part in the defence of their cities.[45] It is likely that the importance of the circus factions in the last decades of Byzantine rule is linked with this development.[46] The consequence of this breakdown of overall military and civilian administration was that Egypt was lost to the Arabs.

Much work remains to be done on Byzantine Egypt. There is need for the reconstitution of dispersed archives, for more local studies like that of R. R é - m o n d o n on the finances of Aphrodito, and for investigations of the social background of the holders of various offices such as dukes, pagarchs, or tribunes. This would be worthwhile not only for its own sake but to illuminate wider areas of Byzantine history. Some of the most striking phenomena of the last unhappy period of Byzantine rule can be found elsewhere too.[47] Fuller understanding of what went wrong in Egypt must help us to recognise what were the essential elements in the measures that enabled the Eastern Empire to recover.[48]

---

[43] J. M a s p e r o, *op. cit.*, 135—48.

[44] Pagarch? mentioned separately at Busiris (J.N. 97, 5; 97, 16); Sebennytos (Samnoud) *ibid.*, 107, 26—7.

[45] J.N. 107, 46; 120, 24 (Alexandria); 115, 10 (Antinoe); 97, 7 force of rebellious pagarchs? in Aikelah rising.

[46] First mentioned by J.N. in connection with Aikelah rising: 97, 4. Both factions support Heraclius' generals: 107, 25; 107, 46. Support rival generals during Arab invasion: 119, 8—9.

[47] Cf. the localisation of the army and the position of the tribune in the Italy of the Exarchate: L. M. H a r t m a n n, *Untersuchungen zur Geschichte der byzantinischen Verwaltung Italiens* (Leipzig, 1889), 56—62; idem, *Geschichte Italiens* (Gotha 1897—1903), Vol. 2, 1, 120—35. With the position of pagarch cf. that of numerarii in Visigothic Spain as in *epistola de fisco Barcinonensi* (of *c. 593*). Mansi X, 473ff.

[48] See J. K a r a y a n n o p u l o s in *Die Entstehung der byzantinischen Themenordnung,* (Munich, 1959) and the problem raised by it.

XIX

GENERALS, FEDERATES AND BUCELLARII
IN ROMAN ARMIES AROUND AD 400

In this paper it will be argued that in Roman armies in
the last decades of the fourth century an important
role was played by federates who were in no sense
contingents provided by an allied people, whether from
within or without the frontiers, but were raised by
Roman commanders by individual recruitment of non-
Romans, wherever they might be found, who enlisted not
for the term of service of a regular soldier but only
for as long as they might be needed. It will be
suggested that the ties between such units and their
commander were very close, with the result that the
position of a late Roman general, a Gainas or Stilicho
was quite different from that of the imperial generals
of earlier periods. It will be argued that 'private
soldiers' or bucellarii came into existence as a consequence of this kind of recruiting.

In literary accounts of campaigns after 378, as for instance
Theodosius' expedition against the usurper Maximus in 388[1] or
against Eugenius in 393 (Zos. IV.57; John Ant. Frg. 187
(FHG.IV.609)), the eastern army is divided into units of two
kinds, Roman and barbarian. This distinction appears in accounts
of every campaign for which we have literary evidence (Gainas in
396: Theodoret HE. V.32.1; Socr. HE VI.6 (text uncertain), cf
Soz. VIII.4.1. Tribigild's revolt in 398: Zos. V.13.2; 17.1;
18.10). The division does not mean that some units were composed
of Roman citizens while others were of barbarians. There is good
evidence that Roman units too included a high proportion of
soldiers of non-Roman origin.[2] The difference appears to be one
between regular units and units that were not part of the regular
army. At any rate the distinction is made so consistently that
it must correspond to a formal division within Roman army
units.[3] Late Roman campaigning armies must have been made up of
regular units together with auxiliaries, entirely or almost entirely recruited from barbarians, that did not count as regular
units.

We have a late Roman army register, the famous Notitia Dignitatum
(Seeck 1876; Clemente 1968). This document seems to represent
the disposition of the army of the Eastern Empire around 394,
while the lists of the West appear to have been brought up to

date until around 420 (Jones 1964: III, 347-80; Mann 1976: 1-8; Demougeot 1975: 1079-1134). The Notitia distinguishes between a number of different classes of units but it shows no sign of a distinction between regular units and foreign irregulars. True there is an important class of crack infantry units which bear the title of auxilia palatina, and there is good reason to suppose that these units were originally recruited from barbarians, and that they continued to include a high proportion of men of barbarian origin (Hoffman 1969: 130-173). But the serving soldiers appear to have been Roman citizens - to judge by the fact that the majority bore the name of Flavius (Hoffman 1969: 76-78). So they would probably not have been classified simply as barbarians. On the other hand the lists of the Notitia do not appear to include all units making up the campaigning armies. Certain tribal units mentioned in the literary sources seem to be missing.[4] Most strikingly the Goths who figure so prominently in the narrative of Theodosius' campaign against Eugenius in which they are said to have lost 10,000 dead (Jord. Get. 145; 20,000 Goths, cf Zos. IV.58; Socr. HE V.25; VII.10), are represented by no more than two regiments (Or. V.20: Uisi; Teruingi), that is at most 2,000 men (Jones 1964: 680-2). It is likely that the bulk of the Goths were enrolled in barbarian regiments which have not been included in the Notitia. Presumably they were sent home and disbanded after the campaign.

Another indication that the lists are incomplete is that the Western field army has been given very few cavalry units (Hoffman 1969: 193ff). The proportion of cavalry in the Western field armies is likely to have been as high as in the East, that is approximately one third. So presumably on campaign the army was accompanied by a considerable number of cavalry units. A high proportion of cavalry is likely to have been recruited from barbarians.[5] In 398-9 in the East the barbarians of Tribigild (Zos. V.15.5; 16.1) and Gainas (Synesius De Prov. II.1 (1260 BC)) certainly included a high proportion of cavalry. Against Radagaisus in 404-6 Stilicho employed a lot of Huns and Alans as allied cavalry in addition to 30 units of regular Roman troops (Zos. V.26). But if allied cavalry has been omitted, the reason is likely to be that allied units (foederati) in general did not qualify for inclusion in the Notitia.

Failure to mention foederati would be quite natural if they were not part of the permanent establishment, but had only been enrolled for a particular campaign. It appears to be a fact that at this period the standing army was not large enough to deal with emergencies as they arose, so that major wars like Stilicho's operations against Alaric in 397 (Claud. IV Cons. Hon. 485ff of AD 398; cf Cameron 1976: 375: some German offers of recruits rejected I. Cons. Stil. 234-5), or 401-2 (B. Get. 401-3, 463-6; cf 105-6), or against Radagaisus in 405-6 (Cod. Theod. VII.13.16-17 (406); Hun and Alan federates: Zos. V.26), were preceded by desperate recruiting campaigns. We also know that Stilicho made agreements with Alaric with a view to having Alaric's Goths as allies in campaigns which he was planning against the government of the eastern Empire (Zos. V.27; 29), and

against the usurper Constantine in Gaul (Zos. V.31). The employment of barbarian allies for the duration had obvious financial
advantages. It enabled the government to manage with a much
smaller, permanent army, as the eastern government at any rate
seems to have done[6] - and to save the cost of the retirement
benefit which was owed to regulars after twenty or more years of
service (Jones 1964: 635f).

That allied peoples beyond the frontiers or client kings provided
units to assist the imperial army on campaign goes back to the
early days of the Roman Empire and continued into the Late
Empire. For instance a large contingent of Huns, under their
king Uldin, helped to defeat Radagaisus in 406 (Oros. VII.37.12;
Marc. Comes s.a. 406; cf Jones 1964: III.38 n. 61). It was an
innovation - and a disastrous one - that units were now also
being provided by allies who were permanently stationed within
the borders of the Empire, whether by agreement, or because the
Empire was no longer strong enough to keep them out (Jones 1964:
199-200). Alaric's Visigoths are, or at least seem to be[7] a
conspicuous example of this kind of ally.

But often barbarian allies or federates mentioned in the sources
do not appear to have been provided by the rulers, or indeed any
collective organisation, of their native people. These federates
appear to be simply individually enlisted mercenaries of barbarian origin. They may have included a very high proportion of
Goths, because a large number of Goths were available, eager to
be enrolled both within the Empire and on the far side of the
Danube, but they may well have included others as well. A fragment of Olympiodorus which tells us that the title of 'federates'
was first given to mixed units in the reign of Honorius (Olymp.
Frg. VII.4 [R. Blockley]) appears to refer to the origin of this
new type of federate unit. Unfortunately our sources which are
very inadequate for this period will not allow us to identify
individual units in the way Procopius' Histories enable us to
identify federate units in the army of Justinian (Jones 1964:
664ff; Halden 1979; 1984; Miller 1912: 114ff; Teall 1965: 294-
322).

But if we cannot identify units we have numerous references to
barbarian troops that are contrasted with Roman troops, and
which do not appear to have had links with any organised body of
tribesmen, whether within the Empire or outside it. What cohesion such bodies of men possessed appears to be the result of
their serving under the same commander in the Roman army.

Barbarian contingents of this kind played a key role in two
important episodes: the fall of Stilicho and the Gainas revolt.
In the case of Stilicho, it is clear that the barbarian units
were recognisably a distinct division of his army, with distinct
leaders, and political attitudes different from those of Roman
units. Numerically they were of a strength comparable but not
overwhelmingly superior to that of the Roman units (Zos. V.33).
Their families were quartered in a number of cities, and evidently identifiable as families of federate soldiers (Zos. V.34.2;

35.5). Their total strength is given as 30,000. After the execution of Stilicho and the massacre of their families these men joined Alaric's Goths. They evidently had nowhere else to go (Zos. V.35.6; 17.1; 18.10; 19.1).

Gainas' forces are consistently described as barbarians and contrasted with the Roman forces of Leo (Zos. V.14.3; 17.1; 18.6; 18.10; 19.2; 21.9). Unlike the force of the mutinous Goth Tribigild, which was recruited from Greutungi settled in Phrygia, (Claud. In Eutr. II.196; Zos. IV.38-39; Chron. Minor I. p.233 [Mommsen]; cf Albert 1984: 89f) Gainas' Goths appear to have been recruited among fellow Goths from the east of the Danube outside the Empire.[8] But there is no suggestion that they were supplied under treaty by a local ruler. The territory was under the government of Uldin, King of the Huns. It is likely that the Goths presented themselves individually, having their families with them (Synesius De Prov. II.1) at Gainas' instigation, and were enrolled by him under officers that he appointed. They were numerous, since the 7,000 reported killed inside Constantinople are said to have been only a fifth of the whole force (Zos. V.19.4; Synesius De Prov. II.2).

In the case of both barbarian armies it is clear that the commander-in-chief himself took a considerable part in recruiting.[9] Gainas is said to have invited Goths into the Empire to enrol (cf n.8). Stilicho preceded the expedition to Greece against Alaric, and the defence of Italy against Alaric's first invasion with expeditions to the northern frontier which culminated in large-scale recruiting of barbarians into the Roman army (cf above). We owe our information to the poems of Claudian, and Claudian's account of recruiting in 396, vague as it is, would fit recruitment into Roman units rather than into barbarian units.[10] There is however no reason why both kinds of recruiting should not have gone on at the same time. Certainly Stilicho must have recruited cavalry. The Notitia includes a large number of infantry units raised by Honorius,[11] but - not counting units stationed in Africa - only two units of cavalry (Not. Dign. Or. VI.59, 60). Presumably the cavalry units were enrolled as federates. Not all the recruiting will have been done by Stilicho personally. Outstanding among his barbarian officers was Sarus sometimes described as 'king' (Marc. Comes. s.a. 406; Jord. 321) sometimes as dux of the Goths (Oros. VII.37.12), who had a large force who stood in a special relationship to him personally (see below).

An officer did not have to be commander-in-chief to build a federate force with a strong sense of loyalty to himself, or at least to obtain the leadership of a coherent body of men. Tribigild the Goth who led a force of mutinous Greutungi through south-western Asia Minor in 399 is a case in point. His official position seems to have been commander of all the barbarian troops [federates] stationed in Phrygia, with the rank of comes militaris (Zos. V.13.2; Soc. HE VI.6.5; Philost. XI.8). These included a number of Greutungi with wives and families settled on land near Nacoleia.[12] They were almost certainly survivors of a band of barbarians that had been defeated by the general Promotus when attempting to cross into the Empire in 386 (Zos. IV.38). Tribigild was a kinsman of Gainas, and therefore does not appear to have been one of the Greutungi himself.[13] At any rate he did not live in Phrygia but in Constantinople. It is not at all clear what factors other than his rank as their commander induced the Greutungi to trust him to the extent of following him into mutiny and rebellion. By far the most likely explanation is that the Goths had taken part in Eutropius' campaign against the Huns, and that Tribigild had led them (Albert 1984). If that was so, the common motive of leader and men was a grievance over inadequate rewards for their contribution to victory. If at the start Tribigild's band was mainly made up of Greutungi, it certainly did not remain limited to members of that tribe. It grew and gathered strength by absorbing large numbers of slaves and perhaps other provincials (Zos. V.13). Tribigild died soon after he had submitted to the command of Gainas (Philost. XI.8), and it is likely that his force joined up with that of Gainas in Thrace and was destroyed together with it (Zos. V.18.9).

Sarus, who was mentioned earlier, was another barbarian officer to make progress towards creating a private army without, however, succeeding in the end. Sarus was of noble birth and heroic qualities and character (PLRE II.978 s.v. Sarus). He commanded a large force under Stilicho in the battle against Radagaisus (Oros. VII.37.12; Marc. Comes s.a. 406). At the time of Stilicho's death he had a powerful following of barbarians. With more luck he might have become another Stilicho - or another Alaric.[14] In the event his following became reduced to 200-300 (Zos. VI.13.2; Olympiod. Frg. 6 [R. Blockley]). He was eventually assassinated. Jones (1964: III.62) suggested that Sarus and his followers were part of Alaric's Goths who had deserted their leader after the Battle of Verona. It is just as likely that he had assembled his men himself. Certainly it seems that the various units of federates in Justinian's armies were closely linked to their respective commanding officers, and had probably been raised by them.[15]

Federates who served the Empire without a guarantee of permanent employment were in a weak position. There was a possibility of their units becoming part of the regular army[16] or they might be used to fill up regular units (Hoffman 1969: 503). But their future must have depended very largely on the support of the general who had enrolled them. The way in which the troops depended for rewards of service on their general, and the pressure which they consequently exerted on him was well understood by Augustine when he wrote to Bonifatius, comes Africae, and a general with his own following of federates[17], to set a limit to the acquisitiveness of his troops. Close bonds were formed between commander and men, with the troops anxious that their general should keep, or if possible, increase his rank in the imperial service, and thus to enhance his ability to look after their interests.[18] In consequence a commander like Stilicho or Gainas, or Bonifatius or Aetius, could be deposed against his will only by assassination or battle. I would suggest that this rather than the command structure of the Western army is the basic reason why the magister militum in the West became the virtual ruler of the Empire.

It is in the context of the individual recruitment of foederati that I would explain the development of the institution of the bucellarii. Bucellarii were a particular kind of armed retainer. The word itself, 'biscuit-men', is obviously a nickname. It is derived from bucellatum the biscuit issued to soldiers on two days out of three. Eventually it became a technical term for armed followers of a particular status. It was not yet so in our period, and it is likely that men described in the sources by words like amici or armigeri or clientes sometimes represent the status which in the time of Justinian would regularly have been described as bucellarii (Diesner 1972: 322f).

The earliest military use of the word occurs in the title of the comites catafractarii bucellarii iuniores, the most senior of the cavalry regiments under the magister militum per Orientem.(Not. Dign. Or. VII.25; cf Hoffman 1969: 273f). A fragment of Olympiodorus informs us that it was in the reign of Honorius that the name ceased to be given exclusively to Roman soldiers (i.e. regulars?) and came to be used to describe certain Goths (Frg. VII.4 [R. Blockley]). This seems to have been the beginning of the use of the term bucellarii to describe a body of soldiers enjoyng so close a relationship to their commander that they appear to be members of a private force rather than of the imperial army. Most of the evidence about bucellarii is much later, fragments of the code of Euric who ruled Visigothic Spain AD 466-85 (Zeumer 1902 = Code of Euric Frg. 310; Thompson 1969: 187f; Claude 1971: 46ff), Procopius' Histories of the Wars of Justinian (Jones 1964: III. 206f; Lecrevain 1980: 267-83; Haldon 1984: 101ff), and papyri of the sixth century or later (Maspero 1912: 6ff; Gascou 1976: 143-56). Bucellarii are known to have been kept not only by military officers but also by some high civil officials and even by private individuals.[19]

The institution has been explained as an example of German influence, the adoption on the part of powerful Romans of a following of armed companions of the kind described by Tacitus in his account of the household of a German noble.[20] Bucellarii have also been seen as evidence of developing 'feudalisation', that is the usurpation of prerogatives of the state by powerful landed magnates (Patlagean 1977: 289ff). There is something in these explanations. There can be no argument that the resemblance of the bucellariate to a German noble's armed following helped its introduction at a time when so many officers were German. Similarly the bucellarii of great landowners like the Apions obviously strengthened the landowners relative to the agents of the imperial government. Nevertheless neither 'German influence' nor 'feudalisation' accounts for the admittedly scanty evidence we have about the origin of the institution. That the armed retainers were known by a Latin name even in a Germanic kingdom shows that this precise type of following must be of Roman origin. This is confirmed by Olympiodorus' statement that the name was given to Romans before it was given to Goths. Olympiodorus and the Notitia suggest that the name bucellarii was first applied to soldiers. This suggests that the institution started in the imperial army rather than on great estates. This deduction is confirmed by the fact that elsewhere than in Egypt the individuals known to have had armed followings acquired them as a consequence of their being, or having been military commanders, and not simply men of great landed wealth.[21] An exception, Rufinus the praetorian prefect of the East, AD 392-5, who is actually the earliest known case of an individual with an armed following, was of course a civilian (Claud. In Ruf. II.76). But his following was not an expression of local landed power - after all Rufinus was in Constantinople while his ancestral property was in Gaul. It was a bodyguard[22] for the man who was ruling the East while the Emperor Theodosius was campaigning against a usurper in the West.

Bucellarii did become a threat to the imperial administration (Cod. Iust. II.10 of 468), but this does not mean that they originated as bodies of private retainers. On the contrary, the 6th century papyrus evidence as interpreted by J. Gascou (1976: 143-56) suggests that the bucellarii of the Apion family and other great houses of Egypt were enrolled at the instigation of the imperial government.

The bucellarii of the Apions were part of the household of these great men and were maintained by them. But it seems that they were enrolled on the instructions of the government (Gascou 1976: 146f on P. Oxy. 156), and that their payment was annona, and therefore presumably counted against the estate's tax bill.[23] They were employed for local police duties like keeping order in the hippodrome, also for tax-collecting. In military emergencies the bucellarii of the various houses were concentrated and put at the disposal of the Duke of the Thebaid (Gascou 1976: 150). This arrangement might be called 'privatisation' of part of the administration of the defence forces.

The head of the house and therefore the patron of the bucellarii might not be an office holder himself. On one occasion it was a woman. But the Apion family produced many holders of high imperial office (PLRE II. s.v. Apion 1-2; Strategius 8; 4 stemma 27), and there is no reason why the family's force of armed retainers might not have originated when one of the Apions held high military office. The relationship between a bucellarius and his 'lord' was one of patron and client.[24] It would therefore not have been limited to the duration of a particular period of office-holding, or even the lifetime of a single generation of 'patron' or bucellarius, but would continue from father to son unless it was deliberately ended by the parties concerned,[25] or by the imperial government.[26]

One might ask why the government helped to build up this potentially dangerous institution. The government's policy can be quite plausibly explained as a response to recruiting problems of the late 4th century and after. As we have seen this was a time when the army had to be expanded in a hurry before major campaigns, and when the commander-in-chief himself led expeditions to the frontier for recruiting purposes before risking confrontation with a major foe. This was the time when at a lower level a leader like Sarus the Goth might build up a band of dependent federates. These men must have faced a serious problem, if as I have argued, they recruited for campaigns rather than for a lifetime of military service: they could not offer their men a certain future. Now the institution of the bucellariate, because it established a formal relationship of patron and client between commander and men, gave the latter the assurance that it would be a powerful man's responsibility to provide for them, without imposing an expensive obligation on the state. I am not suggesting that when Stilicho for instance recruited Germans they all became his bucellarii but that perhaps the most valuable and most influential among them did. In this way Gainas, or Stilicho, or Bonifatius or Aetius (the only one whose followers are actually described as bucellarii) could provide themselves with a core of loyal and reliable men around whom they could build up a much larger military following.

Notes

1. Tribal units. Ambros. Ep. 40.22; Pacat. Pan 12.39.2; Barbarians in Roman units: Zos. IV.31, 45.3.

2. See Hoffmann 1969: 81-3 on evidence of Concordia sarcophagi; ibid 137ff. on the Germans recruited into auxilia in contrast with citizens into legions; ibid 299 on Germans in the scholae. But after 378 Germans were recruited into all kinds of Roman units: Zos. IV. 31.

3. Most clearly in the narrative of the fall of Stilicho: Zos V. 31; 33-5. 4. E.g. Armenians and Iberians of Themistius Or. XVI. 207 a of AD 383; XV. 189d of AD 381 and XVIII 219 of AD 384, also in Stilicho's army in AD 395: see Hoffmann 1969: ii, 191 n.268.

4. E.g. Armenians and Iberians of Themistius Or. XVI.207a of AD 383; XV.189d of AD 381 and XVIII.219 of AD 384, also in Stilicho's army in AD 395: see Hoffmann 1969: ii, 191 n. 268.

5. Cavalry could only be recruited in certain regions of the Empire, especially in the Balkans and North Africa, and also from barbarians across the border, e.g. the comites of Amm. Marc. XVIII.9.4; cf Hoffmann 1969: 243ff.

6. At the expense of regular subsidies to barbarians, and of having to leave one frontier undefended when campaigning on another, cf Croke 1977: 347-67. See also inadequate defence of Mesopotamia in early 6th century: Josh.Styl. Chron. 53, 81.

7. I would argue that Alaric's Goths shared characteristics with the federates assembled by Roman officers discussed below.

8.   Zos. V.219: Gainas tried to lead his men back to their (or only his) homeland. Recruiting: Soc. HE VI.6 καὶ τᾶν τὸ Γότθων ἔθνος ἐκ τῆς αὐτου Χώρας μετεπεμψατο. Soz. VIII.8.1 τοὺς ὁμοφύλους αὐτῷ Γότθων ἐκ τῶν ἰδίων νομῶν εἰς Ρωμαίους μετεπέμψατο I would take this to be outside the Empire, otherwise Albert 1984: 111-2.

9.   Generals were deprived of the right to issue probatoria by Zeno. See Jones 1964: 668 on Cod. Iust. XII.35.17 of AD 472.

10.   Claud. IV Cons. Hon. 485; proiecta pelle Gelonus militat ...in Latios ritus transistis Alani. The recruiting of 401, B.Get 400-3 has no allusions to Romanisation and the Alans are described as externa auxilia, B.Get. 580-1.

11.   See Hoffman 1969: 358-67 (summed up p.365); 15 units before 398, 10 possibly 14 after 398, and, in Hoffman's view, but not necessarily, before 406.   The chronology remains uncertain.

12.   Philos. XI. 8.   They served as cavalry: Claud. In Eutr. II.176 "Geticae dux improbus alae".   Gainas' force too included much cavalry: Synesius De Prov. 2.1 (1260).

13.   Socr. HE VI.6; Soz. VIII. 4.2.   Albert (1984: 89) argues that Tribigild must have been one of the Greutungi, otherwise he would have lacked authority to lead the revolt.   I would argue that his authority came not from being a fellow tribesman but from his Roman rank.

14.   If he had not suffered a setback in Gaul in 407 (Zos. VI 2.4-5), or if he had been appointed successor to Stilicho in 408 (Zos. V. 36.2).

15.   Benjamin 1892 and Haldon 1979; and 1984 assume that foederati of Justinian were recruited by their commanders; Maspero 1912 and Jones 1964: 664f, argued that they were individually recruited and assigned Roman officers like other regular units.

16.   Jones 1964: III, 38 n.62 on Oros. VII. 40.7, perhaps also the post-Theodosian Western auxilia named after barbarians: Attecoti, Marcomanni, Brisigaui, Mauri; cf Jones 1964: III, 355.

17.   Aug. Ep. 220.6.   He clearly had a following even though the word bucellarii is not used.

18.   Hence the barbarians' eagerness for Roman commands. Zos. V.13.1, 17.4 (Gainas).   Claud. In Eutr. II. 178ff; 317-21 gifts and title; cf magister militum rejected. (Tribigild); but Zos. V. 5.4, Claud. B. Get. 535 ff; Zos V. 31, 48.3 (Alaric).

19.   Nov. Theod. II.XV.2 of AD 444: Valerian decurion, cf Emesa; Cod. Iust. IX.12.10 of AD 468 the East generally; see also below on bucellarii of the Apions in Egypt.

20.   Germ. XIII, but bucellarii (at least their 'other ranks') were dependents rather than companions of their chief.

472

21. Stilicho: Zos V.34, but at least not displayed during the consulate in 400 (Claud. Cons. Stil. III 220-3; Bonifatius: Aug. Ep. 220.6; Aetius: John of Antioch Frg. 201.4-5; Aspar: Malalas 371; Belisarius: Procop. BG III.1.18-20.

22. Not mentioned in account of assassination (Claud. In Ruf. II.400).

23. Gascou 1976 on P. Oxy. 156 and P. Wilk. Chrest. 471. It is difficult to believe that Belisarius had undertaken to pay 7,000 bucellarii (Procop. Goth. III. 1. 18-20) for the rest of their lives. Presumably their annona came from taxation. Belisarius gave them presents in addition.

24. Leges Visigothorum 216 cf 217. 10 qui in patrocinio est = bucellarius; cf also Claud. In Ruf. II.76.

25. Or perhaps only by the bucellarius, Leges Visigothorum 18 frg. 310.

26. By a general law like Cod. Iust. XII.10 of AD 468 which presumably orders the disarming and not the dismissing of armed retainers, or by redistributing the bucellarii as after the disgrace of Belisarius (Procop. Hist. Arc. IV.17). The command of Bonifatius 3 (including bucellarii?) passed to his son-in-law, Sebastianus 3 (Hyd. Lem. 99). Aetius married his widow and inherited property (John of Ant. frg. 201-3), and perhaps also his military following. Aetius' bucellarii passed to the Emperor Valentinian III (John Ant. frg. 201.5).

Bibliography

ALBERT, G.	1984	Goten in Konstantinopel. Paderborn.
BENJAMIN, C.	1892	De Iustiniani imp. Aetate Quaestiones Militares. Berlin.
CAMERON, A.D.	1976	Claudian. Oxford.
CLAUDE, D.	1971	Adel, Kirche und Donigtum in Westgotenreich. Sigmaringen.
CLEMENTE, G.	1968	La Notitia Dignitatum. Cagliari.
CROKE, D.	1977	Evidence for the invasion of Thrace in 422. Greek, Roman and Byzantine Studies XVIII: 347-67.
DEMOUGEOT, E.	1975	La Notitia Dignitatum et l'histoire de l'Empire d'Occident au debut du Ve siècle. Latomus XXXIV: 1079-1134.

DIESNER, H-J.   1972   Das Buccelariertum von Stilicho und
                                  Sarus bis auf Aetius. Klio LIV:
                                  321-50.

GASCOU, J.   1976   L'Institution des bucellaires.
                                  Bulletin de l'Institute Francais
                                  d'Archéologie Orientale LXXVI: 143-
                                  56.

HALDON, J.F.   1979   Recruitment and Conscription in the
                                  Byzantine Army 556-950. Vienna
                                  (Sitzungsbericht Oest. Akad. 357).

                     1984   Byzantine Praetorians. Bonn.

HOFFMAN, D.   1969   Das Spatrömische Bewegungsheer und
                                  die Notitia Dignitatum. Dusseldorf
                                  (Epigrapische Studien 7).

JONES, A.H.M.   1964   Later Roman Empire. Oxford.

LECRIVAIN, CH.A.   1980   Les soldats privés au Bas-Empire.
                                  Mélanges d'Archéologie et
                                  d'Histoire de l'École Francaise de
                                  Rome X: 267-83.

MANN, J.C.   1976   What was the Notitia Dignitatum
                                  for? In R. Goodburn and P. Barthol-
                                  omew (eds.) Aspects of the Notitia
                                  Dignitatum: 1-8. Oxford (BAR,
                                  International Series 15).

MASPERO, J.   1912   Organisation militaire de l'Égypte
                                  Byzantine. Paris.

                     1912   φοιδερᾶτοι et στρατιῶται dans
                                  l'Armée Byzantine au VIe siècle.
                                  Byzantinische Zeitschrift XXI: 97-
                                  109.

MÜLLER, A.   1912   Das Heer Justinians nach Prokop und
                                  Agathias. Philologus 71: 101-38.

PATLAGEAN, E.   1977   Pauvreté économique et pauvreté
                                  sociale à Byzance, 4e-7e siecles.
                                  Paris.

SEECK, O.   1976   Notitia Dignitatum. Frankfurt
                                  (repr. 1962).

TEALL, J.   1965   The Barbarians in Justinian's Army.
                                  Speculum XL: 294-322.

THOMPSON, E.A.   1969   The Goths in Spain. Oxford.

XIX

474

WARD, J.H.   1974   The Notitia Dignitatum. *Latomus* XXXIII: 397-434.

ZEUMER, K.   1902   *Leges Visigothorum*, MGH *Legum Sectio I*. Hanover and Leipzig.

XX

THE DEFENCES OF SYRIA IN THE SIXTH CENTURY

In writing about the eastern frontier of the Roman Empire one often comes across the view that there were two lines of frontier defences, an inner line and an outer one. Thus A. Poidebard in 1934 described as the interior limes the line of forts along the military road leading from Bostra via Palmyra to the Euphrates and Sura. He thought that posts to the east of this line constituted an outer limes which had however been much reduced since the loss of Dua Europos[1]. In 1945 R. Mouterde and P. Poidebard in their classical work 'Le Limes de Chalcis' distinguished a first line of defence on the Euphrates from a second barrier organised in depth in the area east of Chalcis[2]. B. Rubin in his 'Zeitalter Justinians' has followed the scheme of Mouterde and Poidebard and talks of fortresses of the front-line and a second system of defences in depth[3]. M. Gichon has explained the failure of the Roman defences of Palestine in the face of Persian and Arab invaders by the defection of the tribes guarding the outer limes, and analyses the fortifications of southern Palestine into an inner and an outer zone of defence[4].

I wish to argue that the distinction between an outer and an inner limes whether at Chalcis[5] or elsewhere has no basis in the ancient sources. It seems to be based on mistaken interpretation of a very small number of passages. In around 528 the Arab chieftain Arethas (Al Arith) of the Kindite family[6] who was probably a refugee in the Roman Empire[7] clashed with Diomedes, the *silentiarius, dux* of Palestine and was compelled to withdraw 'into the inner limes'[8]. Two years later the ally of the Persians, the formidable Al Mundhir[9] raided Syria as far as Antioch and then withdrew 'across the outer limes'[10]. So here we seem to have reference to two distinct zones of limes, an inner and an outer one.

But appearances are misleading. When Theophanes reported the same events, using either Malalas himself or a source also used by Malalas, he changed the key word, substituting

---

* I wish to thank Professor G. W. Bowersock for his paper 'Limes Arabicus', due to be published in Harward Studies in Class. Philol., in which he disproves the existence of a double line of defences on the Arabian frontier.
[1] A. Poidebard, La trace de Rome dans le désert de Syrie: Le limes de Trajan à la conquète Arabe. Atlas (Paris 1934) 127 f.
[2] R. Mouterde – P. Poidebard, Le Limes de Chalcis, organisation de la steppe en haute Syrie Romaine (Paris 1945) 230 f.
[3] B. Rubin, Das Zeitalter Justinians I (Berlin 1960) 273 f.
[4] M. Gichon, The Origin of the Limes Palaestinae and the Major Phases in its Development. Akten 6. Limeskongreß 175 ff.
[5] Malalas XII 295–6 = P.G. XCVII 448 uses expression limes of Chalcis.
[6] G. Olinder, The Kings of Kinda of the family of Akil al-Murar (Lund 1927).
[7] On his story cf. B. Rubin, op. cit. (note 3) 272 f. – S. Smith (Events in Arabia in the 6th century A. D. Bull. School Orient. Afr. Stud. 16, 1954, 425 ff. esp. 446) shows that he was not a phylarch. Malalas and Theophanes are wrong. Otherwise: I. Kawar, The Patriciate of Arethas. Byz. Zeitschr. 52, 1959, 321 ff. esp. 341.
[8] Malalas XII 434 = P. G. XCVII 641: εἰς τὸ ἐνδότερον λίμιτον ἐπὶ τὰ Ἰνδικά. – Date: Th. Nöldeke, Die Ghassanischen Fürsten aus dem Hause Gafnas. Abhandl. d. Preuss. Akad. d. Wiss. (Berlin 1887) 11. – S. Smith (op. cit. [note 7]) dates incident 'about 425'.
[9] G. Rothstein, Die Dynastie der Lahmiden in al-Hira (Berlin 1899).
[10] Malalas XII 445 = P. G. XCVII 656: διὰ τοῦ ἐξωτέρου λιμίτου.

ἐσώτερον, inner, in both places[11]. Since he cannot have had independent knowledge of the 6th century frontier, he must have thought that the seemingly opposite words found in the two passages actually meant the same, namely, up-country, remote. That this was so is confirmed by the fact that Theophanes applied .the word ἐσώτερον to the limes on which Palmyra was situated[12]. This city can never have been anywhere but at the outer edge of the Roman Empire. When Theophanes uses ἐσώτερον he must intend to describe the extreme remoteness of the limes of Palmyra.

That the 'inner limes' is simply the remote, up-country limes is also shown by the fact that Ammianus places Circesium in this zone. Diocletianus fortified this city *cum in ipsis barbarorum confiniis interiores limites ordinaret, ne vagarentur per Syriam Persae*[13]. Circesium lay inside the junction of the Khabur and Euphrates rivers. The Khabur marked the frontier of the two empires: by crossing the river Julian started his invasion of the Persian empire[14]. So there could not have been a second 'outer' limes to the east of Circesium, there simply was no room. Ammianus is pointing out that Diocletian fortified a place even in so remote a region because he was impressed by the recently demonstrated vulnerability of Syria to Persian attack.

Thus an 'inner' limes does not imply an outer one. It simply means a limes which was far inland or up-country[15]. Limes itself has a variety of meanings starting with military highway[16]. It sometimes means a fortified line but can also be used to describe a frontier area without any implication as to its fortification at all[17]. In one of our two accounts of border incidents limes must mean simply frontier zone: it would have been absurd for the fugitive Arethas to retreat precisely into the line of frontier fortification. In the second incident the meaning could be that Al Mundhir broke through the fortified line but much more likely Malalas and Theophanes wish to indicate that he retreated across the border zone.

If there was no double line of fortifications, how were Syria and Antioch, its capital, defended?

It is certain that Diocletian greatly strengthened the fortifications of the eastern frontier[18]. It is likely that his system was based on a line of forts situated at regular intervals along a

---

[11] Flight of Arethas: Theoph. 179, 17 (De Boor) = P.G. CVIII 413. – Retreat of Al Mundhir: Theoph. 178, 15 (De Boor) = P.G. CVIII 404. – Theophanes writing 810–13 often is very close to Malalas' version of events. It has not been established whether this is due to direct use or common sources: RE. V A (1934) 2127 f. s. v. Theophanes (G. Ostrogorsky).

[12] Theoph. 174, 14 (De Boor) = P.G. CVIII 404. In the corresponding passage Malalas has no epithet: XII 426 = P.G. XCVII 628.

[13] Amm. Marc. XXIII 5, 2.

[14] Amm. Marc. XXIII 5, 4–5.

[15] Use of *interior* in sense of remote, far inland, up-country: Cic., Tusc. I 23,54: *interiores nationes*; Antoninus Placentinus, Itinerarium 36 = P.L. LXXII 911 = CSEL. XXXIX 183: *de interiore parte heremi*. In Greek: V. Alex. Acoem. 33 = P. Or. VI 5. In Syriac Josh. Styl., chron. 57 (ed. Wright). Dr. D. Metzer has kindly reminded me that in Ptolemy ἡ ἐντὸς of Libya (IV 4) and of Aethiopia (IV 7) must mean the areas situated furthest from Rome.

[16] A. Piganiol, La notion de limes. Akten 5. Limeskongreß 119 ff.

[17] R. Devréesse (Le patriarcat d'Antioche [Paris 1945] 270 n. 1) by far the best discussion of the whole problem, cites uses of λίμιτον without implication of fortification.

[18] Amm. Marc. XXIII 5, 2; Malalas XII 308. – On *strata Diocletiana* milestones: D. van Berchem, L'armée de Dioclétien et la réforme constantinienne (Paris 1952) 13 f.

military road leading through Damascus and Palmyra to Sura on the Euphrates[19]. Some cavalry units were stationed at strategically situated road junctions further west. Altogether cavalry formations predominated[20]. No doubt this was the only way in which the great empty spaces could be patrolled. But the line had real defensive capacity[21] with (in our area) a legion at Oresa and another at Sura. Circesium on the north bank of the Euphrates had a legion, too[22]. Almost the whole system was situated, unusually, on steppe but within the 100 mm rain line[23]. To the west of the main line, between the 'elbow' of the Euphrates and the city of Chalcis, was a network of roads, fortified road centres and water points which Mouterde and Poidebard following Malalas have caused to be known as the limes of Chalcis[24].

But by the sixth century the defensive arrangements seem to have been changed. Most significantly the defensive line through the steppe has disappeared. In 536 a large group of Arabs allied to the Persians crossed the frontier to seek grazing land in a time of drought[25]. Before 540 Arab allies of the Roman and Persian empires disputed whether some grazing areas known as *strata* were part of the Roman Empire or not[26]. Neither incident could have happened if the frontier had been continuously patrolled by the Roman army. In those years the Arab allies of the Persians claimed that they found little opposition to their raids into Syria[27] and military history confirms their claim[28].

The apparent absence of the frontier troops raises problems. There is no doubt that *limitanei* were still considered a standard part of frontier organisation in the reign of Justinian. Laws about them were republished in the new Code[29]. When Justinian organised the frontier of the re-conquered African provinces he re-established *limitanei*[30]. *Limitanei* are mentioned in a number of widely separated areas of the empire in the sixth century[31]. What then had happened to the units on the *strata Diocletiana*?

Answers can be suggested. Already in the 4th century the government had difficulty in keeping frontier units at a proper standard of military discipline. The archive of Abinnaeus

---

[19] A. Poidebard, op. cit. (note 1) map in Atlas. – D. van Berchem (op. cit. [note 18] 27) lists locations of units mentioned in the Notitia Dignitatum (Or. XXXIII) identified in Syria but enough are still unidentified to leave the pattern uncertain: D. Hoffmann, Das spätrömische Bewegungsheer und die Notitia Dignitatum. Epigr. Studien 7, 1970, 416 ff.

[20] The duke of Syria and Euphratensis commanded 12 cavalry and six infantry units: Not. Dig. Or. XXXIII.

[21] Diocletian's object was to prevent the Persians from overrunning Syria as they had done in the 3rd century: Amm. Marc. XXIII 5, 2.

[22] Not. Dig. Or. XXXV 24.

[23] A. Poidebard, op. cit. (note 1) Atlas: pl. 11.

[24] R. Mouterde – P. Poidebard, op. cit. (note 2).

[25] Marcell. Comes, chron. 536 = Monum. Germ. (Auct. Ant. XI) 105: *ipso namque anno ob nimiam siccitatem pastura in Perside denegata circiter quindecim milia Saracenorum ab Alamundaro cum Chabo et Hercido phylarchis limitem Euphratesiae ingressa ubi Batzas dux eos partim blanditiis partim districtione pacifica fovit et inhiantes bellare repressit.*

[26] On *strata Diocletiana*: D. van Berchem, op. cit. (note 18). – Procopius II 1, 3 ff.

[27] Advice of Alamoundaras (Al Mundhir) in Procopius (I 17, 34) contrasts fortified and garrisoned state of Mesopotamia and Osroene with undefended condition of Euphratensis and Syria. The Arab exaggerated the garrisons and fortification of Mesopotamia.

[28] Esp. Al Mundhir's raids of 523 (Zach. Mityl., chron. VIII 5) and 529 (Theoph. 178, 12 [De Boor]). On Persian invasions see below.

[29] C.J. I 31, 4; 46, 4; XI 60, 3 republish. Th. II Nov. 24 of 443.

[30] C.J. I 27, 2. 8.

[31] A. H. M. Jones, The Later Roman Empire (Oxford 1964) 660.

suggests that from his unit in the Fayum a considerable number of men were permanently absent[32]. We are told of the practice of keeping dead men on the roll so that their commander might draw their pay and rations[33]. In the circumstances some units may have faded out. Moreover the Romans as a rule avoided the stationing of troops in desert or steppe[34]. Diocletian's line was an untypical arrangement. Perhaps the units were simply withdrawn, but if they were withdrawn this is not likely to have been a consequence of Jovian's peace in 364, as has been suggested by Mouterde and Poidebard[35]. The surrender to the Persians of the Nisibis-Singara-Bezabde triangle brought about a great weakening of the eastern frontier. Henceforth the Persians controlled Nisibis, a secure base well supplied with corn and water much closer to potential objectives whether in Mesopotamia or in Syria[36]. But this was no reason why troops should be withdrawn from the edge of the Syrian desert. Quite the contrary. In fact the units seem still to have been in place in the early 5th century[37].

But whenever the line ceased to be held the disappearance of the troops must have raised problems. Their functions would have to be performed in some other way. There was peaceful frontier control. The Romans were concerned who crossed the frontier in either direction[38]. Trade at least with the Persian empire was channelled through the single city of Daras[39]. If nothing else the government was intent on collecting customs' dues[40]. Even when the actual frontier was no longer held by Roman troops, traffic in and out of the empire must still have been controlled. Then there was the problem of resisting armed invasion. This involved two distinct threats: the perpetual menace of nomad raiders and from time to time the danger of invasion by the Persian army. The problems must have been solved somehow. On the solutions employed we have evidence of fortifications, described and actual, and the history of campaigns. We will examine them in turn.

There is a great deal of evidence about fortifications. The difficulty lies in establishing their dates and precise function. Outstandingly informative are the chapters in Procopius 'de aedificiis' which deal with Justinian's fortifications in the provinces of Mesopotamia, Osroene, Euphratensis and Syria[41]. The information is so detailed for the first two provinces that it looks as if Procopius had in front of him an official document. This would seem to

---

[32] R. M. Price (The Role of Military Men in Syria and Egypt from Constantine to Theodosius [unpublished Ph. D. thesis of Oxford University 1974] 225 n. 55) cites evidence from H. I. Bell – V. Martin – E. G. Turner, The Abinnaeus Papyri (Oxford 1962) notably P. Ab. 28, 37, 48, 32, 52. The soldiers were locally recruited and had relatives near the camp: P. Ab. 26, 12, 33 f., 48–59. Possibly absentees continued to draw *annona*: P. Ab. 4 l. 17.

[33] Themist., or. 136 b; Liban., or. XLVII 31; Procopius, hist. Arc. XXIV 5–6.

[34] P. Trousset, Recherches sur le limes tripolitanus (Paris 1974).

[35] R. Mouterde – P. Poidebard, op. cit. (note 2) 237.

[36] Procopius I 17, 25. But he is wrong to suggest that the Persians attacked through Euphratensis before they had won Nisibis. Under Constantius Nisibis belonged to the empire yet his long Persian wars were fought between the Euphrates and Tigris. The fact is possession of Nisibis must have facilitated invasion of Syria along the Euphrates as much, or more, than invasion of Mesopotamia. Nisibis constituted a bridgehead on cultivated land on the Roman side of a belt of desert separating the two empires: L. Dillemann, La haute Mésopotamie orientale et les pays adjacents (Paris 1962) 73 fig. 9. An important book.

[37] V. Alex. Acoem. = P. Or. VI 32.

[38] Cf. Anastasius' regulations for *limitanei* of Libya: SEG. IX 356; G. Olivero, Documenti Antichi dell' Africa Italiana II. Cirenaica (Rome 1933) 135 ff. § 11 deals with frontier control.

[39] Menander Protector § 3 and 5 of peace treaty of 561: FHG. IV 212.

[40] A. H. M. Jones, op. cit. (note 31) 429 ff. 825 f.; G. Tchalenko, Villages antiques de la Syrie du Nord III (Paris 1958) 40 ff.

[41] Procopius II.

have listed buildings by province, and to have had distinct sections for cities and for a much larger number of small forts[42]. It has been pointed out that the smaller forts in Mesopotamia – in the modern meaning of the name – cluster round the margin of cultivated land, that is on the edge of the land roamed by nomads[43]. Unfortunately the account, which is after all part of a literary work, becomes increasingly selective so that the fortifications of Euphratensis do not include mere forts, or only very few, and the section on Syria has only the great cities of Antioch, Chalcis and Cyrrhus (the latter should be in Euphratensis).

Fortunately Procopius can be supplemented by actual remains. There are first of all a number of forts south and south-west of Chalcis, of Justinianic or post-Justinianic date, which Sauvaget has described as the limes of Justinian[44]. Then there are the very large number of fortified enclosures of various shapes and sizes which make up the so called limes of Chalcis. The difficulty in interpreting this evidence lies in the fact that there has been very little excavation and the dating of many of the structures described and mapped by Mouterde and Poidebard is quite uncertain. They probably range from the early empire to the Arab occupation[45]. We are faced with a palimpsest of systems of fortification, successive layers of which have still to be disentangled. But it is significant that the enclosures are densest in the area between Chalcis and the Euphrates around the marshes of the lake of Gabbulon and around Anasartha. They lie across one of the routes into Syria from the Euphrates. They are also situated on the margin of cultivated land. In this the enclosures of the limes of Chalcis and of the limes of Justinian correspond to the smaller forts listed in Procopius' account of the fortifications of Mesopotamia.

There is unfortunately little evidence about the way these forts were used or the people who used them. Especially there is practically no inscriptional evidence for the presence of the Roman army[46]. There are a few building inscriptions, all civilian.

At Bouz el Hanzir south of the lake of Gabbulon a fort situated inside a wider enclosure was built in 506–507 A. D. by order of a bishop, perhaps of Anasartha[47]. At Rasm er Rbeyt a wall and ditch were built by an unknown but orthodox individual in 470–471[48]. In 533–534 two men with the title of financial officials (τραχτευταὶ) built a fortified animal enclosure (πυργοσηχών) at Rasmel Haǧal. They also built a chapel. Their residence was near by[49]. Evidently they were local magnates. At Tell Makroum Mouterde and Poidebard have identified a fortified estate centre of unknown date[50]. At El Touba a land owner built a large fortified farm, including a granary for the public good. The date was between 326 and 353[51].

---

[42] A few places are located in the wrong province. Thus Gabbulon is in Euphratensis instead of Syria while Cyrrhus, properly in Euphratensis, is treated with Syrian cities. Callinicum is placed in Euphratensis though on the north bank of Euphrates. Neocaesarea is mentioned twice. The few exceptions do not invalidate the rule.

[43] L. Dillemann, op. cit. (note 36) 227 fig. 31.

[44] Cf. J. Sauvaget, Les Ghassanides et Sergiopolis. Byzantion 14, 1939, 115 ff.

[45] J. Sauvaget, op. cit. 124 n. 1.

[46] R. M. Price, op. cit. (note 32) 62 ff.

[47] R. Mouterde – P. Poidebard, op. cit. (note 2) 73; IGLSyr. 270.

[48] R. Mouterde – P. Poidebard, op. cit. (note 2) 81. There also is a *tetrapyrgium* of Diocletianic type.

[49] R. Mouterde – P. Poidebard, op. cit. (note 2) 202 ff.; IGLSyr. 316–320 and errata p. 382.

[50] R. Mouterde – P. Poidebard, op. cit. (note 2) 157.

[51] R. Mouterde – P. Poidebard, op. cit. (note 2) 197 ff. – The owner Bellichos, son of Libianus (IGLSyr. 338–340; R. Mouterde – P. Poidebard, op. cit. [note 2] inscr. 30), claims public credit for the expenditure.

At Hanaser (Anasartha) Gregorios Abimenos, a rich man, restored the walls and gates of the city between 594 and 604[52].

It may be significant that some of the magnates of the area, especially from Anasartha, have Arab names or connections. So Mavia, the lady who founded a martyrium of S. Thomas outside Anasartha, was probably a descendant of the formidable Arab princess of the same name who in the 4th century, defeated a Roman army and married a Roman general[53]. The illustrious Silbanus who founded a martyrium at Anasartha was son-in-law of an Arab phylarch and describes himself as powerful among Arabs[54]. Judging by his name, Abimenos, who restored the defences of the city, may well have been an Arab. He may indeed have been a phylarch.

The evidence about builders of fortifications in the limes of Chalcis does not amount to much but such as it is points in one direction. Fortifications were built by private individuals especially the religious and secular magnates to shelter themselves, their neighbours and their crops and animals from marauders. It is also likely that some of the primitively-built walls enclosing towns or villages were put up by the communities. If the imperial government contributed it – uncharacteristically – did not advertise the fact.

The situation is not quite the same in the limes of Justinian, the series of fortresses constructed in the second half of the 6th century, which Sauvaget saw as part of a systematic programme of fortification[55], and Devréesse interpreted as a barrier protecting Apamea and the valley of the Orontes[56]. Some of these works certainly seem to show the hand of the imperial government. The complex of palace, church and barracks at Quasr ibn Wardan built in the style and materials of Constantinople must surely have been put up by the imperial authorities. Presumably this was a headquarters[57]. The same architectural style was employed in a *castrum* or barracks in the centre of Il Anderin (Androna). But this we learn from an inscription was actually built by a private individual for the benefit of his native land[58]. At Idjaz south of Kerratin a wall has a long but vague inscription which implies that it was part of a structure built to safeguard the inhabitants[59]. At Umm there is a fortress described as a ξενέων of St. Theodore which Lassus has interpreted as a barracks for

---

[52] R. Mouterde – P. Poidebard, op. cit. (note 2) 208; IGLSyr. 281. 288. 298. – IGLSyr. 288 suggests an imperial subsidy. He may have been a phylarch; in 281 he is πανεύφημος. In IGLSyr. 288 a πανεύφημος person (name lost) is mentioned between emperors and praetorian prefect.

[53] R. Mouterde – P. Poidebard, op. cit. (note 2) 194 inscr. 20; Socrates H. E. IV 36; Sozomen H. E. VI 38.

[54] R. Mouterde – P. Poidebard, op. cit. (note 2) 193 f. – Idjaz 546–547: see note 59. – Walls of Chalcis 550: Am. Arch. Exp. Syr. III inscr. 305–306, Justinian given credit. – Il Hallâbât 556–557: Princeton Arch. Exp. Syr. III B inscr. 1057. – Androna 559: ibid. inscr. 915. – Quasr ibn Wardan: Barracks 561, ibid. inscr. 906; palace 564, ibid. inscr. 908. – Stabl Autar: ibid. II B 63 ff. III B inscr. 947.

[55] J. Sauvaget, Byzantion 14, 1939, 122 f. – IGLSyr. 297: Umm el Halikil undated. See below note 60.

[56] R. Devréesse, op. cit (note 17) 26.

[57] Described in Princeton Arch. Exp. Syr. II B 26 ff. – Ibid. III B inscr. 908 reads simply πάντα εἰς δόξαν Θεοῦ.

[58] Ibid. III B 45–47 inscr. 915: Φιλοτιμίᾳ Θωμᾷ καὶ σπουδῇ 'Ιακώβου ἀνεψιοῦ αὐτοῦ. . . . . τῇ πατρίδι δι' ὧν εὐγνωμονεῖς ἀνεφάν[ης] σωτήρ. – Reading slightly different in IGLSyr. 1682. – Thomas also provided a public bath: Princeton Arch. Exp. Syr. III B 48–49 inscr. 918 = IGLSyr. 1687.

[59] Ibid. 92–93 inscr. 1016 = IGLSyr. 1598: οὐ φοβήσομαι ἀπὸ μυριάδων λαοῦ τῶν κύκλῳ συνεπιτιθημένων μοι (Psalm III 7). The editor conjectures that the wall was part of a barracks.

troops in transit[60]. At Kerratin (Taroutia) an ex-official of the emperor's private property built fortifications to be a 'bulwark of safety' in the area[61]. The latest of these constructions has already been mentioned. It is part of the work on the walls of Anasartha in the reign of Phocas and this at least appears to have received a financial contribution from the emperor[62].

These fortifications are all more or less in the same area. But they are – I think – too different in date, in place and – as far as this can be established – in building to be considered part of a systematic programme of fortification. I also imagine that normally fortifications put up on government initiative, or with government finance, would record the fact[63]. It is therefore likely that the fortresses of the limes of Justinian too were put up independently of each other, mainly by local inhabitants in response to circumstances which we cannot know. The main function of most of them will have been not strategic but simply to protect the local population[64].

This does not exclude the possibility that some of the forts had a permanent garrison. A locality or a monastery might ask for the protection of soldiers[65]. The government might even be concerned to establish something like a line of fortifications so as to encourage people to live there[66] or simply to make possible a modicum of frontier control[67].

---

[60] J. Lassus, Inventaire archéologique de la région au nord-est de Hama (Paris 1935) 65 inscr. 31: ξενέων τοῦ ἁγίου Θεοδώρου. Not dated. Lassus refers to Wadington 2327. 2524 from Soada. The enclosure with its internal buttresses resembles a fortified, perhaps originally military, enclosure surrounding a church at Androna. Princeton Arch. Exp. Syr. II B 59 fig. 54. This is dated 528. This enclosure must be distinguished from the architecturally metropolitan barracks mentioned earlier.

[61] Princeton Arch. Exp. Syr. III B inscr. 992–993 = IGLSyr. 1630–1631 (509–510 A. D.): ὁ τοῦ βασιλέως πραγμάτων Ἰωάννης πισ[τὸς] πεφυκὼς ἐν πόνοις ὑπηρέτης, i. e. formerly employed in res privata ?

[62] Ibid. III B inscr. 1108 = IGLSyr. 281 (604). 288 (594?): τῆς βασιλείας [πόλις?] δωρήμασιν καταφρογοῦσα βαρ[βάρων] καταδρομῆς.

[63] Often buildings not built by emperor attributed to him: G. Downey, Imperial Building Records in Malalas. Byz. Zeitschr. 38, 1938, 1 ff. 299 ff. The walls of Chalcis (see note 54; Procopius, aed.) were attributed to Justinian. But the other Syrian buildings of Justinian's supposed 'limes' were not. One might add to note 54 Quasr el Mharram: three strong points in a village constructed 551 (J. Lassus, op. cit. (note 60) 143 and inscr. 81) and Abū Habbe a walled enclosure with angle towers built 566 by one Macedonius through his notarios (ibid. 47–51 inscr. 26).

[64] The building of forts will have depended on the extent of the danger from nomads, the availability of money private or imperial and the influence of patrons. Some fortresses were no doubt built with strategic objectives but far fewer than is generally thought. Even Amida was not fortified to defend N. Mesopotamia, but ut accolae suffugium possint habere tutissimum (Amm. Marc. XVIII 9, 1). Callinicum without a garrison and with its walls in disrepair was still a refuge for country folk (Procopius II 21, 32).

[65] Cyr. Scyth., vita Sabae 178. Monastery needs protection. Dux sent imperial money with which the abbot would build a fort. This would later receive a garrison maintained at public expense. This was under Anastasius (491–518) when Arab raiders were active (Evagrius H. E. III 36; Theoph. 141, 1–17 [De Boor]) and it was imperial policy to protect monasteries (John Niciu, chron. 89, 33 [ed. Charles] 125). Justinian carried out the same policy in Sinai (also in Palestine III). According to Eutychius' annales in P. G. CXXL 1070–1071 he responded to request of the monks. Procopius (V 8, 9) says nothing of this but adds that the fortress was to prevent surprise attacks by the Saracens on Palestine. The surviving walls of St. Catherine's monastery are formidable. Entychius describes the garrison as slaves sent with their wives and children to protect the monastery who would receive their supplies from Egypt. The 800 condomae at Pheran (Antoninus Placentinus, Itinerarium = CSEL. XXXIX 186) probably had the same status whatever that was. Perhaps they were burgarii (C. T. VII 14,1 [398]).

[66] C. J. I 27, 2.8: ut alii provinciales videntes eos (sc. limitaneos) ad illa loca se conferant.

[67] C. J. Kraemer (Excavations at Nessana III [Princeton 1958] 122 f.) on the Beersheba edict of Anastasius suggests that there was still a line of garrisons like that of Nessana spread along the southern edge of cultivated Palestine. Cf. also A. Alt, Limes Palaestinae. Palaestina-Jahrb. 26, 1930, 43 ff.

But if the limit of the steppe was intermittently guarded by camps of *limitanei* these areas will not have known so sharp a distinction between soldiers and civilians as existed in earlier periods. At this time all *limitanei* had land which they farmed[68] and they might well not live in their camp[69]. In an emergency, on the other hand, civilians would be taken into the camp and by no means only then. The rich whom Alexander Acoemetus offended by the suggestion that they should distribute their wealth seem to have lived in the camp itself[70]. In some garrisoned localities it seems that the greater part of the population was on the roll of the unit[71]. It even looks as if civilians contributed to the regular payment which frontier troops were obliged to make to their duke[72].

But it is not necessary to assume that all or even most of the forts had soldiers attached to them. The mere existence of the fortified enclosure was of use. Nomads found great difficulty in storming even unsophisticated walls[73]. So a stone fort without garrison could provide protection for civilians and their corn, and the army would benefit from the fortified camp-site and supply base whenever it had to operate in the area[74]. A passage from the 'Chronicle' of Joshua Stylites explains the disadvantage of campaigning in an area lacking in fortification:

The generals of the army informed the emperor that the troops suffered great harm from their not having any town situated on the border. For whenever the Greeks went forth from Tella or Amida to go about on expeditions among the Arabs, they were in constant fear, whenever they halted, of the treachery of enemies, and if it happened that they fell in with a larger force than their own, and thought of turning back, they had to endure great fatigue because there was no town near them in which they could find shelter. For this reason the emperor gave orders that a wall should be built for the village of Daras[75].

It is thus likely that many fortifications had no soldiers attached to them and that Procopius fails to mention a garrison in connection with the great majority of fortifications in the 'de aedificiis' because they were, in fact, not garrisoned[76]. Certainly there are few epigraphic indications of the presence of the army in the forts between the Euphrates and Chalcis. Moreover, these forts, in striking contrast to the fortified towns on the Euphrates, figure very little in military history[77]. It is true that one major invasion halted in this area: the joint

---

[68] C. T. VII 15, 2 (423); Nov. Theod. II, XXIV 14 (443). – Nessana papyri show that soldiers sold land.

[69] Cf. R. M. Price, op. cit. (note 32). – The fort at Nessana was not inhabited by soldiers: C. J. Kraemer, op. cit. (note 67) 16 and 42 on P. Colt. 15. – Cf. also M. Gichon, Das Kastell En Boqeq. Bonner Jahrb. 171, 1971, 386 ff. esp. 399. Fort used for storage and administration in 6th century.

[70] V. Alex. Acoem. 33 (early 5th century Palmyra) = SEG. IX 356 § 10: ὥστε . . . [ἐν] το[ῖς] κάστροις ἰδυιώτας.

[71] A. H. M. Jones, op. cit. (note 31) 662 on Philae, Syene and Elephantine. Perhaps this applies to Nessana too.

[72] Beersheba edict: A. Alt, Die griechischen Inschriften der Palaestina Tertia westlich der Arabia. Wiss. Veröffentl. d. dt.-türk. Denkmalschutz-Komm. II (Berlin – Leipzig 1921) 4 ff.; SEG. VIII 282. The edict mentions a payment made jointly by soldiers and συντελεσταί. So also the edict from Koiser il Hallâbât south of Bostra (Princeton Arch. Exp. Syr. III A 24–42, συντελεσταί on frg. 40).

[73] Procopius II 19, 12; II 9, 3–4.

[74] Cf. E. Wightman, Some Aspects of the Later Roman Defensive System in Gaul. Akten 7. Limeskongreß 46 ff. esp. 48.

[75] Joshua Stylites, chron. (ed. and tr. W. Wright [Cambridge 1882, repr. Amsterdam 1968]) 90. Daras as offensive base: Menander Protector = FHG. IV 213.

[76] In Euphratensis: Zenobia – II 8, 11; Sergiopolis – II 9, 8; Hemerium – II 9, 10; probably Zeugma and Neocaesarea – II 9, 19. In Syria: Chalcis – II 11, 1; Cyrrhus (correctly in Euphratensis). In Phoenicia Libanensis: Palmyra – II 11, 12.

[77] R. M. Price (op. cit. [note 32]) points out this not sufficiently considered fact.

operation of Persians and Arabs in 531. The invader captured the fortified town of Gabbulon and several other places before turning back. The precise circumstances are not clear but it seems that the decisive factor was the arrival of the Roman field army from Mesopotamia which encamped at Chalcis. The Persians at this point did not wish to fight a battle against superior numbers and retired[78]. The garrisons of the limes played no part. Next, the invasion of 540 had not the slightest difficulty in reaching the cities of Syria. It can be objected that this was before Justinian's fortifications had been completed. But I have argued that in Syria at any rate Justinian did not change the defensive organisation in any fundamental way and that the deployment of troops in the limes remained weak and was never intended to bear the main burden of frontier defence. In fact, that if there were forts and troops, they will have resembled those found in Southern Palestine later in the century[79].

The forts on the edge of settled land did not even have to bear the full pressure of the nomads. Defence against tribesmen from over the border was in the hands of tribesmen within. These were organised under phylarchs[80], perhaps one to each frontier province[81], and received subsidies[82]. The Persians proceeded to unite the tribes allied to them under the command of the Lakhmid chieftain Al Mundhir and in this way greatly increased the penetrating power of their raids. After a particularly damaging raid in 529, Justinian imitated the Persian example and placed most, but not all, the allied phylarchs and their tribes under the command of the Ghassanid Harith (Arethas)[83]. Eventually the Ghassanids gained the upper hand over their Lakhmid rivals and in the process became something very like independent allies of the imperial government[84].

The Ghassanid chiefs did not have anything to do with cities. Their headquarters were a camp at Gabija in the Golan. After the Arab conquest Omar treated it as a kind of capital of Syria. There the Ghassanids held court while Arab poets sang their feats of arms[85]. These Arab princes also became builders in the territories roamed by their tribesmen and Arab legend was to add to structures actually put up by them. The Ghassanids furnished a strong if not altogether reliable contingent to the Roman field army. Malalas mentions the figure of

[78] Malalas XII 462, 16 = PG. XCVII 673–676; Procopius I 18, 8. There are discrepancies.
[79] Low profile of army in S. Palestine in late 6th century: P. Mayerson, The First Muslim Attacks on Southern Palestine (A. D. 633–634). TAPA. 95, 1964, 155 ff. esp. 183. 185 f. based on Antoninus Placentius (op. cit. [note 65] 180 f. 187). Also by P. Mayerson, The Desert of Southern Palestine According to Byzantine Sources. Proc. Am. Phil. Soc. 107, 1963.
[80] Procopius I 77, 46. – Before the system was unified under a Ghassanid King it probably resembled the North African arrangement implied in C. T. VII 15, 1 (409); Not. Dig. Occ. XXV–XXXI; August., ep. 199, 46; and on these A. H. M. Jones, op. cit. (note 31) 652 n. 103–104; J. Barradez, Fossatum Africae (Paris 1949).
[81] A phylarch corresponding to each duke? Cf. Malalas XII 443. – Phylarch of Palestine: Malalas XII 446. – Phylarch of Arabia: Just., Nov. CII 1 (536). – Phylarch of Phoenicia Libanensis: Just., ed. IV 2 (555–556).
[82] Suppression of subsidy to Ghassanids in 584: John of Ephesus III 42. – Suppression of subsidies in S. Palestine in 629: Theoph. 335 (De Boor) = P. G. CVIII 689. – 30 lbs. of gold?: Nicephorus, opuscula historica 23 (De Boor). – Various subsidies: A. H. M. Jones, op. cit. (note 31) 612 n. 8. Were subsidies the cause of the flourishing condition of the frontier area?
[83] Procopius I 17, 47.
[84] J. Sauvaget, op. cit. (note 44) passim; R. Devréesse, op. cit. (note 17) 277 ff.; I. Kawar, Procopius on the Ghassanids. Journal Am. Orient. Soc. 77, 1957, 79 ff.; idem, The Patriciate of Arethas. Byz. Zeitschr. 52, 1959, 322 ff.; S. Smith, Events in Arabia in the 6th Century. Bull. School Orient. and Afr. Stud. 16, 1954, 425 ff.
[85] Th. Nöldeke, op. cit. (note 8). – Malalas XII 461 = P. G. XCVII 673.

5000. They also continued their war with the pro-Persian Arabs even when the two empires had made peace. The importance of the family can be judged from the fact that Justinian turned a blind eye to their monophysite Christianity – as he did to that of Theodora the empress. He did not even prevent communications – carried out through Theodora – between Harith and Theodosius, the monophysite patriarch in semi-hiding at Constantinople, with a view to the appointment of a bishop, naturally a monophysite one, for his camps[86]. In this way Harith in 541 set in motion the process which was to lead to the creation of a separate monophysite church organisation by James Bar'adas[87]. When the Ghassanid power was eventually broken by the emperor Maurice there was little defensive strength left in Syria and Palestine[88].

The Ghassanid sphere of authority appears to have been entirely within the frontier of the empire. The centre of their influence was in Batanaea between Damascus and Bostra[89] but it extended as far as the seasonal movements of the nomads as is witnessed by the remains of the hall outside Sergiopolis where the Ghassanid chieftain held audience when the tribesmen had gathered for the festival of S. Sergius on November 15. Some phylarchs came out of the wider Arab world. In 420 Asbetus with his family had moved into the empire from the Persian sphere of influence and was made phylarch of the Arab allies in the province of Arabia[90]. Another Sheikh, Amorcessus, left the Persian sphere around 470 to establish himself, partly at the expense of the empire, on the gulf of Aquaba. The emperor Leo recognised his position and granted the title of phylarch[91]. Abocharabus was ruler of an oasis some way from the frontier. He ceded this to the emperor though its geographic position meant that it could in no real sense become part of the empire. The gift was nevertheless accepted and the ruler rewarded with the phylarchate of Palestine[92]. He played an important, and to himself profitable, role in the suppression of a Samaritan rebellion[93].

One suspects that there was a good deal of movement across the frontier in the course of the annual nomadic migrations and that not only chieftains but their followers also entered the empire in this way[94]. The subsidies paid to Arab allies are likely to have acted as a magnet. Certainly there was considerable infiltration of Arabs into Southern Palestine[95].

[86] W. H. C. Frend, The Rise of the Monophysite Movement (Cambridge 1972) 284 f. 326 ff.; P. H. Charles, Le christianisme des Arabes nomades (Paris 1936) 68 f.

[87] Michael the Syrian, chron. IX 29 (ed. Chabot II 245–246); John of Ephesus, Lives of James and Theodore (ed. E. W. Brooks) = P. Or. XIX 154.

[88] Arrest of phylarch produces raid, all over Palestine and Phoenicia: John of Ephesus III 42. – The kingdom broke up into 15 phylarchates the majority of whom joined the Persians: Michel the Syrian II 372; John of Ephesus III 56, 135–136.

[89] R. Devréesse, op. cit. (note 17) 279, lists inscriptions naming members of family; R. Nöldeke, op. cit. (note 8) 45, buildings attributed to them. IGLSyr. 2553 (Quasr el Heir) and commentary.

[90] Cyr. Scyth., vita Euthymii 10.

[91] Malchus I: FHG. IV 112.

[92] Procopius I 19, 10–11.

[93] Malalas XII 445–447; Exc. de ins. frg. 44, 171 (De Boor); Cyr. Scyth., vita Sabae 70. The phylarch sold 20 000 slaves to the Persians.

[94] Arab tradition locates tombs of the family in Batanaea (R. Devréesse, op. cit. [note 17] 279 n. 1). But the family together with its followers of the tribe Ghassan are said to have migrated from S. Arabia where the inhabitants of Medina belong to the tribe (R. Nöldeke, op. cit. [note 8] 85, see above 487).

[95] C. J. Kraemer, op. cit. (note 67) 24 ff. The influx of Arabs was of course greatly increased by the Arab conquest.

Arab allies were supported and kept in check by a force of Roman regulars led by the two 'commanders of soldiers in Lebanon'[96]. These were surely the two dukes of Phoenicia Libanensis who had their headquarters at Palmyra and Damascus. The force consisted of cavalry. When Antioch was threatened by the Persians in 541 it was moved into the city, 6000 strong. As soon as the Persians broke into the city, the troops rode away[97]. Later Belisarius made the force part of his field army for offensive operations in Mesopotamia. This was not part of its normal role and the commanders were worried about exposing Syria and Phoenicia to Arab attack[98]. I imagine that this force was separate from the *limitanei* discussed earlier. *Limitanei* were intended for defence of their immediate locality[99]. Moreover, the force which so signally failed to defend Antioch would surely have been in action earlier if it had been stationed in the limes of Chalcis zone. Presumably the troops were garrisoned near the headquarters of the two dukes at Palmyra and Damascus. Their normal employment was to intercept Al Mundhir or other nomad raiders or to drive them back if they had broken into the settled areas[100]. Striking forces of this kind together with a certain amount of logistical infrastructure are known from Egypt[101].

The effective strength of the various kinds of Roman units stationed in Syria and Palestine must not be estimated highly. The chaos that broke out when the emperor Maurice exiled the Ghassanid chieftains and ended the family's supremacy over the tribesmen of the empire[102], showed how far the security of the provinces, especially of Palestine, had come to depend on their ability to organise the Arab allies. The lesson then taught was repeated by the Muslim invasion which met with little resistance from local forces[103].

So far we have discussed defence against raiders from the desert. Defence against the Persians was a separate problem which involved the military organisation of the Mesopotamian as well as the Syrian provinces. Two lines of advance were open to the Persians. They could either move along the military roads through Mesopotamia, past the fortified cities of Constantina and Edessa (or alternatively Theodosiopolis and Carrhae) or they could enter the empire near Circesium, cross the Euphrates and then advance with the Euphrates on the right until they struck the military roads leading into the heart of Syria. In the 6th century, Syria was invariably attacked by the latter route.

---

[96] Procopius I 13, 5; II 8,2; II 16, 17; II 19, 33. Procopius usually avoids non-classical titles.

[97] Procopius II 8,2; II 16, 17.

[98] Procopius II 16, 17; II 19, 33.

[99] Cf. C. T. I 27, 28 . . . *adiuvare loca ubi dispositi fuerunt, non longe limitem exeuntes nec ipsi limitanei nec duces eorum*. *Limitanei* scattered over many villages and not necessarily living in barracks would have been hard to concentrate. In 6th century dukes commanded also former field army units permanently stationed in their areas: A. H. M. Jones, op. cit. (note 31) 660 on C. J. XII 35, 18 of 492, and perhaps specially created mobile units.

[100] Dukes responsible for security of Syria and Palestine: Procopius II 19, 34. Palmyra situated across Saracen invasion route: Procopius II 11, 11–12.

[101] R. Rémondon, Soldats de Byzance d'après un papyrus trouvé à Edfou. Recherches de papyrologie 1, 1961, 143 ff. Does Malalas 308 refer to the ducal striking forces – anachronistically?

[102] See note 88.

[103] P. Mayerson, TAPA. 95, 1964, 172 f.: In 630 Mohammed agrees terms of capitulation of Aila with its phylarch or bishop. No Roman officer involved. The *legio decima Fretensis* (Not. Dig. Or. XXXIV 30) had evidently long disappeared. In 629 the vicar (of the duke of Palestine) was able to gather *limitanei* from frontier forts near Mu'ta to defeat Arab invaders but in 634 when the Arabs attacked Gaza they were met by only 300 soldiers from Caesarea (Theophanes: P. G. CVIII 688–689).

Roman defensive measures were of two kinds: fortification and garrisoning of cities and the maintenance of a field army. Procopius shows how the system worked. In 531 the Persians following the advice of their Arab allies, invaded Syria by the Euphrates route, keeping the river on their right[104]. The Persian force met no significant Roman force on the frontier or inland. What induced the Persians to withdraw was the arrival of the Roman field army from Mesopotamia. Before moving out of Mesopotamia Belisarius, the Roman commander, garrisoned a number of cities. Evidently permanent garrisons were small or non-existent[105].

The invasion of 540 caught the Romans in a very weak position because most of the field army had been sent to re-conquer Italy from the Goths. The situation recalls that of the Persian invasion of 359[106]. The Roman commander-in-chief, with such forces as remained to him, was at Hierapolis, the centre where Roman armies preparing to invade Persian Mesopotamia had often assembled. He was too weak to interfere with the Persians' ravaging of Syria in any way. He retired to Edessa. Hierapolis saved itself from the Persians by paying ransom[107]. In the circumstances the cities were entirely at the mercy of the Persians and faced with the choice of paying or being destroyed. The presence of small garrisons at Sura[108], Beroea[109], Chalcis scarcely availed to prolong resistance. The troops at Chalcis were actually hidden by the citizens[110]. Antioch had no garrison. Justinian sent a special force of 300 to hold it; later, and unexpectedly, there arrived the striking force from Lebanon[111]. As a result, the city resisted and was destroyed. After sacking Syria, the Persians returned through Mesopotamia. City after city paid money to be rid of them. Only Daras withstood an attack. Its commander had recently been sent from Italy[112]. In the following campaigning season, Belisarius returned from Italy and proceeded to create a new field army[113]. With this, he launched a not very successful counter-offensive. No doubt he suffered heavy casualties. But in 342 the field army still looked a formidable force which enabled Belisarius to bluff the Persian king into giving up an invasion of Syria and Palestine before it had done too much damage[114].

In the sixth century there was no way in which the Persians could be prevented from penetrating into the empire. The only way to check an invasion was by means of a field army strong enough to defeat or at least to threaten the invading force[115]. Fortified cities provided no kind of barrier and most of them could be captured easily. Nevertheless, they too had an important function. They provided shelter for the inhabitants, their corn and their animals.

---

[104] Procopius I 17, 2; II 34.
[105] Procopius I 18, 1–12.
[106] In 359 the Persians launched a massive invasion of Mesopotamia while the field army was with Constantius in Illyricum. (Amm. Marc. XVIII 5,2; XX 6,1). Then the cities were much more strongly held than in 540.
[107] Procopius II 6,2 ff.; II 13.
[108] Procopius II 5,11.
[109] Procopius II 7,6 ff. Their pay was in arrears and they eventually enrolled with Persians: ibid. 37.
[110] Procopius II 12,2 ff.
[111] Procopius II 6,9; II 8,2.
[112] Procopius II 14,9.
[113] Procopius II 14; II 10; II 16,1–3.
[114] Procopius II 21,20; II 29.
[115] In 544 Chosroes marched straight to Edessa. Nothing tried to stop him: Procopius II 26,1–5.

They also provided bases for Roman armies operating in the neighbourhood. Moreover, while nothing could stop the Persians from overrunning and plundering the countryside, they could not remain in permanent occupation while the cities were not in their hands. Conquest would require systematic reduction of the cities, especially of Daras, Amida and Edessa and the fortified towns along the Euphrates. The only lasting occupation of Syria by the Persians followed the systematic conquest of the cities of Mesopotamia. But the number and strength of such garrisons is unknown. Their primary role will have been to assist the local population to protect themselves. Of greater significance was the mobile reserve including former field army units under the dukes of Lebanon. A great part of the defence against raiders from the desert had been passed on to nomadic allies in the steppe lands inside the frontier. Defence from the Persians depended as before on a combination of field army and fortified cities. Again the impression is that the military effort has been reduced. It had been traditional policy of the Roman Empire since Augustus to hold the frontier with forces large enough to meet any forseeable emergency. This was no longer the case. Neither garrisons nor the field army were kept at a permanent high level. Both were allowed to run down, or were withdrawn and only built up for particular operations – in 541 only after Syria had been devastated. There was also a certain weakening of the military cover of Syria because relatively greater importance was given to operations in Armenia, the chief recruiting area of the Byzantine army, and from the reign of Justinian a separate military command[116].

It is time to sum up the changes in the defensive organisation between the fourth and the sixth centuries. The imperial military effort has been reduced. The line of frontier forts through the desert fringe has been abandoned. Some forts on the desert fringe may have been garrisoned by a Nessana or Syene type of frontier soldier, but probably most of them were not.

The military effort had been reduced but this did mean that the Syrian provinces were no longer defended adequately. The invasions of 541 and 573[117] were very unpleasant but they were also passing incidents. Looking at the century as a whole, nomads and Persians were kept out. The frontier areas in Syria and Palestine at any rate were in a flourishing condition. Agricultural expansion was the rule. The system only collapsed under Phocas but the sorry state of the empire under Phocas was not the result just of defective frontier strategy. But the civil strife and Persian invasion must have terribly weakened the empire when it had to face the Arabs. Moreover, the Arab attack was of a kind which the frontier strategy was not designed to meet. It had the weight of a Persian invasion but was directed against the long desert flank whose defences, especially since the suppression of the Ghassanid monarchy, were designed only to deal with raiding parties[118].

---

[116] A. H. M. Jones, op. cit. (note 31) 271.281; P. Charanis, The Armenians in the Byzantine Empire (Lisbon 1963) 14 ff.

[117] In 573 a two-pronged surprise attack caught the Roman field army completely off-balance, with the result that it was neither able to protect Syria nor defend Daras: Theoph. 247,8–10 (De Boor) = P. G. CVIII 536. Evagrius H. E. V 4.

[118] Even so the first stage of the invasion showed that except for the contribution of Arab tribesmen in the semidesert the structure of the 6th century defensive system was still intact in Southern Palestine. Cf. A. Alt, Das Ende des Limes Palaestinae. Journal Pal. Orient. Soc. 18, 1938, 149.

INDEX